In the centuries since his death in 1626, Francis Bacon has been perceived and studied as a promoter and prophet of the philosophy of science – natural science. Certainly Bacon proclaimed that he could and would fill the vacuum which he saw existing in the study of nature; but he also saw himself as a clarifier and promoter of what he called 'policy', that is, the study and improvement of the structure and function of civil states including the new British state established by the Union of 1603.

In this major new study Mr Wormald shows that Bacon was concerned equally with knowledge of the world of nature and with that of policy. There was indeed a dilemma, about which Bacon was explicit. He resolved it by attending assiduously to both fields, arguing that he would perform in policy in ways which would help progress in knowledge of nature. In his teaching, in his practice, and in the end as things turned out in terms of what was actually achieved, the junction between the two enterprises was effected by his work in history – first in civil history, but also in natural history. His proposed metaphysics of nature, which would reveal the 'real truth' about it, came to nothing: it was his conception and practice of history which provided the answer to his strivings to advance not only policy but also, and in addition, natural philosophy. In thus stressing the inspiration which history provided even for Bacon's study of nature, Mr Wormald here provides a fundamental reappraisal.

FRANCIS BACON

Francis Bacon (1561–1626). Portrait by John Vanderbank, reproduced by permission of the National Portrait Gallery, London.

FRANCIS BACON

History, politics and science, 1561–1626

B. H. G. WORMALD

Coll. Div. Pet. Acad. Cantabr.

CAMBRIDGE
UNIVERSITY PRESS

Published by the Press Syndicate of the University of Cambridge
The Pitt Building, Trumpington Street, Cambridge CB2 1RP
40 West 20th Street, New York, NY 1001, USA
10 Stamford Road, Oakleigh, Victoria 3166, Australia

First published 1993

Printed in Great Britain at the University Press, Cambridge

British Library cataloguing in publication data
Wormald, B. H. G. (Brian Harvey Goodwin)
Francis Bacon: history, politics and science, 1561–1626.
(Cambridge studies in the history and theory of politics)
1. English philosophy. Bacon, Francis, Viscount St Albans 1561–1626
1. Title
192

Library of Congress cataloguing in publication data
Wormald, B. H. G.
Francis Bacon: history, politics and science, 1561–1626/B. H. G.
Wormald.
p. cm. – (Cambridge studies in the history and theory of politics)
Includes bibliographical references and index.
ISBN 0-521-30773-2
1. Bacon, Francis, 1561–1626. 1. Title. II. Series.
B1198. W67 1991
192 – dc20 90-20211 CIP

ISBN 0 521 30773 2 hardback

UP

For Denise

῎Εστω δ᾽ ὦν μηδὲν ἀπείρητον
αὐτόματον γὰρ ουδέν, ἀλλ᾽ ἀπὸ
πείρης πάντα ἀνθρώποισι φιλέει
γίνεσθαι

Herodotus, VII, 9

Let nothing then be untried; for nothing
is accomplished by its own self, but
all things are usually achieved by men
through endeavours.

Transl. HENRY CARY, 1854

Contents

Acknowledgments

In this study, consuming ten years of a lifetime, I acknowledge indebtedness to *The Works of Francis Bacon, Baron of Verulam, Viscount St Alban, and Lord High Chancellor of England*; published in London in fourteen volumes between 1857 and 1874 inclusive. These were collected and edited by James Spedding, Robert Leslie Ellis and Douglas Denon Heath. The first seven volumes consist of (A) Works, Philosophical, Literary and Professional; the second seven volumes consist of (B) The Letters and the Life including occasional works. In notes I shall refer respectively to (A) or to (B), giving volume and page. I am also indebted to *The Philosophy of Francis Bacon, an Essay on its development from 1603 to 1609 with new Translation of Fundamental Texts*, Benjamin Farrington, Liverpool 1964. In my notes I shall refer to Farrington, giving page. I am also indebted to *The Discourses of Niccolo Machiavelli*, translated from the Italian with an Introduction and Notes by Leslie J. Walker; New Introduction and Appendices by Cecil H. Clough, Routledge and Kegan Paul, London 1975. In my notes I shall refer to *Discourses*, giving chapter, section and page.

I extend grateful thanks to my editor at the Cambridge University Press, William Davies, for his encouragement and patience; to Hugh Kearney, who read and criticized the work in typescript; to Hazel Dunn who has produced the typescript; to Maurice Cowling who has provided faithful support; to Nancy-Jane Thompson for assistance and support; and to Susan Beer for copy editing.

CHAPTER I

Introduction

In the course of his lifetime and career Francis Bacon pre-enacted his subsequent reputation. He advertised and in so doing inflated his part as proponent, inaugurator and instigator of a new natural science. Without renouncing them, he played down what he achieved in other realms. In the centuries after his death, in the early times of the efflorescence of the natural sciences, he was often taken at his word. He was acclaimed as hero of a scientific revolution. He was hailed and celebrated, not as prophet only, but as agent and perpetrator of a great transformation. The rest of what he did was largely neglected – though his *Essays*, it is true, furnish the exception. The rest was neglected not only for this reason, namely, the successful 'rise of science', casting much else into shadow; but also because in the matter of this remainder, government, law and the constitution, he turned out – in terms of what he stood for – to be on the losing side in subsequent discords and troubles. Upheavals and civil wars disqualified in people's minds his political and constitutional philosophy, ostensibly discrediting it.

Bacon also pre-enacted this piece of history. His overthrow as Chancellor of England and minister of King James VI and I was the upshot of initiatives which were made in a parliament. This was in 1621. A parliament which assembled in 1640 instituted successful attacks not only on a minister but on King Charles I's entire government. Thus Bacon was victim of a revolution before it took place – a revolution, moreover, which he predicted was likely to occur given the arrival of a certain set of contingencies. Further, because men rejected measures which he urged regarding the implications of the Union of the Crowns of England and Scotland, he was also able to predict the contingencies.

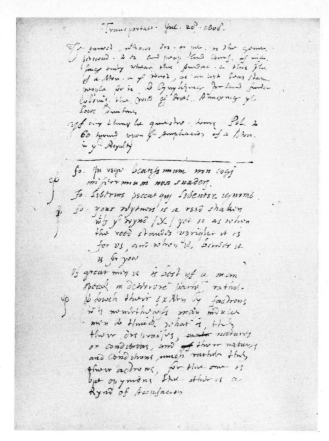

Above and left: manuscript extracts from Bacon's notes, British Library Add. MS 27278, fos. 22 v, 23 and 23 v. © British Library.

The revolution foreseen was a successful assault in a parliament upon the power of the monarch, which, given the financial straits of the latter, consisted of withholding – or, if not refusing – then of remorseless bargaining over supply. Among highly abbreviated jottings dated 1608 under the head 'Poll.',[1] which, because of the contents of these notes, manifestly stands for 'policy', we find Bacon writing: 'The. bring. ye K. low by pov. and empt. Cof.' (The bringing the King low by poverty and empty coffers.) Such a subversion, he observed in the same notes, would be unlikely to occur unless an emergency took place first in Scotland: 'The revolt or troub. first in Sco. for till yt be no dang. of Eng. discont. in dowt of a warre fro. thence.' (The revolt or trouble first in Scotland: for till that be, no danger of English discontent: in doubt of a war from hence.) This rebellion in Scotland took place. Troubles in England were duly triggered. After the accession of King James VI and I Bacon had worked in vain for a closer and more durable union between the Scots and the English. In the House of Commons he pointed out not only the impermanence but the dangers of incomplete unions.

Whether or not the Scots moved in the way he feared, Bacon constructed a long-term strategy for avoiding unmanageable situations in England. Parliaments should continue to be assembled. But they should be implicated, when summoned, in joint exercises, jointly that is to say, with the King's government. Among the 1608 private notes – Commentarius Solutus – under the head 'Poll.' Bacon wrote:

The fairest, without dis. or per. is the gener. perswad. to K. and peop. and cours. of infusing every whear the foundat. in this Ile of a Mon. in ye west, as an apt seat state people for it; so cyvylizing Ireland, furder coloniz. the wild of Scotl. Annexing ye Lowe Countries. Yf any thing be questio. touch. Pol. to be turned upon ye Ampliacion of a Mon. in ye Royalty. The fairest, without disputes(?), discontents(?), distempers(?), discords(?), disfavour(?), disabilities(?) or perils, is the general persuading to King and people, and course of infusing everywhere the foundation in this isle of a monarchy in the West, as an apt seat, state, people for it; so civilizing Ireland, further colonizing the wild of Scotland. Annexing the Low Countries. If anything be questioned touching policy, to be turned upon the ampliation of a Monarchy in the Royalty.[2]

Challenges to the monarch's prerogatives would be parried by investing the attentions and interests of parliaments in projects such as were sketched.

Evidence is abundant that Bacon worked consistently and coherently in this course. We are helped – because he did so – in deciphering the jottings in which he described it. He made of the course an enterprise which he tried to put into practice. He based it on scrutiny of past practices in such matters. He also argued that present circumstances and prevailing conditions favoured it and invited it. Hereinafter I refer to it as a grand strategy. The enterprise can be described as analogous to and comparable with his *Great Instauration*. But by the 1640s revolutions had happened both in Scotland and in England. On the face of things Bacon, his position and his 'course', were consigned to the limbo of failure and defeat. Nevertheless his grand strategy was later implemented to the full, this including, though still without a common law and a common church, a closer and less precarious union between the English and the Scots. In less than a century after Bacon's death both King and people had been persuaded, governments and parliaments working together, into founding 'in this isle a monarchy in the West'. The Crown as restored in 1660 had lost prerogatives which Bacon had defended. But supremacy in matters of war and peace survived. Parliaments and monarchs, the latter retaining supremacy in affairs of war and peace even after 1688, were more closely joined. Britain after that date emerged into the company of greater powers, establishing itself among them. After 1688 the island and the Low Countries even acquired for a time a common ruler. The year 1707 saw the achievement of less fragile union between the northern and the southern nations.

None of these things took place as the result of Bacon's plans. They happened nevertheless because they were possible opportunities and/or properly unavoidable necessities, acted upon by others, which Bacon had correctly perceived. He had conjured up the accurate vision of them. John Robert Seeley (1834–95) introducing *The Growth of British Policy* (1895) remarked that it was only natural 'that while we have entered early into the conception of constitutional history...we have scarcely yet perceived that constitutional history requires the history of policy as its correlative'.[3] But Bacon had already joined the two, recognizing that they could not be divided. A constitution cannot be envisaged apart from what men do with it. What is done cannot be contemplated apart from constitutional arrangements making such actions possible. In the private notes of 1608 'Poll.' means policy – and policy in his usage we shall see, means a science, civil science: policy also means a course or courses of action which this science dictates: policy also means an agency – the royal government – with a recognized duty to under-take the action or actions. In addition, in his usage, policy means constitutional arrangements of a state as a whole – including parliaments – these in their turn requiring or facilitating the action or actions.

In the course of the present century, the authority and prestige of natural science being established and taken for granted, Bacon's part in its origins has in general been graded down. The nature of the scientific revolution and the processes of its emergence have come to be recognized by historians of science as complex. Neither Bacon's claims for himself in natural philosophy, nor his enduring impact in that field can be rated as highly as once seemed possible. Time and studies have seen to that. In this presiding matter of natural philosophy – Bacon himself sharing responsibility for it being a presiding one – he has suffered successively a twofold misfortune: first from having been endowed with too little historical context and second and latterly with too much. In the present century a normal stance of historians is to insist that it is only by furnishing 'contexts' that men's thoughts and deeds in past times become intelligible. According to this teaching in its extreme forms men are functions of contexts. Historians must see to it, they seem to say, that a man is 'cut down to size', that he be 'kept in his place'. Subjects become objects consisting of situations in which they find themselves – or rather of situations into which historians decide to place them. During the later twentieth century Bacon in the matter of natural philosophy has been rightly restored to his times. But also he has been riveted back into them to such a degree that sometimes he barely emerges in this field as different from them. A likely result of such proceedings is that we shall know more about the context than about Bacon.

He conveniently pre-enacted in his life the story of his scientific reputation in after centuries. Declared ambitions and plans in natural philosophy were not successfully matched by output. In parallel with this, as the answering echo of his time, his reputation as exercising controls over posterity's achievements in this field has shrunk in the estimate of investigators. There could for instance be no question of him filling the part of a second Aristotle. Though urgently describing and recommending his procedures, his own efforts resulted in producing little in what came to comprise the sciences of nature. In the other fields – civil history, studying it, writing it, using it for making policy (civil philosophy, a science which he claimed to have invented by emancipating it from morality), the applying of this civil science in government and in law, and in seeking to establish a constitution for the state, areas in which he was close observer and active participator, not only did the verdict of immediate events pronounce against him, he was also to some extent his own detractor – again, so it would appear, in the cause of intended and projected exploits in natural philosophy. He refrained from placing his contributions in other fields unequivocally inside his *Great Instauration*, thus helping to promote questionable conclusions on the matter. On the one hand he described the *Great Instauration* as a 'total reconstruction of sciences, arts and *all human knowledge*' (emphasis added), 'raised upon the proper foundations'.[4] He had already told Lord Burleigh in 1592 that he took *all* (emphasis added) knowledge as his province.[5] On the other hand, as for instance in correspondence with Bishop Lancelot Andrewes[6] or in a letter to the Venetian Fr Fulgentius,[7] he said or clearly implied that *The History of the Reign of King Henry the 7th, De Sapientia Veterum*, Of the Wisdom of the Ancients, and his essays, were outside not inside the *Great Instauration*.

In order to clarify this matter it is necessary to recall other things Bacon said and also other things he did. He said that he knew his way, but not his position. He did not know how far he had got. Concluding *Thema Coeli* – Theory of the Heaven – he wrote: 'Nevertheless I repeat once more that I do not mean to bind myself to these; for in them as in other things I am certain of my way, but not certain of my position.'[8] He also said, writing to Sir Toby Mathew in 1610, that 'My great work goeth forward; and after my manner, I alter ever when I add, so that nothing is finished till all be finished.'[9] Additions brought alterations: alterations carried additions. *The Advancement of Learning*, first published in 1605, was in due course added to, and made part of, the *Great Instauration*. When thus added to the *Great Instauration*, and when republished in 1623, it presented alterations in its contents. But even before alterations and additions were made, the 1605 version lamented the deficiency in civil history writing under which England – and also Scotland – suffered, and urged the need to remedy this. Here Bacon recommended a period which it was especially desirable to cover, this being the stretch of time running from the Union of the Roses to the Union of the Crowns.[10] But in statements he makes elsewhere it is plain that in the years preceding the appearance of the first *Advancement* it was this period of events which he had chosen and marked out for a work in civil history writing from his own pen. In 1623, by which time *Advancement* in its second version was explicitly part of the *Great Instauration*, both the description of this deficient condition in civil history writing, the plea for remedy, together with the special recommendation regarding the series of events to be dealt with, were repeated unchanged save that they appeared in Latin.

With respect to additions, *Advancement*'s version of 1623 included pieces out of *De Sapientia Veterum*. Representing the argument of that book, three fables with his interpretation of them were imported, 'one taken from things Natural, one from things Political, and one from things Moral'.[11] *Advancement*'s version of 1623 contained also two pieces which he styled 'examples of summary treatises'. One of these, entitled *Of the Extension of Empire*, was later republished as an essay in the 1625 collection. There is nothing about the extracts from *De Sapientia Veterum* and nothing about the example of a treatise later appearing as an essay which entitles them to this favoured treatment and to inclusion in the *Great Instauration* which excludes the rest of *De Sapientia Veterum* and the rest of the essays. The second example of a treatise, published in the second *Advancement*, is entitled *Of Universal Justice or the Fountains of Equity, by Aphorisms*. But there is nothing in the contents of this piece, that is to say in its argument and procedure, which entitles it to be thus set apart from Bacon's numerous other exercises when in office in matters of law. The same applies to the content, argument and procedure of the treatise's twin, which was devoted to the topic of extension of empire, whether this piece appears in *Advancement* or as an essay. In content, argument, and procedure, as is true in the case of other essays, it is solid with, and indistinguishable from Bacon's numerous other exercises – including the never-abandoned and interconnected elements of his grand strategy. Not 'analogous to' or 'comparable with', but 'at the very least organically connected with' is the better way of describing the relationship between the grand strategy and the *Great Instauration*. The two stand distinct, it is evident. Nevertheless, they relate together inseparably.

Regarding the *Essays*, Bacon at a late date told Bishop Lancelot

Andrewes in a letter: 'As for my *Essays*, and some other particulars of that nature, I count them but as the recreations of my other studies, and in that sort propose to continue them.'[12] Contents of the *Essays*, as we shall see, relate unmistakably to 'other studies'.[13] Furthermore, on this topic of 'recreations' Bacon in a much earlier letter had explained to the bishop: 'I hasten not to publish; perishing I would prevent. For with me it is thus, and I think with all men in my case; if I bind myself to an argument, it loadeth my mind; but if I rid my mind of the present cogitation, it is rather a recreation. This hath put me into these miscellanies, which I purpose to suppress, if God give me leave to write a just and perfect volume of philosophy, which I go on with though slowly.'[14] On this argument everything he wrote was a 'recreation', and by the same token an essay, since in the process of writing he was clearing his head by unburdening his mind.

Bacon bequeathed a situation which has encouraged while not justifying posterity's misunderstanding. Nor is this the sum of the matter. In addition, as will be seen, in the course of the text of *Novum Organum* he played down his contributions to learning other than in natural philosophy. As for posterity, men in their turn have often either neglected the work he did in areas other than those of the sciences of nature, apart from the essays; or, apart from the essays, been unsympathetic. His history – that of the reign of King Henry VII – has been decried as containing mistakes in plenty. Needless to say, his trial and dismissal as Chancellor and his needlessly total submission scarcely enhanced his subsequent standing. But even had he died holding his high office it is doubtful that he would have fared better at the hands of posterity. For many in later times have dismissed his standpoints regarding the political constitution of the state in England – and specially those regarding the relation therewith of the laws. His conclusions in this sphere, namely that in matters of state as interpreted by government, *salus populi suprema lex*; and that when such emergencies occur procedures and rules at Common Law in their strictness do not apply for men who invoke them, were not peculiar to himself. Unlike his positions in the sciences of nature these conclusions were shared by others both before and also in his own times. In his case they were the upshot of deep study and reflection. Bacon pre-enacted in his own days the story of his later repute, such pre-enactment being illustrated with a singular exactitude in the case of the essays. For of these he himself correctly wrote that they 'of all my other works have been most current'.[15] The statement is as true today as when he made it.

Equally conveniently he showed himself aware not only of the difficulties he himself must face in the things he was trying to do, but also of the hazards which would confront those in later times who attempted to assess his efforts and understand the positions he achieved. In his doctrine about idols of the mind he warned against over-confidence, his own and other men's, in the matter of intellectual perspectives. 'Historical context', passively incurred or thoughtlessly imbibed rather than as far as possible sorted, sifted and chosen, is precisely what he was talking about – with conspicuous originality – in his treatment of idols of the mind. Human individuals, he wrote, are 'circumscribed by place and time'.[16] Place and time condition the ways in which they confront and perceive reality. But he also taught that place and time can be transcended by human individuals. In extremist context doctrine this is denied. The idols cease to be idols. Instead they become the normality and the mediocrity which constitute, so it is implied, the history of mankind.

Writing of idols Bacon explained that one of them is rooted in 'every man's individual nature and custom. Although our persons live in the view of heaven, yet our spirits are included in the caves of our own complexions and customs, which minister unto us infinite errors and vain opinions if they be not recalled to examination.'[17] However, 'the idols of the market-place are [the] most troublesome; which have crept into the understanding through the tacit agreement of men concerning the imposition of words and names'.[18] These idols are 'formed by the intercourse and association of men with each other, which I call idols of the Market Place, on account of the commerce and consort of men there'.[19]

The context doctrine subscribed to by latter-day historians is self-defeating. If uncritically accepted, it must follow that they should themselves shut up shop and retire from business. For they in their turn can scarcely hope to escape the consequences of being prisoners both of themselves and of the times they work in. In fact they persevere. When not carried to extremes their teaching, whether applied to men in the past or to their own endeavours, is the half of a truth. The other not less indispensable half is that men like Bacon help to make their times or those that follow. They do this by trying in conscious choices and deliberate efforts to transcend their times.

If in no case and on no occasion have times been transcended by deliberate choices and conscious efforts it is hard to understand how changes which are of import could have been capable of occurring. If Bacon failed as he did in discovering and establishing a new natural philosophy in a shape which was dominating and decisive for a whole future – inherently an unlikely achievement by any mortal – his endeavours nevertheless did not fail to help a new science in its coming.

While continuing to point men's attention to the idols and the insidious challenge which they present, Bacon proposed that 'a kind of thoughtful prudence'[20] could be used 'to guard against them'.[21] Idols could be 'recalled to examination', defined and reduced. While never claiming that he could always dethrone them or that in given cases he had not fallen victim to idols, he showed himself concerned in all that he wrote to choose a context for himself which was the right one as he saw it for his constructive purposes. Thus an answer to men's questions, how to establish a context for Bacon, is in a pre-eminent degree, and to an extent which is unusual, provided by the man himself. He could not, it is true, choose the times he had been born into. But he explored both past and present. He penetrated even into part of the future. In all his perambulations of learning, in matters divine, human and natural, he was sorting and establishing his context.

He also encouraged others to exercise the same 'kind of thoughtful prudence'. Truth, he ingeminated, is the daughter of time. Time in one shape, that is to say, prevailing social and other kinds of conditioning, obfuscates men's vision of what goes on around them. It also impairs their judgment of men, events and institutions in the past. But on the other hand, whether or not new evidence comes to light, time, if exploited by men aware of the idols and exercising 'thoughtful prudence', illuminates and reveals. The mere passing of time can do this. Indeed it is normally the case that, whether or not fresh information is uncovered, both things are needed; not only men working, but time in its passing. This in itself assists men's work and enlightens them.

Neither Thomas Babington Macaulay (1800–59) nor Leopold Ranke (1795–1886) had specialized commitments to the history of philosophy and science. They wrote about Bacon as statesman, man of the law, counsellor to princes, man of letters and essayist. Both historians ignored his claim to have established a new civil science distinct from moral science. But in the course of tributes to him as thinker and scientist both of them nevertheless noted that he advocated procedures which were to be as applicable in moral and political matters as in things of the world of nature. They also stated or implied that he employed his procedures in both realms. In an essay, first published in 1837 in *The Edinburgh Review*, Macaulay wrote that in the *Novum Organum* he (Bacon)

distinctly and most truly declares that his philosophy is no less a Moral than a Natural philosophy, that though his illustrations are drawn from physical science, the principles which those illustrations are intended to explain are just as applicable to ethical and political enquiries as to enquiries into the nature of heat and vegetation. He frequently treated of moral subjects; and he brought to those subjects that spirit which was the essence of his whole system.[22]

Ranke made the same point in his *Englische Geschichte* (1859–69).[23] Contrasting natural with supernatural – that is, theological – topics, Bacon, he writes, seeks to move the human mind in the direction of natural objects. 'Amongst these he ranks the state of human society, to which all his life long he devoted a careful and searching observation.' His essays 'show wide observation and calm wisdom, and like his philosophical works are a treasure for the English nation…'.[24] Macaulay and Ranke were right in proclaiming the breadth and comprehensiveness of Bacon's aims and procedures. But it is possible to show that in Macaulay's case a historian was right for a wrong reason. When he wrote that Bacon in *Novum Organum* 'distinctly and most truly declares that his philosophy is no less a moral than a natural philosophy' his reference is manifestly to Aphorism CXXVII in Book I.[25] There seems little question that Macaulay mistook the bearings and implications of this aphorism.

Neither Macaulay nor Ranke conceded that there could have been connection and cross-fertilization between Bacon's ideas and actions in a career in politics and the law on the one hand, and his ethical and political philosophy as expressed more formally in his writings on the other. Indeed Macaulay not only ignored the possibility that there could have been a connection, he sharply separated the activities of the statesman/lawyer from the cogitations of the philosopher. Furthermore neither Macaulay nor Ranke noticed that when Bacon produced ethical and political philosophy, he did not apply – and made no claim to be applying – his scheme of induction set out in *Novum Organum* Book II. In these products and also in his wider practical activities in policy – that is to say, in government and in law – *Novum Organum* was not being employed. Instead it was being gestated. Cross fertilization took place not only between thought and action in the fields of ethics and policy. The same transactions were conducted between his efforts in ethics and policy on the one hand and projects in natural philosophy on the other.

Macaulay's essay falls into two neatly contrasted sections in which, as we have seen, statesman/lawyer is separated from thinker/philosopher. In the essay's second part where he deals with philosophy, he praises Bacon almost without qualification, but in the first part we find harsh judgments on his moral character and career as counsellor and minister. In form and also in content the essay distinguishes between 'Bacon seeking for truth' and 'Bacon seeking for the Seals'.[26] 'The moral qualities of Bacon were not of a high order'[27] ... 'His faults were, we write it with pain, coldness of heart and meanness of spirit'[28] ... 'Bacon was a servile advocate that he might be a corrupt judge'[29] ... 'he perverted the laws of England to the vilest purposes of tyranny'[30] ... 'intellectually he was better fitted than any man that England has ever produced for the work of improving her institutions. But unhappily we see that he did not scruple to exert his great powers for the purpose of introducing into those institutions new corruptions of the foulest kind.'[31]

When congratulating his subject's philosophy in the second part of the essay Macaulay adopts the pose of convert and disciple. But both in strictures on Bacon's character and in condemning his standpoint in politics and constitutional matters he falls short of applying the master's teaching. In rulings on his political and constitutional standpoint he neglects warnings about idols of the mind. In the way he assesses the man's character he ignores a salient implication of Bacon's distinction between 'philosophy of man segregate' and 'philosophy of man congregate'.[32] He thus neglects another warning – this time a warning against over-confidence in moral judgments of the radical and comprehensive kind which in his essays Macaulay not seldom administered. '...Moral philosophy', Bacon wrote, 'propoundeth to itself the framing of internal goodness; but civil knowledge' (that is to say policy) 'requireth only an external goodness; for that as to society sufficeth'.[33] Here there is no lack of concern for what goes on inside a man or for the man's expressions of this in his words and deeds. As he revealed in much that he wrote, this distinction implies concern which is profound. But among implications of his distinction is recognition that total penetration from outside a man into his inside, whether by contemporary observers (including friends), by churches, governments or laws under which he lives, or by historians, is not possible. The full sum and true nature of the things that take place inside a man can be known to two agents only – the man in question and his Maker.

By their fruits shall ye know them. Grapes are not gathered of thorns nor figs of thistles. Bacon does not deny this. But outward fruits do not exhaust the contents of what is inside a man. Nor are outward actions and professions necessarily reliable as indication of things inside. Judge not that ye be not judged. This, another evangelical precept, is glossed by Bacon. Judging others is forbidden because it is impossible to do so with certainty. It is because it is impossible that it is wrong. It is true that life cannot be conducted without forming elementary assessments of what to expect in dealing with one's fellows. Bacon does not deny this. In discussing what he calls 'negotiation' or 'business' he teaches that to neglect prudential assessments jeopardizes success in practical matters. But when a man makes such assessments as he should, experience teaches that even these prudential judgments of others, though needed, are fallible.

Bacon made statements based on observations of particular human individuals about the distribution of moral goodness or badness as revealed throughout time and space in human nature. But he wrote in general terms, without (so what evidence we possess suggests) pronouncing judgments on particular human beings. It is true, also, that he tried to probe into the inside of men. It is scarcely feasible to devote oneself to moral knowledge, which he continues to pursue, without doing so. But because possibilities of penetration with any degree of certainty are limited, two consequences follow. First, what he treats are such matters as men's 'characters of dispositions'. Some men are too quick to anger, some too slow; some are too quick to believe and agree, others too slow to do so. These features and other similar ones are like men's passions which he also studies. They are moral matters. They impair fuller communication among men. They may hinder the advancement of learning. Arguably they are alterable or adjustable. But condemnatory stances are not called for when dealing with them. Bacon does not make them comparable with turpitudes which rot the soul. Secondly, when it is a question of aiming to better moral qualities in men, Bacon prefers indirect action. Given that churches, governments, laws, are instituted and administered as they ought to be, these operate upon men's external conduct and in this way beneficially affect them internally. He does not tire of moral philosophy, but he is committed to civil philosophy. This he has established, so he claims, as a distinct discipline.

Moral judgments directed to the roots of a man's being cannot be tested and checked. There are no means of correcting them. To the two constructive functions of friendship – unburdening and purging of passions and clarifying and disentangling of thoughts – Bacon did not add a third – the achievement of certainty in this matter. Macaulay delivered another ruling on Bacon's inmost depths: 'He was, we are convinced, a sincere believer in the divine authority of the Christian religion.'[34] He may be wrong. He may be right. Others have differed widely from Macaulay here. A writer in the twentieth century informs us that Bacon in spite of statements to the contrary was an agnostic.[35] Since there are no means of checking and so of correcting judgments upon a person's inner morality or belief, these exercises should be abstained from as unworthy of the breath, ink or print which is expended. They are not necessary. Further, when delivered amongst contemporaries who are known to one another, the results both in donors and recipients are as likely to be morally harmful as beneficial. As for prudential assessments for conducting social intercourse or for achieving success in public or private business; these, unlike radical judgments, are necessary. But experience shows, as it cannot do in the case of radical judgments, that these too are fallible. For practical purposes, however, these prudential judgments can be corrected.

In writers of history, intellectual perspectives unlike propensities to moral judgments are necessary. Normally they need correcting either by the writer on his own part or by other scholars. But correcting them is possible. Macaulay condemned the constitution under which Bacon lived, the working of which Bacon assisted. Macaulay did so according to the standards of a constitution which succeeded Bacon's only after bitter struggles. Macaulay's un-examined Whig idols were not shared by Ranke. He was neither Whig nor English. He noted that 'the English have taken the side of Coke',[36] not that of Bacon. But he also noted that the latter's support 'for the preponderance of the authority of the sovereign' was 'within

constitutional limits'.[37] Truth being the daughter of time, time in
some instances helps historians by throwing up new evidence about
the past. Neither Macaulay nor Ranke had access to papers in which
Bacon persistently tried to persuade King James to summon
parliaments, or to those other more private already cited writings in
which he sketched the vision of a more parliamentary monarchy in
the future – 'the fairest, without disorder or peril, is the general
persuading to King and people, etc.'. Nevertheless, without this new
evidence Ranke unlike Macaulay in the 1837 essay was able to
perceive that Bacon was no advocate of despotism still less of
tyranny. It can also be noted that it is Ranke, not Macaulay – either
in his essay or in his *History* – who ventured to assess the man as civil
historian.

But in the course of time, also without the new evidence, even the
Macaulay of the 1837 essay recalled to examination his Whig idols
of the market place 'which have crept into the understanding
through the tacit agreement of men concerning the imposition of
words and names'. He began to define, reduce and dismantle them.
In his *History of England* (1848) King James is deprived of Bacon's
counsel and left to himself; that is to say, there is no mention of
Bacon as the toadying mentor introducing new corruptions of the
foulest kind. Even when writing of James, Macaulay states that 'the
time was fast approaching when either the King must become
absolute, or the parliament must control the whole executive
administration'.[38] This is to admit that the time had yet to come.
Under the then constitution of the state, consistently studied and
supported by Bacon, neither a king acting alone nor a king in
parliament rightfully exercised unlimited authority – that is to say,
sovereignty, not as that term was often employed by Bacon himself,
but as it came to be defined by Thomas Hobbes and by others.
Regula xix of Bacon's *Maxims of the Law* together with the editor's
footnote[39] should make this clear: part of Bacon's teaching accords
with the more recent doctrine ('...*potestas suprema seipsum dissolvere
potest, ligare non potest*' – the supreme power can dissolve itself; it
cannot bind itself.) The rest of Bacon's teaching does not accord with
the more recent doctrine.

Bacon has no place in Macaulay's *History of England* save as
scientific benefactor to England and the human race. Nor is there
mention as there is in the essay, of the applicability of his procedures
in moral and political matters. Science in *The History* means natural

science. Dealing with the times after the restoration of monarchy and parliament, Macaulay writes that Bacon had

sown the good seed in a sluggish soil and an ungenial season. He had not expected an early crop, and in his last testament had solemnly bequeathed his fame to the next age. During a whole generation his philosophy had, amidst tumults, wars and proscriptions, been slowly ripening in a few well constituted minds... The discipline through which the nation had passed had brought the public mind to a temper well fitted for the reception of the Verulamian doctrine... Divines, jurists, statesmen, nobles, princes, swelled the triumph of the Baconian philosophy.[40]

The rhetorician in him running away with the historian, Macaulay exaggerates and simplifies. But his judgment does not lack echoes in later times, and understandably so since it contains an element of rightness. 'It is', writes a recent scholar, 'the conscious grasp of the whole problem which sets Bacon apart from his contemporaries, and it is the conscious embodiment of his vision which distinguished the Royal Society from all earlier societies interested in natural phenomena.'[41] 'These new methods', writes another, 'included experiment but did not consist in experiment. They consisted rather in a continuous process of interaction between experiment and reasoning, "a true and perfect marriage between the empirical and rational faculty"'.[42]

Nevertheless the position of Bacon, whether in politics, natural science or political science; whether in himself or in the consequences of his work, is less cut and dried and fuller of subtleties and surprises than many, including Macaulay either in the essay or in the *History* have been able to perceive. Macaulay's conclusion was that while Bacon's way was no road forward in matters of the constitution and conduct of the British state, it provided the path – in his view largely without other and later and additional directions – for subsequent advance on a wholesale scale in all branches of the natural sciences. Taking the longer view – time enabling men to do this – it looks now as if a judgment putting matters precisely the other way round would approach more closely to the truth; it being added in order to make a just measure in this matter that Bacon's provisions for the British state were proposed in terms no less scientific in his intentions than what he offered with respect to the universe of nature.

Further, enthusiasm for 'the Verulamian doctrine', for the philosophy of works not of words, for procedures which begin in observations and end in arts, led him in the essay to drag the

founder out of his due historical context. Macaulay, it will be
recalled, died years before the floodtide of contextualist orthodoxy.
With some exaggeration, he justly grants a place to protestantism:
'...it is chiefly to the great reformation of religion that we owe the
great reformation of philosophy'.[43] But overseas observers and
correspondents, interested in Bacon's enterprise, included clergymen
of the Roman obedience. Macaulay fitly recalls that Latin, 'being a
fixed language, while the living languages were in a state of
fluctuation, and being universally known to the learned and the
polite, it was employed by almost every writer who aspired to a wide
and durable reputation'.[44] One is being reminded accordingly that
for Bacon Latin was not only the tongue of universal communication,
it was also, since it was 'fixed' – words having meanings varying
within stable limits – the vehicle of uniformly accurate thinking
throughout space and time. Most of his work, if not written
originally in this language, was later translated into it.

But though Macaulay talks about Aristotle, he provides no
exposition of Bacon's retained, even reclaimed, connections despite
protests of disaffiliation with Aristotle and the schoolmen. He makes
no references to proclaimed connections with the Pyrrhonians or
Sceptics. The writings of Sextus Empiricus, who had flourished late
in the second century AD, had been rescued after centuries of
oblivion. Bacon nowhere mentions him by name. But his writings
had been a recent fruit of time not lightly to be ignored. There is a
passage in Bacon's works, in due course to be quoted, which is a
possible reference to Sextus Empiricus. The essay mentions Thomas
Hobbes as a disciple. Macaulay does not cite his evidence for this.
There are no references to Hobbes in surviving writings of Bacon,
nor to Bacon in those of Hobbes. On the other hand, despite Bacon's
confessed links with Niccolò Machiavelli, Macaulay omits Machiavelli. Nowadays it is suggested that Macaulay's essay is 'of
interest...chiefly to the student of Macaulay and early Victorian
thought'.[45] Macaulay unduly magnified Bacon's part in producing
change in the sciences of nature. Nevertheless the 1837 essay – in its
second part – contains insights concerning Bacon which are of
enduring validity.

Enclosed with a letter from Calcutta in November 1836 to the
Editor of the *Edinburgh Review* Macaulay delivered his review article
of Basil Montagu's *The Works of Francis Bacon, Lord Chancellor of
England*, London, 1825–34. The article was less than friendly to Basil

Montagu and, as we see, less than friendly to Lord Chancellor Bacon. But it does not merit being consigned exclusively to students of Victorian literature: neither, it can be added, does the book – sixteen volumes of it – which Macaulay had agreed to review. Macaulay writes:

At last I send you an article of interminable length about Lord Bacon. I hardly know whether it is not too long for an article in a Review: but the subject is of such vast extent that I could easily have made the paper twice as long as it is... My opinion is formed, not at second hand, like those of nine-tenths of the people who talk about Bacon; but after several very attentive perusals of his greatest works, and after a good deal of thought. If I am in the wrong, my errors may set the minds of others at work, and may be the means of bringing both them, and me, to a knowledge of the truth. I never bestowed so much care on anything that I have written. There is not a sentence in the latter half of the article which has not been repeatedly recast.[46]

Sentences in this extract recall Bacon's words in *Preface* to *Novum Organum*:

And for myself, if in anything I have been either too credulous or too little awake and attentive, or if I have fallen off by the way and left the inquiry incomplete, nevertheless I so present things naked and open, that my errors can be marked and set aside before the mass of knowledge be further infected by them; and it will be easy also for others to continue and carry on my labours.[47]

Macaulay's essay is unlike the essays of Bacon in the manner in which it is written. Not only is it of 'interminable length' as the author confessed; it is also a masterpiece of what Bacon called 'connection and order'.[48] It scarcely consists of 'dispersed meditations'[49] which is what Bacon aimed to produce when publishing essays. But Macaulay in his offer – 'If I am in the wrong, my errors may set the minds of others at work, etc., etc. – in a measure retraces his subject's purpose and procedure whether in *Essays*, *Novum Organum* or elsewhere. Accordingly Macaulay does not fail to recognize salient characteristics manifested in words and deeds of Bacon's 'moral and intellectual constitution'. Bacon's own phrase for this is 'character of disposition'.[50]

Of these observations there are two which among all of them most admirably hit the mark: first, 'the mode in which he (Bacon) communicated his thoughts was peculiar to him. He had no touch of that disputatious temper which he often censured in his prede-

cessors.'[51] The achievement which Macaulay rated highest was Book
I of *Novum Organum*, 'yet no book', he says, 'was ever written in a less
contentious spirit'.[52] Secondly: 'In the temper of Bacon – we speak
of Bacon the philosopher, not of Bacon the lawyer and politician, –
there was a singular union of audacity and sobriety.'[53] The statement
is marred by words in parenthesis. These however are withdrawn in
The History: there the spirit of Francis Bacon was 'admirably
compounded of audacity and sobriety'.[54]

There are other points of major consequence correctly taken by
Macaulay: 'The knowledge in which Bacon excelled all men was a
knowledge of the mutual relations of all departments of knowledge.'[55] 'And generally', Bacon argued, 'let this be a rule, that all
partitions of knowledges be accepted rather for lines and veins than
for sections and separations; and that the continuance and entireness
of knowledge be preserved.'[56] At the same time, as Macaulay points
out, he was adept in handling differences and distinctions. 'He had
an amplitude of comprehension'[57] and 'his mind was wonderfully
quick in perceiving analogies of all sorts'[58] but this was combined
with 'great minuteness of observation'.[59] He quotes Bacon on the
pitfalls both in seeing differences and also in perceiving likenesses. 'It
is the vice, he tells us, of subtle minds to attach too much importance
to slight distinctions; it is the vice on the other hand, of high and
discursive intellects to attach too much importance to slight
resemblances.'[60] Macaulay agrees with Bacon when the latter
claimed that he was well equipped to avoid both vices.

Macaulay notes that 'what he was as a natural philosopher and
a moral philosopher, that he was also as theologian'[61]: and that 'of
all the sciences that which he seems to have regarded with the
greatest interest' was the science of medicine.[62] 'Great and various
as the powers of Bacon were,...all those powers received their
direction from common sense' – he had 'no arguments to persuade
men out of their senses'.[63] One is reminded accordingly that in this
respect perhaps Hobbes was different. Macaulay also notes in a
verdict consorting ill with the rest of his judgments on his subject as
statesman and lawyer that 'Bacon well knew to how great an extent
the happiness of every society must depend on the virtue of its
members; and he also knew what legislators can and what they
cannot do for the purpose of promoting virtue.'[64] In this matter he
compares him to his advantage with Plato in *The Republic*.
Macaulay's remarks precede a quotation out of *Example of a Summary*

Treatise on Universal Justice or the Fountains of Equity, by Aphorisms.[65]
The aphorism quoted is Aphorism v. Macaulay renders Bacon's
Latin thus:

The end [of laws] is the well-being of the people. The means are the
imparting of moral and religious education; the providing of everything
necessary for defence against foreign enemies; the maintaining of internal
order; the establishing of a judicial, financial and commercial system,
under which wealth may be rapidly accumulated and securely enjoyed.[66]

Another historian needs mention here on account of the standing
his work has retained amongst scholars throughout many decades.
Samuel Rawson Gardiner (1829–1902) wrote the *History of England
from the Accession of James I to the Outbreak of the Civil War*. These
volumes, together with their successors, have become, *faute de mieux*,
the authoritative presentation of English events and personalities of
the period which Gardiner covered. This historian was in full
possession of all the available evidence about Bacon. What he wrote
at the start of dealing with him was on the right lines. 'It is in
Bacon's philosophy that the key to his political life is to be found.'[67]
The statement is imprecise in wording. But it is capable of being
interpreted as the correct judgment. Here Gardiner endorses
Montagu's better verdict and not Macaulay's. The former had
written 'Into active life he [Bacon] entered, and carried into it his
powerful mind and the principles of his philosophy.'[68] Gardiner again
correctly proceeds when he continues like this. Bacon's 'hardest
blows were directed against the error...which regards the Executive
Power and the Representative Body as capable, indeed, of treating
with one another on a friendly footing, but as incapable of merging
their distinct personalities in each other. It was thus that the Great
Contract of 1610 was utterly distasteful to him. The King and the
Lower House, he held, were not adverse parties to enter into
bargains. They were members of the same Commonwealth, each
charged with its appropriate function. It was not well that the King
should redress grievances merely because he expected to receive
something in return. It was not well that the Commons should vote
supplies as the purchase money of the redress of grievances. If the
King wished to have obedient and liberal subjects, let him place
himself at their head as one who knew how to lead them. Let the
administration of justice be pure. Let the exercise of the prerogative
be beneficent. Let Parliament be summoned frequently to throw
light on the necessities of the country. If mutual confidence could be

thus restored, everything would be gained.'[69] These statements accurately express Bacon's views and his objections to the so-called Great Contract. Gardiner's position is also sound when he writes: 'In proclaiming this doctrine, Bacon showed that he had entered into the spirit of the future growth of the constitution; as completely as he showed, in the *Novum Organum*, that he had entered into the spirit of the future growth of European science.'[70]

'He' [Bacon] 'was not one man as a thinker and another man as a politician.'[71] Thus Gardiner rejects the error of Macaulay, whom he describes as 'a great writer who has written of Bacon's political life without understanding either the nature of the man or the ideas of the age in which he lived...'.[72] However Gardiner later spoils his case. The book which had offered these statements about Bacon was published in 1883. Two years later, writing in the *Dictionary of National Biography*, Gardiner, again in full possession of all the evidence and even quoting from Bacon's rough notes of 1608, contrived in his tone of writing, to endorse Macaulay and his Whig idols of the market place, censuring Bacon along much the same lines as his predecessor. For example – Gardiner writes – 'it was this intuitive perception of the source of the danger' (that is, the breach of sympathy between the King and the House of Commons) 'which raises Bacon to the first rank among statesmen, whilst at the same time, his failure to recognise that it was as impossible to bring James and the House of Commons to work together, as it had been to bring Elizabeth and Essex to work together – a failure the causes of which lay in Bacon's moral as well as his intellectual nature – led to the catastrophe of his misused life'.[73] 'The support of power for the sake of doing good became a support of power from which no good was to be hoped... It ought to have been evident to Bacon himself that there never would be any prospect of him being able to accomplish any statesmanlike work.'[74] Here we see a blaming of a man in a course for not knowing in advance something which he could scarcely have known until he had thoroughly tried it. In any case, another 1608 jotting, as yet not quoted in this study and not cited by Gardiner, shows that Bacon proposed for himself an alternative curriculum for King James: 'Adv^t to a gen. Mem. of Aff. Succ. Salsb. and amuz the K and P. wth pasty. and glory' (Advertisement to a general memorial of affairs. Succeed Salisbury [in power], and amuse the King and Prince with pastime and glory.)[75]

As in his natural science, so in his political science, Bacon addressed himself to all times and to all places. King James was genuinely learned: naturally Bacon would try to convince him. But in both spheres his relationship with King James and his failures therein are beside the point; or if they are not, this point remains a thoroughly minor one. The reputation of Aristotle scarcely depends upon his successes or failures in instructing Alexander of Macedon. Of these two Bacon writes: 'But for this excellent person Aristotle I will think of him that he learned that humour of his scholar, with whom it seemeth that he did emulate, the one to conquer all opinions, as the other to conquer all nations.'[76] Bacon's aim, following Aristotle, was to conquer all opinions, not merely those of his king. Unlike Alexander the latter lacked designs to conquer all nations. But Bacon could in his turn have learned from the humour of his scholar in regretting hostile confrontations – not this time with swords and gunpowder, but with words and arguments when seeking learning's advancement. Bacon writes: 'And as Alexander Borgia was wont to say of the expedition of the French for Naples, that they came with chalk in their hands to mark up their lodgings, and not with weapons to fight; so I like better that entry of truth which cometh peaceably with chalk to mark up those minds which are capable to lodge and harbour it, than that which cometh with pugnacity and contention.'[77] The historian, Gardiner, failing to leave Macaulay decisively behind him, neglected furthermore to take the cardinal points which Macaulay had so effectively proposed to establish – Bacon's singular freedom from the vice of contentiousness; recognition that in mind and in action he embodied both caution and also audacity; and that he could perceive both differences and likenesses in equal measure.

In this present study I make comparisons and see differences between the first version of *The Advancement of Learning* (1605) and the second (1623). *De Sapientia Veterum* – 'Of the Wisdom of the Ancients' – and *Novum Organum* – 'The New Instrument for Thinking' – were published in between the two versions. *De Sapientia Veterum* appeared in 1609. The date of *Novum Organum* is 1620. The former handles as the title makes plain a special topic in *Historia Literarum*, the history of letters. Such a branch of history recording the story of human learning and arts had, Bacon observed, been neglected. The importance of this learning and of these arts, he wrote, was 'such as to entitle them to a separate history of their own. And this...I mean to be included in Civil History.'[78] As for *Novum*

Organum, this, he explained to King James, is the same argument as
that of the first *Advancement of Learning* (1605) – 'but sunk deeper'.[79]
Also, I make comparisons and see differences between these four
works on the one hand, and earlier unpublished writings on the
other.

Certainly differences and distinctions are encountered in these
areas, just as they are seen in that of three collections of essays (1597,
1612, 1625). These differences and distinctions are discussed, not
omitting relationships between letters, papers and speeches; and the
publications devoted formally to advancing learning. But the
background, for aught one can tell, stays mainly one of constancy.
The same fundamental notions of approach, the same leading
objectives, the same ways of aiming at and achieving these run all
through. These mature rather than change. This remains the case
despite Bacon's confession that he 'alters ever when he adds'. His
reference here is chiefly to progress in achievement not to notions of
approach, leading objectives and ways of aiming at and arriving at
them. Therefore, except when chronological treatment is properly
relevant and needed – in which cases I endeavour to supply it – the
procedure in this study is prevailingly analytical.

In 1623 Bacon urged the University of Cambridge (his college was
Trinity – it was also to be Macaulay's):

> In modesty of mind to retain liberty of understanding, and not to lay up in
> a napkin the talent which has been transmitted to you in trust from the
> ancients. Surely the grace of the divine light will attend and shine upon
> you, if humbling and submitting Philosophy to Religion you make a
> legitimate and dexterous use of the keys of sense; and putting away all zeal of
> contradiction, each dispute with other as if he were disputing with
> himself.[80]

His point in this last remark is that when deliberating within
themselves men scarcely undertake to manifest skills in debate, or
to contradict out of zeal for contending. I seek to have Bacon hold
discourse with himself, following the way he both recommended in
general in his message to his university, and adopted himself in
dealing for example with Aristotle and with Machiavelli. He
wrote 'so let great authors have their due, as time, which is the
author of authors, be not deprived of his due, which is, further and
further to discover truth...'[81], it being in such a cause that Bacon
advocated a *Historia Literarum*, a history of letters. It is clear from his
treatment of them that Aristotle and Machiavelli were likely to

achieve their places in such a history. He made Aristotle and
Machiavelli discourse with themselves – or, which comes to the same
thing, he disputed within himself concerning their respective
contributions to the advancement of learning.

In writing about Bacon I attempt to bear in mind the wishes and
hopes he himself expressed, and to follow the instructions he himself
imparted. No man can confidently enter into, examine and judge the
state of his soul and its contents. Operations are restricted to
handling the evidence which time has provided. This evidence
relates to the outward man. It consists of things written and of things
done. I have sought to 'walk upon the earth'.[82] Earth in this instance
is composed of such evidence. A measure of speculation is scarcely to
be avoided. But the exercise in speculating will I hope not be of the
kind dismissed by Bacon as 'the fume of subtile, sublime, or delectable speculation'.[83] I have sought to muster 'a kind of thoughtful
prudence'[84] against idols 'either adventitious or innate'[85]; also to
interrelate the statements in his teaching, rejecting sharp separations
between the departments of knowledge in which he makes
contributions: also to combine sobriety and caution with audacity,
despising 'vain apprehensions'.[86] This book consists of an argument
within the mind of its author, but this argument is with the man
Bacon. 'Read not to contradict and confute, nor to believe and take
for granted, nor to find talk and discourse, but to weigh and
consider.'[87] These instructions are conveyed in *Of Studies*, a piece he
published in all three essay collections. If it is complained that
extensive quotation from his writings is burdensome to readers, the
alternative consisting of my own renderings would have proved yet
more burdensome. If it is objected that quotations are so plentiful that
what I provide is an anthology, it is not amiss that readers should
meet again the quality of Bacon's prose. Finally, as readers will find
out, this study is concerned only with Bacon. Only in a minimal way
do I presume to touch upon his impact upon others in the field of
natural science, either immediately after his death or in near or later
times.

Two programmes. Know thyself and know the universe of nature

Did Francis Bacon invent what today is called science? The question poses itself: natural science becomes of consequence, and this man makes a mark and a name for himself in his times which he still retains. Without doubt he made plans which he claimed would launch natural philosophy. To this question, as is likely and natural, there have been conflicting replies. The question, as he would himself have hoped, has been disputed almost ever since his own lifetime. He held that disputation if uncontentiously conducted advances knowledge. Perhaps Voltaire (1694–1778) has turned out to be the fair judge: 'Chancellor Bacon proposed new sciences; but Copernicus and Kepler invented them.'[1] 'Francis Bacon, worthier of esteem in his literary works than in his place as Chancellor, opened a quite new career for philosophy.'[2] But 'the true physics, of which Chancellor Bacon had done no more than point out the road in England...Galileo had first discovered in Italy'.[3] However, it is inappropriate not to add that it is Voltaire not Bacon who might have been put out by suggestions made in yet later times that the origins of modern science have roots in schoolmen and scholasticism.

Nevertheless Voltaire is sufficient authority and also appropriate judge since in his remarks about Bacon, and in all that he wrote, whatever the topic, he illustrates the point that in Bacon's times and his own there is no incompatibility between literature – purity of diction, niceness or elegance in presentation – and instruction in matters of consequence and weight. On the contrary it was commonly held that instruction of this kind was likely to be promoted if offered in alliance with the former – 'Francis Bacon...*in his literary works...opened a quite new career for philosophy* – ' (emphasis added).

The same point is implied in Voltaire's judgment on Bacon's *Essays*. He – Voltaire – correctly understood their purpose: 'Ses *Essais de Morales* sont très estimés; mais ils sont fait pour instruire plutôt que pour plaire; et, n'étant ni la satire de la nature humaine, comme les *Maximes* de M. de la Rochefoucauld' (1613–80), 'ni l'école du scepticisme, comme Montaigne' (1533–92), 'ils sont moins lus que ces deux livres ingénieux'.[4] [His *Essais de Morales* are much esteemed; but they are written in order to instruct rather than to please; and being neither satire, like the *Maxims* of M. de la Rochefoucauld, nor of the school of scepticism like Montaigne, they are less read than these two ingenious b ɔks]. When writing like this Voltaire was not implying that as purposes instructing and pleasing were incompatible. On the contrary: affording pleasure was likely to be a successful way of imparting instruction. Much of Bacon's posterity in England has read his *Essays* not as instruction in philosophy, civil and moral, which is what they are; but instead as literature offered for the purpose of inducing pleasure. Reading the *Essays* in this way is less than intelligent if it is assumed that being pleased, interested or entertained necessarily impedes being instructed.

On the question of inventing natural science the testimony of the man himself should be consulted; and though as we shall see a picture producing coherence is capable of emerging, what Bacon says about this is on the face of things conflicting and confusing. Without doubt he made plans which he claimed would successfully launch natural philosophy. For aught that posterity can certainly tell, he resolutely adhered in their entirety to these plans to his death. On the other hand when interpreting the fable of Prometheus he wrote in *De Sapientia Veterum – Of the Wisdom of the Ancients* (published 1609): 'The perfection of the sciences is to be looked for not from the swiftness and ability of one inquirer, but from a succession.'[5] Also he told Father Fulgentius in 1625: 'I work for posterity; these things requiring ages for their accomplishment.'[6]

But this is not all. In addition he provided in the body of *Novum Organum* itself what ought to be an adequate, accurate and enduring verdict. 'For of Alexander and his deeds Aeschines spake thus: Assuredly we do not live the life of mortal men; but to this end were we born, that in after ages wonders might be told of us' as if what Alexander had done seemed to him miraculous. But in the next age Titus Livius took a better and a deeper view of the matter, saying in effect that Alexander 'had done no more than take courage to despise vain apprehensions'. And a like judgment I suppose may be passed on myself in future ages: 'that I did no great things, but simply made less account of things that were accounted great'. In the meantime, as I have already said, 'there is no hope except in a new birth of science; that is, in raising it regularly up from experience and building it afresh'.[7] Bacon succeeded in making less account of Aristotle and of the Greeks. This is Aphorism xcvii in Book I. Here the resort to policy in order to make his point – to the science of rule in peace and war – and to civil history – needs noting. In another aphorism (cxxx), the last in *Novum Organum*'s first Book, where Bacon concludes his general precepts before advancing to explore the unknown territories of nature with the aid of Book II, he explains: 'Nor again do I mean to say that no improvement can be made upon these. On the contrary, I that regard the mind not only in its own faculties, but in its connection with things, must needs hold that the art of discovery may advance as discoveries advance.'[8]

Is there such a thing as natural science? Evidently so: in the twentieth century it has attained a commanding presence. It establishes by virtue of its successful results that this is a knowledge not insufficiently describing the realities which are claimed to be known. This science was not started by Bacon on his own, but he had the idea of a future for it and his idea came true. This idea was not prophecy. ['I mean not to speak of divine prophecies; nor of heathen oracles; nor of natural predictions.'] According to his essay bearing that title prophecies should be rejected, save in so far as they formed part of revealed (which he called inspired) divinity.[9] Instead he had foresight and vision. He wrote in his last will when he bequeathed his fame to the next age: 'For my name and memory, I leave it to men's charitable speeches, and to foreign nations, and the next ages.'[10] Throughout his life he manifestly respected the power of examples not less than he worked for the truth of his precepts.

'I consider history and experience', he wrote in the second *Advancement*, 'to be the same thing as also philosophy and the sciences…'[11] In later times history and experience, and also philosophy and the sciences, have respectively come to be distinguished as notions or pursuits whereas Bacon in each case had kept them joined. It can reasonably be argued that he achieved more as historian than he did in his pondered and actively conducted experience in statesmanship; and also – further – that it was in the range and resourcefulness of his proficiency in historical knowledge, civil and also natural, that he excelled, rather than in philosophy or in sciences. But even though in the long term his precepts for advancing the natural sciences proved less effective and less conclusive than he hoped, the example he set of devotion in the cause was none the less potent both at home and abroad. Voltaire was right. Bacon pointed out a road. He opened a new career. Like Alexander the Great, King of Macedon, he had 'the courage to despise vain apprehensions'. This audacity sufficed. If not in terms precisely of all his teaching, yet in virtue of moral force and intellectual intensity and integrity, he encouraged others. For example in England Bacon encouraged members of a nascent Royal Society. Things must be done in addition to being thought about and disputed over; and positions adopted, whether ancient, modern, or one's own, must be tested in action in terms of perceived and agreed results.

Here there will be concern with a distinct yet by no means a separate and unrelated question: not Bacon and sciences of nature, but Bacon and fields of study like ethics, government and law. Such matters should consist, he proposes, of two parts: 'The one considereth man segregate...; the other congregate or in society.' But is there, for example, such a thing as a civil science for politics – for man congregate or in society? Niccolò Machiavelli conducted himself as if the thing were possible, basing his operations on civil histories. Francis Bacon, availing himself as will be seen of the efforts of Machiavelli, and like the latter using civil histories, claimed to invent it by distinguishing it from the science of morality. But for politics can there be a civil science? – that is, a degree of exact knowledge of the past and present enabling a degree of experimental knowledge focussed upon what is to come? Bacon, following Machiavelli, hedged his proposals with so many cautions and *caveats* that neither could have been surprised by the question. But they might have been perplexed by an answer which is totally in the negative. Political wisdom is still generally granted to be valid as a concept: in Bacon 'wisdom' and 'science' are interchangeable both as terms and concepts. Even today, when they have slipped apart, the notions and practices respectively of wisdom and science have it in common that each is a compound and mixture of pre-existing knowledge and current experience. A difference remains. Today natural science is much more than a possibility, whereas the feasibility of a civil science is widely and persistently doubted. But it is not to stretch all relevant points to propose that it is possible to descry a dynasty or succession in civil science consisting of Machiavelli, Bacon, Hyde, Earl of Clarendon (1608–74), Montesquieu (1689–1755), David Hume the Scot (1711–76), and Edmund Burke (1730–97). Naturally these civil scientists do not all say the same thing, repeating the conclusions of their predecessors. But neither do the successions of specialists in the sciences of nature. All the above civil scientists were readers and writers of civil histories. All of these save the Scot obtained access to civil experience. But scholars inquiring into these matters prefer to write about particular exponents in civil theory, and historians restrict themselves to accounts of differing political doctrines, presenting their accounts as if they were collections of miscellanies. That there can be continuity in a process of accumulating validity is seldom if ever conceded. But if this is the state of affairs it will be borne in mind that Machiavelli and Bacon both postulated and presupposed in however elementary a manner that the possibility of either natural science or of political science depended not only on labours but on a supply of conditions, man-made or even heaven-sent, of a sufficiently propitious character.

The question of Bacon and sciences of man, ethical, governmental, legal, restores the argument to the starting-point, which is the relation between his efforts and the institution of an effectual natural philosophy. But this takes a different form: not, did he invent it? But, was it the chief or the only thing which he wished and planned to advance? Some of his pronouncements do more than suggest that this is the case.

In *Novum Organum*, published in 1620, he states more than once that natural philosophy ought to be esteemed the great mother of the sciences. 'All arts and sciences, if torn from this root, though they may be polished and made fit for use, yet they will hardly grow.' '...let no man look for much progress in the sciences – especially in the practical part of them – unless natural philosophy be carried on and applied to particular sciences, and particular sciences be carried back again to natural philosophy'.[12] Bacon according to these statements is no more than a natural philosopher for the reason that all sciences are provinces of natural philosophy.

Earlier, he wrote in *The Advancement of Learning*, published in 1605: 'We come now to that knowledge whereunto the ancient oracle directeth us, which is the knowledge of ourselves; which deserveth the more accurate handling, by how much it toucheth us much more nearly.'[13] The ancient oracle is Delphi and its utterance and directive is γνωθι σεαυτον – *Know Thyself.* 'This knowledge, as it is the end and term of natural philosophy in the intention of men, so notwithstanding it is but a portion of natural philosophy in the continent of nature.'[14] This is *Advancement* in its first version (1605): in its second version, published in 1623, he repeats that man's knowledge of himself is enjoined by the oracle: 'but of nature herself it is but a portion'.[15]

In *Advancement* (both versions) it is not natural philosophy as in *Novum Organum* but what he called 'Primitive or Summary Philosophy – *Philosophia Prima*' – a First Philosophy which is the mother or root of all arts and sciences. It is good, he writes, before we enter into 'the distributions and partitions of knowledge', 'to erect and constitute one universal science ... as the main and common way, before we come where the ways part and divide themselves ...'[16] The requirement, he explains, is a science which may 'be a receptacle for all such profitable observations and axioms as fall not within the compass of any of the special parts of philosophy or sciences, but are more common and of a higher stage'.[17] The examples he gives of these profitable axioms and observations differ as between the two versions of *Advancement.* But one of them is provided in both: 'Is not the ground, which Machiavel wisely and largely discourseth concerning governments, that the way to establish and preserve them, is to reduce them *ad principia*, a rule in religion and nature, as well as in civil administration?'[18] The function of this primary philosophy would be to show plainly 'the same footsteps of nature, treading or printing upon several subjects or matters'.[19] Such a science is lacking. It would be 'a thing of excellent use for displaying the unity of nature...'[20] Here, too, natural philosophy seems to be presiding. 'Primitive', 'summary', 'primary' philosophy would not be the mother. But she would promote herself none the less to be the grandmother of natural philosophy's numerous progeny.

As things turned out, despite the deliberate declaration of intent which Bacon planted in these statements, none of this successfully arrived at the destination which he held out in prospect. Notwithstanding the phrases – 'the same footsteps of nature', and 'displaying the unity of nature', the excellent use of primary philosophy would not succeed under Bacon's guidance in establish-

ing that all sciences are parts of natural science. Primary philosophy
in its use would not successfully do so. Nor in the event would
Bacon's use of other philosophy.

In nearly all the things which Bacon said required to be done,
because of lack, deficiency or improvability, he himself attempts to
make contributions. But he has two programmes – not disconnected
indeed, but nevertheless two programmes. He will deal with the
knowledges which men have. He will also deal with those which they
as yet lack. Arts and knowledges which men in a measure possess
already lie in the region of *Know Thyself*. Men at present possess these
arts because there is something of soundness in them. Those of which
men are so far deprived are knowledges of the world of nature.
Received arts in natural sciences are so misconducted, Bacon holds,
that a fresh start is demanded. Bacon has plans in both these
departments. Both plans, both programmes are announced in 1605
in *The Advancement of Learning* and they reappear in the second
version in 1623. They are reannounced when he prefaces *Novum
Organum* in 1620. It is explicitly clear from statements in what he
calls the *Plan* of the latter work that Bacon places the two on the
same level. At a critical juncture in the course of *Novum Organum*,
Book 1, the difference between them is referred to in a trenchant
elucidation.

But the two programmes are related as said. In *Plan of the Work*,
that is to say, in the plan of *The Great Instauration*, Bacon writes that
the first part, which is *The Advancement of Learning* 'exhibits a
summary or general description of the knowledge which the human
race at present possesses. For I thought it good to make some pause
upon that which is received; that thereby the old may be more easily
made perfect and the new more easily approached. And I hold the
improvement of that which we have to be as much an object as the
acquisition of more. Besides which it will make one the better
listened to; for "He that is ignorant (says the proverb) receives not
the words of knowledge, unless thou first tell him that which is in his
own heart". We will therefore make a coasting voyage along the
shores of the arts and sciences received; not without importing into
them some useful things by the way'.[21] Received – rightly received
– sciences lie in the area of the oracle of Delphi's directive to *Know
Thyself*.

In the course of this coasting expedition which he leads in
Advancement, a voyage he re-embarks upon in the book's second

version, he makes observations. We find as we shall see that his utterances whether in the texts of the two *Advancements* or elsewhere are in accord with observations like the following: 'I proceed to those errors and vanities which have intervened amongst the studies themselves of the learned, which is that which is principal and proper to the present argument; wherein my purpose is not to make a justification of the errors, but by a censure and separation of the errors to make a justification of that which is good and sound, and to deliver that from the aspersion of the other...'[22] Again: 'so let great authors have their due, as time, which is the author of authors, be not deprived of his due, which is, further and further to discover truth'.[23] Again: 'the advice of the prophet is the true direction in this matter, *State super vias antiquas, et videte quaenam sit via recta et bona et ambulata in ea.* Antiquity deserveth that reverence, that men should make a stand thereupon, and discover what is the best way: but when the discovery is well taken, then to make progression.'[24] Finally, and most aptly to the point:

Neither is my meaning, as was spoken of Socrates, to call philosophy down from heaven to converse upon the earth; that is to leave natural philosophy aside, and to apply knowledge only to manners and policy. But as both heaven and earth do conspire and contribute to the use and benefit of man; so the end ought to be, from both philosophies to separate and reject vain speculations, and whatsoever is empty and void, and to preserve and augment whatsoever is solid and fruitful...[25]

In handling the philosophy of nature of which mankind has so far deprived itself through procedures he dismissed as so inadequate and misguided that the field lies empty and void, Bacon nevertheless writes in the first *Advancement* (and repeats in the second) in the terms he knows and approvingly allows to be recognizable as those employed by Aristotle.

I may without prejudice preserve thus much of the conceit of antiquity, that Physic should contemplate that which is inherent in matter and therefore transitory, and Metaphysic that which is abstracted and fixed. And again, that Physic should handle that which supposeth in nature only a being and moving; and metaphysic should handle that which supposeth further in nature a reason, understanding and platform. But the difference, perspicuously expressed, is most familiar and sensible. For as we divided Natural Philosophy in general into the Inquiry of Causes, and Productions of Effects; so that part which concerneth the inquiry of Causes we do subdivide according to the received and sound division of Causes. The one part which is Physic, Inquireth and handleth the Material and Efficient Causes; and the other, which is Metaphysic, handleth the Formal and Final Causes.[26]

The two in the first part handle the two ways in which things are brought into being; the two in the second deal first, with the realities which are brought into being, and second with the end or purpose they are designed to serve.

Following Aristotle but not naming him Bacon writes:

For Metaphysic we have assigned unto it the inquiry of Formal and Final causes; which assignation, as to the former of them may seem to be nugatory and void, because of the received and inveterate opinion that the inquisition of man is not competent to find out *essential forms* or *true differences*: of which opinion we will take this hold, that the invention of forms is of all other parts of knowledge the worthiest to be sought, if it be possible to be found. As for the possibility, they are ill discoverers that think there is no land, when they can see nothing but sea. But it is manifest that Plato, in his opinion of Ideas, as one that had a wit of elevation situate as upon a cliff, did descry *that forms were the true object of knowledge*; but lost the real fruit of his opinion, by considering of forms as absolutely abstracted from matter, and not confined and determined by matter; and so turning his opinion upon Theology, wherewith all his natural philosophy is infected. But if any man shall keep a continual watchful and severe eye upon action, operation, and the use of knowledge, he may advise and take notice what are the Forms, the disclosures whereof are fruitful and important to the state of man. For as the Forms of substances (Man only except, of whom it is said, *Formavit hominem de limo terrae, et spiravit in faciem ejus spiraculum vitae*, ['He formed man of the dust of the ground, and breathed into his nostrils the breath of life'] and not as of all other creatures, *Producant aquae, producat terra* ('[Let the waters bring forth...Let the earth bring forth']), the Forms of Substances I say (as they are now by compounding and transplanting multiplied) are so perplexed, as they are not to be inquired; no more than it were either possible or to purpose to seek in gross *the forms of those sounds which make words*, which by composition and transposition of letters are infinite. But on the other side to inquire the form of those sounds or voices which make simple letters is easily comprehensible; and being known induceth and manifesteth the forms of all words, which consist and are compounded of them. In the same manner to enquire the Form of a lion, of an oak, of gold; nay, of water, of air, is a vain pursuit: but to enquire the Forms of sense, of voluntary motion, of vegetation, of colours, of gravity and levity, of density, of tenuity, of heat, of cold, and all other natures and qualities, which, like an alphabet, are not many, and of which the essences (upheld by matter) of all creatures do consist; to inquire, I say, the true forms of these, is that part of Metaphysic which we now define of. Not but that Physic doth make inquiry and take consideration of the same natures: but how? Only as to the Material and Efficient Causes of them, and not as to the Forms. For example, if the cause of Whiteness in snow or froth be enquired, and it be rendered thus, that the subtile intermixture of air and water is the cause, it is well rendered; but nevertheless is this the Form of Whiteness? No; but it is the Efficient, which is ever but *vehiculum formae*. This part of Metaphysic I do not find laboured and performed; whereat I marvel not, because I hold it not possible to be invented by that course of invention which hath been used; in regard that men (which is the root of all error) have made too untimely a departure and too remote a recess from particulars.[27]

He holds that as to 'essential forms or true differences', it is possible to find them. It is possible to do so. Also it is desirable as he explains:

the use of this part of Metaphysic which I report as deficient, is of the rest the most excellent in two respects: the one, because it is the duty and virtue of all knowledge to abridge the infinity of individual experience as much as the conception of truth will permit, and to remedy the complaint of *vita brevis, ars longa*; which is performed by uniting the notions and conceptions of sciences. For knowledges are as pyramides, whereof history is the basis. So of natural history, the basis is natural history; the stage next the basis is Physic; the stage next the vertical point is Metaphysic.[28]

Some few pages later Bacon continued:

As for the doubts or *non liquets* [things not clear, not proven] general or in total, I understand those differences of opinions touching the principles of nature, and the fundamental points of the same, which have caused the diversity of sects, schools, and philosophies, as that of Empedocles, Pythagoras, Democritus, Parmenides, and the rest. For although Aristotle, as though he had been of the race of the Ottomans, thought he could not reign except the first thing he did he killed all his brethren; yet to those that seek truth and not magistrality, it cannot but seem a matter of great profit, to see before them the general opinions touching the foundations of nature. Not for any exact truth that can be expected in those theories; for as the same phenomena in astronomy are satisfied by the received astronomy of the diurnal motion, and the proper motions of the planets, with their eccentrics and epicycles, and likewise by the theory of Copernicus, who supposed the earth to move, and the calculations are indifferently agreeable to both, so the ordinary face and view of experience is many times satisfied by several theories and philosophies; whereas to find the real truth requireth another manner of severity and attention.[29]

He holds, so he argues, that in these matters 'real truth' is attainable given another manner of severity and attention. Book II of

Novum Organum is an instrument for discovering forms. It is metaphysics not physics. He claims there that he has provided the key which will open the way to 'real truth' in the understanding of the *phenomena* of nature. But this ambition – not only for himself – was an early one. It was firm and strong by 1605, the first *Advancement*'s publication date.

Arguing constructively in discourse with Aristotle he wrote in *Advancement* (1605 and 1623) that the

second part of metaphysic is the inquiry of final causes, which I am moved to report not as omitted but as misplaced ... this misplacing hath caused a deficience, or at least a great improficience in the sciences themselves. For the handling of final causes, mixed with the rest in physical inquiries, hath intercepted the severe and diligent inquiry of all real and physical causes, and given men the occasion to stay upon these satisfactory and specious causes, to the great arrest and prejudice of further discovery ... For to say that *the hairs of the eye-lids are for a quickset and fence about the sight*; or that *the firmness of the skins and hides of living creatures is to defend them from the extremities of heat or cold*; or that *the bones are for the columns or beams, whereupon the frames of the bodies of living creatures are built*, or that *the leaves of trees are for protecting of the fruit*; or that *the clouds are for watering of the earth*; or that *the solidness of the earth is for the station and mansion of living creatures*, and the like, is well inquired and collected in metaphysic, but in physic they are impertinent. Nay, they are indeed but *remoraes* and hindrances to stay and slug the ship from further sailing; and have brought this to pass, that the search of the physical causes hath been neglected and passed in silence. And therefore the natural philosophy of Democritus and some others, who did not suppose a mind or reason in the frame of things, but attributed the form thereof able to maintain itself to infinite essays or proofs of nature, which they term fortune, seemeth to me (as far as I can judge by the recital and fragments which remain unto us) in particularities of physical causes more real and better inquired than that of Aristotle and Plato; whereof both intermingled final causes, the one as a part of theology, and the other as a part of logic, which were the favourite studies respectively of both those persons. Not because these final causes are not true, and worthy to be inquired, being kept within their own province; but because their excursions into the limits of physical causes hath bred a vastness and solitude in that tract. For otherwise, keeping their precincts and borders, men are extremely deceived if they think there is an enmity or repugnancy at all between them. For the cause rendered, that *the hairs about the eye-lids are for the safeguard of the sight*, doth not impugn the cause rendered, that *pilosity is incident to orifices of moisture; muscosifontes, &c.* Nor the cause rendered, that *the firmness of hides is for the armour of the body against extremities of heat or cold*, doth not impugn the cause rendered, that *contraction of pores is incident to the outwardest parts, in regard of their adjacence to foreign or unlike bodies* and so of the rest: both causes being true and compatible, the one declaring an intention, the other a consequence only. Neither doth this call in question, or derogate from divine providence, but highly confirm and exalt it...[30]

The wisdom of God is the more admirable, 'when nature intendeth one thing, and providence draweth forth another'. In *De Sapientia Veterum – Of the Wisdom of the Ancients* (1609) when dealing with the fable of Pan, he again wrote about providence, on this occasion moving in the other area of providential control, that of the course of men's civil affairs: – 'all the works of divine providence in the world are wrought by winding and roundabout ways – where one thing seems to be doing, and another is doing really – as in the selling of Joseph into Egypt, and the like'.[31]

The contention Bacon sustains is that the possessions men lack are knowledges of the contents and structures of nature. The things they already possess are in divinity and in knowledges of themselves. To improve what we have means to transform these latter into sciences. There was even a task to be undertaken in the realm of divinity. These things we can do. We are not required to find the form of man as a third tier of a pyramid, after passing through the two stages, first history and next what is analogous to physics, thus reaching the form of man and the truth of what he really is. We already know man's formal cause. It is supplied by divinity. Furthermore, we know already his final cause, that is to say, the purpose for which he was made. This too is provided by divinity. The purpose for which he was made was to glorify the creator by observing in obedience his expressly delivered commandments. These include moral imperatives. They also include intellectual imperatives. Man is enjoined to know, control and order himself. The oracle of Delphi and the oracle of scripture tally in this matter. He is also instructed to know, control and order the rest of creation. He can fulfil neither task unless in his responses he applies the gift of reason. Bacon is explicit about the final cause. He is explicit also about the formal cause, but explicit in a different way. He gives the formal cause when he quotes the words and deeds of creation recorded in the canon of sacred scripture. He succinctly formulates the final cause whenever he describes his own aim in both programmes. This aim, when he defines it, is the glory of God and the relief of man's estate by advancing arts and sciences. Since he has supply of man's formal and final causes he will attempt to transform into sciences what men do with their formal and final causes in the region where it seems invitingly possible. This is man's knowledge of himself – Γνῶθι σεαυτόν – (*Know Thyself*). This has two parts, 'philosophy of man segregate', which Bacon calls Human Philosophy or Humanity; and 'philosophy of man congregate', which he calls civil philosophy or policy.[32] In the reference to Socrates which has been cited above the partition is tersely put as that between 'manners' and 'policy'. In civil history, as he claims and as we shall see, he has *data* for both. With this *data* he seeks to construct axioms.

Fixed markers, as we shall see also, are not always and everywhere suspect and to be avoided. A fixed marker is provided for him in revealed religion for instance. But Bacon as he always makes clear both by injunction and in constant practice remains interrogative. *Recte enim Veritas filia Temporis dicitur, non Auctoritatis*[33] – 'For it is rightly said that truth is the daughter of time, not of authority.' Not authority but time, that is to say, what men can achieve in and through time, rules everywhere save in such departments as Inspired Divinity. Even in this latter since Bacon claimed to profess protestantism, truth had proved to be the daughter of time. More than fourteen centuries were required to have elapsed before a 'reformed' and protestant truth could disclose itself, though it is fair to point out that the older version against which protestants protested had itself arrived only in the fullness of time. According to numerous statements on his part protestant truth having established itself was authoritative for Bacon.

As he expressed himself in these matters, the moral imperatives which protestant truth as a religion projects and enjoins are indispensable ingredients when conducting procedures devoted to the advancement of learning. But it is also expressly his teaching that neither the authority of protestantism nor other comparable kinds of authority, human or divine, can claim lawful presence providing readymade positions in exploring the processes of nature or investigating the affairs of men and nations. It supplies the formal and final causes of men, in this matter not differing from popish truth. But apart from these two services, including as they do indispensable contributions in philosophy moral, protestant truth provides answers to questions neither in philosophy natural nor in philosophy civil. None are available save such as can be discovered by correct procedures.

If a man starts, Bacon says, with doubts, he may discover

certainties. If he proceeds from certainties, he is likely if honest to achieve doubts. Starting with doubts about all previous certainties in natural philosophy/science, rejecting them all and proclaiming a fresh start, he indicates in *Advancement* an undertaking to offer, and in *Novum Organum*, Book II, he achieves the laying out, of the plan the result of which will be certainties in this field of knowledge. This, it will be understood, is subject to the proviso that men have got the *data* of which so far they have been deprived, and that with the help of this material they have succeeded in constructing axioms.

When working as he does from early days in other areas, man's knowledges of man, his formula announced in *Advancement*, Book I, is employed no less. 'If a man will begin with certainties, he shall end in doubts; but if he will be content to begin with doubts, he shall end in certainties.'[34] In these other areas he begins at a point taken to be dependable – witness giving man's formal and final causes; witness that man has a rational soul constructed in the likeness of the creator; and evidence also of instructions on ways in which to employ it. Also, Bacon is aided by other markers to be adopted and retained as time's fruits. If these are retained, not discarded, that is because they accord with observation and experience, not because of their convenience or their expedience. In both areas, human or natural, procedure begins with observations and seeks to complete itself in arts. But in the human department the certainties pursued and achieved plainly are not offered as absolute and final like those promised in the department of nature in *Novum Organum* Book II. Instead they are provisional. They are adjustable in relation with findings as operations proceed. *Novum Organum* – even Book II which, so he proposes, will produce finalities – together with much work elsewhere is presented in the form of aphorisms. Aphorisms, he explains, do not establish final positions. Instead, they serve to prepare and stimulate further thinking and acting, these two in interacting and therefore, it was to be expected, productive interchanges.

When men seek to change what they already possess into sciences, that is to say, when they set out to improve what is valid and valuable in their inheritance the *formula* implies doubting at every stage. Time consists of a present and future in addition to comprising a past. Certainties are sufficient but temporary. They are achieved but also discarded *ambulando* – in courses expecting movement and devoted to it. Bacon does not explain himself in this. The state of affairs is revealed in what he does in extant and improvable arts and also in what he proposes other men should do. On the other hand work in the realms of what as yet we lack can result, as he appears to state the case, in a quicker, more immediate and more certain kind of certainty. Fuller treatment of the topic, Bacon and certainty, like that of Bacon and Aristotle is postponed to a late stage in this argument. Bacon and certainty raises questions about his connections with Pyrrhonians, the exponents of scepticism and of radical doubt.

Doubts are to be cultivated inside sciences. They are also to be directed against impermeable barriers which men erect between sciences. Bacon maintains consistently that sciences however they may differ should not be divided and separated: 'And generally let this be a rule, that all partitions of knowledges be accepted rather for lines and veins than for sections and separations; and that the continuance and entireness of knowledge be preserved.'[35] Failure to observe this rule 'hath made particular sciences to become barren, shallow and erroneous...'[36] For example, Cicero the orator complained of Socrates and his school, that they separated philosophy and rhetoric; whereupon, rhetoric became an empty and verbal art.[37] Copernicus' opinion that the earth rotates, 'which astronomy itself cannot correct, because it is not repugnant to any of the *phenomena*, yet natural philosophy may correct'.[38] We see that medical knowledge if 'destituted and forsaken by natural philosophy, is not much better than an empirical practice'.[39]

Embodying it in his practice, Bacon embraced and maintained the position that no field of study, and no topic or phenomenon within a field of study, could successfully be investigated in isolation. In Aphorism LXX of *Novum Organum* Book I he wrote: '...No one successfully investigates the nature of a thing in the thing itself; the inquiry must be enlarged, so as to become more general.'[40] He repeats the statement or implies it in Aphorism LXXXVIII (twice),[41] also in Aphorism XCIX;[42] also in Aphorism CVI[43] and in Aphorism CX.[44] Writing in *Historia Ventorum*, the History of the Winds, and again making the same point, he explains: 'If men could only bring themselves not to fix their thoughts too intently on the consideration of the subject before them, rejecting everything else as irrelevant, and not to refine with endless and most unprofitable speculations thereon, they would never be so dull as they are wont to be, but by a free passage and transference of their thoughts they would find many things at a distance which near at hand are concealed. And therefore, in the law of nature, as well as in the civil law, we must proceed with sagacity of mind to look for like and analogous cases.'[45]

Men, he maintains, lack reliable information about the nature of nature. Areas to be occupied by natural philosophy are as yet empty. No one knows how widely as an operating discipline its frontiers may extend. Whatever else men have and do, and however else they are constituted, men have and are bodies, comprising bones, sinews, flesh and blood – these latter being made of the same stuff as the remainder of creation. 'Humanity particular', that is, knowledge of man segregate, 'consisteth of the same parts whereof man consisteth, that is, of knowledges which respect the body, and of knowledges which respect the mind'.[46] These twins however distinct may not, at least in earthly life, be separated or divided. Inseparable is too weak a word. Because of 'sympathies and concordances' between the mind and the body in mutual action and reaction the two, Bacon states, are mixed.[47] In the relief of man's estate, the primary purpose of all his exercises, every form of knowledge is implicated. A primary province needing attention is the condition of medicine. Of all the sciences, Macaulay noted, it was the science of medicine 'which he seems to have regarded with the greatest interest'. But the interest was not restricted to medicine which seeks to achieve cures. Studies should be undertaken of the mutual interactions between bodies and minds in persons enjoying normal good health. This in the realm of matters human (but at the point of junction between mind and matter, man and nature) was an area (or areas, for sciences must not be divided and separated) which Bacon as will be seen marked out in *Novum Organum* as a field for possible contributions by himself.

Not unexpectedly there is detectable unity throughout the created universe. Man and the world, he holds, are the work of a single agent. However, as we have seen, Bacon makes statements explicitly excluding the notion that human nature is the same as that of the rest. The respective origins of man and of the universe comprising creatures other than human are different in kind. He bases himself on the Scriptures. 'Knowledges are as pyramides whereof history is the basis.'[48] In this instance knowledge is founded neither on natural, nor on civil, but on sacred history. *Formavit hominem de limo terrae, et spirat in faciem ejus spiravit vitae* ('And the Lord formed man of the dust of the ground, and breathed into his nostrils the breath of life'), and not as of all other creatures *Producant aquae, producat terra*[49] ('And God said, Let the waters bring forth...Let the earth bring forth.') '...it is the works of God, which do show the omnipotency and wisdom of the maker, but not his image. And therefore therein the heathen opinion differeth from the sacred truth; for they supposed the world to be the image of God, and man to be an extract or compendious image of the world; but the scriptures never vouchsafe to attribute to the world that honour, as to be the image of God, but only the work of his hands; neither do they speak of any other image of God, but man.'[50]

Men like other living creatures are endowed with bodies and irrational souls. Unless all these bodies, human and non-human, are inhabited by what Bacon terms irrational souls they are not alive but dead; or else they are creatures like stars, rocks or water which, on the face of things, have never been alive at all. Elsewhere Bacon calls the forces of life 'spirits'. But since men are fashioned in the maker's likeness they are endowed not only with irrational souls but also with souls which are rational, and rational souls comprise intelligence and will. Certainly this looks like starting out not with doubts but with certainties. But Bacon places the contents of sacred scripture beyond his doubts. Secondly, results in his and other men's observation and experience coincide with these deliveries of sacred truth. In regard to man's formal cause, observation and experience reveal that in varying degrees of rational or moral success or failure, his soul is rational and moral. With regard to his final cause, observation and experience witness that throughout time he is in general inquisitive and acquisitive. Without a difference of this kind between humanity and conditions prevailing in the rest of the created order, how could men have made attempts, valid though fragmentary, at knowing themselves and achieving knowledge of their own kind? Also, how could they have set about devising plans, though wrong-headed and useless, to learn about the rest of the world, the rest being a remainder which includes their bodies?

'My great work goeth forward' he tells Toby Mathew in 1609; 'and after my manner, I alter ever when I add. So that nothing is finished till all be finished.'[51] He goes forward with the aid of chosen markers, for instance Inspired divinity. Nevertheless and even so, Bacon did not permit himself to become consolidated unduly or prematurely. Referring, as the present writer refers, to a final *Advancement* when comparing it with the first is an unavoidable misnomer. Perhaps – even probably – if Bacon had lived longer the world would have seen further versions and conceivably even a new *Novum Organum*. There is a near promise of this latter in the last aphorism of Book I (1620) cited earlier in this argument, and also as will be seen a firmer one elsewhere at a later date. Nevertheless the platform from which he starts out and from which he continues to operate conforms in steadiness with declarations made in the first *Advancement* and repeated in the second: 'I do take the consideration in general and at large, of Human Nature to be fit to be emancipate and made a knowledge by itself...'[52] 'so then we have constituted (as in our own wish and advice) the inquiry touching human nature entire, as a just portion of knowledge to be handled apart'.[53] 'Thus then have I explained the doctrine concerning the nature of man undivided and likewise the league between the mind and the body.'[54]

'...that knowledge whereunto the ancient oracle directeth us...is the knowledge of ourselves'.[55] This consists of knowledges of mind and knowledges of body. The two are to be handled 'entire' and 'undivided', that is to say, together. As far as possible neither knowledge is to be cultivated at the expense of, or to the exclusion of the other. Thus Bacon, it is plain, states in both versions of *Advancement* that he holds human nature to be but a portion of the continent of nature. He nevertheless publishes in both versions his declaration of independence for his own and other men's studies of man; for studies, that is to say, of the products of man's mind and will in rightly received arts.

The context of this declaration of independence requires to be noted. Its context is not the doctrine which Bacon expounds that man is made in the maker's image to the extent that he possesses a rational soul. Instead there is a context more immediate. 'I do take', he writes, 'the consideration...of human nature to be fit to be emancipate...etc....chiefly in regard of the knowledge concerning the sympathies and concordances between the mind and body, which being mixed cannot be properly assigned to the sciences of either.'[56]

Nevertheless, the demands of the lesser and immediate context require resort and flight back to the context which is less immediate but greater. *Know Thyself* – this, says Bacon, is the end and term of natural philosophy in the intention of men – that is to say, this is the point at which men recognize that the domain of natural philosophy has come to an end; and that at which another province, that of knowledge of themselves, has begun. But nevertheless, he insists, this knowledge, *Know Thyself*, continues to constitute a province of the continent of nature. It does so because men have not only minds, they also have bodies and physical life. Furthermore, Bacon suspects and observes that bodies affect minds, and minds bodies, in ways to be explored. But Nature's forces cannot find out about nature, collecting histories of themselves and making axioms. Nor can these forces find out about man. Bodies can make no discoveries about minds. Nor can bodies know ways in which they affect minds or are themselves affected by them. It is clear therefore that in both programmes, improving present belongings and acquiring things brand new, minds, men's rational souls and wills, stand first and retain primacy.

Interpreting the wisdom of the ancients in the book with that title published in 1609 Bacon wrote when discussing the fable of *Prometheus*:

Prometheus clearly and expressly signifies Providence: and the one thing singled out by the ancients as the special and peculiar work of Providence was the creation and constitution of Man. One reason for this, no doubt, was that the nature of man includes mind and intellect, which is the seat of providence; and since to derive mind and reason from principles brutal and irrational would be harsh and incredible, it follows almost necessarily that the human spirit was endued with providence not without the precedence and warrant of the greater providence. But this was not all. The chief aim of the parable appears to be, that Man, if we look to final causes, may be regarded as the centre of the world; insomuch that 'if man were taken away from the world, the rest would seem to be all astray, without aim or purpose, to be like a besom without a binding, as the saying is, and to be leading to nothing.[57]

Bacon aims for improvements. He therefore studies minds, their constitution, together with the propensities and obstructions, whether in minds or impinging upon them, which he calls idols. Also he studies men's dispositions and passions. Also aiming for improvements, he explores knowledges in sufficiently valid extant arts which have resulted from the working of minds and wills – moral knowledge, political knowledge (which includes legal knowledge) and divinity. This is an enterprise, as he says, which 'we have constituted (as in our own wish and advice)'.[58] It is a discernible programme from early stages. The other programme, that directed at achieving arts we as yet do not possess, at unlocking secrets of the world of nature, and of the bodies of men, and at discovering essential forms and true differences – this is long pondered. In 1620 it is laid out in Book II of *Novum Organum* to the exclusion of other matters and the other programme.

He fosters two programmes. It is true that in the territory of human self-knowledge his pyramid metaphor requires adjustment. He does not strive upwards towards a summit, starting at ground level. Instead, stationed securely at the apex of a pyramid, he moves outwards horizontally on a number of radii, using or collecting histories and seeking axioms. He nevertheless follows two lines of thought not two forms of thought. The two pursuits are distinct, but they are not separate and divided. This is for two reasons.

First, he will seek to improve arts which are extant and deservedly so, doing this as end in itself. 'I hold the improvement of that which we have to be as much an object as the acquisition of more.'[59] But he will also try to further these extant arts as a means to an end; using this exercise as an introduction to discovering arts which as yet are lacking. 'I thought it good to make some pause upon that which is received; and thereby the old may be more easily made perfect and the new more easily approached.'[60] Therefore a difference in procedure is scarcely to be expected. Neither would it have been countenanced. Nor was it intended. We have to collect histories. Out of these we make axioms. The latter task must be performed in the right way. We must avoid the 'root of all errors' which is that men 'have made too untimely a departure and too remote a recess from particulars'.[61] *Novum Organum*, Book I, though it prefaces Book II's plan for elucidating, not the world of man's knowledge of man, but the universe of nature, straddles both programmes. In both pursuits what is projected begins in observation and is aimed to end in arts.

Secondly the subject matters to which the two programmes are addressed are not separate but joined. There is an area of union between them. Men have minds. They also have bodies, the latter consisting of the same material as the rest of the things in the natural order. Bacon plans to investigate minds, bodies, and also their mutual relationships.

CHAPTER 3

Knowledges are as pyramids, whereof history is the basis – history civil – this latter extended to describe and to include the Common Law of England

'The parts of human learning have reference to the three parts of Man's Understanding, which is the seat of learning; History to his Memory, Poesy to his Imagination, and Philosophy to his Reason. Divine knowledge receiveth the same distribution; for the spirit of man is the same, though the revelation of oracle and sense be diverse.'[1] This pronouncement in the first *Advancement* prefaces the entire enterprise of advancing learning, whether by bettering the world of man's moral and political activities or by probing instead into the universe of nature. Bacon expands and articulates this in the final version. In this second extended pronouncement the parts played by 'individuals', or 'particulars' – the terms are interchangeable – are expounded with the consequence that the function of histories – divine, civil and natural – is explained. 'Knowledges are as pyramides whereof history is the basis.'[2] History is the foundation of sciences because history consists of, or contains particulars and exhibits them. History is the observing and recording by individuals or particulars – divine or human – of individuals or particulars – either divine, human or natural. History

is properly concerned with individuals, which are circumscribed by place and time... And if individuals are found, which are either unique in their species, like the sun and moon; or notable deviations from their species, like monsters, the description of these has as fit a place in Natural History as that of remarkable men has in Civil History. All this relates to the Memory. Poesy, in the sense in which I have defined the word, is also concerned with individuals; that is, with individuals invented in imitation of those which are the subject of true history;...this is the work of the imagination. Philosophy discards individuals; neither does it deal with the impressions immediately received from them, but with abstract notions derived from these impressions; in the composition and division whereof according to the

46

law of nature and fact its business lies. And this is the office and work of
Reason.[3]

'The sense, which is the door of the intellect, is affected by
individuals only.' The images of those individuals 'the human mind
proceeds to review and ruminate; and thereupon either simply
rehearses them, or makes fanciful imitations of them, or analyses
them and classifies them'. 'Wherefore from these three fountains,
Memory, Imagination and Reason, flow these three emanations,
History, Poesy, and Philosophy; and there can be no others. For I
consider history and experience to be the same thing, as also
philosophy and the sciences.' 'Nor', he concludes, 'do I think that
any other division is wanted for theology.' 'Theology...in like
manner consists either of Sacred History, or of Parables, which are
a divine poesy, or of Doctrines and precepts, which are a perennial
philosophy.'[4]

Attentive readers of *Advancement*'s final version will notice that
at another place in it Bacon makes a favourable reference to 'one of
the moderns', who, he wrote, 'remarked on the conceit and
precipitancy of some of the ancients, who in too eagerly fixing their
eyes and thoughts on the memory, imagination, and reason have
neglected the Thinking Faculty, which holds the first place'. Bacon
commented: 'For he who remembers or recollects, thinks; he who
imagines, thinks; he who reasons, thinks; and in a word the spirit
of man, whether prompted by sense or left to itself, whether in
the functions of the intellect, or of the will and affections, dances
to the tune of the thoughts.'[5] This is the comment. And in this
the second *Advancement* he has added to the formula recited in
the first concerning the three 'fountains', Memory, Imagination,
and Reason. Whether 'simply rehearsing' the impact of individu-
als/particulars (in the case of history); or 'making fanciful imitations' (in the case of poetry); or 'analysing and classifying' (in the
case of philosophy); the human mind, he writes, proceeds to
'ruminate' and to 'review' the individuals/particulars which it
observes and absorbs.[6] Ruminating and reviewing – both of these
are thinking.

Between the publishing of the two *Advancements* Bacon produced
Descriptio Globi Intellectualis. His account here differs somewhat but
not materially, save in that he puts a further and evidently closely
related point, namely the decisive function of the thinking faculty
when it deals with similarities and with differences:

With ... individuals and this material the human mind perpetually exercises itself, and sometimes sports. For as all knowledge is the exercise and work of the mind, so poesy may be regarded as its sport. In philosophy the mind is bound to things; in poesy it is released from this bond, and wanders forth, and feigns what it pleases. That this is so anyone may see, who seeks ever so simply and without subtlety into the origins of intellectual impressions. For the images of individuals are received by the sense and fixed in the memory. They pass into the memory whole, just as they present themselves. Then the mind recalls and reviews them, and (which is its proper office) compounds and divides the parts of which they consist. For the several individuals have something in common one with another, and again something different and manifold. Now this composition and division is either according to the pleasure of the mind, or according to the nature of things as it exists in fact. If it be according to the pleasure of the mind, and these parts are arbitrarily transposed into the likeness of some individual, it is the work of imagination ... If on the other hand these same aspects of individuals are compounded and divided according to the evidence of things, and as they really show themselves in nature ... this is the office of reason; and all business of this kind is assigned to reason.[7]

Bacon taught that a man's senses – his sight, hearing, touch, taste, smell – are the doors by means of which the things and the persons outside himself are introduced into his mind. This 'revelation of sense' provides a man with his experience – or rather, if he is to proceed in knowledge, with the first stage of it. The next two stages of his experience – Bacon's and, as he teaches, everyone else's – are when a man thinks about what he thus observes in history and experience (these two being, as he decides, 'the same thing'), perceiving distinctions but also seeing likenesses, and when thereafter he embarks upon actions. But sense 'is affected by individuals only'. 'Individuals' which are circumscribed by place and time, can signify 'particulars' which are not persons but animate or inanimate things – things which are other than human. Particulars can be things and not persons because history is as much natural as civil. But also history is as much civil as natural. Therefore particulars can signify beings who are human – not only their bodies with their members and organs, but also their minds with the processes and products of willing and reasoning which come out of them.

It is not the case that Bacon was or set out to be a natural scientist and no other sort of scientist. Nor is it true that he was more of a natural philosopher than any other kind, though it is also true that in terms of achievement he failed to become as much of a natural philosopher as he planned. One cause which obscures recognition of him as other than exclusively a philosopher of nature has been a less than accurate reception of his signals. Another resides in the circumstance that, because they are 'well-written', works in *Know Thyself* like his *Essays* – which, now as then, 'of all my other works, have been most current', *The History of the Reign of King Henry the 7th* – his long deliberated exercise in civil history writing – and sometimes even the *Advancement of Learning* itself – in its first and English version – came to be classed less as agencies of instruction and therefore of improvement than as 'English literature' in a rendering which the term 'literature' acquires at a later date – that is to say, writings designed with no other purpose than that of furnishing entertainment or interesting pastimes, pleasing or painful, for writer and reader alike – the former being inspired, it is likely, by ambition to excel or – as Bacon himself might have put it – by habits of intellectual self-indulgence. Similarly Bacon's numerous and persisting – and usually no less 'well-written' – exercises in matters of government and law – the separating of which from the aforementioned productions and from the *Great Instauration* as a whole having no justification which convinces – have been segregated and too hastily dismissed as no more than professional.

What he offered in the *Great Instauration* was either work or counsel: 'giving assistance in every case', he said, 'either by work or by counsel'.[8] In nearly all the things which he said required to be done, because of lack, deficiency, or improvability, he himself attempted to make contributions. But it cannot be maintained, considering either execution or advice, that he provided more in knowledges of nature than he did in man's knowledges of himself. The reverse is the case. No one – and not Bacon himself – claims that he succeeded in making startling advances in the former, though it is not the case that he provided nothing. He made contributions in natural history, the basement of the pyramid. He did so also in the achievement of axioms, the next tier above the basement. Nevertheless, surveying as he did what was extant and what was not, the natural branch of philosophy was more deficient in his judgment than the human. He did not, accordingly, succeed in producing more of the former than of the latter.

In promoting philosophy/science, as we have seen, he was determined both when working and when counselling no less to improve what was extant than to fill what were voids: 'the improvement of that which we have' is 'as much an object as the acquisition of more'. Work in philosophy/science could proceed and advance in only one way: it must be founded on prior achievements in history. 'Knowledges are as pyramides whereof history is the basis.' But work in history natural had been more defective up to his times than work in history civil. Indeed, in his judgment the two histories both in antiquity and afterwards lay at opposite poles with respect to their condition. The ancients had history civil. 'For the history of the exemplar states', he wrote in *Advancement*'s first version (1605), 'it is extant in good perfection.'⁹ The moderns had it too, even if not enough of it either in quantity or quality. On the other hand the history natural of both ancients and moderns was pitifully meagre. 'And in a word all the natural history we have, whether in the mode of inquiry or in the matter collected, is quite unfit for the end which I have mentioned, namely, the Foundation of Philosophy.'¹⁰ This is the position in terms of which we find that from start to finish he chiefly conducts himself. In all surveyable fields of natural history, according to conclusions published in the final *Advancement*, nothing prevails save short-measure, deficiency and lack. In both *Advancements* history natural is divided into three – its normal course, its irregularities, and arts, that is to say, nature wrought upon by men. According to the first version, the state of affairs in the first compartment, nature's normal course, is granted to be satisfactory: 'the first of these no doubt is extant and that in good perfection'.¹¹ It is in the second and third compartments where matters are 'handled so weakly and unprofitably'¹² that he is moved to note them as deficient. About these latter two, no change of judgment is found in the final *Advancement*. But in addition, in this final version, the situation even in the first compartment is reviewed only to be deplored. In the matter collected there is no history of the celestial bodies 'exhibiting the actual *phenomena* simply and apart from theories':¹³ 'no history of comets, fiery meteors, winds, rains, storms, and the like: no history of the earth and sea, mountains, rivers, tides, sands, woods, islands and the shape of continents': also, 'there are no accounts of fire, air, earth and water.'¹⁴ Even in the area where 'writers have shown any conspicuous industry, …they have rather filled it with things superfluous (as figures of animals, plants, and the like) than enriched it with sound and careful observations, which should ever be annexed to natural history'.¹⁵

Here in this realm there was next to nothing a man could build on.

In that department both working and counselling Bacon urged the amassing of foundation material. He incited King James: he exhorted every one else, living and not yet born. The King, he said, should take order 'for the collecting and perfecting of a Natural and Experimental History, true and severe (unencumbered with literature and book-learning), such as philosophy may be built upon';[16] so that 'philosophy and the sciences may no longer float in air, but rest on the solid foundation of experience of every kind ...'[17] 'There is none who has dwelt upon experience and the facts of nature as long as is necessary.'[18] He himself bequeathed a posthumously published *Sylva Sylvarum*, Wood of Woods – a collection of natural history and experiments – and three natural and experimental histories published during his life-time; namely, *The History of Winds*, *The History of Life and Death* and *The History of Dense and Rare*. The second of these histories is the best. But all four of these make their appearances late. He wrote yet another natural history – a *History of Comets*. He did not publish this one.

The present writer is not willing for the reason that he is not competent to assess whether the statement in the first *Advancement* – history of nature in its normal course 'no doubt is extant and in good perfection' – is preferable as describing the state of affairs prevailing in this field in Bacon's day to the stand which he takes in *Advancement*'s second version. It is amply evident that on this point, though not on the condition of the two other branches of work in the department of natural sciences, he changes his stance.

A statement equally strong or stronger is contained in *Descriptio Globi Intellectualis*, a work he produced as we have said in the interval between the two *Advancements*:

Now the noblest end of natural history is this; to be the stuff and matter of true and lawful induction; and to draw from the sense enough to inform the intellect ... This is that natural history which constitutes a solid and eternal basis of true and active philosophy; this it is which gives the first spark to the pure and real life of nature; and whose genius being neglected and not propitiated, has caused us to be visited most unhappily by that host of spectres and kingdom of shadows which we see flitting about among the philosophies, afflicting them with utter barrenness in respect of works. Now I affirm and bear witness that a natural history properly adapted to this end is not extant, but is wanting, and should be set down among the deficients. And let no man be so dazzled either by the great names of ancient writers or the great volumes of modern, as to think this complaint of mine unjust.[19]

Two observations should be made. First, in his imagination and vision he came to be vindicated by subsequent time and its fruits. Compared with what was yet unknown, but which could and would be known in the future in natural history, extant knowledge in this field scarcely deserved mention. Secondly, if it be suggested that he chose to sleight by ignoring the accomplishments of others, whether ancients or moderns, in order to promote his own plans for improved natural histories,it is plain that in this matter as in others he throws standpoints he adopts open to inspection: 'And for myself', he wrote in *Novum Organum's Preface*, '... if in anything I have been either too credulous or too little awake and attentive, or if I have fallen off by the way and left the inquiry incomplete, nevertheless I so present these things naked and open, that my errors can be marked and set aside before the mass of knowledge be further infected by them; and it will be easy also for others to continue and carry on my labours.'[20]

By contrast with the final stated assessment of the position in natural history, he maintained, making this evident in word and deed, that in civil history, and also upon it, men could build on what others had achieved – not only providing civil histories which were in short supply for modern times, but work to erect philosophies for man's conduct using civil histories – and chiefly ancient ones – as base. Urging the possibilities inherent in these extant civil histories and their use as foundation material for moral and civil sciences, he explored the possibilities in his practice, not at the end but from an early stage in his life.

When assessing Bacon's attitude to civil history, it will be recognized that his expressed continuing awareness of the presence and chronically damaging sway of the idols of men's minds does not imply that all things in a landscape will always be in flux for him. A man with vision less penetrating could scarcely have arrived at such a notion as that of the idols of men's minds. In men of this calibre, who are both resolute and purposeful and also superlatively endowed intellectually, a vision revealing no landmarks is not likely to be cultivated. Minds constitutionally unstable or disunited, as Bacon's was not, scarcely produce thinkers, still less thinkers who are also active and practical in their commitments. Nor do sceptics, temperamentally negative in all things.

The landscape which Bacon contemplated was not fluid. For him there was not only the one fixed marker, the marker already mentioned – the sacred scriptures of revealed religion. Instead he can observe more than one, acquired either early or at a later stage. Since he provides no history of his thoughts it is scarcely possible to decide which should be classed as which. But two, acquired early or at a later stage, remain fixed – not only the scriptures of the Old and New Testament but also a canon of civil histories, written also in ancient times by the citizens of Greece and Rome. 'For the history of the exemplar states', he writes in the first *Advancement*, 'it is extant in good perfection... In which sequences of story the text of Thucydides and Xenophon in the one, and the texts of Livius, Polybius, Sallustius, Caesar, Appianus, Tacitus, Herodianus in the other, to be kept entire without any diminution at all, and only to be supplied and continued.'[21]

Both of these, the canon of Inspired Scripture and the pagan secular canon which he proposes display unmistakable excellences. They also have it in common that they have become newly available as fruits of time. The Vulgate, the Latin Bible, was among the first books to be printed. This *corpus* of sacred scripture was brought into widespread use by Protestant reformers in the sixteenth century. They did not invent it – they translated, published and advertised it. The contents of the other canon, historians of Greece and Rome in antiquity as Bacon lists them, were rediscovered as texts in the period preceding that of the Protestant reformers. Thus these texts are made accessible for study once more. Of names included in the canon only those of Livy, Sallust and Caesar had, though to a limited extent, been current in intervenient centuries.

But absence of continuous flux in Bacon's landscape, and the visibility and stability of his observed markers, does not carry the consequence that his approach to them is a mindless acceptance. Since these markers deserve, he holds, to be immovable he does not move them. But his adherence is not servile and questionless. His injunctions in *Of Studies* (version of 1625) are: 'Read not to contradict and confute, nor to believe and take for granted, nor to find talk and discourse, but to weigh and consider. Some books are to be tasted, others are to be swallowed, and some few to be chewed and digested; that is, some books are to be read only in parts, others to be read but not curiously' [that is to say, not overcarefully], 'and some few to be read wholly, and with diligence and attention'.[22] Expressing no questioning that the sacred canon was supernaturally inspired and that therefore its contents were inerrable, the

injunctions in *Of Studies* nevertheless apply – and Bacon applies
them – with respect to this first and sacred canon. Further, it will be
seen at a later stage that Bacon requests study of these sacred
scriptures in a search to discover whether some tenets of faith carry
greater weight than others. Similarly he does not read his second and
secular canon in order to contradict and confute it – that is, he does
not join sceptics of his times who had begun to extend scepticism to
cover knowledge in civil history. Ancient scepticism as presented by
Sextus Empiricus was directed against the three divisions of ancient
philosophy, logic, natural science and moral science. Sextus
Empiricus had given moderns a lead, but no more, when he described
all historians as liars.[23] In historical pyrrhonists temperamental
negativity produced not criticism but hypercriticism: 'there is a
disposition contrary to contradict and cross…'[24] There are those
'who deny that we can know anything, and so introduce a wandering
kind of inquiry that leads to nothing…'[25] Bacon does not agree with
such people.

Also, he rejects an opposite disposition, the one which is too easily
persuadable and too little questioning. He does not read 'to believe
and take for granted'. There are those 'who are ready in
deciding…'[26] He opposes doubters who turn doubt into an absolute.
Equally, he disowns men scarcely capable of doubting. Further, he
does not read his secular canon to find talk and discourse. Instead he
studies it to the glory of God and for the use and profit of the human
race. To this combined end he reads it wholly, with diligence and
attention.

But there was a further respect in which Bacon's treatment of his
secular canon was in no way a case of mindless acquiescence. There
was another fashion in which he studied it to the glory of God and
the use and profit of men. It was to be 'kept entire and without any
diminution at all…'[27] It was unimprovable, but it was not sacrosanct.
Here it differed from Bacon's first marker and resembled his
others. This was a 'matter of magnificence, rather to be commended
than required'. Nevertheless, the secular canon should be 'supplied
and continued'. He himself supplied and continued it – and in this
way enlarged it – in his contribution to the history of England – *The
History of the Reign of King Henry the 7th*.

He directs the same discipline – and also, as will be seen, adds his
own supply and continuation – to the procedures, utterances and
axioms of the man who in his *Discorsi* expounds for him the notion

and practice of civil history, not as the ruminating and reviewing of particulars into a simple rehearsal consisting of pure narrative; but as particulars further ruminated into observations, these being mixed with the narrative. Because Machiavelli expounds this mixed history in a further recent fruit of time he becomes another fixed marker. But Bacon reads him not to contradict and confute, nor to believe and take for granted, nor to find talk and discourse, but to weigh and consider and indeed to chew and digest. Though we shall find him declaring that Machiavelli's mixed history was something of which he greatly approved, Machiavelli is never introduced without appended judgments: 'Machiavel wisely and largely discourseth' on the policy and duty of restoring institutions to their first principles:[28] in regard to mixed history 'some grave and wise men have used it':[29] '...a form of writing which Machiavel chose wisely and aptly for government':[30] 'For Machiavel notes wisely': 'a natural man of Italy',[31] that is to say, he was a layman not a divine, but notable all the same as observer of causes and consequences of controversies in the church:[32] in other contexts Bacon writes that 'the authority of Machiavel seemeth not to be contemned':[33] and 'Neither is the authority of Machiavel to be despised.'[34] He rejects him outright on three occasions – or rather he cites three positions culled from his work and condemns them as corrupt.

Of Studies, published in 1597, republished in 1612, and published yet once more in 1625, announces that 'histories make men wise',[35] that is to say, histories civil do so. In *Advancement* (1623 version) Bacon refers to 'the wiser sort of historians'.[36] He does this as will be seen in his study of 'characters of dispositions'. No doubt among writers of histories civil it is chiefly the ones he calls the wiser who make other men wise – but not exclusively these. Inferior historians help. As for the canon, it contains three in antiquity whom he classes among the wiser sort – Livy, Tacitus and Herodian. But it does not follow because he does not mention them as wise that he regarded the rest – Thucydides, Xenophon, Polybius, Sallust, Caesar, Appianus – as unwise. Two writers, each of whom at different places, he describes as the greatest historian of all times, are ancients. One suspects that a third, also an ancient, Tacitus, had not less status in his estimation.[37] All three, Livy, Caesar and Tacitus, have places in his canon. Two among Bacon's 'wiser sort', Philip de Commines and Francesco Guicciardini, are moderns.

According to *Advancement* (1605): '...for modern histories, whereof there are some few very worthy, but the greater part beneath mediocrity'.[38] '...it is an ability not common to write a good history, as may well appear by the small number of them...'.[39] Whole tracts of modern civil history writing are rejected by him: some of it is received, but with reserves: some is accepted *faute de mieux.* 'It is not Saint Augustine's nor Saint Ambrose's works that will make so wise a divine, as ecclesiastical histories, thoroughly read and observed.'[40] But on the other hand, 'I would the virtue and sincerity of it' (that is to say, of ecclesiastical history) 'were according to the mass and quantity'.[41]

He condemned (in the second revision, 1623) much of the producing of universal history as equally worthless...'the laws of regular history are so strict, that they can scarce be observed in such a wide field of matter. For the writer who has such a variety of things to attend to, will become gradually less scrupulous on the point of information..., he will take up with[42] and popular reports...,' rumours. On the other hand 'the affairs of men are not so far separated by the divisions of empires and countries, but they have a connection in many things; and therefore it is certainly of use to have the fates, acts and destinies of one age described and contained as it were on one tablet'.[43] Epitomes are rejected with scorn: 'They are the corruptions and moths of histories...base and unprofitable dregs.'[44] Commentaries are needed but they 'set down a bare continuance and tissue of actions and events without the causes and pretexts, the commencements and occasions, the counsels and orations and other passages of action?'[45]

Even chronicles, histories of times, which are 'the most complete and absolute kind of history',[46] his point being that history (that is to say chronological sequence) and time can be equated, are nevertheless faulty in that

history of times representeth the magnitude of actions and the public faces and deportments of persons, and passeth over in silence the smaller passages and motions of men and matters. But such being the workmanship of God, as he doth hang the greatest weight upon the smallest wires...it comes therefore to pass, that such histories do rather set forth the pomp of business than the true and inward resorts thereof.[47] Moreover, when it does add and insert the counsels and motives, yet from love of grandeur it introduces into human actions more gravity and prudence than they really have; so that a truer picture of human life may be found in a satire than in some histories of this kind.[48]

It is required that historians employ the science of rhetoric. They misuse it if they distract men by describing 'pomp of business', thus feeding their love of grandeur, from matters which are of truest import. '... it not a little embases the authority of a history to intermingle matters of lighter moment, such as triumphs, ceremonies, spectacles and the like, with matters of state'.[49]

According to his paper written at a time when Elizabeth was still Queen:

this is true that in no sort of writings there is a greater distance between the good and the bad, no not between the most excellent poet and the vainest rhymer, nor between the deepest philosopher and the most frivolous schoolman, than there is between good histories and those that bear the same or like title. In which regard, having proposed to write the History of England from the beginning of the reign of King Henry, the eighth of that name [sic], near unto the present time wherein Q. Elizabeth reigneth in good felicity, I am delivered of the excuse wherewith the best writers of history are troubled in their proëms, when they go about without breaking the bounds of modesty to give a reason why they should write that again which others have written well or at least tolerably before. For those which I am to follow are such as I may rather fear the reproach of coming into their number, than the opinion of presumption if I hope to do better than they.

But in the meantime it must be considered, that the best of the ancient histories were contrived out of divers particular Commentaries, Relations, and Narratives, which it was not hard to digest with ornament, and thereof to compound one entire story. And as at the first such writers had the ease of others' labours, so since they have the whole commendation in regard those former writings are for the most part lost, whereby their borrowings do not appear. But unto me the disadvantage is great, finding no public memories of any consideration or worth, in sort that the supply must be out of the freshness of memory and tradition, and out of the acts, instruments, and negotiations of state themselves, together with the glances of foreign histories; which though I do acknowledge to be the best originals and instructions out of which to write an history, yet the travel must be much greater than if there had been already digested any tolerable chronicle as a simple narration of the actions themselves, which should only have needed out of the former helps to be enriched with the counsels and the speeches and notable particularities...

In completing *The History of the Reign of King Henry the 7th*, his contribution to, and continuation of the canon of secular civil histories, he used the 'former helps' – 'freshness of memory and tradition, and... the acts, instruments, and negotiations of state...':

he also employed, as he admitted *faute de mieux*, the inferior (as he also admitted) compositions of Fabyan, Polydore Vergil, Hall, Holinshed, Stowe and Speed.

'...monuments, names, words, proverbs, traditions, private records and evidences, fragments of stories, passages of books that concern not story, and the like, do save and recover somewhat from the deluge of time'.[50] According to the second *Advancement* – in which the list of sources is extended to include genealogies, coins, 'archives and instruments as well public as private' – study of these 'antiquities' helps to 'supersede the fabulous accounts of the origin of nations, and ... fictions of that kind'.[51] He dismisses for his part King Arthur of Britain. Dealing in *Advancement* (both versions) with 'certain credulous and superstitious conceits... and some frivolous experiments' to be found in books on 'natural magic',[52] he charged them with being 'as far differing in truth of nature from such knowledge as we require, as the story of king Arthur of Britain, or Hugh of Bordeaux, differs from Caesar's *Commentaries* in truth of story. For it is manifest that Caesar did greater things *de vero*' (in reality) 'than those imaginary heroes were feigned to do'.[53] The dismissal of King Arthur was less abrupt in *The History of the Reign of King Henry the 7th*. This king chose the name Arthur for his first son according, Bacon wrote, 'to the name of that ancient worthy King of the Britons; in whose acts there is truth enough to make him famous, besides that which is fabulous.'[54]

However Bacon is also somewhat dismissive of the antiquarian investigators despite their acknowledged services in exposing fictions and the fabulous. They are entitled, he wrote, 'to the less authority, because in things which few people concern themselves about, the few have it their own way'.[55] This remark together with the observation that his own labours must be more onerous in the absence of an 'already digested any tolerable chronicle as a simple narration of the actions themselves' suggests that he advocated a division of labour scarcely acceptable to later generations; also, that he did no 'research'. Some will swallow such suggestions. They require to be qualified. It is scarcely conceivable that in his dealing with, and in his work in civil history he defied his own fundamental that thinking and doing – cogitations and relevantly related activity – are and must remain inseparably accompanied each by the other. It is sufficiently evident that in this instance he perpetrated no self-defiance.

Long after Bacon's death an incorporation of the pursuits of antiquarians and historians each into the other took place in Europe and elsewhere. Also, practitioners were promoted into a profession of academics. Professors of history who conducted no 'research' could expect to be frowned on. But it is not the case that Bacon undertook no 'research'. In the course of a career as man of state and of the law he conducted as will be seen plentiful and sustained investigations into the political, ecclesiastical, constitutional and legal past of England – and not only of England. For *The History of the Reign of King Henry the 7th*, while dwelling on presentation (including 'ornament', that is to say, rhetoric), intelligible connections, interpretation; and the 'compounding of one entire story', he resorted to 'the acts, instruments and negotiations of state themselves, together with the glances of foreign histories' – 'the best originals and instructions out of which to write an history'. Inevitably mistakes have been discovered by later researchers. Nevertheless the judgment of Ranke should stand. For modern times and in England 'he furnishes one of the first examples of exact investigation of details combined with reflective treatment...'[56]

Whatever the times or prevailing teachings and assumptions, historians have always depended upon one another, handing on what is true but also distributing what is false. It is scarcely possible in practice that things should be otherwise. Bacon points out that 'the best of the ancient histories were contrived out of divers particular commentaries, relations and narratives...such writers had the ease of others' labours'. When the latter day purist refuses to countenance division of labour among workers between collecting information on the one hand, and interpretation and presentation on the other, he need not deny that within one and the same student there takes place, or should take place, what amounts to this double pursuit. He could also draw on his experience and grant that some historians do more collecting than thinking and little enough of the latter; while others do more thinking than collecting and sometimes not enough of the latter.

With respect to both kinds of duality, the one between men, the other inside the same person, the standpoint of Bacon, though not articulated in this instance, is clear. While the two functions are distinct they are not divisible or separable. The same holds good when, as will be seen, he sets out a future for natural science/ philosophy. He proposes a distinction between two professions: there will be miners to dig and also smiths to hammer and refine what is dug.[57] Each profession is needed by the other. Here the distinction is between *data* for science and science. In the case of civil history the distinction lies inside the *data*. The possibilities of making distinctions are limitless. At the level of generality on which Bacon was presenting these matters there was no need to labour this one.

Except for Livy and perhaps Herodian, all the historians in his canon and all those he lists among the wiser sort had been practising men of affairs. Bacon shows himself aware of this, and that he recognized the implications. Polybius – who had his place in the canon – had written: 'So I should say that history will never be properly written until either men of action undertake to write it ... or historians become convinced that practical experience is of the first importance for historical composition.'[58] Not only is history writing improved when undertaken by men of action, the converse is no less true: conduct of practical affairs is improved when men engaged in them acquire historical knowledge and apply it. Polybius subscribes to this. So do others in the canon and among the wiser. Bacon adds himself to them in what he teaches about, and practises in his history writing and researches. In assessing Queen Elizabeth's merits as a ruler he states:

> it is not to ... closet penmen that we are to look for guidance in such a case; for men of that order ... are no faithful witnesses as to the real passages of business. It is for ministers and great officers to judge of these things, and those who have handled the helm of government, and been acquainted with the difficulties and mysteries of state business.[59]

He also adds himself to members of his canon in what he teaches about, and practises when holding power under King James in the attempted management of state policy. The latter as he aimed to conduct it would be enriched by his researches into the past.

Bacon complains that 'amongst so many great foundations of colleges in Europe' there is no 'education collegiate ... where such as were so disposed might give themselves to histories, modern languages, books of policy and civil discourse, and other the like enablements unto service of estate' ... 'from hence it proceedeth that princes find a solitude in regard of able men to serve them in causes of estate'.[60] In a later age collegiate education included teaching and study of civil histories and books of policy. Bacon had visions resulting from combining together wishes and aims with rigorously examined estimates of practical possibilities. He had ambitions – not only for himself – which were nurtured in this way. But to foreknowledge of things to take place of which he approved and planned for – a burgeoning of natural philosophy/science – a fuller and truer union of the two kingdoms constituting Britain – a shape viable in due course for the constitution of the political state – this latter being cause and consequence of a grand strategy and of 'founding a monarchy in the West' – he did not add an approving prescience of the future tendencies of his desiderated new branch of studies in history and policy at learned institutions.

For amidst these tendencies, professional exponents of historical knowledge in these more recent times have normally been sceptical that practical lessons can be acquired from studying humanity's past. They doubt, for example, that political guidance can be extracted in this way. In the early nineteenth century Georg Wilhelm Friedrich Hegel (1770–1831) announced in Berlin lectures that the only lesson to be learnt from history is that men do not learn from it. Other authorities would add that it is futile to try. This is because they stress not similarities, but differences between the past and the present. Everything that happens in human affairs is assumed to be unique to some marked and decisive degree. Always there are circumstances which alter cases.

Bacon is aware that circumstances alter cases. He also states in the second *Advancement* that the difficulty of civil history is not less great than its dignity: 'For to carry the mind in writing back into the past, and bring it into sympathy with antiquity[61] is a task of great labour and judgment.' In later times readers might expect that he refers to the need and the difficulty of entering into the alien mentalities and world outlooks of generations in the past. They could suppose that his teaching about idols of the mind would be relevant to this. Idols have prevailed in the past as they do in the present: they are difficult but not impossible to dispel: in regard to the past it should be possible, if not to dispel, yet to penetrate and enter into them. This line is not worth pursuing. Bacon does not pursue it.

His task of great labour and judgment is not that of achieving sympathetic penetration into differing and alien past mentalities. According to his expressed understanding mentalities of men in the past had been neither so alien nor so different that they had nothing in common with men in the present. The great difficulty of the labour and task is 'diligently to examine, freely and faithfully to report, and by the light of words to place as it were before the eyes, the revolutions of times, the characters of persons, the fluctuations of counsels, the courses and currents of actions, the bottoms of pretences and the secrets of governments.'[62]

The central and prior topics of civil history, as this passage makes clear, are matters of policy, this not excluding, as he urged, matters of law. For it was another of his complaints about civil histories that too often matters of law were omitted from them. It is not easy to decide how and at what point in the course of this argument the topic of Bacon and the law should be introduced. Clearly the topic requires to be introduced. Bacon neither in action nor in thought lived a life divided into sealed and separate compartments. He adopted the law as a profession and as Lord Chancellor he reached the summit of it. He frequently mentioned or wrote about law not only elsewhere but in *Advancement* (both versions). Not only did he complain in the text of his *History of the Reign of King Henry the 7th* and also in Aphorism XXIX of *Example of a Treatise on Universal Justice or the Fountains of Equity, by Aphorisms* that matters of law were too often omitted from civil histories, he also more than once defined the law – the Common Law of England – as itself and in itself a history.

He described English law in 1614 in *A Memorial Touching the Review of Penal Laws and the Amendment of the Common Law*: 'Wherefore, for the Common Law of England, it appeareth it is no text law.' That is to say, the Common Law is not a law like that of the Romans which the Emperor Justinian had caused to be digested into a code under titles '...but the substance of it consisteth in the series and succession of Judicial Acts from time to time which have been set down in the books which we term Year Books or Reports, so that as these reports are more or less perfect, so the Law itself is more or less certain, and indeed better or worse'.[63] Hence Bacon's pleas for improved law reporting. Later in *A Proposition... Touching the Compiling and Amendment of the Laws of England* he wrote: 'had it not been for Sir Edward Coke's *Reports*... the law by this time had been almost like a ship without ballast; for that the cases of modern experience are fled from those that are adjudged and ruled in former time'.[64]

'It is too long a business', he declared in this same paper, 'to debate whether *lex scripta aut non scripta*, a text law or customs well registered, with received and approved grounds and maxims, and acts and resolutions judicial from time to time duly entered and reported, be the better form of declaring and authorising laws'. But in 'all sciences, they are the soundest that keep close to particulars; and sure I am there are more doubts that rise upon our statutes, which are a text law, than upon the common law, which is no text law'.[65] The Common Law, being no text law, no code, was instead a history. It was no less and also no more than the record of a series of particulars, in this resembling civil histories which specialized in matters not of law but of government. Compiling and amending the laws of England – which was Bacon's purpose – meant cleansing and confirming the record of them. 'There is to be made a perfect course of the law *in serie temporis*' (in order of time), 'or Year Books (as we call them), from Edward the First to this day'.[66] According to Aphorism LXXVI of *Example of a Treatise on Universal Justice or the Fountains of Equity, by Aphorisms* (included in the final *Advancement* 1623): 'Let these judgments' (of the judges in their courts) 'be digested in chronological order, and not by method and titles. For such writings are a kind of history or narrative of the laws. And not only the laws themselves, but the times also when they passed, give light to a wise judge.'[67]

It requires therefore to be recorded – this being as good a place as any at which to do so – that for Bacon – in his observation – the Common Law of England constituted not only another civil history, but also another fixed marker, another – in this case not so recent but nevertheless constantly emerging – fruit of time, and another secular canon – a canon moreover which was capable of being supplied and continued and which required such treatment. Furthermore the Common Law comprised a field where men did not read to contradict and confute, nor to believe and take for granted, nor to find talk and discourse, but to weigh and consider for purposes of action and practice which were indispensable and urgent.

Nevertheless, just as the sacred canon – the sole canon which could neither be supplied nor continued – came first for him, so the secular canon of Greek and Roman civil histories – this in its turn being followed by Machiavelli's work on it in the shape of his mixed history – have priority as markers among Bacon's expressed interests over his rendering of the Common Law into a species of civil history. This latter stands in a fourth place. According to the evidence it is a distinct, congruent, not in any way negligible, but subsidiary field of interest. This lies in parallel with his explanations that law is part of civil policy just as government is part of civil policy, but that the latter is the senior of the two.

The central and prior topics of civil history are matters of state. 'The laws of regular history are…strict'[68] not only in regard to reliable information, they are also strict with respect to subject matter. …'revolutions of times', that is, changes which mark off one period from another: 'characters of persons', that is, 'characters of dispositions': 'the fluctuations of counsels': 'the courses and currents of actions', that is, the causes and consequences of things done: 'the bottoms of pretences', that is, purposes lying behind claims: in short the secrets of governments.

'A bare continuance and tissue of actions without the causes and pretexts, the commencements and occasions, the counsels and orations' is not enough. To 'any tolerable chronicle as a simple narration of the actions themselves' there requires to be added, 'the counsels and the speeches and notable particularities'. It is 'the true and inward springs and resorts of business'[69] which need to be presented in histories. 'For as when I read in Tacitus the actions of Nero or Claudius, with circumstances of times, inducements, and occasions, I find them not so strange.' By contrast, Suetonius, who handles them 'not in order of time', makes them 'monstrous and incredible'.[70] 'For they be not the great wars and conquests (which many times are the works of fortune and fall out in barbarous times) the rehearsal whereof maketh the profitable and instructing history; but rather times refined in policies and industries, new and rare variety of accidents and alterations, equal and just encounters of state and state in forces, and of prince and prince in sufficiency, that bring upon the stage the best parts for observation.'[71] A history, which he purposed to write, proceeding from the Union of the Roses under King Henry VII to the Union of the Crowns happily consummated under King James VI and I would manifestly exhibit such 'rare variety of accidents and alterations'. 'Above all things (for this is the ornament and life of civil history) I wish events to be coupled with their causes…'[72] 'For it is the true office of history to represent the events themselves together with the counsels…'[73]

Aiming to avoid two unconstructive dispositions, the one that so easily doubts that it can never stop doing so, the other so easily persuadable that it scarcely doubts at all, Bacon offers a canon of civil historians and a few outside it whom he styles the wiser. Duly weighing them, reading them wholly, diligently and attentively, he accepts them as superior in their conformity to standards of what histories should be about and thus as models for civil histories which required still to be written including his own. He also accepts them as conveying knowledge which is reliable on these matters and thus capable of being employed as material for civil philosophy. Again it will be recalled that Bacon practised in the law. He maintained that law reporting in the past left much to be desired. But he did not conclude that what Law Reports reported was fiction. The Common Law, the existence of it and the practice of it, needfully assumes that in one realm at least men can find a sufficiently reliable account of events which took place in the past. Since practice of the law in the present depends upon it having been practised in the past, the law and its practice are correctives to historical pyrrhonism. Such a consideration has no place among Bacon's surviving arguments. Nevertheless, it is scarcely difficult to understand why he credits the law – which is itself a history – with being reliable and acceptable as a record of the human past.

But why does he regard his civil histories proper as being capable of bearing the weight he aims to lay upon them? Why in the sphere of natural history, does he discard, for instance, the work of Gesner, the modern, and in antiquity that of Pliny the Elder whose natural history had been another recent daughter of time – Giovanni de Matociis who flourished in the early fourteenth century had disentangled his text from that of his nephew, Pliny the Younger – while comparable ancient and also certain modern civil historians are received into his embraces and retained there? The answer to the first part of this question we must disclaim knowledge of – that is to say, if we decline to accept his expressed judgment that all such work is defective as *data*. His answer to the second part can be elucidated. His reasons, all of them sufficiently evident, for accepting his civil historians as supplying *data* which is reliable and true are mutually sustaining.

Arguments for accepting the general veracity of events recorded by civil histories in the canon are not explicit. They are embedded in positions which Bacon consistently adopts. They fall under two distinct but related heads – the providence of God and the experience of mankind. Histories of providence, he writes in *Advancement* (1605), have dealt with 'the notable events and examples of God's judgments, chastisements, deliverances, and blessings...'[74] In the second version he adds that 'some pious writers have written on these matters, *sed non sine partium studio*[75] – but not without partisanships. He has more to contribute on this topic than these writers normally achieve. Amongst the deliverances and blessings of divine providence is transmission of the canon of sacred scripture. Providence in its omnicompetence and beneficence does not change. But it would scarcely be omnicompetent and beneficent if what it transmits to men as beneficent turns out to be mendacious. Bacon according to numerous statements accepts what is contained in the sacred canon as reliable. The argument for truthfulness of content is no different in the parallel case of the secular canon of civil histories.

For the History of Times (I mean of civil history), the providence of God hath made the distribution. For it hath pleased God to ordain and illustrate two examplar states of the world, for arms, learning, moral virtue, policy, and laws; the state of Graecia and the state of Rome; the histories whereof, occupying the middle part of time, have more ancient to them histories which may by one common name be termed the Antiquities of the World; and after them, histories which may be likewise called by the name of Modern History.[76]

We have no extant histories of the first and earliest times, 'the antiquities of the world'. Histories are extant in the latest and modern times, though most of these are beneath mediocrity. In the times which are between the two and in the middle we have exemplar states. Exemplar states would scarcely be exemplar if we possessed no histories of them. God's providence or pleasure in ordaining them would have failed in omnipotence if in addition it had not ordained exemplar historians. But this it has done. 'For the history of the exemplar states it is extant and in good perfection.'[77] If this history, extant and in good perfection, is untrustworthy and untruthful in its content, providence would have been omnicompetent. But it would also have been mendacious.

   Here a tenet of faith has invaded the province of science, or rather its groundwork which is history. Divine providence as in itself no fiction, as omnicompetent, beneficent and no liar or cheat was a tenet of faith in Christendom. According to Bacon in *Of Atheism* (1612 and 1625) and to Cicero – it had also been a tenet of faith among pagans in antiquity. He quotes the latter on the religion of the Romans: 'It is in piety only and religion, and the wisdom of regarding the providence of the Immortal Gods as that which rules and governs all things, that we have surpassed all nations and

peoples'.[78] The case is parallel with that of the form of man
the province of science has likewise admitted an incursion by a
of faith. The two incursions are linked and interrelated. For ⌐
divine providence which has ordained the form of man, establishiɴ
it in the first place but also holding it afterwards in constancy.

But while it is not the case that his acceptance of the authority oɫ
the sacred canon – according to Bacon's many statements – is subject
to confirmation in experience, this *corpus* of inspired divinity in the
territory of science requires to be confirmed in this way. The
implication is that this is inspired divinity's teaching. In this
teaching man is commanded to proceed to know and to control
himself and the rest of creation, though after his Fall this knowledge
and control can be acquired only in sweat and hard labour.
Therefore by and in themselves the two interconnected tenets of faith
are not sufficient. Standing alone they can give no credibility to the
events recorded by historians of the secular canon.

Since within the territory of science more than faith is needed,
human experience is appealed to. This experience is available. It is
found to confirm inspired divinity. If the nature of man is constant,
situations in his affairs will be likely to recur and civil history will be
prone to repeat itself. But this constancy and one of its likely
consequences – repetitions and recurrences – are fully observable in
the events of the secular canon. They are observable no less, it may
be added, in those of the sacred canon when it is the deeds of men
which are presented there. Furthermore, constancy and recurrence
are evident to Bacon in his experience of civil affairs in his own times
and in his acquaintance through modern histories with times in the
recent past. Present experience and acquaintance with preceding
and near events corroborate the evidence presented by the secular
canon – and though this is not needed, its authenticity being secure
in advance – by the sacred one too, when it is men's doings which are
described there.

In Bacon's case, reading civil histories no less than writing them
is thinking. Ruminating and reviewing the contents not of one but
of two canons, together with other narratives; and also consulting his
own experience, for Bacon all past civil history is contemporary in
and with itself and also with his own times and experience. In
governmental affairs and also in legal affairs, much is changeless,
especially things in state concerns and legal matters which are of the
chiefest import. If these change, they often do so only to recur. It is

...lgments or perceptions of this kind which in
...on the urgency of the question – How can
...ical nor over credulous in disposition, be
...s recorded in the secular canon are in general

...s in the final *Advancement* – 'I consider history and
...pe the same thing...'[79] History, written civil history,
...ence, are the same thing because the latter is the extension
...present of what is recorded in the former. But history –
...en civil history – and experience are also the same thing
...cause the content of the latter repeats much of what has been
recorded in the former. It is true that he holds that particulars/
individuals, civil as much as natural, are circumscribed by space and
time. But despite circumstances altering cases, a limitation which he
admits, particulars/individuals of the human variety transcend
space and time in some respects. Historians in a period long
afterwards have taught that human individuals are exclusively
related to their spatial and temporal environments – to their contexts
in other words. These historians have held that to assume otherwise
is to invite anachronism. Certainly these historians successfully make
their point. But Bacon insists that 'men's labour...should be turned
to the investigation and observation of the resemblances and
analogies of things, as well in wholes as in parts'.

In the class of 'wholes' he for instance writes in *De Sapientia Veterum – Of the Wisdom of the Ancients* (1609) under *Orpheus; or Philosophy*:

But howsoever the works of wisdom are among human things the most
excellent, yet they too have their periods and closes. For so it is that after
kingdoms and commonwealths have flourished for a time, there arise
perturbations and seditions and wars; amid the uproars of which, first the
laws are put to silence, and then men return to the depraved conditions of
their nature, and desolation is seen in the fields and cities. And if such
troubles last, it is not long before letters also and philosophy are so torn in
pieces that no traces of them can be found but a few fragments, scattered
here and there like planks from a shipwreck; and then a season of
barbarism sets in, the waters of Helicon being sunk under the ground, until,
according to the appointed vicissitude of things, they break out and issue
forth again, perhaps among other nations, and not in the places where they
were before.[80]

Still in the class of 'wholes', a variant, shorter and sharper version
of a civil cycle is presented in *Of Vicissitude of Things* (1625): 'In the

youth of a state arms do flourish; in the middle age of a
learning; and then both of them together for a time; in the decli
age of a state, mechanical arts and merchandise.'[81] In the class
'parts' he for instance makes an addition to what he provides
Advancement's first version about 'appendices to history'. Appendice.
to history consist of 'orations, letters and brief speeches or sayings'.
In 1623 he adds what follows on the topic of 'brief speeches or
sayings' which he calls apophthegms:

Neither are Apophthegms...only for pleasure and ornament, but also for
use and action. For they are (as was said) 'words which are as goads',
words with an edge or point, that cut and penetrate the knots of business
and affairs. Now occasions are continually returning, and what served once
will serve again; whether produced as a man's own or cited as an old
saying.[82]

The contention that civil history since it repeats itself can therefore
be self-confirming in its veracity is an argument no doubt which is
circular. In this it resembles other arguments in matters of
consequence. He reads the two canons in the light of his experience.
He sees his experience in the light of events in the two canons. But
there is perhaps a further consideration. While it remains true –
Bacon not denying it – that observed and reported details of civil
history being gone beyond recall, cannot be tested like those of
natural history, most of nature being most of the time more
manifestly repetitive, he could still have argued that a general
veracity in recorded civil history is retrospectively tested in the
workability or otherwise of axioms of civil policy constructed out of
the material provided in the record of past events, giving their causes
and consequences.

'*Sequitur Historia Civilis specialis, cujus dignitas atque autoritas inter
scripta humana eminet*'[83] – 'I come next to Civil History, properly so
called, whereof the dignity and authority are pre-eminent among
human writings. For to its fidelity are entrusted the examples of our
ancestors, the vicissitudes of things, the foundations of civil policy,
and the name and reputation of men.'[84] According to this un-
compromising pronouncement in the second *Advancement* (1623),
civil history in its dignity and authority holds a place next under the
sacred scriptures, writings which are not human but divine. But
though this conclusion, absent from *Advancement* in its first version, is
offered only in the second, it cannot be rated as a recent achievement.

'y and illustrated vividly in remarks no less
 ising, but more illuminating, which Bacon
 ɪ Q. Elizabeth reigneth in good felicity';
 y, even earlier than that at which the first
 He makes them in a paper already quoted –
 ay – where he meditates a purpose to write on the
 d or defectively presented history of England – not on
 of it, but on a sufficiently telling part of it.

ɔks which are written do in their kinds represent the faculties of the
ɪ of man: Poesy his imagination; Philosophy his reason; and History
ɪs memory. Of which three faculties least exception is commonly taken to
memory; because imagination is oftentimes idle, and reason litigious. So
likewise History of all writings deserveth least taxation, as that which
holdeth least of the author, and most of the things themselves. Again, the
use which it holdeth to man's life, if it be not the greatest, yet assuredly is
the freest from any ill accident or quality. For those which are conversant
much in poets, as they attain to great variety, so withal they become
conceited; and those which are brought up in philosophy and sciences do
wax (according as their nature is) some of them too stiff and opinionate,
and some others too perplexed and confused. Whereas History possesseth
the mind of the conceits which are nearest allied unto action, and
imprinteth them so, as it does not alter the complexion of the mind neither
to irresolution nor to pertinacity.[85]

It is not possible that history should have stood higher in Bacon's
reckoning than philosophy. Philosophy is the theatre in which men
exercise their faculty of reason. Nor in the philosophy he himself
pursues and produces is he stiff and opinionated or perplexed and
confused. For him history nevertheless is that to which least
exception is commonly taken and that which deserves least taxation.
At an early date therefore, just as in 1623, he assigns merit to history
giving it a pre-eminence outstripping other disciplines. History
displays 'least of self' and most of the things themselves. It 'holdeth
use to man's life'. In itself it directs to action. In itself it discourages
irresolution. It also discourages pertinacity – persisting obstinately,
that is to say, in a point or on a course where it is wrong or when it
requires to be changed. Here he writes about all history, not only
about his secular canon. Further, since in this piece he does not
employ the epithet 'civil', no doubt natural history would share the
same status if or when it was extant. But the context makes it clear
that it is primarily civil history which he discusses. This context is his
purpose to write on the history of England.

The then Bishop of Lincoln, John Williams (1582–1650), in a remark which looks like subscription on his part to historical pyrrhonism, told Bacon in 1625 that much civil history at bottom was little more than the historian who wrote it. Williams appeared not to agree that histories present least of the author and most of the things themselves. Bacon, as he made clear, while rejecting historical pyrrhonism, knew what the bishop had in mind. Under the head of civil history's difficulty Bacon complains in the final *Advancement* (1623) about historians who 'impress on their works the image not so much of their minds as of their passions, ever thinking of their party, but no good witnesses as to facts';[86] '– some are always inculcating their favourite political doctrines'. He has further things to say about bias. Writing (again in 1623) about 'Narrations and Relations of actions (as the Peloponnesian War [Thucydides], the Expedition of Cyrus [Xenophon], the Conspiracy of Cataline [Sallust] and the like)', he asserted that these 'cannot but be more purely and exactly true than the Perfect Histories of Times…' But on the other hand '(seeing that everything human is subject to imperfection, and good is almost always associated with evil) it must certainly be confessed that relations of this kind, especially if published near the time of the actions themselves (being commonly written either in favour or in spite), are of all other histories the most to be suspected'. The remedy he offers is 'that as these very relations are commonly put forth not by one side only, but by both, according to their several factions and parties, a way may be found to truth between the extremes on either hand…'[87] As observers like François de La Mothe Le Vayer and Voltaire pointed out at later dates, it is precisely such needed counter-relations and counter-narrations that are so often lacking in the civil historiography of antiquity. Bacon could scarcely have been unaware of so notable a deficiency. Nevertheless he robustly scorned discouragement.

Nor had Bishop Williams' disparaging statement about civil histories endorsed the doctrine that all of them should be dismissed as worthless – far from it. Bacon had written to Williams in 1625 telling him

I find that the ancients (as Cicero, Demosthenes, Plinius Secundus, and others), have preserved both their orations and their epistles. In imitation of whom I have done the like to my own; which nevertheless I will not publish while I live. But I have been bold to bequeath them to your Lordship, and Mr Chancellor of the Duchy. My speeches (perhaps) you will think fit to publish. The letters, many of them, touch too much upon late matters of state, to be published; yet I was willing they should not be lost.[88]

The bishop's reply ran in full like this:

It is true that those ancients, Cicero, Demosthenes, and Plinius Secundus, have preserved their orations (the heads and effects of them at the least) and their epistles; and I have ever been of opinion, that those two pieces are the principal pieces of our antiquities. Those orations discovering the form of administering justice, and the letters the carriage of the affairs in those times. For our histories (or rather lives of men) borrow as much from the affections and phantasies of the writers, as from the truth itself, and are for the most of them built altogether from unwritten relations and traditions. But letters written *e re nata*, and bearing a synchronism or equality of time *cum rebus gestis*, have no other fault than that which was imputed unto Virgil, *nihil peccat, nisi quod nihil peccet*; they speak the truth too plainly, and cast too glaring a light for that age, wherein they were, or are written.

Your Lordship doeth most worthily therefore in preserving those two pieces, amongst the rest of those matchless monuments you shall leave behind you; considering that as one age hath not bred your experience, so it is not fit it should be confined to one age, and not imparted to the times to come. For my part therein, I do embrace the honour with all thankfulness, and the trust imposed upon me with all religion and devotion.[89]

In *Advancement* (both versions) Bacon handled orations and letters under two heads; under Memorials – 'preparatory history' – and also under Appendices to history. In the first version under the latter we find:

For all the exterior proceedings of man consist of words and deeds; whereof history doth properly receive and retain in memory the deeds, and if words, yet but as inducements and passages to deeds; so are there other books and writings, which are appropriate to the custody and receipt of words only; which likewise are of three sorts; Orations, Letters, and Brief Speeches or Sayings. Orations are pleadings, speeches of counsel, laudatives, invectives, apologies, reprehensions, orations of formality or ceremony, and the like. Letters are according to all the variety of occasions, advertisements, advices, directions, propositions, petitions, commendatory, expostulatory, satisfactory, of compliment, of pleasure, of discourse, and all other passages of action. And such as are written from wise men are of all the words of man, in my judgment, the best; for they are more natural than orations, and public speeches, and more advised than conferences or present speeches. So again letters of affairs from such as manage them or are privy to them are of all others the best instructions for history, and to a diligent reader the best histories in themselves.[90]

The parallel passage in the second *Advancement* carries no change of substance except that the last statement is left out. Bacon was content to leave the topic of appendices to history asserting not that letters are the best histories in themselves but that they are the best materials for histories. This is second thoughts. Abolishing a distinction between history and experience helped action both in writing civil histories and in building axioms upon them. Abolishing a distinction between history and materials it should employ scarcely assisted action either in writing civil histories or in building upon them.

As it turned out the exchange between Bacon and Bishop Williams in 1625 all but constituted the appendix to the history of Bacon. He was dead within a year from the date of it. When the bishop told him 'considering that one age hath not bred your experience; so it is not fit it should be confined to one age; and not imparted to the times to come', Williams confirmed in a final summary articulation both Bacon's wishes and also his teachings and practice. Throughout, and up until these last months, and with no apparent breaks and hesitations, Bacon stands by and illustrates in his works and counsels his early contention that compared with all other human writings civil history – all of it, though no doubt in differing degrees of attainment – 'holdeth least of the author and most of the things themselves'; and that because it does so, it conduces to action and invites it. The early judgment and the consistent conduct culminate in the 1623 announcement: '*Historia Civilis…cujus dignitas atque authoritas inter scripta humana eminet*' – 'Civil history, …, whereof the dignity and authority are pre-eminent among human writings.'[91]

But here, as in many other contexts where civil history is written about or discussed, that other 1623 pronouncement, namely that history and experience are 'the same thing', will be recalled and duly regarded. Not only civil history, but civil experience and not least Bacon's own civil experience, must needs hold 'least of the author and most of the things themselves'. As Ranke noted of Bacon 'all his life long he devoted a careful and searching observation' to the state of human society. Civil history and his own civil experience were the *media* through which he did so all his life long.

The second *Advancement* (1623) contains his judgment, stronger than in 1605, that the current condition of natural history is to be deplored. It also contains his ruling on civil history and its foremost dignity and authority amongst human writings. Truth, Bacon continues to insist is the daughter not of authority but of time. But intermittently time and civil history are interchangeable terms in his usage. With the exception of inspired divinity, truth, as he persists in asserting, is not the offspring of authority when authority consists of prestige, might, weight, influence, either in persons or institutions. But the word 'authority' can be used in another way implying eminence, even pre-eminence, in responsible assistance and reliable advice or guidance whether in private or public life. For Bacon, while still placing it beneath inspired divinity ('the use of which it holdeth to man's life, if it be not the greatest, etc.'), it is a leadership in this kind of authority which civil history early possesses as inherent and residing in itself. Civil history continues to retain this leadership for him.

Such a starting point, this turning out to be a sustained standpoint, recalls Cicero's in his dialogue *De Oratore*: *Historia vero testis temporum, lux veritatis, vita memoriae, magistra vitae, nuntia vetustatis...*' 'history...bears witness to the passing of the ages, sheds light upon reality, gives life to recollection and guidance to human existence, and brings tidings of ancient days[92] –'. But it is Bacon not Cicero who locates civil history's singular excellence in the circumstance that it presents least of the author and most of the things outside himself than other sorts of men's writings are likely to do. Writing or studying civil history is not working in a vacuum which is what many philosophers do; nor is it creative activity in a void which is what many poets indulge in. It is a pursuit which confronts and handles particulars which are outside the writer or reader and which claim standing for themselves first and foremost in virtue of being – or of having once been – real.

Bacon explained to King James in the final *Advancement* that 'all History...walks upon the earth, and performs the office rather of a guide than of a light; whereas Poesy is as a dream of learning; a thing sweet and varied, and that would be thought to have in it something divine; a character which dreams likewise affect. But now it is time for me to awake, and arising above the earth, to wing my way through the clear air of Philosophy and the Sciences'.[93] 'All history' suggests that history natural is capable of being included, but again the context shows that it is history civil of which Bacon was writing.

Poets and poetry have their uses and functions. Bacon extols them. He states as will be seen that poets are like civil historians in providing keen and accurate observation of human nature – of men's passions and 'characters of dispositions'. According to the second *Advancement* which repeats points made about poetry in the first:

As for Narrative Poesy...the foundation of it is truly noble, and has a special relation to the dignity of human nature...Poesy seems to bestow upon human nature those things which history denies to it;...a sound argument may be drawn from Poesy, to show that there is agreeable to the spirit of man a more ample greatness, a more perfect order, and a more beautiful variety than it can anywhere (since the Fall) find in nature. And therefore, since the acts and events which are the subjects of real history are...far from being agreeable to the merits of virtue and vice, Poesy corrects it,...since true history wearies the mind with satiety of ordinary events, one like another, Poesy refreshes it,...So that this Poesy conduces not only to delight but also to magnanimity and morality...[94]

It accommodates the show of things to the 'desires of the mind, not (like reason and history) buckling and bowing down the mind to the nature of things...it has so won its way as to have been held in honour even in the rudest ages and among barbarous peoples, when other kinds of learning were utterly excluded'.[95] In this last statement Bacon refers to the wisdom which he described disguised as fables in the most ancient Greek poetry; and which he expounded in *De Sapientia Veterum* in 1609. Men's rational faculties, he explained, being temporarily in abeyance, the imagination of poets employed itself effectively as a substitute.

Though Bacon expressed himself carefully, not underrating but instead encouraging poets and poetry in later ages and other lands, he consistently taught that unless men begin by walking upon the earth in company with civil history, buckling and bowing down their minds by observing humanity's conditions, and embracing the guidance concerning them which civil history provides, they will be incapable of rising above the earth and will meet small success in ascending into the clear air of philosophy and sciences. Plainly it is not only his judgment about the defective state of natural history, but also his conclusion about the inherent qualities and merits of civil history, notwithstanding much poor quality in its composition in the modern era, which from early days animates and propels Bacon. But doubtless as in much else of his thinking and practice the two positions are distinct while remaining inseparable and indivisible.

In history civil which was extant and in its modern shape improvable, and in sciences of human conduct which, whether extant and improvable, or for which, being absent, historical foundation material was available, Bacon, as things turned out, did more both counselling and working to improve received arts in this field than he did for the universe of nature either in collecting its history or in building its sciences. Judged by the distribution of attention between the world of nature and that of human affairs in terms of the evidence regarding his efforts which survives, Bacon looks less like a natural philosopher than a political and moral philosopher. It is not the argument here that this is what he planned. There is plenty of evidence that this is not what he intended. The programme in human self-knowledge was an end in itself. It was also a means to an end. With respect to this end, the programme for nature, what happened was that time of which truth is the offspring intervened for him unfavourably on this occasion, bringing not truth he had hoped to contribute, but death before he could do so.

CHAPTER 4

Logic – idols of the mind – rhetoric

'So generally', he wrote in *Advancement* (both versions), 'men taste well knowledges that are drenched in flesh and blood, civil history, morality, policy, about the which men's affections, praises, fortunes do turn and are conversant.'[1] These knowledges, drenched in flesh and blood, belong in the department of *Know Thyself*. Bacon well tasted them in his thinking and in his actions, the two working in tandem, and sought to advance them all. Civil history being history was not philosophy. But the two others, morality and policy, belonged to that department. Philosophy concerning man according to Bacon had two parts. 'For it considers man either segregate, or congregate and in society. The one I call the Philosophy of Humanity, the other Civil Philosophy.'[2]

Civil history was either extant as in and for the times of antiquity – here civil history was not improvable, though it was capable of being supplied and continued – or it was improvable as in and for the epoch of modernity. Bacon, killing two birds with one stone, supplied and continued the former and also improved the latter by planning, writing and publishing the substantial first section of a history of England to run from the Union of the Roses to the Union of the Crowns. Civil history according to Polybius 'will never be properly written until either men of action undertake to write it, ... or historians become convinced that practical experience is of the first importance for historical composition'. As Bacon put it himself, 'it is for ministers or great officers of state to judge of these things' – that is to say of 'the real passages of business' – and to write about them in histories. Nourished in his own civil experience *The History of the Reign of King Henry the 7th* appeared in 1622 after his tenure of power had come to an end. Thus he writes in it as experienced statesman for the benefit of statesmen. But evidence he himself provides dates the plan from a time when the Queen was still reigning. Continued interest in the matter had been displayed in a letter to the Lord Chancellor, Ellesmere, in April 1605, not without the hint that the latter had offered him encouragement. 'For as Statues and Pictures are dumb histories, so histories are speaking Pictures. Wherein if my affection be not too great, or my reading too small, I am of this opinion, that if Plutarch were alive to write lives by parallels, it would trouble him for virtue and fortune both to find for her a parallel amongst women.' Here his reference is to Queen Elizabeth. 'But I confess unto your Lordship I could not stay here, but went a little furder into the consideration of the times which have passed since king Henry the 8th; wherein I find the strangest variety that in like number of successions of any hereditary monarchy hath ever been known.'[3] The deficiency in English/British history writing was forcibly referred to in the first *Advancement* which appeared later in the same year. This same complaint was made again in 1623 in the second version.

Morality, Philosophy of Humanity, which considers 'man segregate', was extant and, so he said, defective; but again, so he argued, capable of being improved. It was with the aid of civil history, he proposed, that this could be done. As for policy, Civil Philosophy, which is 'doctrine concerning man congregate', for this, also, the source of *data* is civil history. He divides civil policy into three. Civil policy, as he sees it, was extant in one of its sections – 'conversation'. It was also arguably extant in another – 'government' or 'wisdom of state'. Machiavelli had worked there. But it was absent in another section which Bacon called 'negotiation' or 'business': for this he offered contributions in both *Advancements* and also in essays. But in policy – Civil Philosophy – in all its departments, even when arguably extant, as in 'conversation' and in Machiavelli's government or wisdom of state – he examined, in his thinking and practice laboured in, and copiously enriched the current stock.

Among the received arts, logic and rhetoric in his judgment were in no sense defective compared with parts of civil history, moral knowledge, and parts of civil knowledge. On the other hand, as we shall see, logicians harboured pretensions and made promises which, according to Bacon, they could not honour or justify. Logic like rhetoric was not among the arts drenched in flesh and blood 'about the which men's affections, praises, fortunes do turn and are conversant'. On the contrary 'that part of human philosophy which regards Logic is less delightful to the taste and palate of most minds, and seems but a net of subtlety and spinosity...'.[4] This 'same "dry light" parches and offends most men's soft and watery natures'.[5] But logic and rhetoric were connected with the arts drenched in flesh and blood because they were needed by them and indispensable to them. '...to speak truly of things as they are in worth, rational knowledges' (in this instance logic and rhetoric) 'are the keys of all other arts. And as the hand is the instrument of instruments, and mind is the form of forms, so these are truly said to be the arts of arts. Neither do they only direct, but likewise confirm and strengthen; even as the habit of shooting not only enables one to take a better aim, but also to draw a stronger bow.'[6] '...judgment by syllogism, as it is a thing most agreeable to the mind of man, so it hath been vehemently and excellently laboured'; this was for the reason that 'men' – men different from those who found logic 'but a net of subtlety and spinosity' – 'did hasten to set down some principles about which the variety of their disputations might turn'.[7]

Dealing here with 'rational knowledges', Bacon intended not such knowledges 'as reason produceth (for that extendeth to all philosophy)'[8] – including philosophy concerned with morality and policy, knowledges drenched in flesh and blood – 'but of such knowledges as do handle and inquire of the faculty of reason'. Rhetoric is included in these rational knowledges because it is the science of verbal communicating in order to persuade and convince men. More precisely rhetoric exists in an overlap with that part of logic which is devoted to *traditio* – tradition in the sense of handing on or communicating. 'It appeareth...that logic differeth from rhetoric not only as the fist from the palm, the one close, the other at large; but much more in this, that logic handleth reason exact and in truth, and rhetoric handleth it as it is planted in popular opinions and manners. And therefore Aristotle doth wisely place rhetoric as between logic on the one side, and moral and civil knowledge on the other as participating in both.'[9] Bacon follows. He places rhetoric as between logic and moral knowledge. In its own fashion rhetoric for Bacon is drenched in flesh and blood.

Bacon had little complaint about rhetoric and two complaints about logic. These two were both grave ones. But despite these latter two main complaints extant logic and also rhetoric were used by him in both his adopted programmes. His complaints about logic – both grave – were first that the logic which was extant and which was derived from Aristotle, however correctly applied and however acutely conducted, cannot to the extent claimed add to the sum of knowledge, that is to say, in every area and department including knowledges in the realm of nature. Second, there is 'a much more important and profound kind of fallacies in the mind of man' than those which 'the common logic' could successfully eliminate. These deeper fallacies 'I find not observed or inquired at all... '[10] The force of this profounder type is such 'as it doth not dazzle or snare the understanding in some particulars, but doth more generally and inwardly corrupt the state thereof. For the mind of man is far from the nature of a clear and equal glass, wherein the beams of things should reflect according to their true incidence; nay, it is rather like an enchanted glass, full of superstition and imposture, if it be not delivered and reduced.'[11] Even if logicians could be converted to recognizing this, their logic would be incapable of changing it.

The state of affairs to which Bacon refers is the challenge presented by *Idola* (spectres, apparitions), the idols of the mind. 'Be it known', he writes, 'how vast a difference there is between the Idols of the human mind and the Ideas of the divine. The former are nothing more than arbitrary abstractions; the latter are the creator's own stamp upon creation, impressed and defined in matter by true and exquisite lines. Truth therefore and utility are here the very same things: and works themselves are of greater value as pledges of truth than as contributing to the comforts of life.'[12] In a passage like this Bacon not only makes clear why he calls *Idola* idols. He also proclaims that the highest utilities are engendered by truth. Here it needs to be recalled that for him humanity is as much the creator's creation as the natural universe; that in this statement 'matter' includes human matter; and that in the action of divine providence human affairs no less than the processes of nature carry impressed and defined upon them and in them the stamp of the creator. Bacon's warnings about idols apply in both his programmes.

One of the idols is rooted in 'every man's own individual nature and custom... Although our persons live in the view of heaven, yet our spirits are included in the caves of our own complexions and customs, which minister unto us infinite errors and vain opinions if they be not recalled to examination.'[13] Also there are 'false appearances that are imposed upon us by words'.[14] '...it must be confessed that it is not possible to divorce ourselves from these fallacies and false appearances because they are inseparable from our nature and condition of life: so yet nevertheless the caution of them...doth extremely import the true conduct of human judgment'.[15]

This is Bacon writing in the first *Advancement*. According to the second:

idols are imposed upon the mind, either by the nature of man in general; or by the individual nature of each man; or by words, or nature communicative. The first of these I call Idols of the *Tribe*, the second the Idols of the *Cave*, the third the Idols of the *Market-Place*. There is also a fourth kind which I call the Idols of the *Theatre*, super-induced by corrupt theories or systems of philosophy, and false laws of demonstration. But this kind may be rejected and got rid of, so I will leave it for the present. The others absolutely take possession of the mind, and cannot be wholly removed...Nor (to say truth) can the doctrine concerning Idols be reduced to an art; all that can be done is to use a kind of thoughtful prudence to guard against them. The full and subtle handling of these however I reserve for the New Organum, making here only a few general observations touching them.[16]

The full and subtle handling referred to had been published in the interval between the two *Advancements*.

Introducing *Novum Organum*, he writes:

Now the idols or phantoms, by which the mind is occupied, are either adventitious or innate. The adventitious come into the mind from without; namely, either from the doctrines and sects of philosophers, or from perverse rules of demonstration. But the innate are inherent in the very nature of the intellect, which is far more prone to error than the sense is....And as the first two kinds of idols are hard to eradicate, so idols of this last kind cannot be eradicated at all. All that can be done is to point them out, so that this insidious action of the mind may be marked and reproved...; and to lay it down once for all as a fixed and established maxim, that the intellect is not qualified to judge except by means of induction, and induction in its legitimate form.[17]

Bacon throughout does not change his teaching in this matter and his doctrine is presented in writings written earlier than *Advancement*. His position is clear. Though if we separate the teaching from his conduct in practice, it is perhaps less so. The idols 'generally and inwardly corrupt the state' of the understanding. They absolutely take possession of the mind. It is not possible to divorce ourselves from them. They cannot be wholly eradicated. Doctrine concerning them cannot be reduced to an art. Common logic cannot deal with them. Teachers of the common logic are not even aware of their menace. Nor does he claim that his new induction can infallibly eliminate them. Though the idols figure largely, together with much else in *Novum Organum* Book I, Book II is not a device devoted wholly and exclusively to getting rid of them. The worst idols are those of the market place 'which have crept into the understanding through the tacit agreement of men touching words and names' – 'words or nature communicative' – that is to say, human nature communicative.

On the other hand, as Bacon insists, it is imperative to assail these idols. And this he does. If we examine his practice his position is not that success in warfare against them is impossible. Success is not guaranteed. But it is possible. The idols may be remarked and reproved. 'A kind of thoughtful prudence' can guard against them. Caution, warning and knowledge of them, can constitute victory on perhaps more than half the battlefront.

He writes in the final aphorism of *Novum Organum*'s second book:

For man by the fall fell at the same time from his state of innocency and from his dominion over creation. Both of these losses however can even in this life be in some part repaired; the former by religion and faith, the latter by arts and sciences. For creation was not by the curse made altogether and for ever a rebel, but in virtue of that charter 'In the sweat of thy face shalt thou eat bread', it is now by various labours (not certainly by disputations or idle magical ceremonies, but by various labours) at length and in some measure subdued to the supplying of man with bread; that is, to the uses of human life.[18]

This statement is relevant in all assaults on idols of the tribe and idols of the cave. It is also relevant in combating the others.

The sacred canon of inspired divinity which incorporates ancient Hebrew wisdom contains a history of a voluntary defection by a deed of simple disobedience – not by action wrong in itself – on the part of the first man and the first woman from a privileged original high estate. The penal consequences of this were inherited by the race as a whole. To individual men and women inspired divinity presents in addition a cure for these liabilities. The remedy is religion and this projects moral imperatives. To this Bacon adds another cure, advancement in arts and sciences. This as he expressly maintains is no novelty. On the contrary, the purpose in advancing arts and sciences is the glory of God and the relief of man's estate. This also, translated by Bacon into his own idiom, is an imperative transmitted by inspired divinity. These two imperatives deriving from the same oracle cannot be separated. Arts and sciences if kept bonded with religion and morality can be made to progress. Bacon, it is true, nowhere expressly links the dominion of the idols with man's Fall. It is just as likely that he classes this dominion as a consequence of man's creatureliness. But religion is as much a resource for this latter condition as it is for the results of the Fall. His notion of idols, whatever his thoughts concerning their origin, does not, it is evident, turn him aside in any of his projects, still less frustrate him in advance and deter him in all of them.

Doctrine about idols, their nature, scope, together with instructions about how to handle them, is in itself a notably original contribution on Bacon's part. It is also a conspicuous instance of his capacity for combining a singular caution with a no less singular audacity. His caution is so cautious that what would now be termed ideology, not truth, seems indicated as the sole likely outcome of all inquiries into matters divine, human and natural. If this be the case Bacon would have been seeking to forward and practise a cause embodying a lie. He would have been re-enforcing the impact of ancient pyrrhonism revived, and presenting itself in contemporary forms. Though he acknowledged a vast debt to this pyrrhonism and used it, he decisively rejected it. He would also have been anticipating relativistic teachings of those historians and sociologists of later times who would imprison men's minds and wills inside a succession of historical contexts.

But he has insisted that there is no true utility and no true relief of man's estate without true truth. This truth, though with respect to some areas of knowledge – those in *Know Thyself* – it will be partial and provisional, will still be truth. This being so, his caution does not stand alone. It is not synonymous with lack of resolve. It is combined with, and completed by audacity. He announces a promise. The promise embodied in word and deed is that given time and also labours philosophy and sciences, whether rightly received extant arts or arts not yet discovered, can be made to flourish 'on the solid foundation of experience of every kind and the same well examined and weighed'.[19]

In a first consideration of the case it might seem that, while it is evident that Bacon teaches that idols adversely affect and frustrate advances both in the departments of *Know Thyself* and also in that of investigating nature; he indicates that difficulties in the one are chiefly in the mind studying, but that in the other difficulties are chiefly in the thing studied. For he writes: 'The subtlety of nature is greater many times over than the subtlety of the senses and understanding.'[20] Nature is unknown, or rather, what is known of her should assure us that she is alien and intractable.

And therefore Velleius the Epicurean needed not to have asked, why God should have adorned the heavens with stars, as if he had been an *aedilis*, one that should have set forth some magnificent shews or plays. For if that great work-master had been of an human disposition, he would have cast the stars into some pleasant and beautiful works and orders, like the frets in the roofs of houses; whereas one can scarce find a posture in square or triangle or straight line amongst such an infinite number; so differing an harmony there is between the spirit of Man and the spirit of Nature.[21]

By contrast, man is not unknown. The requirement that there be sciences in nature is because she is unknown. The need for sciences in *Know Thyself* is the opposite. It arises from the circumstance that the strengths and weaknesses in man, his virtues and his vices, are known. Bacon writes in *Advancement* (both versions) under the branch of policy which he calls negotiation or business:

As for the true marshalling of men's pursuits towards their fortune, as they are more or less material, I hold them to stand thus. First, the amendment of their own minds; for the remove of the impediments of the mind will sooner clear the passages of fortune, than the obtaining fortune will remove the impediments of the mind. In the second place I set down wealth and means; which I know most men would have placed first, because of the general use which it beareth towards all variety of occasions. But that opinion I may condemn with like reason as Machiavel doth that other, that monies were the sinews of the wars; whereas (saith he) the true sinews of the wars are the sinews of men's arms, that is, a valiant, populous, and military nation;...In like manner it may be truly affirmed, that it is not monies that are the sinews of fortune, but it is the sinews and steel of men's minds, wit, courage, audacity, resolution, temper, industry and the like....To conclude this precept, as there is order and priority in matter, so is there in time, the preposterous placing whereof is one of the commonest errors; while men fly to their ends when they should intend their beginnings, and do not take things in order of time as they come on, but marshal them according to greatness and not according to instance; not observing the good precept, *Quod nunc instat agamus.* [Attend to present business.][22]

Also, under the branch of policy consisting of government, he writes in his essay *Of Empire* (1612, 1625): 'The difficulties in princes'

business are many and great: but the greatest difficulty is often in
their own mind ... For it is the solecism of power to think to command
the end, and yet not to endure the mean.'[23]

From this difference it might seem to follow that in Bacon's
teaching and in his practice studies in *Know Thyself* – knowledges
drenched in flesh and blood – are less difficult than studies in the
other department, that of nature. This inference is incorrect, and,
contrary to expectation, the situation displayed by Bacon is nothing
less than completely the opposite. In *Know Thyself* difficulties abound
in the mind of the inquirer. But contrary to what seemingly ought to
follow from the circumstance that man unlike nature is known, in
Know Thyself difficulties also abound in what is inquired into. For in
Know Thyself it is knowledge of men's outsides rather than of their
insides upon which the inquirer has inevitably to depend. This matter
is hard to hold in focus because despite Bacon's stand in insisting
upon nature's impenetrability, in *Novum Organum* Book I he offers
assurances that once we have the right procedure successful results
will be easy to come by; and moreover that in *Novum Organum* Book
II this right procedure will be available. In *Know Thyself* no such
assurances of easy results are given, and certainly in this field there
will be no *Novum Organum* Book II. In both departments 'in the sweat
of thy face shalt thou eat bread' – and in similar wise make sciences.
But in regard to nature as contrasted with the realm of *Know Thyself*
Bacon argues that he has, if not a short cut, yet a possible sure
passage in the end into and through all obstacles.

Leaving the idols aside, as both he and logicians do, but for
different reasons – he knows about them, logicians do not – Bacon
proposes to establish as his other complaint that logic, to the extent
claimed, is inadequate on its own for discovering new knowledge,
that is to say in all departments and all areas, not excepting that of
nature. 'The induction which the logicians speak of... whereby the
principles of sciences may be pretended to be invented... their form
of induction, I say, is utterly vicious and incompetent'[24] '... where the
point is not to master an adversary in argument, but to command
nature in operation, truth slips wholly out of our hands, because
the subtlety of nature is so much greater than the subtlety of words'.[25]
'It is true that in sciences popular, as moralities' (*moralia*, matters
moral), 'laws, and the like, yea, and divinity... that form may have
use; and in natural philosophy likewise, by way of argument or
satisfactory reason,... but the subtilty of nature and operations will

not be enchained in those bonds'.[26] ' ... the logic which is received, though it be very properly applied in civil business and to those arts which rest in discourse and opinion, is not nearly subtle enough to deal with nature; and in offering at what it cannot master, has done more to establish and perpetuate error than to open the way to truth'.[27]

Granted, however, that its limitations are recognized, Bacon sanctions the use of the instrument he calls the common logic as practised and taught by Aristotle in antiquity and at universities in later times, including Bacon's university, which was Cambridge, when he studied there at Trinity College. Certainly it is not suggested that he devoted himself to syllogistic exercises as ends in themselves. He had better ways of spending his time. Nevertheless the common logic is applied in, and is certainly neither contradicted nor disregarded when he practises, as he does, in the fields where it is 'very properly employed' – that is to say, in the arts which are received and soundly extant and which he sets himself to improve; those being morality, laws, divinity, and civil business. Logic, like rhetoric, needed no great mending, save only that a new and different logic, his own induction, must be substituted for procuring so far absent knowledges in the realm of nature, this constituting his other and parallel programme. But even with respect to his new induction, the common logic like rhetoric will assist by communicating not only instructions about itself but also the results it may succeed in achieving. For all these purposes the common logic and also rhetoric are indispensable.

Bacon did not need to mend rhetoric. Instead he used it. Rhetoric is

a science certainly both excellent in itself and excellently well laboured. Truly valued indeed, eloquence is doubtless inferior to wisdom ... Yet in profit and in popular estimation wisdom yields to eloquence; for so Solomon says: 'the wise in heart shall be called prudent, but he that is sweet of speech shall compass greater things'; plainly signifying that wisdom will help a man to a name or admiration, but that it is eloquence which prevails most in action and common life.[28]

Approved studies of the art survive – Aristotle's *Rhetoric* and Cicero's dialogues. There are also famous examples of its practice in orations by the latter and by Demosthenes. Such instances of the art in action 'have doubled the progression in it'.[29] Good examples exhibited in practice, Bacon held, can be as effective for teaching as precepts.

Sometimes they are more effective. Bacon provides examples of rhetoric's use in his own performances, thus adding impetus to its 'progression'. If the true purpose of rhetoric is to persuade men in matters of moment, and not to be a vehicle for self advertisement, self-amusement or the entertainment or hoodwinking of others, Bacon no doubt often fails in convincing his audiences. Therefore it can scarcely be argued that indubitably he advanced the art. There is evidence on the other hand that whether or not his speeches convinced, they stirred the respect of those who heard them. Though he himself provides such evidence, as we shall see, it is none the less acceptable. He would scarcely have provided it if he had known or suspected that other evidence existed by means of which his statements could have been refuted.

But in any case rhetoric, civil history writing in the Greek and Roman secular canon, and the common logic, the latter used in a sphere proper to itself, were in his assessment exceptions among knowledges as being acceptable and usable as they stood. It is true that like Erasmus of Rotterdam, he assailed recent excesses in rhetorical practice: ' ...four causes concurring, the admiration of ancient authors, the hate of the schoolmen, the exact study of languages, and the efficacy of preaching, did bring in an affectionate study of eloquence and copy of speech...This grew speedily to an excess...'[30] 'But yet notwithstanding it is a thing not hastily to be condemned, to clothe and adorn the obscurity even of philosophy itself with sensible and plausible elocution.'[31]

Bacon writes in both *Advancements*:

to stir the earth a little about the roots of this science, as we have done of the rest; the duty and office of rhetoric is to apply reason to imagination for the better moving of the will. For we see reason is disturbed in the administration thereof by three means; by illaqueation or sophism, which pertains to logic; by imagination or impression, which pertains to rhetoric; and by passion or affection, which pertains to morality. And as in negotiation with others, men are wrought by cunning, by importunity, and by vehemency; so in this negotiation within ourselves, men are undermined by inconsequences, solicited and importuned by impressions or observations, and transported by passions. Neither is the nature of man so unfortunately built, as that those powers and arts should have force to disturb reason, and not to establish and advance it: for the end of logic is to teach a form of argument to secure reason, and not to entrap it: the end of morality is to procure the affections to obey reason, and not to invade it; the end of rhetoric is to fill the imagination to second reason, and not to oppress it: for these abuses of arts come in but *ex obliquo* (indirectly), for caution.[32]

'And', he continues, 'therefore it was great injustice in Plato, though springing out of a just hatred of the rhetoricians of his time, to esteem of rhetoric but as a voluptuary art, resembling it to cookery, that did mar wholesome meats, and help unwholesome by variety of sauces to the pleasure of the taste.'

Condemnation of excesses and faults is more than offset by Bacon's commendation of rhetoric as an art, by thorough employment of it on his own part, by praise of its condition, and by approving explanations of its use: – 'the duty and office of rhetoric, if it be deeply looked into, is no other than to apply and recommend the dictates of reason to imagination, in order to excite the appetite and will'.[33] 'The end of rhetoric is to fill the imagination to second reason, and not to oppress it.'[34] Rhetoric is 'Imaginative or Insinuative Reason'.[35] This art like all arts can be and has been abused and misused. Logicians, he argues, misapplied their art in misguided impotent attempts to increase the sum of knowledge in natural philosophy/science. The art of rhetoric is abused if civil historians distract men by describing 'pomp of business', feeding their love of grandeur, when they should be directing them to 'matters of truest import'. But resorting to Thucydides for testimony in defence of eloquence, he claims that: 'no man but speaks more honestly than he thinks or acts. And it was excellently noted by Thucydides as a censure passed upon Cleon, that because he used always to hold on the bad side, therefore he was ever inveighing against eloquence and grace of speech; as well knowing that no man can speak fair of courses sordid and base; while it is easy to do it of courses just and honourable.'[36]

Rhetoric rightly used, not divided and separated from philosophy/science, but harnessed into unity with it, makes and sustains society. When men 'give ear to precepts, to laws, to religion, sweetly touched with eloquence and persuasion of books, of sermons, of harangues, so long is society and peace maintained –'.[37] In both programmes he uses rhetoric conjoined with philosophy/science, in this way undoing the fault of Socrates and his school who according to Cicero – now strongly seconded in his own judgment – separated the two. He uses rhetoric combined with philosophy/science in parliaments, in councils and in law courts when making contributions in government and in law. He employs rhetoric everywhere throughout the *Great*

Instauration – that 'total reconstruction of sciences, arts, and all human knowledge, raised upon the proper foundations',[38] a rebuilding which, though not in every case explicitly, includes not only *Novum Organum* but efforts in both *Advancements*, in *Wisdom of the Ancients*, in civil historiography, in *Essays* and elsewhere. In *Novum Organum* he states: 'I have on my own part made it my care and study that the things which I shall propound should not only be true, but should also be presented to men's minds, how strangely soever preoccupied and obstructed, in a manner not harsh or unpleasant.'[39] *The History of Life and Death* is one of the specimens he himself provides of a Natural and Experimental History of the type he demands: but it too is presented to men's minds in a manner neither harsh nor unpleasant.

His notion that rhetoric is 'imaginative or insinuative reason' aptly describes much of his practice in speaking. In any case memory, imagination, reason – all three when in exercise are thinking as he said. Ben Jonson wrote regarding the effect of Bacon's oratory: 'No man ever spake more neatly, more pressly, more weightily, or suffered less emptiness, less idleness, in what he uttered.'[40] But the judgment is no less true of Bacon as writer than as speaker. Walter Raleigh according to Bacon's chaplain pronounced on his pre-eminent excellence, comparing him with two of his eminent contemporaries in both attainments.[41]

Macaulay in his essay reminds readers that in the middle of the sixteenth century 'a person who did not read Greek and Latin could read nothing, or next to nothing. The Italian was the only modern language which possessed anything that could be called a literature. All the valuable books then extant in all the vernacular dialects of Europe would hardly have filled a single shelf.'[42] It must be pointed out therefore that in addition to striving to invent natural philosophy/science; to efforts to reinvent civil history proper for England by supplying and continuing that of the ancients; to claims and attempts to invent a civil science by erecting it upon civil histories and by applying it in his English civil experience; to proposals and outlines towards inventing a civil history of letters, Bacon in the process of proceeding in these creative activities took part together with others in England in inventing yet something more – a language at its early but formative stage.

If found to be denouncing 'literature and book learning' as he berates them for instance when presenting King James with *Novum*

Organum, everything he himself writes, whether in Latin or in English, proves that he cultivates an emotive power in address and presentation and that he does not reject what is now termed style. As for book-learning, he does not repudiate books. A pyrrhonistic preacher having written a piece which is included in the sacred canon complained at the finish: 'of making many books there is no end; and much study is a weariness of the flesh. Let us hear the conclusion of the whole matter: Fear God, and keep his commandments: for this is the whole duty of man.'[43] This preacher suggested a dilemma which for Bacon could not have existed. Much study was indeed a weariness of the flesh, but this experience of discomforts and sufferings was as things ought to be. Keeping the commandments could not be fully achieved, nor the whole duty of man fulfilled, unless men attempted to promote the advancement of learning. Bacon writes: 'For the opinion of plenty is amongst the causes of want, and the great quantity of books maketh a show rather of superfluity than lack: which surcharge nevertheless is not to be remedied by making no more books, but by making more good books...'[44]

He told the King in 1623 that he was 'a man naturally fitted rather for literature than for anything else'.[45] By that date he had himself contributed more 'good books' in the shape of *Advancement* (in two versions), *De Sapientia Veterum* (reprinted during his lifetime), *Novum Organum* (in two books), *The History of the Reign of King Henry the 7th* (fragments survive of projects to write histories of Henry's successors), and *Essays* (two books of them – a third would be added in 1625). On its own the common logic is incompetent in dispelling idols of the mind. Also it is incapable on its own of penetrating the secrets of nature. These positions being accepted, Bacon does not cast out the common logic where it is properly applicable as in moral matters, laws, divinity and civil business, or the science of rhetoric, or literature, or book-learning. Literature or book-learning according to his teaching comprises or includes human learning and arts as hitherto achieved; and this spectacle of attainments or of efforts deserves, he argues, a history of its own. Even when devoted to knowledges less evidently drenched in flesh and blood than 'civil history, morality and policy', he casts out, or ignores, or improves and thus supersedes, these disciplines and exercises of men only when they exhibit pretensions to advancing knowledge by no procedures or by wrong ones.

CHAPTER 5

Policy a great part of philosophy – Bacon's engagements in policy

In neither of his programmes is 'method' the word which Bacon adopts when describing what he holds to be the correct way in achieving knowledge. 'Method' – Μεθοδος – was a Greek term for this achievement and for the discovery of truth. According to Aphorism xxxvi of *Novum Organum*, Book I: 'One method of delivery alone remains to us; which is simply this: we must lead men to the particulars themselves, and their series and order; while men on their side must force themselves for a while to lay their notions by and begin to familiarise themselves with facts.' This is Bacon in *Novum Organum*. But it is Bacon when translated.[1] Understandable though it be that we should find him rendered in this way, this is not what he wrote either in this instance or in many other comparable ones. His words in Aphorism xxxvi are: *Restat vero nobis modus tradendi unus et simplex*[2] – one mode. Elsewhere it is the same – one mode, one road, one manner, one way, one rule – one almost anything, but not one method – and this despite the fact that when literally rendered Μεθοδος means finding or making and then pursuing a road. In his usage the word has its place. But this, though of the greatest import for him, has a range more limited. As we shall see he adopts the term 'method' not for discovering knowledge but as the mode of describing one of the ways in which to communicate it.

The sciences we possess, he writes in *Novum Organum*, have come largely from the philosophers of Greece in antiquity.[3] He refers principally but not exclusively to sciences of nature. In his judgment these latter constitute not possessions but deprivations. But it will be recalled that he rejected sharp separations between knowledges both with respect to subject matters and also to procedures for studying them. The wisdom of ancient Greek philosophers, he writes, was 'professorial and much given to disputations'.[4] They had accepted that some 'methods' in pursuing knowledge were better than others. But they could reach no agreement. Both as cause and effect of this, their wisdom in his judgment was *de haut en bas*, pursuing 'magistrality' as much as truth. Also, their disputations were disputatious.

> Nor does the character of the time and age yield much better signs than the character of the country and nation. For at that period there was but a narrow and meagre knowledge either of time or place; which is the worst thing that can be, especially for those who rest all on experience. For they had no history, worthy to be called history, that went back a thousand years; but only fables and rumours of antiquity. And of the regions and districts of the world they knew but a small portion…[5]

On this point – that Greeks in antiquity had no history – the reference it is clear is not to natural but to civil history, though this latter he puts in conjunction, it is true, with geography.

This last statement is like an echo of the complaint of Thucydides, whose work was the first of time's fruits in Bacon's secular civil canon. In the early pages of *The History of the Peloponnesian War* Thucydides referred to the difficulty of finding accurate information not only about the distant past but even about recent events.[6] He made no mention of Herodotus, his predecessor as civil historian of the Greeks. Nor did Bacon mention Herodotus. When Bacon alluded elsewhere to Aristotle's deficiency in history and experience, again, as will be seen, it is a lack not only of natural but of civil history with which he charged him. For Bacon whole tracts of the Greek period in antiquity were occupied and presided over not by historians but by poets. These latter, he maintained, had wrapped up a pre-existing perished wisdom in allegories and fables. The poets were followed in the case of the Greeks, mainly not by historians but predominantly by philosophers; and the poets, in his judgment, had been better philosophers than the philosophers.

We have noted that in the second *Advancement* Bacon makes a favourable reference to 'one of the moderns', who 'remarked on the conceit and precipitancy of some of the ancients, who in too eagerly fixing their eyes and thoughts on the memory, imagination, and reason have neglected the Thinking Faculty, which holds the first place'.[7] Bacon had introduced three fables out of *De Sapientia Veterum* into the text of the second *Advancement*, 'one taken from things Natural, one from things Political, and one from things Moral'.

These three were 'Of the Universe, according to the Fable of Pan', 'Of War, according to the story of Perseus', and 'Of Desire, according to the fable of Dionysus'. Bacon makes his statement about 'the Thinking Faculty, which holds the first place' in the interpretation of the fable of Pan, given in the second *Advancement*, as we have said. The statement is not to be found in the version of Pan which he offers in *De Sapientia Veterum*. But as we know he alters ever when he adds – or adds ever when he alters. By the year 1623 he had had plenty of time to think about thinking. Accordingly, the formula in the first *Advancement* is added to and expanded: whether 'simply rehearsing' the impact of individuals/particulars (in the case of history); or 'making fanciful imitations' (in the case of poetry); or 'analysing and classifying' (in the case of philosophy); the human mind, he had written, first proceeds to 'ruminate' and to 'review' the individuals/particulars which it observes and absorbs.[8] Ruminating and reviewing – both of these are thinking.

The passage concerning the thinking faculty in the rendering of the fable of Pan which Bacon provided in 1623 runs as follows:

Pan delights in the nymphs, that is in spirits; for the spirits of living creatures are the delight of the world. And with reason is he styled their leader, for each of them follows its own nature as a guide, round which after their own fashion they leap and frisk in endless variety and constant motion. And therefore one of the moderns has ingeniously referred all the powers of the soul to motion, and remarked on the conceit and precipitancy of some of the ancients, who in too eagerly fixing their eyes and thoughts on the memory, imagination, and reason, have neglected the Thinking Faculty, which holds the first place. For he who remembers or recollects, thinks; he who imagines, thinks; he who reasons, thinks; and in a word the spirit of man, whether prompted by sense or left to itself, whether in the functions of the intellect, or of the will and affections, dances to the tune of the thoughts; and this is the frisking of the Nymphs.[9]

Handling this fable in his *De Sapientia Veterum* (1609) Bacon wrote that the 'ancients have given under the person of Pan an elaborate description of universal nature'.[10] 'A noble fable this, if there be any such; and big almost to bursting with the secrets and mysteries of Nature. Pan, as the very word declares, represents the universal frame of things or nature.' 'Now the office of Pan can in no way be more lively set forth and explained than by calling him god of hunters. For every natural action, every motion and process of nature, is nothing else than a hunt. For the sciences and arts hunt after their works,[11] human counsels hunt after their ends…'[12]

As for the tale that the discovery of Ceres was reserved for this god, and that while he was hunting, and denied to the rest of the gods, though diligently and specially engaged in seeking her; it contains a very true and wise admonition – namely that the discovery of things useful to life and the furniture of life, such as corn, is not to be looked for from the abstract philosophies, as it were the greater gods, no not though they devote their whole powers to that special end – but only from Pan; that is from sagacious experience and the universal knowledge of nature…[13]

Writing of the most ancient poets of Greece in the *Preface* Bacon stated: 'I do certainly for my own part (I freely and candidly confess) incline to this opinion – that beneath no small number of the fables of the ancient poets there lay from the very beginning a mystery and an allegory.'[14] 'Imagination is oftentimes idle.'[15] In this instance it had been conspicuously and extensively active according to Bacon. In this case, according to Bacon, 'he who imagines, thinks'.[16] The fables, he argued, were more than they seemed. The poets – 'Homer, Hesiod and the rest'[17] – deliberately put wisdom into fables, and the wisdom they put into them was such, he held, as could demand the attention of men in his times.

According to Bacon their performance was not the beginning of valid human arts and learning. He stated that the learning which the poets presented in their fables was a learning which had preceded them. Moreover, he announced what he held to be the sources of it. In the jottings of July 1608 we find:

Discoursing skornfully of the philosophy of the Graecians wth some better respect to ye Aegiptians, Persians, Caldes, and the utmost antiquity and the mysteries of the poets.[18]

Since the poets of Greece were better philosophers than the philosophers of Greece, it follows that the poets' predecessors must have been better philosophers than the Greek ones. On the other hand, though Bacon claimed that he could name the sources, he had no knowledge of the content of the performance of these pre-Greek and other than Greek savants, apart from what the most ancient Greek poets had used their imaginations to embody in their poetry. Hence the performance of the latter was for Bacon the beginning, so far as any evidence survived which he knew of – or which he knew of and could trust, of valid human arts and learning.

Bacon did not suggest that the ancient Greek peoples who received the fables from their poets continued to interpret them as the poets had done and as he did. Nor did he affirm, as a disciple of

his, the Neapolitan Giambattista Vico (1668–1744), later argued in
Scienza Nuova (1725), that the poets had done nothing consciously
and rationally deliberate when making and propagating fables thus
pregnant with hidden meanings. Instead his argument was that the
poets were consciously and rationally well aware of what they did.
In *De Sapientia Veterum* (1609) Bacon interpreted these fables for the
benefit and profit of his times, propounding his interpretations as
confirming what he held already on other grounds. He went the
length in one place of conceding that the inventors of the fables had
not put as much into them as he had done: 'For I find the wisdom
of the ancients to be like grapes ill-trodden: something is squeezed
out, but the best parts are left behind and passed over.' Clearly it is
not possible to dismiss his expressed belief in what he was doing as
other than genuine.

We note that not only did he include parts of *De Sapientia Veterum*
in the second *Advancement* he also, still pursuing and interpreting this
ancient hidden wisdom, produced a separate tract of which the date is
uncertain. In *De Principiis atque Originibus*, On Principles and Origins
according to the Fables of Cupid and Coelum, etc. again he
expounds ancient teaching concealed within the most ancient myths
of the poets; though it needs to be added that in this tract he goes
on to discuss the teachings of philosophers both early and late: 'This
fable' (Cupid),

with the following one respecting Coelum, seems to set forth in the small
compass of a parable a doctrine concerning the principles of things and the
origins of the world, not differing in much from the philosophy which
Democritus held, excepting that it appears to be somewhat more severe,
sober, and pure. For the speculations of that philosopher, acute and diligent
as he was, could not rest nor keep within bounds, nor put a sufficient check
and control over themselves. And even the opinions which are veiled in the
parable, though somewhat more correct, are yet no better than such as
proceed from the intellect left to itself and not resting constantly on
experience and advancing step by step; a fault to which I suppose the
primitive ages were likewise subject.[19]

He explains that Cupid

is represented by the ancient sages in the parable as without a parent, that
is to say, without a cause, – an observation of no small significance; nay I
know not whether it be not the greatest thing of all. For nothing has
corrupted philosophy so much as this seeking after the parents of Cupid;
that is, that philosophers have not taken the principles of things as they are
found in nature, and accepted them as a positive doctrine, resting on the

faith of experience; but they have rather deduced them from the laws of
disputation, the petty conclusions of logic and mathematics, common
notions, and such wanderings of the mind beyond the limits of nature.
Therefore a philosopher should be continually reminding himself that
Cupid has no parents, ...[20]

Nevertheless in continuing with discussing the philosophers as this
tract proceeds, Bacon writes: 'for I wish to deal quite fairly with
every man's opinions, and to give them the benefit of a favourable
construction.'[21]

The *Preface* to *De Sapientia Veterum* explains that 'the most
ancient times (except what is preserved of them in the
scriptures) are buried in oblivion and silence: to that silence
succeeded the fables of the poets: to those fables the written records
which have come down to us...'[22] But in *Advancement* (1605) he had
already noted that:

> it is generally to be found in the wisdom of the more ancient times; that as
> men found out any observation that they thought was good for life,
> they would gather it and express it in parable or aphorism or fable. But for
> fables, they are viceregents and supplies where examples failed: now that
> the times abound with history, the aim is better when the mark is alive.[23]

The first poets of Greece in recently published texts were doubtless
another gift of time. But the age of poetry and poets of this kind had
passed long ago to be succeeded by epochs which in the times Bacon
referred to in the above passage boasted histories. Here again as in
the statements in *De Sapientia Veterum*'s *Preface* Bacon's reference is
to histories civil.

The wisdom conveyed by the most ancient poets of Greece, as
Bacon saw it and expounded it, concerned matters civil, matters
moral, things natural; and also the mechanical arts. He provided
explanations of thirty-one fables. In civil philosophy ten pieces are
offered. Six are given in the field of moral philosophy. Two relate
either to moral or to civil philosophy. Eight pertain to natural
philosophy. Four are general, that is to say, four relate in all spheres.
One concerns the arts mechanical. Behind his interpretations in civil
and moral philosophy is backing from sacred history or from civil
history or from his civil and moral experience. He apprehended and
comprehended the experience of the most ancient ages of mankind
as conformable with that of his own times. Pieces relating to natural
philosophy and those relevant in all areas are backed by notions
germinating in his head, notions which would burst into flower in

Novum Organum, Book I. But support provided by civil history and by his civil experience is detectably present even in pieces which are general in their bearing.

Two pieces general in bearing, but detectably revealing buttressing afforded by civil history and civil experience are the *Flight of Icarus*; also *Scylla and Charybdis* (Fable XXVII) and *Sphinx* (Fable XXVIII). 'Moderation, or the middle way', he wrote under the former,

'is in Morals much commended; in Intellectuals less spoken of, though not less useful and good; in Politics only, questionable and to be used with caution and judgment... Now for the passage between *Scylla and Charybdis* (understood of the conduct of the understanding) certainly it needs both skill and good fortune to navigate it. For if the ship run on *Scylla*, it is dashed on the rocks, if on Charybdis, it is sucked in by the whirlpool: by which parable (I can but briefly touch it, though it suggests reflexions without end) we are meant to understand that in every knowledge and science, and in the rules and axioms appertaining to them, a mean must be kept between too many distinctions and too much generality, – between the rocks of the one and the whirlpools of the other. For these two are notorious for the shipwreck of wits and arts.[24]

Under *Sphinx*, he explains that he finds its riddles consist of two varieties:

one concerning the nature of things, another concerning the nature of man; and in like manner there are two kinds of kingdom offered as the reward of solving them; one over nature, and the other over man... the riddle proposed to Oedipus, by the solution of which he became King of Thebes related to the nature of man; for whoever has a thorough insight into the nature of man may shape his fortune almost as he will, and is born for empire...[25]

It will be noted that in *De Sapientia Veterum*, Bacon's contribution to the history of learning, arts and sciences, it is moral and civil knowledge – knowledges in *Know Thyself* – both in the fables of the poets and also in the sources which he considered to have preceded them – which are for him the first in time of all the valid arts which mankind had acquired, for the reason that these knowledges seemed not lacking in some sufficient connections with experience. By contrast, it was not these, but knowledges of the realm of nature which were restricted, as in the fable of Pan, to helpfully provoking, inspired, and inspiring hints, and to sagacious guesswork: or else they consisted of preceding teachings, veiled as under the fable of Cupid, which were 'no better than such as proceed from the intellect left to itself and not resting constantly on experience...', a fault to which

I suppose the primitive ages were likewise subject. It can be noted therefore that the fables concerning moral and civil knowledge are not only prominently numerous, they carry messages more positive and more encouraging than do the fables devoted to knowledge of the natural order.

Interpretations of fables in *De Sapientia Veterum* which are plainly and primarily in civil philosophy are not the majority. Nor are those which are plainly and primarily in moral philosophy. Nor are those which recognizably apply in both disciplines. Taken together, however, these three groups constitute a majority. But according to Bacon, whether explicitly or implicitly, throughout a constant course on his part of a lifetime's interacting contemplations and practice in the *Know Thyself* programme, it is always required of civil philosophy and of moral philosophy, both here and elsewhere, that they be taken together. Civil philosophy in its applications, as it is in process of being constructed, though distinct from moral philosophy is not separable from it. In the study of man there are two parts – mind and body, these two being distinct yet indivisible. 'Humanity particular consisteth of the same parts whereof man consisteth; that is, knowledges which respect the body, and knowledges which respect the mind.'[26] But in the study of man, this time when the processes and products of his mind and will are inquired into, there is also partition into two – moral philosophy and civil philosophy. Once again, though these are distinct, they are not divisible. As in the case of the first partition, so also in the second, the subject to which the partition relates is a single entity. Man's inside, his morality, affects his external conduct. But, equally, forces operating from outside a man's self, government, church, laws, affect his inside and his morality. Therefore these outside agents will conduct themselves, Bacon insisted in his teaching and also in his practice, in accord with moral requirements. 'And generally let this be a rule, that all partitions of knowledges be accepted rather for lines and veins than for sections and separations; and that the continuance and entireness of knowledge be preserved.'[27]

Bacon dedicated *De Sapientia Veterum* to Lord Treasurer Salisbury who was Chancellor of Cambridge University. In this dedication the Chancellor was informed that the source from which *politia*, policy, was drawn was philosophy; and, further, that policy was a great part of philosophy.[28] 'And if any man think', Bacon continued, 'these things of mine to be common and vulgar, it is not for me of course to say what I have effected; but my aim has been, passing by things obvious and obsolete and commonplace, to give some help towards the difficulties of life and the secrets of sciences.'[29]

Here it needs to be recalled that in 1604, Bacon had been appointed King's Counsel and that in 1607 he was created Solicitor General. He continued to seek high offices and thereafter attained to higher ones. Conditions prevailing as he judged and described them in improvable arts – government, law, morals – invited attention devoted to them. In addition his birth and prospects, coinciding with his expressed desires and hopes, did the same. His father, Sir Nicholas Bacon, had been Lord Keeper of the Great Seal. William Cecil, Lord Burleigh, was his uncle by marriage. Since 1584 he had been elected to the House of Commons in successive parliaments. He made speeches in these assemblies. Outside parliaments, in addition, he had tendered unsolicited advice on matters of state. In 1593 he offended the Queen by the contents of speeches he made in the Commons. He was reported to have asserted amongst other things that: 'in histories it is to be observed that of all nations the English care not to be subject, base, taxable'.[30] His speeches concerned the privileges of the Commons in the matter of bills for levying subsidies. He grieved, he wrote, that the Queen 'should retain an hard conceit' of things he had said. 'It mought please her sacred Majesty to think what my end should be in those speeches, if it were not duty and duty alone. I am not so simple but I know the common beaten way to please.'[31] Here a foretaste is provided of Bacon's civil philosophy as it relates to the topic of counsel. The favour he did not receive from Queen Elizabeth he obtained in due course from King James VI and I.

In 1592 he had written to his uncle, Burleigh:

I confess that I have as vast contemplative ends, as I have moderate civil ends; for I have taken all knowledge to be my province; and if I would purge it of two sorts of rovers, whereof the one with frivolous disputations, confutations and verbosities, the other with blind experiments and auricular traditions and impostures, hath committed so many spoils, I hope I should bring in industrious observations, grounded conclusions, and profitable inventions and discoveries; the best state of that province.[32]

Here what he calls his contemplative ends are in natural not in civil philosophy. Nevertheless, though he claims his civil ends to be moderate, the province of all learning includes civil philosophy.

According to *De Interpretatione Naturae Proœmium*, Concerning the

Interpretation of Nature – Preface, an early unpublished piêce presumably preceding the publication of the first *Advancement* (1605), Bacon's civil ends can scarcely be assessed as more moderate than his other aspirations: 'Believing that I was born for the service of mankind, and regarding the care of the commonwealth as a kind of common property which like the air and the water belongs to everybody, I set myself to consider in what way mankind might best be served, and what service I was myself best fitted by nature to perform.' Here, 'the care of the commonwealth' covers more than politics and economics. But the phrase can scarcely be taken to exclude these matters.

Now among all the benefits that could be conferred upon mankind, I found none so great as the discovery of new arts, endowments and commodities for the bettering of man's life... And it was plain that the good effects wrought by founders of cities, law-givers, fathers of the people... extend but over narrow spaces and last but for short times; whereas the work of the Inventor, though a thing of less pomp and shew, is felt everywhere and lasts forever.

'For myself', he continued, 'I found that I was fitted for nothing so well as for the study of Truth; as having a mind nimble and versatile enough to catch the resemblances of things (which is the chief point), and at the same time steady enough to fix and distinguish their subtler differences...'

'Nevertheless', he went on,

because my birth and education had seasoned me in business of state; and because opinions (so young as I was) would sometimes stagger me; and because I thought that a man's own country has some special claims upon him more than the rest of the world; and because I hoped that, if I rose to any place of honour in the state, I should have a larger command of industry and ability to help me in my work; for these reasons I both applied myself to acquire the arts of civil life, and commended my services so far as in modesty and honesty I might, to the favour of such friends as had any influence. In which also I had another motive: for I felt that those things I have spoken of – be they great or small – reach no further than the condition and culture of this mortal life; and I was not without hope (the condition of Religion being at that time not very prosperous) that if I came to hold office in the state, I might get something done too for the good of men's souls.

When I found however that my zeal was mistaken for ambition, and my life had already reached the turning point, and my breaking health reminded me how ill I could afford to be so slow, and I reflected moreover that in leaving undone the good that I could do by myself alone, and applying myself to that which could not be done without the help and consent of others, I was by no means discharging the duty that lay upon me, – I put all those thoughts aside, and (in pursuance of my old determination) betook myself wholly to this work.[33]

It is of little consequence that *De Interpretatione Naturae Proœmium* cannot be precisely dated. It is of greater import to recognize that pursuit of two programmes implied in the longer term no mutual disjunctions. Bacon's ambition was confronted and puzzled by this dilemma as he made evident. But policy, though not natural philosophy, was nevertheless philosophy. Study in it was commitment to truth. Further, the same mind and will were at work employing the same procedures whichever programme was being pursued. Moreover the dilemma – 'leaving undone the good that I could do by myself alone' or 'applying myself to that which could not be done without the help and consent of others' – this, on his own showing, would be temporary. In due course interpretation of nature, once embarked upon in practical activity, would require no less than affairs of state and law, the help and consent of other men.

Bacon as we have seen discusses both civil history and civil philosophy in *Advancement* (1605). But there is notably more about civil history in that book than there is about civil philosophy. There is plainly more about civil philosophy in *De Sapientia Veterum* (1609) than there are dealings with this topic in *Advancement* (1605). Neither in the letter to Lord Burleigh – recently quoted – nor in *De Interpretatione Naturae Proœmium* – also recently quoted – is Bacon explicit that policy – civil philosophy – is a great part of philosophy. Nor in either document is he explicit that action in policy contributes to the redress and relief of man's estate. But when he addresses Lord Salisbury and the university in the dedications prefacing *De Sapientia Veterum* in 1609 he makes both affirmations; at the same time making clear that there is connection between making them and his own embarkment into active political life. Here it will be noted that the dating of Bacon's jottings outlining the grand strategy under the head 'Poll.' (policy) was 1608, the year preceding the publication of *De Sapientia Veterum* with its dedications. Not only does policy by commitment into action become a great part of philosophy; but also his aim – both in the contents of *De Sapientia Veterum*, so large a part of which consists of themes civil and moral, and also in his commitments in policy – 'has been to give some help towards the difficulties of life'. In the same year – 1609 – he wrote to Isaac

Casaubon in similar terms: 'For indeed to write at leisure about that which is to be read at leisure matters little; but to bring about the better ordering of man's life and business, with all its troubles and difficulties, by the help of sound and true contemplations – this is the thing I am at.'[34]

Scarcely any of the positions characterizing *Advancement* (1605) and *Novum Organum*, Book I (1620) are not embodied already in early writings antedating *Advancement*. Bacon did not publish these early writings. One of these, *De Interpretatione Naturae Proœmium* has been mentioned and cited already. *Valerius Terminus of the Interpretation of Nature* is another early piece. There he set down 'this position or firmament, namely *that all knowledge is to be limited by religion, and to be referred to use and action*'.[35] This pronouncement may be rendered thus: search for knowledge is to be directed by religion and the way in this search is to make sure that it is grounded in use and action, not in speculation alone. This position is to be distinguished from another, which also is directed by religion: 'But yet evermore', he wrote in *Valerius Terminus of the Interpretation of Nature* 'it must be remembered that the least part of knowledge passed to man by this so large a charter from God must be subject to that use for which God hath granted it; which is the benefit and relief of the state and society of man.'[36]

Both this latter and also the former position comprise part of the message of *Advancement* and of *Novum Organum*, Book I. But the former – namely that 'all knowledge is to be limited by religion and to be referred to use and action', is the part of the message which becomes activated at the time when he has entered into active pursuit of a political career. It becomes activated because Bacon himself has become politically activated. The great part which this latter event plays – not only in the *Know Thyself* programme but also in that devoted to investigating nature – is the addition of an enduringly propelling thrust behind the message delivered at the outset, that speculation/contemplation must always be joined with use and action. Contemplations become 'sound and true' when they are not leisured, consisting, that is to say of leisurely speculation alone; but instead when they are combined inseparably with use and action. It can be objected that thinking is action and that action is thinking and that the distinction between cogitating and doing is artificial and arbitrary. But Bacon as Macaulay noted was a philosopher not disdaining the aids of common sense.

When he dedicated *De Sapientia Veterum* (1609) he addressed first the Chancellor of the university and next the university itself which, as he reminded it, was 'his nursing mother'. 'Nor', he told the professors, doctors and scholars, 'shall I take too much to myself (I think), if by reason of that little acquaintance with affairs which my kind and plan of life has necessarily carried with it, I indulge a hope that the inventions of the learned may receive some accession by these labours of mine.'[37] This statement could refer, it is true, to the opportunities afforded by high place in the state for promoting measures to forward the programme for exploring nature. But on the other hand it is no less possible and at the same time more likely that it refers to the words which immediately follow: 'Certainly I am of opinion that speculative studies when transplanted into active life acquire some new grace and vigour, and having more matter to feed them, strike their roots perhaps deeper or at least grow taller and fuller leaved.'[38]

Bacon's wisdom of the ancient poets of Greece pertained as said to matters civil, to matters moral and to matters natural, but preponderantly it pertained to matters civil and moral, that is, to matters standing under the oracle's directive to *Know Thyself*. What he told the University of Cambridge and its Chancellor is plain foretaste and prefiguring in 1609 of what he announced in *Plan of the work* of *the Great Instauration* in 1620 – namely that improving what we have already is not only in itself a worthy and valid ambition, but that the enterprise can also constitute an introduction into discovering sciences we are as yet deprived of. Policy is a great part of philosophy. But not only so. Not only is policy a great part of philosophy – or rather precisely because it is so great a part of it, Bacon's programme and commitment in policy is capable not only of offering help in 'The difficulties of life', but of providing in addition entrances into discovering secrets of the sciences not of human nature, but of nature. 'And generally let this be a rule, that all partitions of knowledges be accepted rather for lines and veins than for sections and separations; and that the continuance and entireness of knowledge be preserved.'[39]

The part of his main message which is communicated here is that speculative studies when transplanted into active life acquire new force. Thinking and action both benefit if conducted in deliberate interchange. In *Advancement* (1605)[40] the philosopher had been enjoined to 'keep a continual watchful and severe eye upon action, operation and the use of knowledge' – that is to say, the building of knowledge by using it, applying it, and so testing it in action.[41] Another part of his main message had also already been delivered in *Advancement*. Dwelling upon this other part was inappropriate in a book devoted to the exertions of 'Homer, Hesiod, and the rest'; though without this omitted part it would scarcely have been possible to interpret the results of their exertions and to see what Bacon claimed to see in them. This omitted part consisted of the announcement in *Advancement* that the times men now lived in abounded with history – with civil history – and that knowledges were as pyramids whereof history – not poetry – was the basis.

The point of junction between these two parts of his main message is first that memory – history – civil history – writing it or reading it and thus handling a series of particulars – is thinking; and second that civil history is not only thinking, but in itself conduces and invites to action of the right kind – action which is neither irresolute nor pertinacious. That is because civil histories are accounts of moral and/or civil actions. Listing as he does in *Advancement* (both versions) three sorts of civil histories proper, one of them was specifically 'Narrations and Relations of actions'.[42] Of this kind he wrote, while making his due reservations, that it 'cannot but be more purely and exactly true'[43] than a history of times. But all three varieties provided accounts of action. His own *History of the Reign of King Henry the 7th* which as we shall see was a mixture of all three would do so. Lives recite actions. Times contain them. Narrations or relations of actions are restricted to them and specialize in them. Seeking help for his own enterprise in civil history he had seen the need of, but failed to find, 'any tolerable chronicle as a simple narration of the actions themselves'.[44]

Morality and policy not only imply actions, they consist of actions. In both spheres men do things and launch themselves into actions – it not being forgotten that, in spheres were action is appropriate, inaction can be no less decisive in its consequences than action. 'For all the exterior proceedings of man', he wrote in *Advancement* (1605 version) 'consist of words and deeds; whereof history doth properly receive and retain in memory the deeds, and of words, yet but as inducements and passages to deeds...'[45] Bacon states in *De Sapientia*'s dedication to Cambridge University – he had already in effect said the same in *Valerius Terminus of the Interpretation of Nature* and in *Advancement* (1605) – that 'speculative studies when translated into active life acquire some new grace and vigour, and having more matter to feed them, strike their roots perhaps deeper'.[46] The converse, namely that active life translated into speculative studies endows the latter with grace and vigour which they previously lacked, is no less true. Indeed, it comes to the same thing. It is required that things be done in addition to being thought and argued about. In civil history and in civil policy things are done, Bacon claims, in addition to being thought about and disputed over. In civil history and in civil policy at the time he published *De Sapientia* with its dedications he had started to do these things himself. In natural history and natural philosophy things up to now had been chiefly deliberated and disputed about. There had been little action in the shape of history-making and experiments.

The first position, that history, writing it or reading it, is thinking, speculation, contemplation – this was not stated in so many words till 1623 in the second *Advancement*, when he wrote of 'ruminating and reviewing' not only in the spheres of poetry and philosophy; but also in that of history. By that time history includes natural history. The second position, that history relates things outside a man's self, things consisting of action and therefore generating action, had been advanced, though not fully so in all the implications, before the first *Advancement*'s publication date, and at a time when the Queen was still reigning. Again, Bacon's reference was to history civil.

A third section of his message is that philosophy should consist of middle axioms. This third section is contained in his rendering of the fable of *Scylla and Charybdis*: 'in every knowledge and science, and in the rules and axioms appertaining to them, a mean must be kept between too many distinctions and too much generality, – between the rocks of the one and the whirlpools of the other. For these two extremes are notorious for the shipwreck of wits and arts.'[47] History, dealing with particulars, is itself thinking and itself conduces to action. But it still nevertheless falls short of being philosophy. Axioms of high generality attain the status of philosophy. But these, implying as they do, too few distinctions, are useless according to Bacon's consistent and persistent teaching. On the other hand too many distinctions are implied by axioms which distinguish themselves scarcely – if at all – from the particulars which they profess to handle. Only middle axioms, avoiding both extremes, and presenting neither too few distinctions nor too many, produce results which are worth the effort.

In discussing *Scylla and Charybdis* in 1609 Bacon speaks of every knowledge and science. But as we see civil science and moral science are conspicuously foremost in the contents of *De Sapientia Veterum*. Sciences – every knowledge and science – can be made sound only by constructing in them and using in them middle axioms. But Bacon had started to produce middle axioms in the field of the Common Law while the Queen was still reigning. To her *Maxims of the Law* had been dedicated. As he explained in the *Preface*:

there be two contrary faults and extremities in the debating and sifting out of the law, which may be best noted in two several manner of arguments: some argue upon general grounds, and come not near the point in question; others, without laying any foundation of a ground or difference or reason, do loosely put cases, which, though they go near the point, yet being so scattered, prove not; but rather serve to make the law appear more doubtful than to make it more plain.[48]

According to *Advancement* in 1605 and to the version of 1623 where the argument was repeated with little change:

all those which have written of laws, have written either as philosophers or as lawyers, and none as statesmen. As for the philosophers, they make imaginary laws for imaginary commonwealths, and their discourses are as the stars, which give little light because they are so high. For the lawyers, they write according to the states where they live what is received law, and not what ought to be law ... There are in nature certain fountains of justice, whence all civil laws are derived, but as streams.[49]

In addition 'civil laws vary according to the regions and governments where they are planted'.[50] Here Bacon stated a purpose to produce a work, writing, he implied, as a statesman and taking into account both the universal immutable fountains of justice and the observable differences between regions and governments.

In *A Proposition touching the Compiling and Amendment of the Laws of England* he argued the case as we have seen that the Common Law could better establish itself by attending to the historical record of which in truth it consisted. He told the King in this paper that 'some little helps I may have of other learning which may give form to matter'.[51] This other learning could be rhetoric, or it could be philosophy. In this same paper he did not omit to advertise his own efforts. For 'the treatise *de Regulis Juris*', (rules or maxims of law), 'I hold it of all other things the most important to the health, as I may

term it, and good institutions of any laws... but I have seen little of
this kind, either in our law or other laws, that satisfieth me... In this
I have travelled myself... and will go on with it'.[52]

In *Advancement* the philosophers and lawyers complained of are
those – so one should assume – who fail to resort to middle axioms.
Further, the request in this business is for philosophers who are also
statesmen. Laws are part of policy. The point about differences
between minds – some better at finding distinctions – others apter at
seeing resemblances – with the implication that it is middle axioms
which are required, is put vigorously much later in Aphorism LV,
Book I, *Novum Organum* (1620) where the predominant concern is
with sciences of nature.[53] The point is to be found also in *Of Studies* in
1612 and in 1625. In both versions of this essay Bacon enlists
schoolmen as good teachers of how to make distinctions, and refers
to lawyers as well capable of instructing men in perceiving
resemblances.[54]

This call for middle axioms is voiced at another place in *Advancement*
(both versions) where the reference is to what Bacon calls the
longitude and latitude of sciences. He makes it clear that, regarding
their latitude, 'generally let this be a rule that all partitions of
knowledges be accepted', but never as presenting impassable barriers.
Applying this rule, as he argued elsewhere, remedies 'the complaint
of *vita brevis, ars longa*; which is performed by uniting the notions and
conceptions of sciences'.[55] 'The one' – the latitude – 'giveth rule how
far one knowledge ought to intermeddle within the province of
another... the other' – the longitude –

> giveth rule unto what degree of particularity a knowledge should descend:
> which latter I find passed over in science, being in my judgment the more
> material; for certainly there must be somewhat left to practice; but how
> much is worthy the inquiry. We see remote and superficial generalities do
> but offer knowledge to scorn of practical men; and are no more aiding to
> practice, than an Ortelius' universal map is to direct the way between
> London and York. The better sort of rules have been not unfitly compared
> to glasses of steel unpolished where you may see the images of things, but
> first they must be filed: so the rules will help, if they be laboured and
> polished by practice. But how crystalline they may be made at the first, and
> how far forth they may be polished aforehand is the question; the
> inquiry whereof seemeth to me deficient.[56]

In this much compressed passage Bacon contrives to include not
only his teaching on the interrelation between theory and practice;

and his instruction on keeping close to particulars; he inserts for
good measure a pointer to middle axioms. For he prints in his
margin the words *de Productione Axiomatum* – Concerning the Production of Axioms. But manifestly the argument for middle axioms
is also put – and put, too, in sharpness and in force when he
deciphered *Scylla and Charybdis*, that fable which suggests 'reflections
without end', and which advertises the alternative perils threatening
the wrecking of men's wits and arts. Here, though mentioning
'intellectuals' in general, the sciences which he has expressly in
mind, are morals and policy in particular. It is true that the
argument is anticipated at an earlier stage when as we have seen he
debates within himself whether embracing policy or devoting himself
to natural philosophy is the better course. Describing his personal
qualifications, he claims he can fix and distinguish subtler
differences; but also, 'which is the chief point', that he can catch
resemblances. Here he states a personal claim. But in the *Flight of
Icarus* also *Scylla and Charybdis* he shows that he can excel in another
fashion. Interpreting an age in which as he contends imagination
performed the functions of reason, he displays for men of his times his
own 'imaginative or insinuative reason'. His rhetoric applies and
recommends 'the dictates of reason to imagination in order to excite
the appetite and will'.

The case that if there be axioms they have to be middle ones might
seem barely to merit the airing. Axioms in policy – that is in
government and in law – handling questions which are specific and
practical and seeking answers which are no less specific and practical
could usefully take no other form. But the case required stating.
Policy is philosophy and a great part of it. Therefore axioms are
'middle' in another way. As philosophy they stand on the one hand
between the histories which are thinking, and on the other, the
actions which histories precipitate. Needless to say this picture of
three, with axioms placed in the middle, is not a static pattern. As
inquiries proceed as they ought to do, the pattern is to be in
continual recurring movement.

CHAPTER 6

Morality and policy I

In the first *Advancement of Learning* (1605) and also in the second (1623) Bacon teaches that in man's knowledges of man, since there are two forms of exertion or energy, it follows that there are two areas of study. There is man segregate – morality; also there is man congregate and in society – policy or philosophy civil. He seeks to establish that these two are distinct, but also that they interact and cannot be divided. That there are two such areas on the one hand of exertion or energy, and on the other of study, and that these are distinct but nevertheless interacting and inseparable, these propositions are set down in the first *Advancement*. He reasserts them in the second version. In both versions he also propounds that morality is concerned with the inside of men – with the inward exercises of memory, imagination and reason, which are 'the three parts of man's understanding'; and that also morality embraces for study the mind's idols, the movements of will, of passions, and of what he calls 'different characters of dispositions'. In addition, he never forgets that men consist not only of minds but of bodies, and that these interact or intersect. On this Bacon is insistent. He does not incessantly stress it. But he presents sufficient reminders.

On the other hand, policy is concerned with external conduct, with men's actions and speech in state, church and society. Further, while making it plain – again at the start in the first *Advancement* – that Machiavelli makes contributions in studying man congregate in the sub-department of government, he maintains nevertheless – in the final *Advancement* only – not in the first – that it is he, Bacon, who emancipates policy (philosophy of man congregate) from morality (philosophy of man segregate) as a field for justifiably independent

inquiries, thus constituting it a distinct province of learning.[1] He does
not state that this is Machiavelli's achievement; instead, that it is he,
Bacon, who achieves it. His relationship with this Florentine in civil
science will be further explored at a later stage in this argument.

In the meantime it must be stated and stressed that morality –
moral knowledge – retains its place prominently in Bacon's explorations. It does so in its own right; and also because of its link with
divinity:

> And if it be said that the cure of men's minds belongeth to sacred Divinity,
> it is most true: yet Moral Philosophy may be preferred unto her as a wise
> servant and humble handmaid. For as the Psalm saith, *that the eyes of the*
> *handmaid look perpetually towards the mistress,*[2] and yet no doubt many
> things are left to the discretion of the handmaid, to discern of the mistress'
> will; so ought Moral Philosophy to give a constant attention to the doctrines
> of Divinity, and yet so as it may yield of herself (within due limits) many
> sound and profitable directions.

Machiavelli noted Roman proficiency in policy. Bacon noted the
same, agreeing with him that the Romans had excelled in that way.
Writing of them, he states that the greatest wits of those times
applied themselves 'very generally to public affairs; the magnitude
of the Roman Empire requiring the services of a great number of
persons'.[3] But also and in addition to the observations recorded by
Machiavelli, he notes that the Romans were adept in studying moral
knowledge: 'the meditations and labours of philosophers were
principally employed and consumed on moral philosophy, which to
the heathen was as theology to us'.[4] The difference between us and
them is that we do not substitute morality for divinity; instead we
hold the former to be handmaid to the latter.

Morality is 'that knowledge which considereth of the Appetite and
Will of Man'.[5] The end of moral knowledge is 'to procure the
affections to obey reason and not to invade it'.[6] He writes the same
of rhetoric: 'the duty and office of rhetoric, if it be deeply looked
into, is no other than to apply and recommend the dictates of reason
to imagination in order to excite the appetite and will'.[7] This sharing
of a definition need perplex no one. Rhetoric like other sciences
cannot be divorced from moral knowledge and moral requirements.
Bacon, like Aristotle, places the science of rhetoric 'as between logic
on the one side, and moral and civil knowledge on the other, as
participating of both'.[8] Rhetoric participates in logic since it cannot
dispense with reasoning, and logic is an organization of the conduct

of reasoning: moreover rhetoric helps logic by its onflow of ornament of words. Rhetoric participates in moral and civil knowledge since these are also indispensable in its task of persuading, prompting, activating men into approved moral or civil conduct. In the one case – moral – rhetoric's effect can activate what should be working already inside men: in the other case – civil – its effect can shew itself in their external conduct. Men's outward responses can come forward to meet this agent, rhetoric, which works and impinges from outside them.

Morality is 'that knowledge which considereth of the Appetite and Will of Man',[9] and inquiries into moral knowledge are required according to both versions of *The Advancement of Learning*. These inquiries will be possible and perhaps productive if men resort both to surviving studies of the subject and also to civil historians and to other recorded or as yet unrecorded experience; that is to say, to their own.

In efforts to promote moral philosophy Bacon proposes that authors have been like men teaching writing, but giving no instruction on how to hold pens. 'Accurate draughts and portraitures of good, virtue, duty and felicity' are needed. But it is also necessary to explain 'by what method and course of education the mind may be trained and put in order for the attainment of them ... '.[10] This aspect of moral knowledge has been neglected, Bacon suggests, because 'men have despised to be conversant in ordinary and common matters which are neither subtle enough for disputation, nor illustrious enough for ornament'.[11] The example of Virgil who wrote both *Georgics* and *Aeneid* should induce second thoughts. Virgil 'got as much glory of eloquence, wit and learning in the expressing of the observations of husbandry, as of the heroical acts of Aeneas ... '[12]

Since the business was 'really to instruct and suborn action and active life ... '[13] moral knowledge ought to be partitioned: a first section should comprise 'the Exemplar or Platform of Good'. Here few difficulties emerge. The Exemplar had been 'excellently laboured';[14] we have the sacred canon of inspired scripture: also the *ancilla*, the moral philosophy of Roman pagan philosophers. There should be a second part. The end of morality is 'to procure the affections to obey reason and not invade it'.[15] The purpose of a department to be added to the subject as hitherto conceived would be discovery of 'rules how to accommodate the will of man'[16] to the

Exemplar or Platform of Good. This would be a Georgics of the mind, it being understood that after precepts imparting strategies had been discovered for the Georgics not foregoing the aids of religious practice, they would be used in continued combination with religious practice.

But in constructing such strategies 'as in all things which are practical, we ought to cast up our account, what is in our power and what not; for the one may be dealt with by way of alteration, but the other by way of application only'.[17] The farmer cannot command the nature of the soil or the seasons or the weather. Similarly before a physician sets to work he must accept and try to understand 'the natural temper and constitution of the patient' and also 'the variety of accidents'[18] to which he may be subject. 'Now in the culture of the mind', wrote Bacon 'and the cure for its diseases three things are to be considered; the different characters of dispositions, the affections and the remedies...'[19] It remains likely that neither men's 'different characters of dispositions' nor their affections and passions nor the effects and impacts of internal or external agents can easily be altered: 'Yet the inquiry into things beyond our power ought to be as careful as into those within it; for the exact and distinct knowledge thereof is the groundwork of the doctrine of remedies, that they may be more conveniently and successfully applied...'[20]

The case here is precisely on a par with that of idols of the mind. 'Exact and distinct knowledge' is cause and also effect of Bacon's caution. 'Exact and distinct knowledge' is the groundwork for seeking remedies both for idols and for 'characters of dispositions'. It is not the case that he holds that – or acts as if – no remedies are available. As in the realm of policy a man must 'take courage to despise vain apprehensions'.[21] Both reason and will, distinct yet inseparable, must be equally at work in these matters. If the will is irresolute or disinclined to find answers, the reason is hamstrung at the outset. If the will is firm and eager in searching for them it must turn to the reason with its 'exact and distinct knowledge'. But as in the realm of policy a man's will must exert itself again resolutely and audaciously at the right moment, truth being no less the daughter of timing than of time. Precipitancy, boldness, is not the same as audacity and should not be confused with it. Precipitancy dispenses with 'exact and distinct knowledge' when it decides that things are unalterable. Equally it dispenses with this when it concludes the opposite and tries to alter them.

touching impossibility…if any man will take to himself rather that of Salomon, *Dicit piger, Leo est in via* – The slothful man saith there is a lion in the path than that of Virgil, *Possunt quia posse videntur* – They find it possible because they think it possible – I shall be content that my labours be esteemed but as the better sort of wishes: for as it asketh some knowledge to demand a question not impertinent, so it requireth some sense to make a wish not absurd.[22]

'Different characters of dispositions' – the first version reads 'several characters and tempers of men's natures and dis- positions' – [23]what lies behind these expressions? The meaning is explained more plainly in the first version. What Bacon wants done is put more clearly in the second. According to the former the differences refer to such observable facts as that 'there are minds which are pro- portioned to great matters, and others to small…' or 'that there are minds proportioned to intend many matters, and others to few' or 'that there is a disposition in conversation…to soothe and please, and a disposition contrary to contradict and cross…'[24] Among such examples the earlier contributions provided in *Of Studies* (1597) cannot be omitted – though the essay has been extensively cited already. 'Read not to contradict, nor to believe, but to weigh and consider.'[25] The injunction is repeated word for word in the version of the essay published in 1612. In the 1625 version it is repeated and fortified. 'Read not to contradict and confute, nor to believe and take for granted, nor to find talk and discourse, but to weigh and consider.'[26] This full statement of 1625 is preceded by another not less full in 1620. Aphorism LXVII of *Novum Organum* Book I runs like this: excess of intemperance 'is of two kinds: the first being manifest in those who are ready in deciding, and render sciences dogmatic and magisterial; the other in those who deny that we can know any thing, and so introduce a wandering kind of inquiry that leads to nothing; of which kinds the former subdues, the latter weakens the understanding'.[27] Some men, it is plain, have a propensity propelling them in the one direction, that of outright rejection and disbelief. Others, it is not less clear, display a disposition urging them into the opposite course, that of passive acceptance and credulity.

In *Advancement*'s second version Bacon describes what he wants inquired into, constructed and presented in a 'full and careful treatise'[28] and does so in words not to be found in 1605:

Not however that I would have these characters presented… (as we find them in history or poetry, or even in common discourse), in the shape of

complete individual portraits, but rather the several features and simple
lineaments of which they are composed, and by the various combinations
and arrangements of which all characters whatever are made up, showing
how many, and of what nature these are, and how connected and
subordinate one to another; so that we may have a scientific and accurate
dissection of minds and characters, and the secret disposition of particular
men may be revealed; and that from the knowledge thereof better rules
may be framed for the treatment of the mind.[29]

And' [here Bacon repeats a point made in 1605] 'in truth I cannot
sometimes but wonder that this part of knowledge should for the most part
be omitted both in Morality and Policy, considering it might shed such a
ray of light on both sciences.[30]

He proposes that this neglect can be remedied. 'Knowledges are as
pyramids whereof history is the basis': '…among the poets (heroic,
satiric, tragic, comic) are everywhere interspersed representations of
characters…' But these generally are 'exaggerated and surpassing
the truth'.[31]

far the best provision and material for this treatise is to be gained from the
wiser sort of historians, not only from the commemorations which they
commonly add on recording the deaths of illustrious persons, but much
more from the entire body of history as often as such a person enters upon
the stage; for a character so worked into the narrative gives a better idea
of the man, than any formal criticism and review can; such is that of
Africanus and Cato the Elder in Livy, of Tiberius, and Claudius, and Nero
in Tacitus, of Septimius Severus in Herodian, of Louis XI, King of France,
in Philip de Comines, of Ferdinand of Spain, the Caesar Maximilian, and
the Popes Leo and Clement in Francesco Guicciardini.

He continues:

For these writers, having the images of those persons whom they have
selected to describe constantly before their eyes, hardly ever make mention
of any of their actions without inserting something concerning their nature.
So some of the relations which I have met with touching the conclaves of
the popes present good characters of the Cardinals; as the letters of
ambassadors do likewise of the councillors of princes.

Here are materials 'surely rich and abundant'[32] for constructing the
treatise. The parallel statement in the original *Advancement* offers
'history, poetry, and daily experience' as matter from which this
science could be created. But though Bacon suggests as in the second
version 'Relations which Italians make touching Conclaves'[33] as
examples of this available, suitable and inviting material, the
original version is thinner. No wiser sort of historians are listed and
no mention is made of the superiority of their character studies in

that these are worked into the narrative and not added as *appendices* and concluding assessments.

Proposals for this treatise are not restricted to treatment of 'characters which are impressed by nature'; in addition (here both versions are the same) the work should handle characters as they are affected ' ... by sex, by age, by region, by health and sickness, by beauty and deformity, and the like; and again, those which are caused by fortune, as sovereignty, nobility, obscure birth, riches, want, magistracy, privateness, prosperity, adversity and the like'.[34] Bacon allows that such matters as these have been touched on in Aristotle's *Rhetoric* and also here and there in the writings of others.[35] But such needful studies have not been incorporated into moral philosophy which is where they belong.

Next on the list should come a science of 'the affections and perturbations'. Today these are commonly known as passions or emotions. According to Bacon 'the mind in its own nature would be temperate and staid; if the affections, as winds, did not put it into tumult and perturbation'.[36] 'And here again', he complains, 'I find it strange, that Aristotle should have written divers volumes of ethics, and never handled the affections, as a principal portion thereof;[37] yet in his *Rhetoric*, where they are considered collaterally and in a second degree (as they may be moved and excited by speech), he finds a place for them, and handles them acutely and well, for the quantity thereof.' But apart from Aristotle's contribution which is valuable so far as it goes, poets and civil historians, he insists, ought to be regarded as the best teachers of such knowledge. In their works a man can see passions vividly represented and analysed. It is poets and civil historians who have shown how these may be kindled and excited or pacified and restrained,

and how again contained from act and further degree; how they disclose themselves, though repressed and concealed; how they work; how they vary; how they are enwrapped one within another; how they fight and encounter one with another; and many other particularities of this kind; among which this last is of special use in moral and civil matters; how, I say, to set affection against affection, and to use the aid of one to master another; like hunters and fowlers who use to hunt beast with beast, and catch bird with bird...[38]

It is upon such a base that civil government dispensing rewards and punishments is erected and conducts itself – 'seeing those predominant affections of fear and hope suppress and bridle all the rest'.[39] Here he adds nothing to what he writes in the first *Advancement*.

Bacon concludes proposals for this part of a Georgics of the mind with a section about agents which unlike others are more evidently within man's command to control. Here again philosophers have failed: 'philosophers ought carefully and actively to have inquired of the strength and energy of custom, exercise, habit, education, imitation, emulation, company, friendship, praise, reproof, exhortation, fame, laws, books, studies, and the like'.[40] In the first version the list is identical except that 'example' had been another item. These, he writes, are things which rule in morals. These are the agents by which minds are moulded. These form the ingredients from which medicines may be made to maintain or recover the health of men's minds so far as this can be done by remedies merely human. Men should explore these things and produce axioms, investigating a common experience; that is to say, their own findings together with what is recorded by civil historians and poets.

Bacon, it is evident, did not forsake the conviction that examples, past or present, of conduct in action are often more effectual than precepts. He gave instructions in *Of Great Place* (1612 and 1625): 'In the discharge of thy place set before thee the best examples; for imitation is a globe of precepts; and after a time set before thee thine own example; and examine thyself strictly whether thou didst not best at first. Neglect not also the examples of those that have carried themselves ill in the same place... '[41] It is scarcely torturing evidence to suggest that in all his pursuits – not excluding, we have seen, his struggles to establish natural philosophy/science – he hoped he had not set worthless examples.

In 1617 when taking his place in Chancery as Lord Keeper he referred to his predecessor in that office, 'of whom I learn much to imitate and somewhat to avoid'.[42] In the same year when instructing Sir William Jones, appointed Lord Chief Justice of Ireland, Bacon told him: 'I will lead you the short journey by examples and not the long by precepts.'[43] After his eclipse and overthrow in 1621 he reminded King James that there had been examples of men disgraced in the past who had been recalled to favour and service.[44] In 1622 he sent Bishop Andrewes a similar reminder. Also he told the bishop at the start of his letter: 'Amongst consolations, it is not the least to represent to a man's self like examples of calamities in others. For examples give a quicker impression than arguments.'[45] All the same, Bacon did not argue that the advantage over precepts accruing to examples ruled philosophers with their axioms out of court. Actions speak louder than words. But if at some previous stage nobody writes or speaks words, there would perhaps be no subsequent actions. The two modes are distinct, but also inseparable. They will move in tandem.

Bacon showed himself aware that demands and projects for moral and civil sciences will provoke objections from practical men. Theories of practice – are these necessary? Are they even possible? 'If any man ... do judge that my labour is but to collect into an Art or Science that which hath been omitted by other writers as matter of common sense and experience, and sufficiently clear and self-evident, he is welcome to his opinion; but in the meanwhile let him remember that I am in pursuit not of beauty but of utility and truth ... '[46] Elsewhere – *Advancement* (both versions) as we have already seen – the defence is stronger. 'For certainly something must be left to exercise and practice ... ' 'For we see that too remote generalities (unless they be deduced) give little information, and do but offer knowledge to the scorn of practical men; being of no more avail for practice than an Ortelius' universal map is to direct the way between London and York.' ' ... rules and precepts will help if they be laboured and polished by practice but not otherwise'.[47] Rule and precept on the one hand – practice on the other – neither of them can be investigated and rendered improvable solely in itself and when excluding the other.

Bacon wrote in *Advancement* (1605) that 'moral philosophy is more difficile than policy.'[48] He nevertheless claimed that moral philosophy was capable of improvement. He proposed to improve civil philosophy – policy. But in process of trying to do this during his career, he concluded he had invented it, professing as much in 1623 in the second *Advancement*. Previously, as he stated the matter it had subsisted under the wing of moral knowledge. But it remained the case that, if not his recommended studies devoted to such topics in moral knowledge as exploring 'characters of dispositions', investigating 'affections and perturbations' (that is, passions or emotions), and measuring the impact of other agents which he listed as affecting the minds of mankind; yet the practice among men of the moral virtues need fare none the worse and could be promoted if civil knowledge could be increased in Bacon's proceedings of interlocking thought and action.

Moral knowledge according to Bacon's instructions as we have seen ought to be partitioned. The first section comprises the Exemplar or Platform of Good. We already possess this Exemplar or Platform. A second part should consist of 'rules how to accommodate the will of man to the Exemplar or Platform…' As things turned out these rules – axioms – constituting a second section had to wait: 'moral philosophy is more difficile than policy'. It remained no less difficile than policy according to the second version of *Advancement*. On the other hand essays in the second and third collections indisputably deal with matters mentioned under Bacon's Georgics of the mind, and he repeated requests for these Georgics in the *Advancement* of 1623. But – and this is of first relevance here – the essays, covering two distinct yet inseparable interacting departments, are 'civil and moral'. Moreover, the civil department could prove to be prior to the moral. This is illustrated in and by the title of the final collection in 1625 – *The Essays or Counsels Civil and Moral*. ' …moral philosophy propoundeth to itself the framing of internal goodness; but civil knowledge requireth only an external goodness, for that as to society sufficeth'. For this reason the latter, civil knowledge, is the easier and the former the more difficult of the two. But the promoting of 'only an external goodness' in itself encourages with no added difficulties a goodness which is internal. Thus the 'sufficiency' achievable by civil knowledge exceeds what is stated in Bacon's definition of it. Its sufficiency is greater than immediately meets the eye.

Of Custom and Education (1612 and also 1625) illustrates this more comprehensive 'sufficiency' which policy can attain. The essay reads:

> …if the force of custom simple and separate be great, the force of custom copulate and conjoined and collegiate is far greater; for there example teacheth, company comforteth, emulation quickeneth, glory raiseth; so as in such places the force of custom is in his exaltation. Certainly, the great multiplication of virtues upon human nature resteth upon societies well ordained and disciplined. For commonwealths and good governments do nourish virtue grown, but do not much mend the seeds; but the misery is that the most effectual means are now applied to the ends least to be desired.[49]

Morality and policy according to Bacon would be advanced or retarded each in company with the other. Civil policy indirectly but effectually serves moral education at least in adults by being itself skilfully conducted and successfully advanced. When men 'give ear to precepts, to laws, to religion, sweetly touched with eloquence and persuasion of books, of sermons, of harangues, so long is society and peace maintained ... '[50] Civil government and laws, the dispensing of rewards and punishments, the providing of examples, the employing in right causes of rhetoric in pulpits and elsewhere, these move men from outside themselves to constrain and encourage them to observe the Exemplar or Platform of Good. In this case, not by internal strategies applied by a completed Georgics of the mind, but instead as the result of impacts generated by grand strategy put into effect from outside men, their minds and wills can be moved towards compliance with an extant and securely valid Exemplar or Platform.

In August 1604, as already noted, Bacon was appointed King's Counsel. In June 1607 he was made Solicitor General. He was appointed Attorney General in October 1613. In June 1616 he was made a Privy Councillor. Early in 1617 he became Lord Keeper of the Great Seal. By early 1618 he was Lord Chancellor of England. The year of his dismissal and disgrace was 1621. But before he achieved power and place under the King, during the time when he was holding them, and after he had lost them, this civil science in terms both of claim and of performance, the two being taken together, was the science he was most productive in inventing. Was what he invented here also right and true? It is likely that this contribution was as right and as true as anything he produced either in moral science or in natural science; it being brought to mind suitably often that the promoting of civil science was certainly an end in itself, but that it was also – as he explained was his adopted plan and chosen mode of proceeding – a means to the end not only of improving moral conduct but of successfully launching the sciences of nature.

But what he offered in civil science, since doubt is never to be excluded, was provisional. He altered and added, knowing his way, but not always certain of his position. What he offered was subject always to confirmation or alteration by the further findings of what it was based on in the first instance, namely experience – that of others in the past and his own in the present – the two ruminated and reviewed in terms of causes and consequences of things done or omitted. Items in this programme of strategy fit the circumstances of his times. They conform with what should be done and could be done given needs and possibilities. But while fitting and being congruent with precise and actual situations, these items were worked up and presented in terms of positions transcending time and place. Bacon's proposed civil courses are inseparable from roots in his civil historical investigations.

He frequently referred in the same breath to 'kingdoms and estates'. For example, of the two 'examples of treatises' placed in the second *Advancement*, the one carrying the title *Of Extension of Empire* was republished as an essay in the 1625 collection entitled *Of the True Greatness of Kingdoms and Estates*. Perceiving distinctions yet also remarking resemblances, Bacon's civil science was constructed as applying in both kingdoms and estates, that is to say in both monarchies and republics. Bacon makes generalities in middle axioms out of observable and observed particulars of the past, doing this in order to help him handling for the present and future further observable and observed particulars. The enterprise consists of 'industrious observations' and 'grounded conclusions'[51] in organized interplay. Bacon, pre-eminently studying examples presented by ancient Rome and by his own land – but always not neglecting other states of antiquity and of modern times – bridges forms and evident differences between states both in time and in space.

For example he told the House of Commons in 1610: 'the King's Sovereignty and the Liberty of Parliament are as the two elements and principles of this estate; which, though the one be the more active the other more passive, yet they do not cross or destroy the one the other, but they strengthen and maintain the one the other. Take away liberty of Parliament, the griefs of the subject will bleed inwards: sharp and eager humours will not evaporate, and then they must exulcerate, and so may endanger the sovereignty itself. On the other side, if the King's Sovereignty receive diminution or any degree of contempt…it must follow that we shall be a *meteor* or *corpus imperfecte mistum*; which kind of bodies come speedily to confusion and dissolution…and herein it is our happiness that we may make the same judgment of the King which Tacitus made of Nerva. *Divus Nerva res olim dissociabiles miscuit, Imperium et Libertatem*: The divine Nerva did temper things that before were thought incompatible or insociable, Sovereignty and Liberty.'[52] Feudal institutions, as Bacon pointed out in an earlier debate, are a foreign body in the scheme of things. The Civilians 'tell us, that all the laws *de feodis* are but additionals to the ancient civil law, and that the Roman Emperors in the full height of their monarchy never knew them; so that they are not imperial'. Whatever the Common

Lawyers might assert to the contrary about Tenures in England, 'they are', in a due historical perspective, 'not Regal nor any point of Sovereignty'.[53] Therefore tenures need not be so greatly difficult to part with as part of Lord Salisbury's bargain in the so-called Great Contract.

It could be objected that Bacon's vision is Europocentric. But little of politics outside Europe, ancient and modern, was known or knowable in his time. Therefore his policy, both the *data* and the conclusions stretched rather through time than through space. Moreover in the times after his death extra-European polities have increasingly been superseded by European political forms. A further objection could be that Bacon ignored the complications introduced into politics by economics. This is scarcely true. Considering his proposals in the essay *Of Seditions and Troubles* (1625) and in that *Of Usury* (1625), it can be argued that he was one of the early promoters of political economy. For example: '...money is like muck, not good except it be spread'. On the other hand it is true that agonizing economic or fiscal dilemmas becoming as stubborn a circumstance as any with which politics has to deal is something he could scarcely have foreseen.

Bacon's civil policy unites two elements which came later to be divided and named respectively 'political thought' and 'con-stitutional history'. He aimed to marry and to join together what has been and what is, with what could be and what ought to be. This 'what could be and what ought to be' is not to be dismissed as utopian. It is illustrated as capable of entry into the world of reality by the best of what has been and the best of what is. The material of his science, as we know, is civil history – its course and the records of it. Despite contending 'characters of dispositions', and not-withstanding warring passions – loves, hates, prides, cruelties, neg-lects, greeds – civil history for him is not an amorphous on-rushing flood, but a tolerably rational process; and this process, he taught, is capable of being made more rational in the future. Civil history's course is the upshot of the play between human contributions and that of stubborn circumstance – of human thoughts and human actions in this interplay, causing and creating experience. But human thoughts and actions in the future can be and should be controlled by experience sifted. This experience in the past, and this science in the future, are fully under human calculation – that is, thought; and fully under human control – that is, action. But there remains a control and a judgment of another sort, that of stubborn circumstance. Bacon associates this other control and this other judgment with the proceedings of deity. If men prefer an alternative, Machiavelli provides one and calls it Fortune, but of the kind which men cannot make for themselves and which is irresistible. The latter element manifests itself most visibly in the great breaks which Bacon calls 'vicissitudes'.

How can the course of civil history be held to be rational? How can a perceived rationality arise out of actions which are the result of the free will of men, not to mention events proceeding from the free will of deity? Civil histories as adequately presented, as for example those in his civil secular canon, recount causes and effects: and civil affairs are prevailingly conducted in terms of necessities. Bacon shows himself to be no less aware of the play of necessities than Machiavelli had been. The former provides explicit discussion of necessities in the matter of treaties between states when he interprets the Fable of *Styx*.[54] Men's actions in civil matters are not less free than at other times. But normally in civil matters they are governed in terms of sufficient perceptions of necessities both in the perceiving of them and in the choice of them. This business, Bacon argued, can be improved. True there are the great breaks – vicissitudes, the interventions of deity/fortune. But civil affairs continue to be conducted in despite of these. After such episodes men proceed as before in civil matters.

Civil histories exhibit least of their authors and most of the things themselves. Civil histories thus present a sufficiency of the indwelling nature of policy. Bacon insists as a central point in his studies of the world of nature that *Natura parendo vincitur*: in order that nature be conquered – that is, understood and harnessed – nature must be obeyed.[55] Similarly and no less, in order that policy be understood and successfully constructed and conducted – constructing and conducting science, whether natural or civil, being two aspects of one and the same operation – policy in its indwelling nature demands and in Bacon's case receives obedience. The indwelling nature of policy is defined as the contemplating, the weighing, and the making of decisions for action amidst the whole range of perceived necessities. Action in policy is directed to changing, or to preventing changes, in relationships between realities, these latter being men as such or men who staff civil institutions. Action will consist of commands, of persuasion, or of force. Action is deemed to impose itself as a necessity for the reason that the consequences of inaction are calculated to prove more inconvenient in terms of civil peace and justice than the consequences of action.

Bacon sees the course of civil history as circular and repetitive, hence as a starting point for his science. ' ... experience is the best guide'; he told the House of Commons in February 1607, 'for the time past is a pattern of the time to come'.[56] His civil policy is aimed at making the future course of civil history more rational. Becoming more rational it will become less circular and more linear: that is to say, he endeavours to promote improvements. Arts and sciences are capable both of improvement and of decline. But the subject-matter, the material in which and upon which arts and sciences work, remains as a whole constant. It, the material, is not subject as a feature of it – inbuilt and overall – to qualitative change which tends to necessary deterioration. Nor, on the other hand, does qualitative change – overall and inbuilt – tend to necessary progress in betterment.

Machiavelli, in his *Preface* to his Book II of *Discorsi*, analysed reasons why 'men always, but not always with good reason, praise by-gone days and criticise the present'.[57] 'The first of them is, I think, this. The whole truth about olden times is not grasped, since what redounds to their discredit is often passed over in silence, whereas what is likely to make them appear glorious is pompously recounted in all its detail.'[58] 'Another reason is that, since it is either through fear or through envy that men come to hate things, in the case of the past the two most powerful incentives for hating it are lacking, since the past cannot hurt you nor give you cause for envy. Whereas it is otherwise with events in which you play a part... '[59] Similarly, Bacon writes in *Novum Organum*, Book I Aphorism LXXXIV: 'As for antiquity, the opinion touching it which men entertain is quite a negligent one, and scarcely consonant with the word itself. For the old age of the world is to be accounted the true antiquity; and this is the attribute of our own time, not of an earlier age of the world in which the ancients lived; and which, though in respect of us it was the elder, yet in respect of the world it was the younger. And truly as we look for greater knowledge of human things and a riper judgment in the old man than in the young, because of his experience and the number and variety of the things which he has seen and heard and thought of; so in like manner, from our age, if it but knew its own strength and chose to essay and exert it, much more might fairly be expected than from the ancient times, in as much as it is a more advanced age of the world; and stored and stocked with infinite experiments and observations.'[60]

Neither Machiavelli nor Bacon displayed any favourable prepossessions regarding the past. But neither did they display any favourable prepossessions regarding the future. It was because of its overall constancy that the course of civil history had been circular. It was also because of this same overall constancy that the course of it was improvable. Neither improvement nor deterioration are ineluctable. Apart from what men (and deity/Fortuna) could think and also do, there is no tendency in events bringing either decline or progressive betterment. Bacon in his aphorism quoted above did not state that the present was 'better' than the past. Nor did he say that the future would be better still. What he argued was that things since antiquity could have been improved – given accumulations of experience – but that improvement had not been taken in hand. It can be added that in Bacon's case what he held regarding the course of civil history – because what he held was what he saw – was carried over into his studies of the universe of nature. Indeed nature is unknown, he taught. But at least it is taken as granted neither that the universe of nature is bound into a process of dissolution, nor that it is in the grip of a process leading in the opposite direction. 'Truth is to be sought for not in the felicity of any age, which is an unstable thing, but in the light of nature and experience, which is eternal' (*id est* not everlasting, but basically constant while it lasts).[61]

Regarding the tone of all Bacon's work in policy, it is not hubristically hopeful. 'Religion, progressive enlightenment, the perpetual vigilance of public opinion, has not reduced his empire, or disproved the justice of his conception of mankind.' This is John Emerich Edward Dalberg Acton (1834–1902) writing not of Bacon but of Machiavelli in his introduction to L. E. Burd's edition of *Il Principe* published in 1891 in London. But granted that as we shall see Bacon repudiated Machiavelli's 'evil arts', as he called them, the statement in the matter of tone or flavour is as true of the one as it is of the other, since in each case it is civil history in general which is the man's source. Bacon did not write as Machiavelli did that 'all men are wicked'.[62] On the other hand there is no sign that he disagreed with Machiavelli's other general assessment of mankind – 'men do not know how to be either magnificently bad or perfectly good'.[63] But given even only mediocrity, much can be done. In the essay *Of Goodness and Goodness of Nature* (1612 and 1625) Bacon writes: 'divinity maketh the love of ourselves the pattern, the love of our neighbours but the portraiture'.[64] In the essay *of Wisdom for a Man's Self* (1612 and 1625) he writes: 'Divide with reason between self-love and society.'[65] Though he does not say so here, the author of these essays recognized that self-love prompts and encourages deference to the claims of society and of the state.

The trumpeted new beginnings of 1776 (the events which produced the United States in North America), of 1789 (France, the Jacobins and Napoleon's Empire), of 1917 (Russia and the Bolsheviks), lay far in the future. All three were to manifest utopian elements. But at the end of the twentieth century these fresh starts lie far in the past and experience here as in other matters has not discredited Bacon's civil policy. Utopian elements in the above over-confident trans-formations – especially in regard to establishing equality – have been exposed as such by time. Bacon posited what he saw, namely division of labour, stratification, class societies, and inequalities. These features – if less oppressively in less barbarous regions – have endured. Though tied to civil history his policy, like Machiavelli's, is not backward looking as we have argued. Return to origins – stand in the ancient ways – yes indeed: but also look around and study present circumstances. 'Surely every medicine is an in-novation', he writes in the essay *Of Innovations* (1625), 'and he that will not apply new remedies must expect new evils; for time is the greatest innovator: and if time of course alter things to the worse, and wisdom and counsel shall not alter them to the better, what shall be the end?' But 'It is good also not to try experiments in states, except the necessity be urgent, or the utility evident...'[66]

Since morality and policy can be and ought to be inseparable and since policy can and ought to contain law, despotism for Bacon is ruled out. It is equated by him with tyranny. Too much government in the shape of compulsion is as normally obnoxious as government of which there is too little and which is weak. But his civil policy assumed – because he has concluded from studies – that *régimes* can become 'constitutional' in structure. All states, ancient and modern, to a greater or a lesser degree apply or should apply safety valves, that is to say, assemblies to register grievances. Without a degree of consent or compliance government founders. Government for Bacon, it is true, ought not to be totally at the mercy of assemblies – as the formula defining responsible government came to be stated in later times. Nevertheless he equates all true government with responsible government. Principles are laid down in the opening aphorisms of *Example of a Treatise on Universal Justice or the Fountains of Equity, by Aphorisms.* This treatise as a whole is concerned as Bacon states with one 'title' only, namely that laws be certain.[67] The treatise as it proceeds becomes highly technical. But Aphorism I reads: 'In Civil Societies either law or force prevails. But there is a kind of force which pretends law, and a kind of law which savours of force rather than equity. Whence there are three fountains of injustice; namely, mere force, a malicious ensnarement under cover of law, and harshness of the law itself.'[68] According to Aphorism v: 'The end and scope which laws should have in view, and to which they should direct their decrees and sanctions, is no other than the happiness of the citizens. And this will be effected, if the people be rightly trained in piety and religion, sound in morality, protected by arms against foreign enemies, guarded by the shield of the laws against civil discords and private injuries, obedient to the government and the magistrates, and rich and flourishing in forces and wealth. And for all these objects laws are the sinews and instruments.'[69] This is the aphorism which was quoted and approved of by Macaulay. According to Bacon – and also to Hobbes – assemblies are or should be available to supply aids and advices. In France for example the Estates General met in Bacon's lifetime in 1614. He advised King James frequently in the matter of summoning a parliament.

Given that civil states have normally existed in proximity with one another, not in history and time only, but also in space – even if separated by seas – Bacon considered and urged his findings regarding the conduct in peace and war of dealings between them. However firmly governments may be set upon pursuing peace, they must be always ready for war. They should make it unmistakably evident both at home and abroad that they are vigilant in maintaining this readiness. King James was free to cherish for himself the Beatitude, *Beati Pacifici*. He should pay equal attention to making it understood everywhere that as the motto of kings of Scots, his ancestors, warned: *Nemo me impune lacessit*,[70] No one with impunity provokes me. Regarding relations between civil states Bacon makes another point. No one – and not he – denies that wars between states bring cruel and painful miseries – these, though, also occur in peacetime. But according to Bacon it is observable that societies are never so prone to decay as when, as in long periods without external warfare, they feel safe enough to relax. ' ...in a slothful peace', he writes in the essay *Of the True Greatness of Kingdoms and Estates* (1612 and 1625), 'both courages will effeminate and manners corrupt'.[71]

If unfortunately in dealings between states it is normal that civil imperatives sometimes conflict with moral ones, Bacon made a contribution to discussing this topic. *Of Simulation and Dissimulation* (1625) distinctly intimates that if in state interest moral law requires to be broken, this is best done by men accepting and in general attempting to serve the moral law; by men, that is, who are aware of what they do if they break it. 'Dissimulation is but a faint kind of policy or wisdom; for it asketh a strong wit and a strong heart to know when to tell truth, and to do it: therefore it is the weaker sort of politics that are the great dissemblers.'[72] 'Certainly the ablest men that ever were have had all an openness and frankness of dealing, and a name of certainty and veracity: but then they were like horses well managed, for they could tell passing well when to stop or turn; and at such times when they thought the case indeed required dissimulation, if then they used it, it came to pass that the former opinion, spread abroad, of their good faith and clearness of dealing, made them almost invisible.'[73] 'There be three degrees of this hiding and veiling of a man's self. The first, Closeness, Reservation, and Secrecy ... '[74] ' ... (to say truth) nakedness is uncomely, as well in mind as body; and it addeth no small reverence to men's manners and actions if they be not altogether open.' 'Therefore set it down, that an habit of secrecy is both politic and moral... '[75]

For the second [degree] which is dissimulation; it followeth many times upon secrecy by a necessity; so that he that will be secret must be a dissembler in some degree. For men are too cunning to suffer a man to keep an indifferent carriage between both, and to be secret, without swaying the balance on either side. They will so beset a man with questions, and draw him on, and pick it out of him, that, without an absurd silence, he must show an inclination one way; or if he do not, they will gather as much by his silence as by his speech.[76]

'But for the third degree, which is simulation and false profession, that I hold more culpable and less politic, except it be in *great and rare matters*' [emphasis added]. ' ...a general custom of simulation (which is this last degree) is a vice rising either of a natural falseness or fearfulness, or of a mind that hath some main faults... '[77] Regarding simulation and dissimulation 'there be three disadvantages... The first, that simulation and dissimulation commonly carry with them a show of fearfulness, which in any business doth spoil the feathers of round flying up to the mark. The second, that it puzzleth and perplexeth the conceits of many, that perhaps would otherwise cooperate with him, and makes a man walk almost alone to his ends. The third and greatest is, that it depriveth a man of one of the most principal instruments of action, which is trust and belief.' 'The best composition and temperature is, to have openness in fame and opinion; secrecy in habit; dissimulation in seasonable use; and a power to feign, if there be no remedy.' Evidently Bacon's observations relate to conduct between men. But governments consist of men. There being no requirement – and little suitability – that he be explicit on the point, his observations relate to conduct between governments. Bacon recognized that in statecraft extreme situations occur and that in 'great and rare matters' extreme courses require to be adopted. But he rejected an unashamedly immoral *Raison d'Etat*. Ongoing courses pursued in means or in ends by governments, regularly in defiance and mockery of the moral sense and moral traditions of mankind – these were evidently morally objectionable. But also they were objectionable in policy. In due time they were liable and likely to defeat themselves and to prove counter-productive.

Nevertheless for Bacon, though not guile, yet armed force is the *ultima ratio*, the last resort, of all rulers in their external dealings. The same is true inside the states which they rule. Recognizing the need for, and himself practising moral persuasion, and being also well aware of the experience of moral force, Bacon does not adopt the manicheanism which rejects the force which is physical. Following Machiavelli he recommends citizen armies. But 'the strength of a veteran army (though it be a chargeable business), always on foot, is that which commonly giveth the law, or at least the reputation, among all neighbour states, as may well be seen in Spain'.[78] However in his case states are not envisaged as what Hobbes called them, namely, little but armed camps. Rather, Bacon envisages civil states as containing not only classes but also institutions, these constituting, when taken in sum, what would come later to be called 'civil society'. Individuals and institutions, all are subject to civil governments, but these institutions will not be ruled directly, and without intermediaries, by civil governments. Churches, corporations, administrations in localities, universities, inns of court,

parliaments, even armies considered internally and within themselves, all these constitute civil society. Civil states control their
religions, but state religions employ separate distinctive castes to
conduct them. When men 'give ear to precepts, to laws, to religion,
sweetly touched with eloquence and persuasion of books, of sermons,
of harangues, so long is society and peace maintained'.[79] There is a
process working both ways. Morality improves society: but also
society improves morality: 'But if the force of custom simple and
separate be great, the force of custom copulate and conjoined and
collegiate is far greater; for there example teacheth, company
comforteth, emulation quickeneth, glory raiseth; so as in such places
the force of custom is in his exaltation.'[80]

Public doctrines and cults of a religious nature have normally
been indispensable parts of the *apparatus* of civil states. Such public
doctrines and cults underpin and promote in civil states teachings
concerning moral practice. Just as policy and morality are linked,
similarly morality and divinity are linked. State divinity must be
part of policy. Bacon proposed and sought to maintain a closed circle
consisting of these three items – each of them distinct but not
separate.

In *Of Unity in Religion* (1625) he set down that 'Religion being the
chief band of human society, it is a happy thing when itself is well
contained within the true band of Unity.'[81] Both for religion's sake
and for the sake of the state, it is the duty of the civil magistrate to keep
men united in religion and to enforce by the laws outward conformity
to public doctrine and cult. Bacon's recommended device for
achieving this unity was his express persuasion that a distinction
should be established between matters essential and fundamental in
religion and things indifferent. Again, he recommends this in general
terms, and not as a particular device for England only. Men must
continue conforming with public cult. But they could recognize that
in doing so they were accepting amidst fundamentals elements which
were inessential, and therefore harmless to conscience. He attempted
to persuade others of the validity of his distinction in three surviving
documents, *An Advertisement Touching the Controversies of the Church of
England* (1589), *Certain Considerations Touching the better Pacification and
Edification of the Church of England* (1604) and the essay *Of Unity in
Religion* (1625).

Given the existence of governments and also of laws, a condition
of affairs which had largely prevailed in the West in antiquity and

in after times, Bacon pondered and pronounced on relations between the conduct of governments and the administration of laws – between, that is to say, public law and private law. Conduct of government and administration of law comprise two departments respectively involving actions of government and proceedings of lawyers. The two are equally indispensable. Each must be retained. On the one hand there is the general interest of the state; and on the other the particular and private interests of particular individual subjects or citizens.

But as Bacon explains in Aphorism III of *Example of a Treatise on Universal Justice or the Fountains of Equity, by Aphorisms*: 'Private right depends upon the protection of public right. For the law protects the people, and magistrates protect the laws; but the authority of the magistrates depends on the sovereign power of the government, the structure of the constitution, and the fundamental laws. Wherefore, if this part of the constitution be sound and healthy, the laws will be of good effect, but if not, there will be little security in them.'[82] In Aphorism IV he proceeds: 'It is not however the only object of public law, to be attached as the guardian of private right to protect it from violation and prevent injuries; but it extends also to religion, arms, discipline, ornaments, wealth, and in a word, to everything that regards the wellbeing of a state.'[83]

Therefore, for particular cases and instances where public right and private right interact a working relationship between the two requires to be protected institutionally, ensuring that neither will be abandoned or in principle sacrificed. In such intersections conduct will be analogous with that in which state imperatives conflict with moral ones. In both cases, both of which constitute abnormalities, decisions are best made by men who are aware of what they do. Bacon stood for conduct according to morality in all normal cases. Similarly in cases where procedures according to law would normally be applied it was Bacon's natural assumption that such a course of conduct would continue.

Bacon wrote in the essay *Of Judicature* (1612 and 1625):

Judges ought above all to remember the conclusion of the Roman Twelve Tables, *Salus populi suprema lex*; and to know that laws, except they be in order to that end, are but things captious, and oracles not well inspired. Therefore it is an happy thing in a state when kings and states do often consult with judges; and again, when judges do often consult with the king and state: the one, when there is matter of law intervenient in business of state;

the other when there is some consideration of state intervenient in matter of law. For many times the things deduced to judgment may be *meum* and *tuum*, when the reason and consequence thereof may trench to point of estate: I call matter of estate, not only the parts of sovereignty, but whatsoever introduceth any great alteration or dangerous precedent, or concerneth manifestly any great portion of people. And let no man weakly conceive that just laws and true policy have any antipathy; for they are like the spirits and sinews, that one moves with the other.[84]

While on a higher level of generality law for him is part of policy, Bacon as will be observed refers here to law and policy as distinct.

In a parliament too, and especially in a parliament, such conflicts of interest and principle, Bacon argued, could be and should be confronted and resolved. Given as he insisted that the rule of just laws and the incidence of true policy must both be upheld, parliaments very properly constituted a clearing house or sorting shop. On the prerogative claim to exact Impositions, as one of the 'parts of sovereignty', Bacon speaking in May 1610 in the House of Commons began with a text from the sacred canon: *State super vias antiquas, sed videte quaenam sit via recta, et ambulate in ea* – stand in the ancient ways, but look also into present experience in order to see whether in the light of this experience ancient ways are right. If they are found to be so, walk in them. He had, he inferred, duly investigated the ancient ways and he recommended standing and proceeding in them. He had, he said, long been a parliament man. Within that time

he did observe that the parliament had received divers inhibitions from the Queen to restrain them from debating the matter then in question, wherein he took this difference; and that if the matter debated concerned the right or interest of any subject or the Commonwealth, if in that case an inhibition came, he for his part would not advise the House to desist, but to inform the King of the liberty of the House and so to proceed.[85]

In a case of a clash of this sort, as in consultations between kings or states and their judges, he proposed no formula to cover the outcome, nor in such cases was any particular outcome predictable, as he was careful to make clear. 'But if the matter in question were an essential thing which concerned the Prerogative and the power of the crown, then the House did always desist from proceeding any further upon such inhibitions received.'[86]

He told the House that, of the events he thus cited, two of them had taken place under Queen Elizabeth and one under Queen

Mary. The two former concerned first, succession to the throne; second, control of matters ecclesiastical: the precedent from Queen Mary's reign related to that queen's household. Impositions were in this same class – 'an essential thing which concerned the Prerogative'. But Impositions were also different. Unlike the three other cases cited, Impositions also and in addition 'concerned the right or interest of any subject or the Commonwealth'. 'Commonwealth' in Bacon's usage of the term was the sum total of private rights and interests. Both parties were involved – rights and interests which were private – rights and interests which were public, namely those of government. Government was the reigning monarch in due exercise of the several 'parts of sovereignty'. 'And therefore he persuaded the House to present these matters of Impositions as grievances to the Commonwealth (which the King had given us leave to do), that is, to petition him, but not to question his power and prerogative to impose.'[87]

Later in the same year he spoke again on this matter:

And it please you, Mr Speaker, this question touching the right of Impositions is very great, extending to the prerogative of the King, on the one part, and the liberty of the subject on the other; and that in point of profit and value, and not of conceit or fancy.... my proposition is, that the King by the fundamental laws of this kingdom hath a power to impose upon merchandise and commodities both native and foreign...There appeareth not in any of the King's courts any one record, wherein an imposition laid at the ports hath been overthrown by judgment; nay more, where it hath been questioned by pleading...Bates was the first man *ab origine mundi* (for anything that appeareth) that ministered that plea...Whereupon I offer this to consideration. The King's acts that grieve the subject are either against law and so void, or according to strictness of law and yet grievous; and according to these several natures of grievance there be several remedies. Be they against law? Overthrow them by judgment. Be they too strict and extreme, though legal? Propound them in Parliament. For as much then as impositions at the ports, having been so often laid, were never brought into the King's courts of justice but still brought to parliament, I may most certainly conclude that they were conceived not to be against law. And if any man shall think that it was too high a point to question by law before the Judges, or that there should want fortitude in them to aid the subject; no, it shall appear from time to time in cases of equal reach, when the King's acts have been indeed against law, the course of law hath run, and the Judges have worthily done their duty.[88]

Bacon tendered advice on counselling rulers, and also on the dilemmas facing counsellors, whether these be inside or outside a ruler's parliament, cabinet or council. '...it were disproportion enough', he wrote in the essay *Of Wisdom for a Man's Self* (1612 and 1625),

for the servant's good to be preferred before the master's; but yet it is a greater extreme, when a little good of the servant shall carry things against a great good of the master's. And yet that is the case of bad officers, treasurers, ambassadors, generals, and other false and corrupt servants; which set a bias upon their bowl of their own petty ends and envies, to the overthrow of their master's great and important affairs... And certainly it is the nature of extreme self-lovers, as they will set a house on fire, and it were but to roast their eggs; and yet these men many times hold credit with their masters, because their study is but to please them, and profit themselves; and for either respect they will abandon the good of their affairs.[89]

Bacon reiterated that advisers should counsel rulers according to their interest and business; that they should advise them not in terms of what goes on inside their 'characters of dispositions', their quirks and humours – though no doubt it is helpful if these latter can be penetrated – but in terms instead of events and situations occurring and existing, whatever rulers might be surmising, in an observably outside world which was real. Nevertheless the praising of rulers has a due place in the counselling of them. *Advancement* (both versions) together with his numerous papers addressed to King James exude praise of the reigning monarch seemingly to excess. Bacon has his explanation ready at hand. He writes in *Of Praise* (1612 and 1625): 'Some praises come of good wishes and respects, which is a form due in civility to kings and great persons, *laudando praecipere*' (to advise by praising); 'when by telling men what they are, they represent to them what they should be... '[90] Flattery in his practice would be a way of teaching the monarch his business.

According to the essay *Of Counsel* (1612 and 1625): counsellors 'should not be too speculative into their sovereign's person. The true composition of a counsellor is rather to be skilful in their master's business than in his nature; for then he is like to advise him, and not feed his humour.'[91] Though it should scarcely require to be enunciated, this rule as Bacon showed himself aware, was easier to proclaim than to apply. As he said of himself, he was not so simple that he did not know 'the common beaten way to please'. In the *History of the Reign of King Henry the 7th* when commenting upon Empson and Dudley, agents of that monarch's avarice, he observed that 'kings do more easily find instruments for their will and humour than for their service and honour...'[92]

Princes, he wrote in *Of Counsel* (1612 and 1625) should 'know their counsellors as well as their counsellors know them'. Bacon advises princes on choosing their counsellors:

It is in vain for princes to take counsel concerning matters, if they take no counsel likewise concerning persons; for all matters are as dead images, and the life of the execution of affairs resteth in the good choice of persons. Neither is it enough to consult concerning persons, *secundum genera*, (according to their class), as in an idea or mathematical description, what the kind and character of the person should be; for the greatest errors are committed and the most judgment is shown, in the choice of individuals. It was truly said, *optimi consiliarii mortui* (the best counsellors are the dead:) books will speak plain when counsellors blanch; therefore it is good to be conversant in them, specially the books of such as themselves have been actors upon the stage.[93]

Rulers should be versed in civil history no less than the men who counsel them.

'In the youth of a state arms do flourish; in the middle age of a state, learning; and then both of them together for a time; in the declining age of a state, mechanical arts and merchandise. Learning hath his infancy... then his youth... then his strength of years, when it is solid and reduced...'[94] *Of Vicissitude of Things* which offers these conclusions appeared only in 1625 in the last collection. But elsewhere Bacon provided plentiful evidence revealing that he located his own times with respect to the Kingdom of Great Britain as being well capable of introducing an epoch of flourishing learning. In this epoch, moreover, arms and learning could well prosper together. Learning could be solid and reduced – that is, reduced to truth – not only, as he hoped, in the shape of natural, but also in that of civil philosophy. The latter could *inter alia* direct government conduct in diplomacy and in its use of fleets and armies.

'So when any of the four pillars of government are mainly shaken or weakened (which are Religion, Justice, Counsel and Treasure), men had need to pray for fair weather.'[95] He makes this statement in *Of Seditions and Troubles*. This was published in the essay collection of 1625. He composed it at an earlier date. The four pillars, it may be noted, are entities implying actions. But in each case those are institutionalized. None of the four pillars with the exception of counsel had been mainly shaken or weakened according to Bacon's expressed judgments. Even on counsel he produced as will be seen a second opinion. However with counsel conducted as it ought to be, all things could be improved with the result that even greatness, civil, moral, and material, could be at hand.

Policy in Bacon's usage of the term is a part of philosophy. It is a science. Though sometimes as in the extract from *Of Judicature* quoted above, he employs 'policy' to mean government as contrasted with law – government being the senior partner – more often the term policy includes both science of government and science of law. Policy is also a course of action or actions which science dictates. Science implies action. Policy is also an agency, a government, which undertakes action or actions. It is also the constitution of a state within which such actions can and require to take place. These four aspects are firmly interconnected. Each of the uses of the term should inescapably imply the existence or activity of the others. Therefore Bacon employed one and the same word to cover all of them. Since, following Machiavelli, he taught that constitutions and laws flow out of governments as the result of their actions, this interconnectedness between the several aspects of policy had existed in what for Bacon were past pre-scientific times.

Since Bacon aims to promote science in the present for the sake of the future, the four aspects of policy remain interconnected. But the items he listed in his abbreviated notes of July 1608 under the head 'Poll.' are also and further interconnected since they are parts of a single grand strategy which he conceives as requiring, and as being capable of fulfilment. What was the objective? Precisely the purpose for which Macaulay declared him to be so suitably endowed; 'Intellectually he was better fitted than any man that England has ever produced for the work of improving her institutions. But, unhappily we see etc. etc.'[96] But according to evidence it was this work of improving institutions which Bacon set out to achieve.

In pursuing policy, as in the conduct of natural philosophy/ science, a man needs to know what takes place, takes place that is to say in a course of events, whether civil or natural. He needs also to know what takes place in procedures for study and handling, whether the field he engages in be that of civil affairs or that of the universe of nature. Given the sufficing quantity and the high quality of the *data* in civil histories and in civil experience, which latter included 'seeing Fortune', 'for though she be blind, she is not invisible'[97] – as he put it in the essay *Of Fortune* (1612 and 1625) – Bacon perceived in the former department compared with what was visible to him in the latter, solid foundations to build upon – not only the realities of what was taking place, but in addition the procedure for handling these realities. 'Bacon embraced as his own all the *business* and knowledge of the age.'[98] The italics are the present writer's. The statement is Edward Gibbon's (1737–94) when he compared him with Tribonian, prominent jurist and Quaestor of the Palace under the Emperor Justinian. Whatever may have happened in the case of Tribonian, Gibbon in that of Bacon correctly assigned the strategic priority to business, though it needs to be added that in Bacon's case business and knowledge were not mutually exclusive. Bacon's business was a knowledge, namely policy; and not only in that branch of it which comprised government and law but also in the department described by him specifically as that of 'negotiation or business'.

'The bringing of the King low by poverty and empty coffers.'
'The revolt or trouble first in Scotland: for till that be, no danger of
   English discontent: in doubt of a war from thence.'
'The greatness of some particular subjects, popularity (?)
   Salisbury acceptable to the Lower House of Parliament. question'
'The greatness of the Lower House in Parliament.'
'Confederacy and more strait amity with the Low Countries.'
'Limiting all Jurisdictions. More regular.'
'Qu. what use of presbytery.' the presbyterians
'Books in commendation of monarchy mixed, or aristocracy.'
'Persuade the King in glory, *aurea condet saecula*, that he establish
   golden age.'
'New Laws to be compounded and collected: Lawgiver *perpetuus
   princeps* – perpetual prince.'
'Restoring the Church to the true limits of authority, since Henry
   the 8th confusion.'
'Choice of persons active and in their nature stirring, and assure
   them.'
'Advertisement to a general memorial of affairs,
   Succeed Salisbury, and amuse the King and Prince with pastime
   and glory.'
'It is like Salisbury hath some further intention upwards.
   To win him to the point of policy.

Surdis modis, cave aliter' (in noiseless ways, in other things stay alert).

'Finishing my treatise of the Greatness of Britain with aspect *ad politiam*' (to policy).

'the fairest, without disputes (?) discontents (?) distempers (?) discords (?) disfavour (?) or peril, is the general persuading to King and people, and course of infusing everywhere the foundation in this isle of a monarchy in the west, as an apt seat, state, people for it; so civilizing Ireland, further colonizing the wild of Scotland. Annexing the Low Countries.'

'If anything be questioned touching policy, to be turned upon the ampliation of a Monarchy in the Royalty.'

'Making some collection touching the authority of the Privy Council, as it appeareth in our books of Law…'

'Still to consider how to make use both in state and for my particular of my project of Amendment of Laws.'[99]

Items in the above list propose government action, rooted as this would be in his general studies in civil histories, chiefly ancient. But some of the items in addition required more specific researches into a past which was local, namely the past of the kingdom of England. Under the head 'Limiting all Jurisdictions. More regular' and under 'Books in commendation of Monarchy mixed, or aristocracy' Bacon's plans are manifested in his attempts to clarify and establish the political constitution of the state. His leading pronouncements on this topic are set out in 1606 in a paper dealing with a dispute which had arisen concerning the jurisdiction of the Council of Wales and the Marches. But he pursued the same objective in speeches delivered in King James' first parliament. Two of these have already been noted. In these speeches as in the paper on the Welsh Council, he offers what he has found to be the relevant and therefore cogent civil history. Conclusions are presented with the evidence with which they have been arrived at. It is thus available to others. This evidence is not adduced in support of an already made up mind. Examples are not chosen to dance attendance upon the discourse. On the contrary the discourse is directed by the examples. It is possible though not verifiable that on the prerogative claim to impose dues on certain classes of merchandise Bacon became more doubtful in the end than he had been at first. Throughout these debates in the House of Commons he did not lose the respect of other

members. This was his boast. Neither then nor later has this claim
been refuted.

*A View of the Differences in Question betwixt the King's Bench and the
Council in the Marches* (1606)[100] was Bacon's leading pronouncement on
his theme 'Limiting all Jurisdictions. More Regular.' He first
recounted the origin and early course of the dispute. The rest of the
paper it will be noted is conducted in the form of a debate. A man
named Farlie, he explained, was imprisoned by the Marches Court
for contempt. Complaining to the King's Bench, he obtained a writ
to remove his body and cause. 'This writ (for that none of that
nature had ever taken place at the Council) was not obeyed.'
Instead, the Lord President, 'considering the inconvenience that
might grow by contentions of Courts, and that it properly belonged
to the wisdom of His Majesty as a point of government and not of
law, to compose such differences as may fall out,...referred the
whole cause to the judgment of the state.'

The King...first commanded the Judges to proceed no further till his
pleasure were known; and then in person vouchsafed to hear the reasons of
both parts: and finding no just exception (as it seemed) against the Lord
President's proceedings, only referred to his Council the examination of
particulars for reconciling and maintaining both Courts in their rights. To
this purpose when their Lordships gave hearing, it was not denied by the
reverend Judges that the order of the Council of the Marches, whereupon
this question grew, was just; nor that their instructions gave them warrant
for it: besides it was granted that the Council there was an absolute Court,
and to be controlled by none save the high Court of Parliament, for matters
within the jurisdiction thereof.

Then the judges changed their ground. It seems that it was in
Shropshire that the affair had begun. The judges maintained that
'the four shires of Salop, Hereford, Worcester, and Gloucester, were
not contained in the Act of Parliament by which' (so they
maintained)

that Council was established; and howsoever they were expressed in the
Commissions of our Kings, yet the regal Prerogative by law did not extend
so far as to erect a Court of Equity for trial of suits; and therefore the causes
of those shires must return to Westminster and the course of Common Law.
Upon this assumption...the King's Bench (upon reasons to them
known)...thought good to proceed...And hereupon it came to pass
(though doubtless against the purpose of those honourable persons)...that
the Lord President of Wales...was publicly disgraced,...the Court of the
Marches, being the King's Council, was brought in contempt; and his

Majesty's prerogative...was laid open to more exception than in former times it had been.

And this being the plain and true progress of this business, it may be considered, first, whether Farlie were a worthy Sampson to shake at once so many pillars of this state; then whether the exemption of the shires was not brought in question only for supply to maintain the writ...and lastly whether it will not be a great derogation both to the King and Council to have the sovereignty of his government either cried down with the strong voice of law, or referred to Parliament and there made subject to popular dispute.

Next Bacon examines more widely the issues in debate.

For the King's power it is alleged: that the Council of the Marches had a royal foundation; and was first established by Edward the 4th to govern by his instructions and commission both the counties of Wales and the shires adjoining; and that it hath continued King after King to this present day, as by divers records and infinite precedents testifying the continued practice thereof, and by nothing to the contrary that can be produced, shall hereafter appear. To this answer is made: First in general, that the Prerogatives of our Kings are only given them by law; and then in particular, that by the law they have no power to establish a Court of equity; and therefore neither the Council board of right can decide any matter between party and party, neither any court or council that hath not a proper establishment by law.

To this Bacon gives his answer:

first to the general, that the King holdeth not his prerogatives of this kind mediately from the law but immediately from God, as he holdeth his Crown; and though other prerogatives by which he claimeth any matter of revenue, or other right pleadable in his ordinary courts of Justice, may be there disputed, yet his sovereign power, which no Judge can censure, is not of that nature; and therefore whatsoever partaketh or dependeth thereon, being matter of government and not of law, must be left to his managing by his Council of State. And that this is necessary to the end of all government, which is preservation of the public, may in this particular appear. For no doubt but these grave and worthy ministers of justice have in all this proceeding no respect but to their oaths and the duties of their places, as they have often and deeply protested; and in truth it belongeth not to them to look any higher, because they have charge but of particular rights. But the State, whose proper duty and eye is to the general good, and in that regard to the balancing of all degrees...will happily consider this point above law: That Monarchies in name do often degenerate into Aristocracies or rather Oligarchies in nature by two insensible degrees. The first is when prerogatives are made envious or subject to the constructions of laws; the second when law as an oracle is affixed to place. For by the one the King is made accomptable and brought under the law; and by the other the law is overruled and inspired by the Judge, and by both all tenures of favour, privy Counsel, nobility and personal dependencies (the mysteries that keep up states in the person of the Prince) are quite abolished, and magistracy enabled to stand by itself.

Venice, Poland, the Mayors of the Palace in ancient France are cited.

And what greater strength had the League there of late than the exorbitant greatness of the Parliament of Paris? And from hence also in the time of Henry the 3rd, our Parliament challenged power to elect and depose the Lord Chancellor, Treasurer, and Chief Justice of England, as officers of the State and not of the King. Whether then these popular titles of limiting prerogatives for subjects' birthrights and laws may not unawares, without any design or thought of the authors, open a gap unto new Barons' wars, or other alteration and inconvenience in government, the wisdom of the state is best able to discern. And therefore all I conclude is this, that the ordering of these matters doth belong thereunto.

Yet God forbid (as one said) that we should be governed by men's discretions and not by the law. For certainly a king that governs not thereby can neither be comptable to God for his administration, nor have a happy and established reign.

The 'one' who had made these observations was King James himself in his *True Law of Free Monarchies.*

But God forbid also upon pretence of liberties or laws government should have any head but the King...But because I assure myself that no soul living will charge His Majesty with any manner of encroachment upon the subjects' rights, I confess I marvel, and some perchance may doubt, why we should be so curious to wrest that right from his hand which all his progenitors have enjoyed heretofore.

Again to the particular of his power to establish Courts of equity it is further said: That by the ordinance of God it properly belongeth to a King to administer justice and judgment to his people...

Here Bacon quotes from the sacred canon, from the Book of the Prophet Isaiah and also from the Book of Proverbs and from that of Exodus. 'And our own law', he continued,

giveth no less power to our Kings; for as Bracton saith: *Rex habet ordinariam potestatem et omnia jura in manu sua.* And their practice in all times doth confirm as much. For King Alfred first divided the land into shires and provincial law days. William the Conqueror brought in the Exchequer, and kept the Chancery and Common Pleas at his court. Henry the 3rd settled the Common Pleas at Westminster. Edward the 3rd erected the Admiralty and Duchy. Edward the 4th the Councils of Star Chamber and the Marches. Henry the 8th set up the Courts of Requests, of Wards and

Liveries, and the Council at York. And though some of these were since approved by Statute Law, yet the author and life giver of them all was the prerogative of our Kings, which must of necessity be impeached in all, if denied in any.

Besides we say that in the King's prerogative there is a double power. One which is delegate to his ordinary judges in Chancery or Common Law; another which is inherent in his own person, whereby he is the supreme judge both in Parliament and all other Courts; and hath power to stay suits at the Common Law; yea *pro bono publico* to temper, change and control the same...Nay our acts of Parliament by his sole authority may be mitigated or suspended upon causes to him known. And this inherent power of his, and what participateth thereof, is therefore exempt from controlment by any Court of Law. For saith Britton lib. I, *We will that our jurisdiction be above all jurisdictions in our realm*: so as we have power to give or *cause judgments to be given as shall seem to us good, without other form of process, where we may know the true right as judge*. Now this free jurisdiction the King exerciseth by his Councils, which are not delegations of power, but assistances thereof inherent in himself. And upon this ground the Council Table judgeth matters in equity when they are referred unto them. And the same sufficient warrant have these Councils in the Marches and the North for all their proceedings, though they had no other law. For that this is also a Council of Estate, and not a bare Court of Law, may appear, First by the style thereof both in the instructions and statute itself: Secondly by the Institution, which was to assist the Prince of Wales as well in matters of government as law: Thirdly, by their oath, which is the same with the oath of a Councillor of State: Fourthly, by their authority to make pro-clamations: and fifthly by the attendance of their Pursuivants and Serjeant at Arms. So by all this it may appear both that this Council was duly established by the King's prerogative, if it had no other right, and that therefore it ought to be subject to no controlment but his.

Next, the judges' contention that Shropshire, Hereford, Worcester and Gloucester 'are not intended to be Marches of Wales' is refuted, for example:

We have records to show of orders from Henry the 3rd at several times for the fortifying of Shrewsbury, Hereford, Bridgenorth, and Worcester, as special frontiers against the Welsh. For after that William Rufus and Henry the first had driven the Welshmen into narrower room; specially after the conquest of Wales by Edward the First, and his new division thereof into shires, these countries beyond Severn were also no more called Wales, but the Marches thereof...

Finally Bacon adduces his considerations of convenience or inconvenience; that is to say, he lists possible and likely future aspects of this affair.

if *salus populi* be *suprema lex*, then though law and usage and prerogative were all against us, yet *bonum publicum* should be always preferred. The consequents then of this renting and discountenancing the government in Wales may probably be these: it will be a dangerous beginning of innovation in the general government of the land. For if the King's Prerogative, the ancient and main foundation upon which this jurisdiction was built, be thus questioned and shaken, then of necessity the Council of York must fall after this: which is not denied; and the Court of Requests must follow; and happily other Courts of equity, which may be seen to be blemished in the handling of this cause. And what further way may be opened to Parliament or lawyers to dispute more liberties, may rather be feared than discovered at the first.

Ruining the Marches court will encourage papists who are numerous in those parts. It will imperil the union between England and Wales 'by breaking of their great traffic, their mutual alliances, and their equality of right'. 'And why should not both again spoil one another when they have no common justice to keep them in fear?' Rioting and brawling will be less restrained in the area: the old condition of 'borderers and highlanders' will return. Who will control insolences and oppressions by the Marcher lords and who bridle disorderly gentry? The hearing of cases in courts at Westminster will become slower and even more encumbered than at present. The past orders and judgments of the Marches court will be overthrown. 'And his Majesty of right should repay all the fines levied there since the beginning of that Court.' Besides all these, other inconveniences call for reflection: there would be acknowledgment of wrong and usurpation in the crown time out of mind:

The condemning of the acts and instructions of so many former kings: The present disparagement and overthrow of a Council of Estate…can it be denied that by means of this Court, established as it now is, all those countries both of Wales and the Marches have been reduced from barbarism, poverty and disorder, and thus long been maintained in civility and peace? or can any just and important exception be taken against their present proceedings? Or is there any ground of all this ado to satisfy present or after times?

Finally, ' …if it be once carried out of his royal hand he shall hardly or never recover like power: and what incongruity soever time shall discover the remedy will be past.'

Under 'New Laws to be compounded and collected: Lawgiver *Perpetuus Princeps* (Perpetual Prince)', and under 'Still to consider how to make use both in state and for my particular of my project of Amendment of Laws' a number of initiatives on his part could be adduced. Several of these have been cited already in this study. The scraps which have survived recording his first speech in the House of Commons in the Queen's reign relate to such projects. Even after fall and disgrace, he continued to offer help and advice in this matter to her successor. He informed King James in March 1622 that 'the laws of the most kingdoms and states have been like buildings of many pieces, and patched up from time to time according to occasions, without frame or model.'[101] The plight of English Common Law, it is true, was less extreme than this. But he urged, if not in this paper yet elsewhere in others, that work was nevertheless required. Above all it was needed in setting the record straight; that is by attending to law reporting; and in making maxims out of this record – which was a history – for help in handling future court cases. It was likely also that there were laws obsolete, laws repetitive, and laws contradictory. These should be inspected in order to weed them out if found to be so.

He informed the King that 'this kind of work, in the memory of times, is rare enough to show it excellent; and yet not so rare as to make it suspected for being impossible, inconvenient, or unsafe…' He cites his numerous examples. Moses, Lycurgus and Solon are recalled. He reminds the King that four of the kings of Rome had been lawgivers. 'For it is most true, that a discourser of Italy' (namely Machiavelli) 'saith: *there was never state so well swaddled in the infancy as the Roman was, by the virtue of their first kings*…Which was a principal cause of the wonderful growth of that state in aftertimes'.[102] He mentions the *Decemviri*, Sylla, Caesar, Augustus, Justinian, the Athenian *Sexviri*. He adds for later times Edgar, King of the West Saxons, Alfonso the Wise, King of Castile and Louis XI, King of France.

The note touching restoring the church to the true limits of authority is alas incapable of a complete elucidation: the destructive accidents of time – have afforded little evidence towards explaining what he planned to do about Henry VIII's 'confusion' or even what he meant by the term. Despite the early statement of purpose while the Queen still reigned 'to write the history of England from the beginning of the reign of King Henry the Eighth of that name', and despite Prince Charles's later reported interest in a study by Bacon of the rule and proceedings of that monarch, Bacon failed to produce such a book. However a statement in his fragmentary *The Beginning of the History of Great Britain* presents perhaps a clue. Describing King James VI and I he writes that he was a king 'that besides his universal capacity and judgment, was notably exercised and practised in matters of religion and the church; which in these times by the confused use of both swords are become so intermixed with considerations of estate, as most of the counsels of sovereign princes or republics depend upon them ... '[103] Henry VIII's policy in matters of religion and the church – whether in internal or in external affairs – was indeed marked 'by the confused use of both swords ... ' Bacon, writing in *Of Unity in Religion* (1625) stated: 'There be two swords amongst Christians, the spiritual and temporal; and both have their due office and place in the maintenance of religion ... '[104] Henry VIII's religious policy – both internally and externally – indeed became 'intermixed with considerations of estate' by this his confused use of the two swords. Furthermore he used parliaments in addition to assemblies of the clergy to effect his changes in religion. King James, on the other hand, did not offend in these respects. Being 'notably exercised and practised in matters of religion and the church'; King James gave Bacon the less to do in this department of affairs. On the other hand we have already seen that policy as he envisaged it embraced the state's decisions and teachings regarding matters spiritual, and that he advanced proposals regarding the condition and prospects of the protestant religion as established in doctrine and in cult by statute law in the Church of England. Following and observing his own standards – that is, keeping free of 'intermixtures of considerations of estate' – Bacon offered his two papers, *An Advertisement Touching the Controversies of the Church of England* (1589) and *Considerations Touching the Better Pacification with Edification of the Church of England* (1604). The note: 'Qu. what use of the presbytery', is not neglected in these papers. With respect to both of these papers an 'intermixture of considerations of estate' no doubt remained; but only in that 'Religion being the chief band of human society, it is a happy thing when itself is well contained within the true band of unity'.[105] Needless to say, conformity, according to Bacon, in the public cult was obligatory regardless of men's inward dispositions. As for the established public doctrine, open challenging of it according to Bacon was rightly punishable by the laws.

CHAPTER 7

Morality and policy II

Four points respecting the 1608 notes require above all to be remarked. The first is this: it is true we see Bacon in his theses referring to 'amendment of laws' as his 'project'; and we know that under this head he submitted plans for amending, compiling or digesting laws. Nevertheless his chaplain and biographer records that Bacon's profession of the law was '(as himself said) but as an accessory, and not his principal study'.[1] The chaplain adds that 'notwithstanding that he professed the law for his livelihood and subsistence, yet his heart and affection was more carried after the affairs and places of estate'.[2] But William Rawley's testimony agrees with Bacon's own testimony. It accords with his words and deeds. '...all the exterior proceedings of man consist of words and deeds; whereof history doth properly receive and retain in memory the deeds, and if words, yet but as inducements and passages to deeds'.[3] It is upon Bacon's words and deeds that this book, which if not strictly a history of Bacon, is nonetheless a history, attends and relies. According to his words and also to his deeds his heart and affection were more carried after the affairs and places of estate than towards matters of the law. But nevertheless 'His principal study', dilemmas notwithstanding, certainly was twofold. It was statecraft rather than law. It was also the universe of nature.

The information conveyed in these two last sentences introduces the second cardinal point respecting the notes of July 1608, though it is a point which as yet has not been mentioned when they have been cited in this text. The notes contain the substantial section headed 'Poll.' But they contain also entries concerning private affairs, money matters and gardening plans. In addition however there is much material relating to Bacon's preoccupation with his programme for investigating nature. For example, we find: 'The finishing the 3 Tables de Motu, de Calore et frigore, de sono.'

'The finishing of the Aphorismes, Clavis interpretationis, and then setting foorth ye book...'[4] Clavis interpretationis was the title which he thought of first as that for *Novum Organum.*

'Imparting my Cogitata et Visa with choyse, ut videbit^r.'

'Ordinary discours of *plus ultra* in Sciences, as well the intellectual globe as the materiall, illustrated by discouvery in o^r Age.'

'Discoursing skornfully of the philosophy of the graecians wth some better respect to ye Aegiptians, Persians, Caldes, and the utmost antiquity and the mysteries of the poets.'

'Comparing the case of that wch lyvy sayeth of Alexander. Nil aliud q^m bene ausus vana contemnere.'[5]

'Ordinary Cours of Incompetency of reason for naturall philosophy and invention of woorks...'

'To procure an History of Marvailes; Historia naturae errantis or variantis, to be compiled wth Judgm^t and without credulity and all the popular errors detected...'

'To procure an History mechanique to be compiled wth care and diligence...'[6]

'Endevor to abase the price of professory sciences and to bring in æstimation Philosophy or Universality – name and thing.'[7]

Extensive Notes on the topic of motion are to be found in the jottings: '*Inquisitio Legitima de Motu*'[8]: 'First to inquire the severall kyndes or diversities of mocion.'[9]

It should be mentioned in this connection that in the field of the universe of nature *Cogitata et Visa* (Things Thought and Things Seen) was completed at about this time. This writing provided something of a foretaste of *Novum Organum* – both books of it. Sending the piece to Bishop Lancelot Andrewes in 1609 he told him: 'I hasten not to publish; perishing I would prevent. And I am forced to respect as well my times as the matter. For with me it is thus, and I think with all men in my case: if I bind myself to an argument, it loadeth my mind; but if I rid my mind of the present cogitation, it is rather a recreation. This hath put me into these miscellanies; which I purpose to suppress, if God give me leave to write a just and perfect volume of philosophy, which I go on with slowly.'[10] *Thema Coeli* and also *Descriptio Globi Intellectualis* can both be dated as composed in 1612. *De Fluxu et Refluxu Maris* would seem to date from before the year 1616. The chaplain Rawley reports that: 'I myself have seen at the least twelve copies of the *Instauration*, revised year by year one after the other, and every year altered and amended in the frame thereof, till at last it came to that model in which it was committed to the press.' In his Latin version Rawley spoke here not of *The Instauration*, but of *Novum Organum*.[11]

The debate within himself in *De Interpretatione Naturae Proœmium*, which has been cited earlier is in itself manifestly inconclusive. It is all the more inconclusive since it is well known that despite its conclusion Bacon nevertheless proceeded to ponder his civil histories and to pursue his civil ambitions. He had written that though 'a man's own country has some special claims on him' and that 'I was not without hope that if I came to hold some office in the state I might get something done, too, for the good of men's souls' '(the condition of religion being at that time not very prosperous)'... But 'I put all those thoughts aside'. He had done no such thing. Letters of Bacon to Sir Toby Mathew and to Isaac Casaubon have been earlier quoted, but not fully. In dating (1610) they nearly coincide. The letter to Sir Toby Mathew primarily refers to the programme for nature: 'My great work goeth forward; and after my manner, I alter ever when I add. So that nothing is finished till all be finished.' But this letter also alludes to the parallel programme: 'This I have written in the midst of a term and parliament.'[12] The letter to Casaubon points sharply to the programme in *Know Thyself*: 'For indeed to write at leisure that which is to be read at leisure matters little; but to bring about the better ordering of man's life and business, with all its troubles and difficulties, by the help of sound and true contemplations, this is the thing I am at. How great an enterprise in this kind I am attempting, and with what small helps, you will learn perhaps hereafter.' But in this letter Bacon also refers to the programme for nature: 'You are right in supposing that my great desire is to draw the sciences out of their hiding places into the light.'[13]

Further illumination of the man's mind is contained in a statement in a long letter dated 1620(?). Despite the letter's superficially irrelevant topic – the matter of appointing a Lord Treasurer – it contains characteristic profundity relevant both in this and in other matters: 'Neither am I so simple or unwrought in business as to think that (all) things can be executed at once, for he that thinks all things can go on at once, I should think his head were full of wind.

But on the other side, he that shall consult or provide but for one thing at once shall never overcome any great difficulties ... '[14] To this statement from the *Know Thyself* programme, there can conveniently be added from the other programme, that of inquiries into nature, the statement which Bacon made in the *History of Winds*: 'If men could only bring themselves not to fix their thoughts too intently on the consideration of the subject before them, rejecting everything else as irrelevant, ... , they would never be so dull as they are wont to be, ... they would find many things at a distance which near at hand are concealed.'[15] Further, we cannot afford to ignore remarks under 'negotiation or business', his science concerned with dealing with others but also concerned with handling himself. 'We should imitate nature which doth nothing in vain;' a man should 'well interlace his business, and bend not his mind too much upon that which he principally intendeth ... nothing is more impolitic than to mind actions wholly one by one'.[16]

He pursued the two courses with equal purpose. Policy had a priority for him but of one kind only: it had a priority in providing procedure and consequently in lending it. This was for the reason first that as we have seen he found civil history to be in a better and more usable condition than natural history; and second, as we shall later more fully see, because he found Machiavelli to have been a sounder and more accomplished user of civil history than Aristotle had been of natural history. Such advantages will be imported into the area where they are lacking and thus needed, namely into natural history and natural philosophy/science. Bacon's conclusion reached before the Queen's death that civil histories exhibited least of their authors and most of the things themselves summed up the above two considerations. What this comes to is that if Bacon was in any way inventor or innovator – which was what he intended – in natural philosophy/science, he was this or did this in that he immersed himself also in policy as being for the above two reasons largely an inescapable undertaking; and one moreover which for the purposes of the parallel work did not need to be escaped from.

Bacon's twofold study was not pursued along the route of a suspect middle way between two commitments with nothing of consequence achieved in either. Whatever the force of his dilemma its result was not compromise. Instead his study was persistingly devoted to policy, preponderantly in the field of government, and equally to the realm of nature – each for its own sake – but the former being a means to the latter. This is the message of indications and suggestions in the *Sapientia Veterum*'s *Dedications* and also of *Plan* of the *Great Instauration*: there he explained that he would make 'pause upon that which is received; and thereby the old may be more easily made perfect and the new more early approached'.

Policy as Bacon made clear includes law. He was committed to the law and worked in it. But policy embraces much else besides. According to the 1608 notes and the rest of what he said and did, the foremost and what he called 'the fairest' element in the grand strategy was not the amendment of laws. Instead it was 'the general persuading to king and people, and course of infusing everywhere the foundation in this isle of a monarchy in the west, as an apt seat, state, people for it...' Civilizing Ireland, colonizing remoter parts of Scotland; and annexing in alliance the Low Countries were included in 'the fairest'. The urgent and essential precondition of all this was a fuller naturalization of the Scots. This was as yet unprocurable. Bacon feared the possible consequences of an imperfect union. But he claimed nevertheless that his 'general persuading' was 'the fairest'. It could be 'without disputes (?) discontents (?) distempers (?) discords (?) disfavour (?)'. Matters of laws and of the constitution directly confronted would be likely to prove controversial and contentious, whereas it could reasonably be calculated that the structure and balance of the state constitution could be settled as a by-product of 'the fairest'. Also it would be 'without peril'. In 'the fairest', dangers could be confronted and averted which were external, those namely from foreign powers – and also those which were internal; perils, that is to the monarch's regal position and 'the parts of sovereignty'.

But with respect to internal dangers 'the fairest' was no smart ploy to protect the Crown's prerogatives, nor, for that matter, a device to safeguard the prospects and rights of parliaments. According to Bacon's arguments the foundation of Britain as a power base, which would be second to none and equal to any, was an ambition both good and possible in itself. In addition to being good and possible it could rightly be said to be necessary. Things in state relations seldom stand still. If the ruler of Britain did not seize or create opportunities the kingdom would be likely to fall prey to opportunities seized or created by others. Frenchmen have had a foothold in Scotland. Spaniards sought to gain one in Ireland. Bacon argued this position in those portions which he completed – or which have survived – of 'my treatise of the Greatness of Britain'. He also pressed the case elsewhere, the case that Britain was an 'apt seat' for power in terms of geography; and that this British state did not generate a servile oppressed populace. The kingdoms were constitutionally tempered. In these newly united states the peoples were ruled by the laws. Moreover both peoples, English and Scottish, were proficient in war.

Preceding pages have presented two cardinal points. A third is that, though regularly a member of the House of Commons, Bacon does not reveal himself as content continually to address audiences from afar, whether these latter consisted of his fellow members, of the King and Council of State, or of the world in general. If the powerful minister, the Earl of Salisbury could not be won 'to the point of policy', he, Bacon, would aim to succeed him, if not as Lord Treasurer, yet as a chief minister in power with the King. He himself would attempt to preside over and to see to the fulfilment of the points of policy.

'Persuad. the K. in glory, Aurea condet saecula.'[17] – Persuade the King in glory, that he should found a golden age. 'Adv^t to a gen. mem. of aff. Succ. Salb. and amuz the K and P. wth pasty. and glory'[18] – Advertisement to a general memorial of affairs. Succeed Salisbury, and amuse the King and Prince with pastime and glory.[19] These notes introduce fully the fourth point. They pointedly suggest that Bacon did not set out relying upon the King's active support for success in carrying out his strategy. It would be enough if, recognizing that in this latter matter his counseller was 'skilful in his master's business', the King agreed and did not oppose.

Bacon, then, would resort not only to thoughts and writings but if possible also to actions. Sure enough, notwithstanding normal misgivings about how he ought to be spending his time and energies, he wrote to the King when Salisbury died and offered the monarch his services in 'business of estate'. In 1612 he told him 'I have looked on others, I see the exceptions, I see the distractions, and I fear Tacitus will be a prophet, *magis alii homines quam alii mores*'[20] – other men rather than other ways of doing things. In 1616 he was already Privy Councillor and was seeking the Lord Chancellorship. He wrote in that year: 'I dare promise, that if I sit in that place your business shall not make such short turns upon you as it doth, but when a direction is once given, it shall be pursued and performed, and your Majesty shall only be troubled with the true care of a king, which is to think what you would have done in chief, and not how for the passages.'[21]

William Harvey (1578–1657), who discovered that the blood circulates in living bodies, was appointed Physician Extraordinary to the King. At one time he was also physician to Bacon. As reported by John Aubrey, Dr Harvey had a point as things turned out when he said that 'He [Bacon] writes philosophy like a Lord Chancellor', speaking, as Aubrey adds, 'in derision'.[22] Harvey was referring to the Chancellor's natural philosophy, by which it seems he was not impressed. The converse to Harvey's statement is also true. He (Bacon) conducted his Chancellorship like a philosopher – a civil philosopher. Harvey's point, though he was unaware of its validity, was that Bacon asserted plainly, and more than once, that his civil philosophy could have a link with his natural philosophy and that the former could help to lead him into the latter. In the case of both sciences, he would – as will be seen – chiefly succeed in advancing them in and by means of his capacities as thinking student of civil histories, as reflecting man of civil experience, and as pondering writer of civil history – these three capacities interacting.

In a letter of 1616 he went on to urge another relevant and closely related point for the King's consideration: 'I do presume also...that I have always been gracious in the lower house, I have some interest in the gentlemen of England, and shall be able to do some effect in rectifying that body of parliament men, which is *cardo rerum*, the core of things.' In this same letter he also confirmed Rawley's observation that office of state rather than profession of law was his objective. A Chancellor as a counsellor could and would do other than confine and enclose himself in matters of equity and law. 'For let me tell your Majesty that that part of the Chancellor's place, which is to judge in equity between party and party, that same *regnum judiciale*...concerneth your Majesty least, more than acquitting of your conscience for justice. But it is the other parts, of a moderator amongst your Council, of an overseer over your judges...that importeth your affairs and these times most...I will add also, that I hope by my care the inventive part of your Council will be strengthened,...'[23]

'This is true', Bacon wrote in the essay *Of Empire* (1612), repeating the statements in 1625,

that the wisdom of all these latter times in princes' affairs is rather fine deliveries and shiftings of dangers and mischiefs when they are near, than solid and grounded courses to keep them aloof. But this is but to try masteries with fortune. And let men beware how they neglect and suffer matter of trouble to be prepared; for no man can forbid the spark, nor tell whence it may come. The difficulties in princes' business are many and great; but the greatest difficulty is often in their own mind.[24]

Thoughts expressed in the letter to the King of 1620 should be coupled with such statements in *Of Empire*. The matter discussed in the letter was that of appointing a Lord Treasurer...'it is not a Commission of Treasury' – which had existed since Salisbury's death – 'that can help...but that your Majesty is to make choice of an officer, as heretofore it hath been'. There should be a Lord Treasurer. Not only so. What was needed, Bacon urged, was fidelity and judgment but also 'invention and stirring and assiduity and pursuit, with edifying one thing upon another'.[25] In the letter he complained of

a course taken and almost grown into a principle that it should so be, which is that your business in this kind goes on by one and by one, and not at once, and rather by shifts to stop gaps from time to time, than by any sound establishments...it is good for your Majesty, nay necessary as the case is, that your business be set forward in many parts at once, and that you be kept from straits afar off, and not only eased a little when they press you.[26]

In the essay *Of the Greatness of Kingdoms* (1612) he explained that

the speech of Themistocles, which was arrogant in challenge, is profitable in censure. Desired at a banquet to touch a Lute, he said, he could not fiddle; but he could make a small Town become a great City. This speech at a time of solace and not serious, was uncivil, and at no time could be decent of a man's self. But it may have a pretty application. For to speak truly of politics and Statesmen, there are sometimes, though rarely, those that can make a small estate great, and cannot fiddle. And there be many that can fiddle very cunningly, and yet the procedure of their Art is to make a flourishing estate ruinous and distressed. For certainly those degenerate Arts, whereby divers politics and Governors do gain both satisfaction with their Masters and admiration with the vulgar, deserve no better name than fiddling; if they add nothing to the safety, strength and amplitude of the States they govern.[27]

In the 1625 version of the above there are verbal changes. But he also adds a passage: 'There are also (no doubt) counsellors and governors which may be held sufficient (*negotiis pares*), able to manage affairs, and to keep them from precipices and manifest inconveniences; which nevertheless are far from the ability to raise and amplify an estate in power, means and fortune.'[28] This addition serves to link the complaints and charges made in *Of Empire* and in *Of the Greatness, etc.* with the civil proceedings of Salisbury: 'fine deliveries', 'shiftings of dangers and mischiefs', 'fiddling', making 'a flourishing estate ruinous and distressed', 'degenerate Arts' – no doubt these terms describe a wider range of examples of impolicy or absence of policy than Salisbury had provided. But nevertheless these descriptions cover the minister's conduct in civil matters, especially in the affair of the Great Contract.

They do so because at the time of the Treasurer's death when Bacon made his offers to the King he expressed himself in sharply adverse criticism of the late minister. He wrote: 'It is no new thing for the greatest king to be in debt'. The King should understand that his coffers could not be instantly replenished.

My second prayer is that your Majesty in respect of the hasty freeing of your state would not descend to any means or degree of means which carrieth not a symmetry with your majesty and greatness. He is gone from whom those courses did wholly flow. To have your wants and necessities in particular as it were hanged up in two tables before the eyes of your lords and commons, to be talked of for four months together ... To stir a number of projects for your profit, and then to blast them, and leave your Majesty nothing but the scandal of them: To pretend even carriage between your Majesty's right and the ease of the people, and to satisfy neither; these courses and others the like I hope are gone with the deviser of them; which have turned your Majesty to inestimable prejudice.[29]

However he expressed not one but two judgments upon Salisbury at the latter's death: 'Your Majesty', he wrote, 'hath lost a great subject and a great servant. But if I should praise him in propriety, I should say that he was a fit man to keep things from growing worse but no very fit man to reduce things to be much better.'[30] To this should be added the testimony of Rawley, Bacon's chaplain:

He [Bacon] was no heaver of men out of their places, as delighting in their ruin and undoing. He was no defamer of any man to his prince. One day, when a great statesman was newly dead, that had not been his friend, the King asked him, *what he thought of that Lord which was gone?* He answered *that he would never have made his Majesty's estate better, but he was sure he would have kept it from being worse,* which was the worst he would say of him ...[31]

Of Great Place (1612) records an instruction: 'Reform without bravery or scandal of former times and persons.'[32] In the version of 1625 this advice is extended: 'Neglect not also the examples of those that have carried themselves ill in the same place; not to set off thyself by taxing their memory; but to direct thyself what to avoid.

Reform, therefore, without bravery or scandal of former times and persons; but yet set it down to thyself, as well to create good precedents as to follow them.'[33] The result of the addition inserted into *Of the Greatness etc.* (1612) when this essay in 1625 becomes *Of the True Greatness of Kingdoms and Estates* – namely when he concedes that there were statesmen who proved capable of preventing conditions from sharply worsening – was that Bacon was able candidly to present both his harsher and also this more lenient verdict. It will be allowed that the two assessments of Lord Treasurer Salisbury are reconcilable.

The notes made in 1608 were not the musings of a moment. They were the summary of a strategy of 'reform without bravery or scandal of former times and persons'. Elements mentioned in the notes antedate the summer of 1608 when he wrote them down. It is not possible to establish the date when he began to compile the treatise *Of the True Greatness of Britain* which according to the notes he promised himself he would finish. But as already noted his first recorded speech in the House of Commons in 1593 addressed the topic of amendment of laws. *Maxims of the Law* is even earlier in date than this speech. *Advancement* (1605) touches not only on amendment of laws which Bacon certainly held to be needed; it also recommends attention to the state constitution as a whole, it being likely that this also would be required. The wisdom of a lawmaker, he wrote in *Advancement*, should take into consideration 'what influence laws touching private right of *meum* and *tuum* have into the public state'.[34] Bacon's paper on the Council of Wales devoted to this subject in 1606 has already been summarized. But arguably the most remarkable surviving contribution antedating the 1608 jottings – and appropriately the most remarkable since it concerned what Bacon was to call the 'fairest' item in the strategy – was the speech delivered in the Commons in February 1607.

Bacon had written two papers for King James on the union of the Kingdoms. He stated in the first that

there hath been put in practice in government these two several kinds of policy in uniting states and kingdoms; the one to retain the ancient forms still severed, and only conjoined in sovereignty; the other to superinduce a new form agreeable and convenient to the entire estate. The former of these hath been more usual, and is the more easy; but the latter is more happy. For if a man do attentively revolve histories of all nations, and judge truly thereupon, he will make this conclusion, that there were never any states

that were good *commixtures* but the Roman. Which because it was the best
state of the world, and is the best example in this point, we will chiefly insist
thereupon.
So likewise the authority of Nicholas Machiavel seemeth not to be
contemned; who enquiring the causes of the growth of the Roman Empire,
doth give judgment, there was not one greater than this, that the state
did so easily compound and incorporate with strangers.[35]

In February 1607 Bacon urged the House of Commons in a
long oration to ·agree to a full naturalization of King James's
northern subjects. This speech on the safety, unsafety, union,
disunion, expansion, contraction, wealth, poverty, of kingdoms and
estates and of their commonwealths is as closely argued and as
substantial and cogent in its parade of examples as anything he
propounded in policy. Referring in the second paper to the first of
the two he had sent the king on the union of the kingdoms he
described the former as having been written 'scholastically and
speculatively', while this, the present paper, is 'actively and politicly'
framed. 'For I hold nothing so great an enemy to good resolution as
the making of too many questions: specially in assemblies which
consist of many.'[36] But when addressing the Commons in February
1607 he guards against the opposite excess: 'to avoid confusion,
which ever more followeth of too much generality, it is necessary for
me... to use some distribution of the points or parts of Naturalisation'.[37]

Avoiding too many distinctions and at the same time eschewing
too much generality, his distribution of 'points or parts' covers
different aspects of naturalization – but not too many of them. In
addition he lists the likely consequences both of naturalizing Scots
and also of refusing them this status. Some of the alleged
inconveniences, he claimed, arising from a decision to naturalize
deserve less weight than men attach to them. We are likely, he says,
to incur greater inconveniences by not taking this course, than by
embracing it. Finally, if we decide to take it, there are sizeable
advantages and benefits to be reaped. Members, he says, should
raise their thoughts, lay aside private considerations, and 'take upon
them cogitations and minds agreeable to the dignity and honour of
the estate'.[38]

With respect to alleged inconveniences he holds that fear of a large
influx of people from the north is unjustified. '... in this point, which
is conjectural, experience is the best guide; for the time past is a

pattern of the time to come. I think no man doubteth (Mr Speaker) but his Majesty's first coming in was as the greatest spring-tide for the confluence and entrance of that nation. Now I would fain understand, in these four years' space, and in the fullness and strength of the current and tide, how many families of the Scottishmen are planted in the cities, boroughs and towns of this kingdom'.[39] Supposing that such influx takes place, we are not, as things stand at present, overpopulated. Even if we become so, what, he asked, could be the worst effect of a 'surcharge of people'?

Look into all histories, and you will find it none other than some honourable war for the enlargement of their borders, which find themselves pent, upon foreign parts; which inconvenience, in a valorous and warlike nation, I know not whether I should term an inconvenience or no... And certainly... I hope I may speak it without offence, that if we did hold ourselves worthy, when soever just cause should be given, either to recover our ancient rights, or to avenge our late wrongs, or to attain the honour of our ancestors, or to enlarge the patrimony of our posterity, we should never in this manner forget the considerations of amplitude and greatness, and fall at variance about profits and reckonings; fitter a great deal for private persons than for Parliaments and Kingdoms.[40]

Under this same head, that is to say, feared inconveniences whereby Scotsmen gained and Englishmen lost, he corrects a misconception. In the matter of gifts of mind and body there is little to choose between the two peoples. Both are valiant, hard, active and comely. The Scots are not so tractable to government. But neither are the English. Both peoples resemble the Romans with qualities incident to martial nations. Fierce horses are better of service, but hard to manage. He adds another point: 'in all the line of our kings none useth to carry greater commendation' than Edward I:

Amongst his other commendations... none is more celebrated than his purpose and enterprise for the conquest of Scotland; as not bending his designs to glorious conquests abroad, but to solid strength at home; which nevertheless if it had succeeded, could not but have brought in all those inconveniences... that are now alleged.

If it were good for us then, it is good for us now.

Under the second head – inconveniences prospectively resulting from declining to naturalize, he said:

wherein that inconvenience which above all others, and alone by itself, if there were none other, doth exceedingly move me, and may move you, is a position of estate, collected out of the records of time, which is this: that wheresoever several kingdoms or estates have been united in sovereignty, if that union hath not been fortified and bound in with a further union, and namely that which is now in question, of Naturalization, this hath followed, that at one time or other they have broken again.[41]

He cites Rome's treatment of the Latins, comparing it with the case of Sparta, which, unlike Rome, was grudging of naturalization and came to grief. The incomplete union of Aragon with Castile likewise broke apart; similarly that of Florence with Pisa, and that of Turkish power with Transylvania, Wallachia and Moldavia. On the other hand, 'we shall find that wheresoever kingdoms and estates have been united, and that union corroborate by the bond of mutual naturalization, you shall never observe them afterwards upon any occasion of trouble or otherwise, to break and sever again'. Where full naturalization takes place unions stay firm – not only in the case of ancient Rome and her annexed peoples, but in other more recent instances – France and its provinces, Spain and its provinces – and England where a heptarchy gave place to a monarchy.[42]

'And so (Mr Speaker) against all these witty and subtile arguments, I say that I do believe, and would be sorry to be found a prophet in it, that except we proceed with this Naturalization (though perhaps not in his Majesty's time, who hath such interests in both nations) yet in the time of his descendants, these realms will be in continual danger to divide and break again.'[43] 'Whosoever useth not foresight and provision for his family is worse than an unbeliever.'[44]

Finally Bacon argues the beneficial consequences of a true union founded upon naturalizing the Scots. First, the state at last becomes secure and safe because it is defensible. *Testudo intra tegumen tuta est* – the tortoise is safe inside her shell. 'The more ancient enemy...hath been the French; and the more late the Spaniard.' France had Scotland, Spain has tried to have Ireland. In future neither could have a foothold in the shape of ally or accomplice. Second, opportunity will arise for greatness. 'Scotland united, Ireland reduced, the sea provinces of the Low Countries contracted, and shipping maintained' this kingdom of England 'is one of the greatest monarchies, in forces truly esteemed, that hath been in the world.'[45] The Kingdom of God, the tiny grain of mustardseed, becomes the greatest of trees. So it is with human and earthly states. We should refer our counsels to greatness and power, preferring such counsels to considerations of utility and wealth. Indeed to seek primarily the latter is to forfeit success. For a nation's material wealth, public or

private, depends on its moral, political and military strength. As
Solon explained to Croesus, King of Lydia, iron is stronger than
gold. 'Neither is the authority of Machiavel to be despised' when he
urges that men not monies are the sinews of war.[46] The great states
of the past had started not wealthy but poor – Persia, Macedon,
Rome, the kingdoms founded by invaders who overthrew Rome's
power, the Ottomans. Recently Switzers had defeated the Duke
of Burgundy on the field of battle. '...all which examples,
(Mr Speaker) do well prove Solon's opinion of the authority and mastery iron hath over gold'.[47] The Kingdom of Spain does not deserve
to fulfil – nor does it succeed in fulfilling – the prophecy, *Video solem
orientem in occidente*, I see the sun rising in the west, in virtue of having
'ravished from some wild and unarmed people mines and store of
gold'. Why therefore should we, 'seated and manned as we are with
the best iron in the world', think of nothing but reckonings, audits
and *meum* and *tuum*? 'But I have spoken out of the fountain of my
heart. *Credidi propter quod locutus sum.*'

Bacon persuades himself as he attempts with rhetoric and the
common logic to persuade others. He produced no 'Advertisement
to a general memorial of affairs' – which is what the notes proposed
that there ought to be. His addresses, taken as a whole, constitute
this 'general memorial'. There are two phases in his attempt and in
the addresses embodying it. In the first phase he approaches
audiences severally. Speeches in parliament have already been cited.
He advises the King as we have seen on naturalizing the Scots. In *An
Advertisement touching the Controversies of the Church of England*: in
*Considerations Touching the Better Pacification and Edification of the Church
of England*, and in the paper on the jurisdiction of the Council of
Wales he counsels himself and the world in general. In the second
phase the proposals are not sent far and wide but are for the King
only. They contain instructions on how to manage parliaments. The
prime device for binding together monarchs and parliaments
remains abidingly unchanged – the joint founding of a monarchy in
the West. But to the grand strategy a sub-strategy for detailed
handling of parliaments required to be added. Bacon proceeded to
supply it.

The two phases overlap. In the letter in which he offered to
undertake 'business of state', telling King James he feared Tacitus
would be a prophet – other men rather than other ways of doing
things – he made no mention of parliaments. But he also wrote

another paper at this time. It carries no date. It is not known whether it was sent to the King. It may be on a par with the 1608 notes, that is to say, thoughts in the form of *memoranda*. But in this case thoughts are much more than notes and are fully articulated. In parenthesis it may be interjected that this is the paper where he delivered the milder of his two verdicts on conduct of affairs by the late Lord Treasurer, confirming with his own pen what his chaplain reported of his words in conversation.

He went on:

So that although your Majesty hath grave counsellors and worthy persons left, yet you do as it were turn a leaf, wherein if your Majesty shall give a frame and constitution to matters, before you place the persons, in my simple opinion it were not amiss. But the great matter and most instant for the present, is the consideration of a Parliament, for two effects: the one for the supply of your estate; the other for the better knitting of the hearts of your subjects unto your Majesty...; for both which, Parliaments have been and are the ancient and honourable remedy.

He continued:

Now because I take myself to have a little skill in that region... and though no man can say but I was a perfect and peremptory royalist, yet every man makes me believe that I was never one hour out of credit with the lower house: my desire is to know your Majesty will give me leave to meditate and propound unto you some preparative remembrances touching the future parliament.[48]

The year 1613 is the date of another paper of thoughts:

Having settled my opinion after some meditation, I conclude with myself it is fit for the King to call a Parliament, or at least not fit for any man to dissuade it ... Parliament hath been the ordinary remedy to supply the K.'s wants: and it is a great confession of weakness in a body if it cannot brook the ordinary remedy... In point of fame and observation, there is no great difference whether it be said abroad, the K. is in necessity and the parliament hath denied to relieve him: or thus, the K. is in necessity and dare not call a Parliament to put the affections of his people to a trial... I conceive the sequel of good or evil not so much to depend upon Parliament or not Parliament, as upon the course which the K. shall hold with his Parliament.[49]

Next, he conveys to King James results of further meditations:

The matter of Parliament is a great problem of estate, and deserveth apprehensions and doubts. But yet I pray your Majesty remember that saying *Qui timide rogat docet negare*, A man who asks timidly invites a denial. For I am still of the opinion (which I touched in general in my former letter to your Majesty) that above all things your Majesty should not descend below yourself;...and that your Majesty should proceed with your Parliament in a more familiar, but yet a more princely manner...that the good or evil effect like to ensue of a Parliament resteth much upon the course which your Majesty shall be pleased to hold with your Parliament; and that a Parliament simply in itself is not to be doubted.[50]

As to this 'course': 'Put off the person of a merchant – rest upon the person of a king...Certainly when I heard the overtures last Parliament carried in such a strange figure and idea...methought... it was almost contrary to the very frame of a monarchy, and those original obligations which it is God's will should intercede between King and people...' Your Majesty should

make this Parliament but as a *coup d'essay* and accordingly that your Majesty proportion your demands and expectation. For as things were managed last, we are in that case, *optime disciplina mala dediscere* – the best teaching is to learn from things that go wrong. Until your Majesty have tuned your instrument you will have no harmony...And if it be said, his Majesty's occasions [empty coffers] will not endure these proceedings *gradatim*, yes surely. Nay I am of opinion that what is to be done for his Majesty's good, as well by the improvement of his own as by the aid of his people must be done *per gradus* and not *per saltum*; for it is the soaking rain and not the tempest that relieveth the ground.[51]

I propose

that this Parliament may be a little reduced to the more ancient form (for I account it but a form), which was to voice the Parliament to be for some other business of estate, and not merely for money: but that to come in upon the bye...And let it not be said that this is but dancing in a net, considering the King's wants have been made so notorious; for I mean it not in point of dissimulation but in point of majesty and honour; that the people may have something else to talk of and not wholly of the King's estate; and that parliament-men may not wholly be possessed with those thoughts; and that if the King should have occasion to break up his Parliament suddenly, there may be more civil colour to it...I am settled in this, that somewhat be published besides the money matter...

Lastly, put it about that there are means available for the King on his own to restore his estate. Else parliament men are likely to conceive him to be at their mercy.[52]

In the 'Undertakers' Parliament' of 1615 Bacon spoke like this:

And in short every novelty useth to be strengthened and made good by a kind of undertaking. But for the ancient Parliament of England, which moves in a certain manner and sphere, to be undertaken, it passeth my reach to conceive what it should be. Must we all be dyed and dressed, and no pure whites amongst us? Or must there be a new passage found for the King's business by a point of the compass that was never sailed by before? Or must there be some forts built in this House that may command and contain the rest? Mr Speaker, I know but two forts in this House which the King ever hath; the fort of affection and the fort of reason: the one commands the hearts, the other commands the heads; and others I know none.[53]

After the spectacle of fiasco which this parliament presented Bacon drafted yet another letter to the King, but again without title, address or date. He dismissed the argument that experience of the last two parliaments was unpropitious. 'Nothing doth encourage me more than that which I do remember of those Parliaments...not indeed alone, but joined also with the remembrance of former Parliaments further back.' Demosthenes, he recalled, had asserted '*Quod ad praeterita pessimum id ad futura optimum* (What has been very bad with respect to the past – is most good with respect to the future)'...when things have gone amiss by accident and error or mishandling, and not of their proper disposition. For nothing is to a man either a greater spur or a greater direction to do over a thing again than when he knows where he failed. If things have gone astray through mismanagement they can be put right when mismanagement is corrected. It is not from the nature of the institution of parliament that things have gone wrong. Recognize, he urged, the true nature of parliament and adapt management accordingly.

this one advice may flow which I shall now give which is so far from tending by any acting, or minting, or packing or canvassing, or any the like devices, as it tendeth wholly to the restoring of that great Council to the natural use and ancient splendour and dignity thereof, from which it hath in latter time, I will not say degenerated, but certainly receded; whereby it will also appear that we shall need no other foundation than that that is laid in a blessed time, which is a good King and a good people; and that there is not requisite any great or laborious engine to draw kindness out of the affections of the subjects; but that it is only like the opening of a spring-head, which with a little cleansing will run frankly of itself.[54]

Bacon continued tendering comparable advice up to and including the year 1621, in which year a parliament assembled and accomplished his disgrace and fall.

Restore an institution to the principles of its origin. This is what Machiavelli had advised. Stand, Bacon recommended, in the ancient ways: '*state super vias antiquas, et videte quaenam sit via recta et bona et ambulata in ea*. Antiquity deserveth that reverence, that men should make a stand thereupon, and discover what is the best way; but when the discovery is well taken, then to make progression.'[55] In *Of Great Place* (1612 and 1625) the two versions of this formula, Machiavelli's and his own – this having been culled from the canon of sacred scripture – are conflated: 'Reduce things to the first institution, and observe wherein and how they have degenerate; but yet ask counsel of both times; of the ancient time, what is best, and of the latter time what is fittest.'[56]

However in the case of parliaments as we see Machiavelli's version held its own. In addition to what has been cited already, the contents of a fragmentary draft speech for 1621 should be noted:

As the king himself hath declared unto you the causes of the convoking of this Parliament, so he hath commanded me to set before you the true institution and use of a Parliament, that thereby you may take your aim, and govern yourselves the better in Parliament matters: for then are all things in best state when they are preserved in their primitive institution; for otherwise ye know the principle of philosophy to be, that *the corruption or degeneration of the best things is the worst*.[57]

In a further note concerning advice to be given to both houses we find '*Nosce te ipsum*. I would have the Parliament know itself…'[58] That is to say, a parliament should be instructed in order to know the history of itself as an institution.

The two major features in this story of a sub-strategy – or rather of a sub-science for a sub-strategy – requiring to be noted are, first, the evident interplay between Bacon's parliamentary experience, his researches into parliamentary history, and his conclusions. His first position is that parliaments have been either for laws, business of state – or for money. This is what he said in his first speech in the Commons in the Queen's reign. His second position is that parliaments ought to be for business of state and for money too. His third position is that in the past parliaments had indeed been assembled for both these purposes simultaneously.

'The kings of this realm have used to summon their Parliaments or estates for three ends or purposes; for Advice, for Assent, and for Aid.'[59] Concerning the quality of the advice which a parliament could offer he wrote:

For Advice, it is (no doubt) great surety for kings to take advice and information from their Parliament. It is an advice which proceedeth out of experience; it is not speculative, or abstract. It is a well-tried advice, and that passeth many reviews, and hath Argus eyes. It is an advice that commonly is free from private and particular ends, which is the bane of counsel; for although some particular members...may have their private ends, yet one man sets another upright; so that the resultate of their counsels is for the most part direct and sincere. But this advice is to be given with distinction. In things which lie properly in the notice of the subjects they are to tender and offer their advice by bill or petition, as the case requires. But in those things that are *Arcana Imperii*, and reserved points of sovereignty...there they are to apply their advice to that which shall be communicated unto them by the King...[60]

As we have seen he had laboured to explain and to maintain this distinction in the House of Commons in earlier times. But in addressing the King on the part he must play in grand strategy it was precisely his argument that matters normally held to be '*Arcana Imperii*, and reserved points of sovereignty' could properly and also fruitfully be 'communicated' to his parliaments.

Needless to say, though he had boasted to the King of his status and standing in the lower House, it was not about the latter but about parliaments as a whole that he addressed him on this as on other occasions. 'The King's Sovereignty and the Liberty of Parliament are as the two elements and principles of this Estate'[61] (May 1610). Bacon even proposed (1613) that 'his M. could wish the ancient statutes were put in ure of holding a Parliament every year'.[62] A parliament is 'in effect the perfection of monarchy; for that although monarchy was the more ancient and be independent, yet by the advice and assistance of Parliament, it is the stronger and the surer built...' 'When the King sits in parliament...he is in the exaltation of his orb.'[63] The note made in 1608 – 'the greatness of the lower House in Parliament' referred as much to the future as to the present: the note illustrates Bacon's penetration in civil affairs and therefore his foresight in them. As things turned out, it was in a House of Commons that the case in 1621 against himself came to be launched.

The second major feature in this story of Bacon's sub-strategy is that the King, instructed by his privy counsellor, should use caution founded in 'exact and precise knowledge'. Knowing his ground, he should prepare his action. He should then launch himself into it with audacity. '...your Majesty should proceed with your Parliament in a more familiar, but yet a more princely manner'. The King should refrain from direct requests for supply. This latter would come in on the bye once a parliament was taking its requested and due part in some great business of state. Such conduct would mean not bargaining and 'merchandising' prerogatives as in the affair of the Great Contract; but instead communicating '*Arcana Imperii* and reserved points of sovereignty' and inviting cooperation. Bacon in 1621 submitted a draft proclamation in which the King announced his intention to do so.[64] The draft was not accepted.

In the science of policy Bacon promises in the first *Advancement* work of his own on laws.[65] He does no such thing for the field of government in the first *Advancement*.[66] In the second *Advancement* he not only promises, but provides work in this field. He inserts into the text *The Example of a Summary Treatise on the Extension of Empire*; this being followed by the promised work on laws, namely *The Example of a Summary Treatise on Universal Justice or the Fountains of Equity, by Aphorisms*. It is in the second *Advancement* and only there that he claims to have invented policy as a distinct discipline. He makes this claim, in short, – and also introduces the examples of summary treatises – only after he has attempted practice as a man of state. Here we see, as he insists ought always to be the case, first the active man, and next the active man becoming the writer.

He addresses the King in the second *Advancement* like this: 'On this subject' ('the Art of Empire or Civil government which includes œconomics'), 'as I before said, I have imposed silence on myself.' He had refrained from contributing in this topic in the first *Advancement*. '…though perhaps', as he continued in the second version

I might not be entirely unqualified to handle such topics with some skill and profit, as one who has had the benefit of long experience, and who by your Majesty's most gracious favour…has risen through so many gradations of office and honour to the highest dignity in the realm and borne the same for four whole years; and, what is more, being one who has been accustomed for eighteen successive years to the commands and conversation of your Majesty (whereby a very stock might be turned into a statesman), and who also, besides other arts, has spent much time in the study of laws and histories. All which I report to posterity, not through any vain boasting, but because I think it is of no little importance to the dignity of literature, that a man naturally fitted rather for literature than for anything else, and borne by some destiny against the inclination of his genius into the business of active life, should have risen to such high and honourable civil appointments under so wise a king. But if my leisure time shall hereafter produce anything concerning political knowledge, the work will perchance be either abortive or posthumous. In the meantime, now that all the sciences are ranged as it were in their proper seats, lest so eminent a seat should be left entirely vacant, I have determined to mark as deficient only two parts of civil knowledge, ...[67]

There follow the *Example of a Summary Treatise on the Extension of Empire* and the *Example of a Summary Treatise on Universal Justice or the Fountains of Equity, by Aphorisms.*

Bacon's mention of possible further exercises in 'political knowledge' is accompanied, as we see, by a warning. Two enterprises fit the announcement that he had work on hand which perchance would prove either abortive or posthumous. One of these, his treatise *Of the True Greatness of Britain*, was abortive and not even posthumous. The project survives as a fragment. The other, *Considerations Touching a War with Spain*, was published in 1629 after the author's death, and hence was posthumous. It was abortive – or, rather, aborted in one respect. The third part was omitted and deliberately so when the treatise came to be printed. This third part offered plans in detail for conducting a war.

Differences between these two undertakings and, for example, the essay *Of Empire* and the trial treatise on the *Extension of Empire* are manifest. The unlikenesses are none the less inessential. The essay *Of Empire* and the trial treatise are cast in general terms. They are founded on the observation of wide-ranging particulars: the results are addressed back to particulars again – but to particulars in general. The fragmentary treatise and *Considerations Touching a War with Spain* are similarly based on observation and study of far-ranging particulars. They range, that is to say, beyond the special case of the United Kingdom. In this respect they resemble the naturalization speech of February 1607. But they, like this and other speeches, *memoranda* and proposals, are directed back, if the phrase be permissible, to this particular particular, the United Kingdom. They elaborate general doctrine derived from many cases which is applicable given the right circumstances in all cases. Kingdoms and estates expand in strength, in moral and material sway, or in territory; or else they contract in these things and fall back and behind. '...for whatsoever is somewhere gotten is somewhere lost'.[68] Standing still is temporary, precarious and partly illusory. If one among the powers is not in the course of ascending or of decline, another or others will be in the process of doing the one or the other. Bacon's argument both in the fragmentary treatise and in *Considerations Touching a War with Spain* – as in the 1607 speech on naturalization – is that the United Kingdom could be and should be the one to avoid contraction and decline and that instead it should expand in its capabilities. This said, a major difference is clear between the fragmentary treatise and most of the rest which Bacon contributed on the art of empire or civil government.

In the fragment he begins and proceeds like this:

The greatness of kingdoms and dominions in bulk and territory doth fall under measure and demonstration that cannot err: but the just measure and estimate of the forces and power of an estate is a matter than the which there is nothing among civil affairs more subject to error, nor that error more subject to perilous consequences. For hence may proceed many inconsiderate attempts and insolent provocations in states that have too high an imagination of their own forces: and hence may proceed, on the other side, a toleration of many grievances and indignities, and a loss of many fair opportunities in states that are not sensible enough of their own strength, therefore... I have thought good, as far as I can comprehend, to make a true survey and representation of the greatness of this your kingdom of Britain; being for mine own part persuaded, that the supposed prediction *Video solem orientem in occidente* – I see the sun rising in the West – may be no less true a vision applied to Britain than to any other kingdom of Europe; and being out of doubt that none of the great monarchies which in the memory of times have risen in the habitable world, had so fair seeds and beginnings as hath this your estate and kingdom; whatsoever the event shall be, which must depend upon the dispensation of God's will and providence, and his blessings upon your descendants. And because I have no purpose vainly and assentatorily to represent this greatness as in water, which shows things bigger than they are, but rather as by an instrument of art, helping the sense to take a true magnitude and dimension; therefore I will use no hidden order, which is fitter for insinuations than sound proofs, but a clear and open order: first by confuting the errors or rather correcting the excesses of certain immoderate opinions, which ascribe too much to some points of greatness which are not so essential, and by reducing those points to a true value and estimation: then by propounding and confirming those other points of greatness which are more solid and principal, though in popular discourse less observed: and incidently by making a brief application, in both these parts, of the general principles and positions of policy unto the state and condition of these your kingdoms. Of these the former part will branch itself into these articles: First, that in the measuring or balancing of greatness, there is commonly too much ascribed to largeness of territory. Secondly, that there is too much ascribed to treasure or riches. Thirdly, that there is too much ascribed to the fruitfulness of the soil, or affluence of commodities. And fourthly, that there is too much ascribed to the strength and fortifications of towns or holds. The latter will fall into this distribution: First, that true greatness doth require a fit situation of the place or region. Secondly, that true greatness consisteth essentially in population and breed of men. Thirdly, that it consisteth also in the valour and military disposition of the people it breedeth: and in this, that they make profession of arms. Fourthly, that it consisteth in this point, that every common subject by the poll to be fit to make a soldier, and not only certain condition or degrees of men. Fifthly, that it consisteth in the temper of the government fit to keep subjects in heart and courage, and not to keep them in the condition of servile vassals. And sixthly that it consisteth in the commandment of the sea. And let no man so much forget the subject propounded, as to find strange that there is no mention of religion, laws, policy. For we speak of that which is proper to the amplitude and growth of states, and not of that which is common to their preservation, happiness and other points of well-being.[69]

In the measuring or balancing of greatness, there is commonly too much ascribed to largeness of territory. For the reasons and from the examples adduced, it is safely concluded that 'largeness of territory is so far from being a thing inseparable from greatness of power, as it is many times contrariant and incompatible with the same'. 'But to make a reduction of that error to a truth, it will stand thus, that then the greatness of territory addeth strength, when it hath these four conditions: first, etc., etc., etc., etc., etc., etc.'[70] The treatise continues in this vein, confuting errors 'or rather correcting the excesses of certain immoderate opinions, which ascribe too much to some points of greatness which are not so essential, and by reducing these points to a true value and estimation'. Bacon examines the conditions under which greatness of territory need not be a liability; he also explains in what circumstances money can rightly be viewed as the sinews of war. Either Bacon did not complete this treatise, or else he finished it and did not publish it, large bits having since been lost. In either case the question arises – why? Answers can be found on the trivial level. He forgot to do so or he could not find the time. But he seems to forget little and to find time when he wishes, making deliberate choices of priority. An answer on a deeper level, though not provably a correct one is ready at hand. This will be offered in the next chapter.

CHAPTER 8

Morality and policy III

A difference between undertakings conducted in natural and those in moral and civil matters, a difference implanted in the subject matter, at once conferred on works in the latter an advantage with respect to prospective advances. Natural sciences need two parts: a speculative/theoretic part which is the inquisition of causes; and an operative/practical part which is the production of effects. Aphorism III, *Novum Organum*, Book I, reads: 'Human knowledge and human power meet in one; for where the cause is not known the effect cannot be produced. Nature to be commanded must be obeyed; and that which in contemplation is the cause is in operation as the rule.'[1] Aphorism IV, *Novum Organum*, Book II, reads: 'Although the roads to human power and to human knowledge lie close together, and are nearly the same, nevertheless an account of the pernicious and inveterate habit of dwelling on abstractions, it is safer to begin and raise the sciences from those foundations which have relation to practice, and to let the active part itself be as the seal which points and determines the contemplating counterparts.[2] Bacon thus accepts and teaches that the two are related and inseparable. Each operates upon the other and each is adjusted by the other: Nevertheless the two parts must be kept distinct.

Now although it be true, and I know it well, that there is an intercourse between Causes and Effects, so as both these knowledges, Speculative and operative, have a great connection between themselves; yet because all true and fruitful natural philosophy hath a double scale, a ladder ascendant and descendant, ascending from experiments to the invention of causes, and descending from causes to the invention of new experiments; therefore I judge it most requisite that these two parts be severally conducted and handled.[3]

In the first *Advancement* he states that the case in philosophy civil is no different: 'For as in civil matters there is a wisdom of discourse, and a wisdom of direction; so is it in natural.'[4] Nevertheless the cases are not comparable and in the final version of *Advancement* the statement is withdrawn. This is another instance of second thoughts. For the world of *Know Thyself* a speculative/theoretic part is not needed. At the outset, in the first *Advancement*, it is made clear that the form of man is already known – 'For as to the Forms of substances Man only except, etc., etc.'[5] – It is true that this is to forget for a time but not for ever that men's bodies are not only human but part of, and conjoined with, the rest of creation. But *reculer pour mieux sauter*.

The book of God's works other than man's mind and will has hitherto been unread. A speculative and theoretic part is therefore required for the whole of creation other than man's mind and will. 'If then it be true that Democritus said *that the truth of nature lieth hid in certain deep mines and caves*[6]; ... it were good to divide natural philosophy into the mine and furnace, and to make two professions or occupations of natural philosophers, some to be pioneers and some smiths; some to dig, and some to refine and hammer.' It is true that stages in constructing moral, governmental and legal philosophy can be called divisions, and Bacon does so in the original *Advancement*. In *Know Thyself*, as in all sciences, 'our road does not lie on a level, but ascends and descends; first ascending to axioms, then descending to works'.[7] But distinctions can be made to proliferate and should not be multiplied more than is needed for action. Stages in constructing philosophy in human self-knowledge, when compared with what is required in philosophy natural, for which he proposes two 'professions or occupations', are but alternating phrases in a single undertaking. One rather than two professions or occupations may prove right in the end for philosophy natural. But that is a state of affairs lying as yet in the future.

Nature – including man's body – as distinct from man's mind, his will and their products, is unknown, lying hid in certain deep mines and caves: 'The object of the natural history which I propose'[8] – this being so far non-existent –

to give light to the discovery of causes and supply a suckling philosophy with its first food. For though it be true that I am principally in pursuit of works and the active department of the sciences, yet I wait for harvest-time, and do not attempt to mow the moss or to reap the green corn. For I well know that axioms once rightly discovered will carry whole troops of works along with them, and produce them, not here and there one, but in clusters. And that unseasonable and puerile hurry to snatch by way of earnest at the first works that come within reach, I utterly condemn and reject, as an Atalanta's apple that hinders the race.[9]

In the enterprise of investigating nature an operative/practical part must wait upon establishment of a speculative/theoretic part. Before men grasp at profits and benefits from nature they must discover its forms and 'the real truth' of things. In the other and parallel programme restraint is still called for. Seeking immediate utilities is to be eschewed. This is for the sake of greater advantages obtainable with patience and at later stages.

But there need be no holding back arising from needs and duties to construct in the first place a speculative/theoretic part. Certainly human particulars vary in time and in space. Dispositions and characters of men differ. Bacon studies these differing characters of disposition and says that they ought to be investigated further. Men are inflicted with incubuses in the shape of idols of the mind. Bacon seeks to expose and to demolish these idols. One type of character of disposition and one of the idols of the mind are indistinguishable the one from the other. Idols of the cave are prison-houses into which men insert themselves by virtue of their personal 'complexions and customs'. The argument of Aphorism LXVII of *Novum Organum* Book I, confirms that a distinction here is otiose.[10]

Men in addition are moved by passions and affected by numerous agencies, states of living and conditions. Again, some of these latter seem indistinguishable from idols of the mind. Bacon lists, investigates and requests more inquiry into passions, conditioning agencies and states of living. Nevertheless all human differences and difficulties, however deeply rooted and however extensively they proliferate, take place and are seated within a structure which throughout time and space is uniform, stable and known. With respect to man's body, although it is stable and uniform, alas it cannot be said to be known. But everywhere and always men's rational souls, their minds and their wills, however affected by conditions and however assailed by passions and idols, singly or in combination, survive or reappear. This is known. Experience confirms the oracle of Holy Scripture concerning the form of man. His rational faculties together with his passions, these latter confronting or combining with the former, are identifiable and in that respect constant in form throughout all ascertainable tracts of time and experience.

'If the present be compared with the remote past, it is easily seen that in all cities and in all peoples there are the same desires and the same passions as there always were.'[11] 'Let no one despair ... of being able to effect that which has been effected by others; for, as we have said ... men are born and live and die in an order which remains ever the same.'[12] Machiavelli, not Bacon, provided these observations. Bacon agreed, not because – though he studied him – Machiavelli said so, but because the two men consulted the same sources, these being extant civil histories, chiefly ancient ones, together with the sacred scriptures of the Hebrews and of the Church.

In addition to those used by Machiavelli, Bacon, as we have seen, claimed to possess another source, the earliest poets of Greece – though as already stated it is not easy to see how he could have annexed the latter source unless he had in the meantime plentifully consulted the former. Studying the surviving earliest Greek poets he was led to question that rational capabilities had been stable throughout time without a break. There seemed to have been an epoch when, passions remaining the same, imagination acquired the function of reason and embedded truth in fables: 'The inventions and conclusions of human reason (even those that are now trite and vulgar) were as yet new and strange ... The understandings of men being then rude and impatient of all subtleties that did not address themselves to the sense.'[13] But this interlude did not undermine, indeed it served to confirm the position that human nature, though changeful, varies within limits which are fixed. First, imagining substituted itself for reasoning. Imagining is thinking. Like all else that takes place imagination in men's minds 'dances to the tune of the thoughts'.[14] In this instance its products successfully served mankind in times of an abeyance of reasoning. Second, the truths which were cloaked in fables 'must be regarded as neither being the inventions nor belonging to the age of the poets themselves, but as sacred relics and light airs breathing out of better times, that were caught from the traditions of more ancient nations, and so received into the flutes and trumpets of the Greeks'.[15]

For the study of mankind, the particulars contained in the *data*, in poetry ancient and modern, in history civil, both properly so-called and in Bacon's extensions of it; and also in history as every man's daily experience – these particulars proffer and provide their own speculative theoretic correlatives. They infuse and incorporate themselves into the *data* and display themselves adequately in and through it. Human particulars manifest not only cases of action or inaction, they are also witnesses to, and functions of a will which is always adequately free and of a soul which throughout time is sufficiently rational and moral. In man's study of man works need not be postponed. In this department, indeed, it would be unreasonable and puerile not to proceed at once. Bacon omits construction of a speculative/theoretic dimension and a resultant temporary priority in these fields because it is provided already.

Therefore since the form – the formal cause of man – is known, it follows that unlike natural philosophy, moral philosophy and civil philosophy – conversation, negotiation (or business) and government/law – are undivided sciences and single undertakings. All work in *Know Thyself* is operative/practical. What survives of the treatise *Of the True Greatness of Britain* reveals that it would have been operative/practical. But it is clear that there remained a further question for Bacon. It is also clear that he tried to answer it. Would the treatise *Of the True Greatness of Britain* have been operative/ practical enough? What was the form of delivery, of writing, most conducive to providing soundly operative/practical science, one which would surely come home to, and move the audiences Bacon addressed? For these audiences, it will be understood, were already engaged in or committed to action, whether in secular and ecclesiastical government, in councils, in parliaments, in law courts; or in business and social transactions more private and personal.

In 1609, the year after the note about 'Finishing my treat. of ye great. of Br. wth. aspect ad pol.',[16] Bacon, as we know, published his *De Sapientia Veterum*, stating in the Dedication to the Chancellor of Cambridge University that his aim 'has been to give some help' not only in penetrating 'the secrets of sciences' but 'towards the difficulties of life'.[17] In the same year, as we have also seen, he wrote to Isaac Casaubon: 'For indeed to write at leisure that which is to be read at leisure matters little; but to bring about the better ordering of man's life and business, with all its troubles and difficulties by the help of sound and true contemplations, that is the thing I am at.'[18] Bacon dedicated the essay collection of 1612 to Henry, Prince of Wales. The prince died in that year. Therefore this dedication was discarded. But it survives. It reads: 'To write just treatises requireth leisure in the writer, and leisure in the reader, and therefore are not so fit, neither in regard of your Highness' princely affairs, nor in regard of my continual services...'[19] For this reason, in the collection of 1612, he submits, he explains, not treatises but essays. He was already aware that the essays published in 1597 had won him an audience and made an impact. These had been three times reprinted after their first publication. The collection of 1597 had contained ten essays. That of 1612 comprised thirty-eight; that is to say, the original ten are reprinted, and twenty-eight new ones are added. The 1612 collection provides a marked increase in the number of essays devoted directly or indirectly to topics in policy. The collection of 1625 presents fifty-eight essays and yet further attention is directed to policy. All the 1612 essays reappear, often in an expanded form. Twenty new essays are included. In the dedication of this last collection to George Villiers, Duke of Buckingham and Lord High Admiral, Bacon, looking back on two previous collections, concluded: 'my Essays, which of all my other works, have been most current; for that, as it seems, they come home to men's business and bosoms'.[20]

In order to be effectively operative/practical, two demands impose themselves, each requiring to be met. There is the demand embodied in the message, the advancement of learning and a correct procedure for this. There is also the requirement that the message be conveyed in a way that does not frustrate but instead promotes advancement and continuing correct procedure. It is not possible to meet the first demand without fulfilling the second. Form of writing, handing on, delivery (*traditio*) – these matter no less than content and message. Since the enterprise is cooperative and progressive, the form of delivery carries equal weight with invention or discovery itself. Inner and outer – the two cannot be divided.

He writes in the first *Advancement*:

for as the doctrine of Syllogisms comprehendeth the rules of judgment upon that which is invented, so the doctrine of Method containeth the rules of judgment upon that which is to be delivered...Neither is the method or the nature of the tradition material only to the *use* of knowledge, but likewise to the *progression* of knowledge: for since the labour and life of one man cannot attain to the perfection of knowledge, the wisdom of the Tradition is that which inspireth the felicity of continuance and proceeding. And therefore the most real diversity of method is of method referred to use, and method referred to Progression...the latter whereof seemeth to be *via deserta et interclusa* – a way shut up and untravelled. For as knowledges are now delivered, there is a kind of contract of error between the deliverer and the receiver: for he that delivereth knowledge desireth to deliver it in such form as may be best believed, and not as may be best examined; and he that receiveth knowledge desireth rather present satisfaction, than expectant inquiry; and so rather not to doubt, than not to err; glory making the author not to lay open his weakness, and sloth making the disciple not to know his strength. But knowledge that is delivered as a thread to be spun on, ought to be delivered and intimated, if it were possible, *in the same method wherein it was invented*: and so is it possible of knowledge induced. But in this same anticipated and prevented knowledge, no man knoweth how he came to the knowledge which he hath obtained. But yet nevertheless, *secundum majus et minus*, a man may revisit and descend unto the foundations of his knowledge and consent; and so transplant it into another, as it grew in his own mind. For it is in knowledges as it is in plants: if you mean to use the plant, it is no matter for the roots; but if you mean to remove it to grow, then it is more assured to rest upon roots than slips. So the delivery of knowledges (as it is now used) is as of fair bodies of trees without the roots...'[21]

In this way Bacon discusses method in the first *Advancement* (1605), making no changes save verbally in the second. Method according to the common logic and also according to Bacon is the term for the way or ways by which knowledge is transmitted. Method, being a term in logic, works in practice in alliance with rhetoric. He also holds that transmitting, delivery, *traditio*, is in a manner part of, and constitutive of knowledge. For knowledge is to be delivered as a thread to be spun upon: 'the life and labour of one man cannot attain etc.': 'it is in knowledges as it is in plants...if you mean to remove it to grow...it is more assured to rest upon roots than slips'. Recipients should be more than presently satisfied, they should be moved to expectant inquiry.

In writing to the Margaret Professor of Divinity at Cambridge University, inviting the professor to translate the recently published first *Advancement* into Latin, he expressed himself in similar terms:

I will open myself what it was which I chiefly sought and propounded to myself in that work; that you may perceive that which I now desire to be pursuant thereupon...I have this opinion, that if I had sought my own commendation, it had been a much fitter course for me to have done as gardeners use to do, by taking their seeds and slips, and rearing them first into plants, and so uttering them in pots, when they are in flower, and in their best state. But for as much as my end was merit of the state of learning to my power, and not glory; and because my purpose was rather to excite other men's wits than to magnify my own; I was desirous to prevent the incertainness of my own life and times, by uttering rather seeds than plants;

And therefore the privateness of the language considered wherein it is written excluding so many readers, ... I must account it a second birth of that work, if it might be translated into Latin.[22]

Bacon declines to describe his mode, rule, way or road as 'method'. Though for him form and content are inseparable, he guards his usage, reserves the term 'method' and applies it only to delivery of knowledge – to *traditio*. For example, in the section on medicine in *Advancement*: 'they be the best physicians, which being learned incline to the traditions of experience, or being empirics incline to the methods of learning'.[23] The final *Advancement* affirms that the best physicians are those who 'being distinguished in practice do not reject the methods and generalities of art'. Terminological exactitude is indispensable. Given the part played by cooperation, and therefore by communication in all the things he undertakes, there are grounds enough why Bacon should have abandoned it. He retains it. He does so because distinctions are needed for embarking into business – in this case, the business of communicating. The spine of the right route and highway is to secure enough particulars and in consequent interchange between thinking and acting to keep close to them. This stays firm and undeviating throughout all undertakings. It remains beyond the level of doubts and experiments. In the business of delivering, in *traditio*, by contrast, this constancy is absent. In *traditio*, delivery, Bacon makes experiments, doing so till the end. He does so in the interests of achieving effectively operative practicality.

In discussing 'method', just as he renders the term 'policy' inclusive on one level of generality and exclusive on another, similarly he makes the term 'method' inclusive on one level and exclusive on another. For example: 'Another diversity of Method, whereof the consequence is great, is the delivery of knowledge in Aphorisms or in Methods... but the writing in aphorisms hath many excellent virtues, whereto the writing in Method doth not approach.'[24] In this passage transition from level to level is unusually abrupt. But it is clear that 'writing in aphorisms' both is and is not method – just as law both is and is not policy. It is also plain that in that writing in aphorisms is not method, Bacon continues to prefer it as his choice for *traditio*, delivery. In that it is method, he continues to experiment. 'I would erect and constitute one general inquiry, which seems to me deficient touching the Wisdom of Tradition.'[25] He erects and constitutes this inquiry by experiment throughout his practice. 'I do allow...of particular Methods of tradition.'[26] This, too, he continues to do up to his death.

At the start in *Maxims of the Law* Bacon has found the major part of his answer, for aphorisms are both right science and best method of delivery. In his maxims – axioms – of the law content and form are more than inseparable, they coincide and are identical. In *Advancement* (1605) aphorisms are extolled and their virtues further elaborated. Elsewhere he argues that some of the ancients had profitably used them.[27] As at the start, so at the end, aphorisms hold their own: the final *Advancement* presents as we know two examples of treatises; the one, on government, is unmistakably aphoristic; the other, on law, is explicitly 'by aphorisms'. However, in the first *Advancement* in addition to commending this procedure, the answer which he has at the start, Bacon announces experiments.

In *Advancement* he recommends treatises in more than one subject – implicitly in 1605, explicitly in 1623. On the topic of 'characters of dispositions' he proposes, as we have seen, 'a full and careful treatise'. In three aspects of divinity he wants treatises. According to memoranda for 1608 he is preparing a treatise on the greatness of Britain. According to *A Proposition* &c 1617: '*For the Treatise De Regulis juris*, I hold it of all other things the most important to the health, as I may term it, and good institutions of any laws:...it must be made useful...by discourse and deducement in a just tractate. In this I have travelled myself...and will go on with it...'[28] But treatises (so entitled), by contrast with essays (so entitled) – witness the collection of these latter which appeared in 1612, entitled *The Essays of Sir Francis Bacon, Knight, the King's Solicitor General*, are not published in the period between the two *Advancements*. It is true that *Wisdom of the Ancients* (1609) is not described as an essay; but neither does Bacon call it a treatise. The latter form however is not renounced for ever. The treatise method is embarked upon not only as part of the text of the second *Advancement* in the shape of the two examples of summary treatises. It is also employed in the period after the publication of this second version (1623). In the cause of operative practicality Bacon still conducts experiments. He experiments even to the extent that he translates and republishes the first of the two summary treatises presented in the second *Advancement* as an essay in the 1625 collection. On the one hand, then, yet more essays, civil and moral, appear in 1625. On the other hand, *Considerations Touching a War with Spain*, completed after 1623, is indubitably a treatise. It is described in the text as a 'little extract of a treatise'.[29] While still an 'essay' in intent and content – a trial, an attempt – it differs vastly from an essay not only in bulk but in structure.

Considerations Touching a War with Spain is not writing in aphorisms. Instead, it is the marshalling of arguments. It springs from the same source as the essays and other papers, speeches and notes. It is based, as he tells readers, in 'long – continued experience in business of estate, and much conversation in books of policy and history'.[30] Also, like the rest of the author's pieces it is put out with a progressive intent: it is to be considered and carried forward by others: 'all that I shall say in this whole argument will be but like bottoms of thread close wound up, which with a good needle (perhaps) may be flourished into large works'.[31]

Considerations etc. has been worked up and worked out from earlier and successive bottoms of thread. Varying the metaphor, as Bacon does, citing to Buckingham a Spanish proverb as indicating procedure: 'he that tieth not a knot upon his thread loseth his stitch'.[32] Bottoms of thread, stitches tied into them, date from the reign of the Queen. Spain does things rather 'by treasure and expense than by forces and valour' [1592–3]. Spain will not be feared by a nation 'seated, manned, furnished and policied as is England' [1592–3].[33] 'England is well sited geographically: the people is military: it is provisioned in every needed way: policy has endowed it with a constitution: under this the people are not oppressed'.[34] 'We know to how many states the King of Spain is odious and suspected; and for ourselves we have incensed none by our injuries, nor made any jealous by our ambition. These are in rules of policy the firmest contracts' [1592–3].[35] 'Scotland united, Ireland reduced, the sea provinces of the Low Countries contracted, and shipping maintained is one of the greatest monarchies, in forces truly esteemed, that hath been in the world.'[36] Because they have successfully 'ravished from some wild and unarmed people mines and store of gold',[37] Spain 'does not fulfil prophecy, *Video solem orientem in occidente*'. Why therefore should we, 'seated and manned as we are with the best iron in the world, think of nothing but reckonings, audits, and *meum* and *tuum*': (1606–7).

Considerations had been anticipated in its theme by *A short view to be taken of Great Britain and Spain* [? 1619] and by *Notes of a Speech concerning a War with Spain* [? 1623]. According to the former: 'His

Majesty now of England is of more power than any of his
predecessors.' 'The footing we had in France was rather a greatness
of trouble unto us than of strength.' 'Instead of the departure from
this broken dominion we had in France, his Majesty hath brought
another whole kingdom to England.' The back door (Scotland) for
an enemy (in this case France) is closed. 'The joining of Scotland
hath made us an entire island, which by nature is the best
fortification and the most capable of all the advantages of strength
that can by art be added to nature; whereby we may be able at one
and the same time both to undertake any action abroad and defend
ourselves at home without either much danger or great cost.' We
have amity with the Low Countries. There is little amiss with either
spirits and hearts or with goods and services in our kingdom. If it be
judged that the King of England in comparison with the King of
Spain is poor, the latter 'knows well enough he shall find it otherwise
whensoever he shall undertake to attempt us or we them '. Further,
his (the King of Spain's) 'root will be found a great deal too narrow
for his tops'. In distances his dominions lie far asunder. He can
assault, but not so well defend. 'He hath ambition to the whole
empire of Christendom. These are motives wherein all Christian
princes are interested.'

  'Let us now betwixt his Majesty and the United Provinces
consider how the particular causes of both nations do importune us
both to the undertaking thereof.' Who hath been so thirsty of our
blood as Spain? In the future there is no likelihood of safety. He (the
King of Spain) knows for his part the peril he stands in should we be
the first to move. It is to be expected that he will launch assaults at
any time. Action first on our part not only prevents hurts, it is also
a matter of fitness and honour. These considerations...do seem to
invite his Majesty: 'in every part considerable in the design, we may
find something to persuade us, that seems to be a kind of offer (both
in Religion, Policy, and Nature) proffered unto his Majesty as the
Prince most fittest for entertaining it.'[38]

  Notes for a draft speech about war with Spain had set out that
three conditions are required in such a war, a just quarrel, sufficient
forces and provisions, and a prudent and politic choice of designs
and actions. On the first condition, justice, he does not elaborate in
these notes. He proceeds with the second: 'You do not see in true
discourse of State and War that we ought to doubt to be overmatched.
To this opinion you are led by two things which lead all men; by

Experience and by Reason.' Spain 'is a nation thin sown of men, partly by reason of the sterility of their soil; and partly because their natives are exhausted by so many employments in such vast territories as they possess...there is not in the world again such a spring and seminary of military people as in England, Scotland and Ireland.' The flow to Spain of treasure from the Indies can be cut off at sea.

This war if we go roundly on with supplies and provisions at the first, the war in continuance will find itself...That it is not a little to be considered that the greatness of Spain is not only distracted extremely and therefore of less force; but built upon no very sound foundations; and therefore they can have the less strength by any assured and confident confederates...if every bird has his feather, Spain would be left wonderful naked. But yet there is a greater confederation against them than by means of any of these quarrels or titles; and that is contracted by the fear that almost all nations have of their ambition, whereof men see no end.[39]

Such points and much of the foregoing material are built into, and even taken for granted and not pressed in *Considerations Touching a War with Spain*. With one exception, the defining of a just war, salient points and arguments scarcely vary throughout the preceding pieces and their consummation in *Considerations etc*. For example, he writes in this treatise, Spain is 'no giant and no overmatch for this estate'. The man who thinks so 'takes greatness of kingdoms according to their bulk and currency and not after their intrinsic value'.[40] 'Although therefore I had wholly sequestered my thoughts from civil affairs, yet because it is a new case and concerneth my country infinitely, I obtained of myself to set down...what I thought pertinent to this business.'[41] The case was not new in the relations between states in general: nor was it new in the concerns of English governments in particular. Therefore it was no new case in the thoughts and works of Bacon. He writes to Buckingham: 'somewhat I have been, and much have I read; so that few things which concern states or greatness, are new cases unto me'.[42] But it is a new case now, because it is acutely relevant to present affairs.

The differences between *Considerations etc*. and preceding statements on, or relating to this matter – that is to say, what is new in it – are twofold. First, there is difference in form. Earlier attempts to persuade are translated into a treatise. The piece is delivered according to an order and an unfolding structure. It is not only announced in these terms; it is conducted strictly in accord with the stated programme. The three conditions required for a war, a just quarrel, sufficient forces and provisions, a prudent choice of designs – the three heads are dealt with in turn. Having handled the first, Bacon proceeds to the second: 'to speak in a human and politic sense' – in the preceding section, as will be seen, he has been arguing in the fields of morality, divinity's handmaid –

to speak in a human and politic sense, I am led to think that Spain is no overmatch for England, by that which leadeth all men; that is experience and reason. And with experience I will begin, for there all reason beginneth. Is it fortune (shall we think) that in all actions of war or arms, great and small, which have happened these many years ever since Spain and England have had anything to debate one with the other, the English upon all encounters have perpetually come off with honour and the better? It is not fortune, sure; she is not so constant. There is somewhat in the natures and natural courage of the people, or some such thing.[43]

As in earlier and preceding pieces, not fortune, but this 'or some such thing' is examined.

But before I proceed further, it is good to meet with an objection, which if it be not removed, the conclusion of experience from the time past to the time present will not be sound and perfect. For it will be said that in the former times (whereof we have spoken) Spain was not so mighty as now it is; and England, on the other side, was more aforehand in all matters of power. Therefore let us compare with indifferency these disparities of time, and we shall plainly perceive, that they make for the advantage of England at this present time. And because we will less wander in generalities, we will fix the comparison to precise times; comparing the state of Spain and England in the year '88, with this present year that now runneth. In handling this point, I will not meddle with any personal comparisons of the princes, counsellors and commanders... that were then and that now are in both kingdoms... but only rest upon real points, for the true balancing of the state of the forces and affairs of both times.[44]

Therefore, this being a treatise which is civil history mixed – for even when handling scholastic morality on the topic of just wars, he introduces as will be seen Thucydides and 'time' – Bacon was constrained to insert a section more extended than normal which is plain narrative. 'I will make a brief list of the particulars themselves in an historical truth.'[45] This includes coverage of the sea campaign of '88 in which King Philip II's Invincible Armada was dispersed and defeated.

The second difference between *Considerations Touching etc.* and all work preceding it dealing with England and Spain, is one not of form but of content. *Considerations Touching etc.*, unlike earlier discussions and investigations, examines for interacting theory and practice the notion of justice in a war. The effect of this is a clarification and refinement of roughnesses and crudities in earlier exercises, attempts and drafts. For instance, in his speech arguing for naturalizing the Scots, while it is fair to note that when King Edward I is mentioned he is praised not for 'glorious conquests abroad', but for 'solid strength at home',[46] in other parts of this speech 'counsels of greatness and power'[47] and 'honourable war for enlargement of borders'[48] are recommended. For instance again, in *Example of a Summary Treatise Touching Extension of Empire* (reprinted, as we have noted, as an essay entitled *Of the True Greatness of Kingdoms and Estates* in 1625) Bacon writes: 'Incident to this point is for a state to have those laws or customs which may reach forth unto them just occasions (as may be pretended) of war. For there is that justice imprinted in the nature of men; that they enter not upon wars (whereof so many calamities do ensue) but upon some, at the least specious, grounds and quarrels.'[49] The tone of this passage can be attributed to the fact that he is writing here not in morality but in policy. 'Civil knowledge requireth only an external goodness, for that as to society sufficeth.'[50] Policy is not the same as morality: therefore, since it is distinct, it requires to be studied in its own right. 'civil knowledge, which is commonly ranked as a part of ethic, I have already emancipated and erected into an entire doctrine by itself...'[51] But it does not follow that because it is an entire doctrine by itself, it is therefore separable from morality, existing and applicable in isolation from it. Agreed that civil goodness is external, it is not licensed to be counterfeit. *Considerations Touching etc.* in that part where Bacon writes in morality not in policy, dispels possible and perhaps likely misunderstandings on this point.

In *Considerations Touching etc.* possible and perhaps likely misunderstandings are strained and drained away. What we see is neither change of ground nor of direction, but continuing application of that which leadeth all men, experience and reason. The treatise does not advocate gratuitous wars; nor resort to arms for its own sake; nor hostilities at any price; nor entering upon wars with no more than 'specious grounds and quarrels'. 'I speak not of ambitious predatory wars'.[52] War, when no other arbiter is available, is an appeal to the deity.[53] Therefore, whatever the war, the *casus belli* must be just. Wars cannot be honourable unless they are just. He goes the length of

stating in *Advancement* (1623) when introducing his *Example of a
Summary Treatise Touching the Extension of Empire* that extension is one
of the three political duties.[54] Further, he concludes the piece by
stating: 'no man can, by taking thought (as the Scripture saith) 'add
one cubit to his stature in this little model of a man's body; but in the
great frame of kingdoms and commonwealths it is in the power of
princes or states to add amplitude and greatness to their kingdoms…
But these counsels are commonly not observed, but left to take
their chance'.[55] But neither in war with Spain nor in any other war
should the aim be extension of the bounds of empire for its own sake;
the increase, that is to say, of the amount of ground – together with
people living on it – in which empire – that is to say, government –
is exercised. In the position worked out by Bacon which is the same
as that of Machiavelli he is opposed to this.

It is true that under some conditions extension of bounds can be
right – in circumstances, that is, when it is necessary: the likely
alternative being loss by one state of its territorial base by erosions,
subversions or annexations arranged or conducted by another.
Dealings of English governments with Scotland, and relations of
English governments with Ireland, these precisely constitute cases in
point. Experience, both our own and that of others recorded in civil
histories, tells us that the power and territorial expanse of states rises
and falls. If one is not expanding another will be likely to be doing
so. The same experience tells us that in this process no state has ever
successfully contracted out and achieved immunity. Reason seeks
explanations why this ongoing quasi-mechanical condition of things
never comes to an end; and why no state including the United
Kingdom of Great Britain can expect to escape from or emerge from
it. The conclusion reason reaches is that it is fear which chiefly drives
the mechanism. Fear is the cause of wars and a justified fear is a just
cause of a war. Other motives, ambitious predatory ones are often in
play. Other causes, superhuman ones (Bacon and Machiavelli agree
on this) are in addition always at work. But on the human level fear
is more fundamental than other motives because it operates even
when other motives are not present.

In most circumstances and in general, accumulation of territorial
possessions is a bad reason for going to war. According to *Example of
a Summary Treatise on the Extension of Empire* (reprinted as the essay *of
the True Greatness of Kingdoms and Estates*), 'The Romans, though they
esteemed the. extending the limits of their empire to be great

honour to their generals, when it was done, yet they never rested upon that alone to begin a war.'[56] *Considerations Touching etc.* is dedicated to Charles, Prince of Wales. But it is not suggested in seriousness, despite the treatise's opening flourish – 'It was a Charles that brought the empire first into France – a Charles that brought it first into Spain – why should not Great Britain have its turn? –'[57] that a Charles from England and Scotland should compete for a title which claimed institutional links with Caesars in Roman antiquity.

'I speak not of ambitious predatory wars.'[58] 'I shall make it plain that wars preventive upon just fears are true defensives, as well as upon actual invasions'; and again, that 'wars defensive for religion … are most just …'[59] The first ground of war with Spain is in the nature of a plaint for the recovery of the Palatinate; but the second is 'a just fear of the subversion of our civil estate: a just fear of the subversion of our Church and religion'.[60] It is impossible that a threat to the former should not also be a threat to the latter. At other places he explains that hurt to either is harm to the other. 'So then, the war is not for the Palatinate only, but for England, Scotland, Ireland, our King, our Prince, our Nation, all that we have.'[61] In this two things are to be proved: 'the one, that a just fear (without an actual invasion or offence) is a sufficient ground of a war, and in the nature of a true defensive; The other, that we have towards Spain cause of just fear; I say, just fear … not out of umbrages, light jealousies, apprehensions far off, but out of clear foresight of imminent danger'. Concerning the former proposition, 'it is good to hear what time saith. Thucydides, in his inducement to his history of the great war of Peloponnesus, sets down in plain terms that the true cause of that war was the overgrowing greatness of the Athenians, and the fear that the Lacedaemonians stood in thereby; and doth not doubt to call it a necessity imposed upon the Lacedaemonians of a war; which are the very words of a mere defensive; adding, that the other causes were but specious and popular.'[62]

Bacon quotes from an English version of Lorenzo Valla's Latin translation of Thucydides – as yet the translation made by Thomas Hobbes did not exist: 'the truest cause of this war, though least voiced, I conceive to have been thus; that the Athenians, being grown great, to the terror of the Lacedaemonians, did impose upon them a necessity of a war: but the causes that went abroad in speech were etc. etc.'[63] He also quotes other sources on preventive war : also the wars of Christendom against the Ottoman Turks. Dcmosthenes, he recalls, 'exposeth to scorn wars which are not preventive'.[64] Clinias, the Caudian (in Plato in his *Laws*)

speaks desperately and wildly as if there was no such thing as peace between nations; but that every nation expects but his advantage to war upon another. But yet in that excess of speech there is thus much that may have a civil construction; namely that every state ought to stand upon his guard, and rather prevent than be prevented. His words are *quam rem fere vocant pacem, nudum et inane nomen est*; *re vera autem omnibus adversus omnes civitates bellum sempiternum perdurat...*

This it is true, is the objection and not the proposition, and it is refuted; 'but yet (as I said before) it bears that much of truth, that if general malignity and predisposition to war (which he untruly figureth to be in all nations) be produced and extended to a just fear of being oppressed, then it is no more a true peace, but a name of a peace.'[65]

Bacon refers to the Athenian Iphicrates as recorded by Thucydides in his history:

as for his opinion...it demands not so much towards a war as a just fear, but rather cometh near the opinion of Clinias; as if there were ever among nations a brooding of a war, and that there is no sure league but impuissance to do hurt. For he, in the treaty of peace with the Lacedaemonians, speaketh plain language; telling them there could be no true and secure peace, except the Lacedaemonians yielded to those things, which being granted, it would be no longer in their power to hurt the Athenians, though they would. And to say truth, if one mark it well, this was in all memory the main piece of wisdom in strong and prudent counsels, to be in perpetual watch that the states about them should neither by approach nor by increase of dominion, nor by ruining confederates, nor by blocking of trade, nor by any the like means, have it in their power to hurt or annoy the states they serve: and whensoever any such cause did but appear, straightways to buy it out with a war, and never to take up peace at credit and upon interest.[66]

He recalls the balancing of powers reportedly attempted by Henry VIII of England, Francis I of France and Charles V of Spain and the Empire:

And the like diligence was used in the age before by that league (wherewith Guicciardine beginneth his story, and maketh it, as it were, the calendar of the good days of Italy), which was contracted between Ferdinando King of Naples, Lorenzo of Medici Potentate of Florence, and Ludovico Sforza

Duke of Milan, designed chiefly against the growing power of the Venetians; but yet so, as the confederates had a perpetual eye one upon another, that none of them should overtop.

To conclude, therefore;...howsoever some schoolmen, (otherwise reverend men, but better with penknives than with swords), seem precisely to stand upon it, that every offensive war must be *ultio*; a revenge, that presupposeth a precedent injury or assault; yet neither do they descend to this point (which we now handle) of a just fear; neither are they of authority to judge this question against all the precedents of time. For certainly, as long as men are men (the sons, as the poets allude, of Prometheus and not of Epimetheus) and as long as reason is reason, a just fear will be a just cause of a preventive war; but especially if it be part of the case that there be a nation which is manifestly detected to aspire to monarchy [that is to say, a monarchy which is universal in scope] and new acquests, then other states (assuredly) cannot be justly accused for not staying for the first blow, or for not accepting Polyphemus's courtesy, to be the last that shall be eaten up.[67]

Bacon reverts to Clinias the Caudian whom he has cited before and proceeds to cite again:

even in the *tenet* of that person that beareth the resolving part and not the objecting part, a just fear is justified for a cause of an invasive war, though the same fear proceed not from the fault of the foreign state to be assailed. For it is there insinuated, that if a state, out of the distemper of their own body, do fear sedition and intestine troubles to break out amongst themselves, they may discharge their own ill humours upon a foreign war for a cure.

This, Bacon recalls, was the advice given by Admiral Jasper Coligny to King Charles IX of France; namely, to make war in Flanders to help extinguish civil war in France. This counsel, Bacon recalls, was not prosperous. Nor will he embrace or countenance counsels of this kind: 'For I will never set politics against ethics; especially for that true ethics are but as a handmaid to divinity and religion.'

Surely St Thomas (who had the largest heart of the school divines) bendeth chiefly his style against the depraved passions which reign in making wars, speaking out of St Augustine: *nocendi cupiditas, ulciscendi crudelitas, implacatus et implacabilis animus, feritas rebellandi, libido dominandi, et si quae sunt similia, haec sunt quae in belli iure culpantur.* And the same St Thomas in his own text, defining of the just causes of a war doth leave it upon very general terms: *requiritur ad bellum causa justa, ut scilicet illi, qui impugnantur, propter aliquam culpam impugnationem mereantur*: for *impugnation culpae* is a far more general word than *ultio injuriae*. And thus much for the first proposition of the second ground of a war with Spain; namely, that a just fear is a just cause of a war; and that a preventive war is a true defensive.[68]

He had embarked, he explained, into matters of divinity's handmaid, morality in seeking to elucidate the grounds of justice in making war. But for Bacon as for Machiavelli the spheres of religion and those of matters of state were not sharply separable. A state's public religion is part of its policy. Since religion is 'the chief band of human society', a state's public religion is the preponderant part of its policy. It is the indispensable basis for the state's unity and coherence. Since this is so conformity with a state's public religion is enforced by the laws.

When Queen Elizabeth 'did whet the laws against' the papists in England 'reason of state' was added to and imposed itself upon 'matter of conscience and religion'.[69]

Only this is true; that the fear of the subversion of our religion from Spain is the more just, for that all other Catholic princes and states content and contain themselves to maintain their religion within their own dominions, and meddle not with the subjects of other states; whereas the practice of Spain hath been,...to intermeddle with foreign states, and to declare themselves protectors general of the party of catholics through the world. As if the Crown of Spain had a little of this, that they would plant the Pope's law by arms, as the Ottomans do the law of Mahomet.[70]

In doing so, Bacon contended, Spain, together with the Ottomans, wrongly differed not only from other states in his own times but from all states ancient and modern. These controlled their religions as part of their policy, not meddling with the religion of subjects or citizens of other states.

It was this practice on the part of the Crown of Spain and not the 'Pope's law' as such which was his chief ground of objection both in this argument and also elsewhere. No doubt 'the Pope's law' sheltered superstitions, aiding and abetting them. Bacon defines these in *Of Superstition*, both in the 1612 version and also in that of 1625.[71] But he also said, despite his own avowed protestantism, that the religion of protestants was no less capable of harbouring and cultivating superstitions both in doctrine and in public cult. In addition to containing essentials and also matters indifferent which latter were harmless, religions known to and referred to by Bacon throughout times and places – that of the ancient Grecians as revealed in their poetry; that of the ancient Romans containing not only superstitions but valid teachings as we have seen about providence; that of the ancient Hebrews; that of the Ottomans; and also the religions of modern papists and protestants – all these displayed as he described them tenets and practices both good and bad, indispensable truths but also harmful falsehoods, these elements being intermingled. Protestants, he pointed out, had invented a superstition 'in avoiding superstition, when men think to do best if they go furthest from the superstition formerly received. Therefore care would be had that (as it fareth in ill purgings) the good be not taken away with the bad.'[72] Bacon added this statement in 1625 to the 1612 essay *Of Superstition* in which (as we have seen) he also described the superstitions of popery. But in *An Advertisement Touching the Controversies of the Church of England* (1589) he had made the same point, this time concerning protestants in England: 'it is a consideration of much greater wisdom and sobriety to be well advised, whether in the general demolition of the institutions of the Church of Rome there were not (as men's actions are imperfect) some good purged with the bad'.[73]

Bacon nowhere states that the sacred canon of Scripture constitutes in itself the true religion. Instead he treats it as if it were a history – a history of the deeds and words of men – but also of the deeds and words of divine providence. On the other hand in *Advancement* (both versions) he identifies or intimately interrelates inspired divinity – theology – with this sacred canon. Moreover, its contents are for him – so he presents the matter – without error and acceptable as in no way fallible. Beside the sacred canon – in addition to it – as he explains as *Advancement* approaches its conclusion (each version complementing the other), he desiderates the undertaking of three works: 'Introduction only is made to three Deficients; namely the Doctrine concerning the legitimate Use of the Human Reason in Divine Subjects; the Doctrine concerning the Degrees of unity in the Kingdom of God; and the Emanations of the Scriptures.'[74] The subject of the first treatise he here proposes is self-evident. The second treatise would explain what elements in the Christian religion are essential and what are matters indifferent. The third treatise would amount to a book of aphorisms collected out of the sacred canon stating religion's ever-changeless but ever-freshly flowing truths. 'For he that will reduce a knowledge into an art, will make it round and uniform: but in divinity many things must be left abrupt...'[75] 'What we want is a concise, sound, and judicious collection of annotations and observations on particular texts of Scripture; neither dilated into common places, nor chasing after controversies, nor reduced into method of art, but entirely unconnected and natural.'[76] Needless to say, none of the results of the three proposed works, should these be undertaken, would make changes in the public doctrine and cult unless lawful authority decided to introduce them.

This item, endorsement by Bacon of public doctrine and cult of a religious nature, this latter maintained by the laws, seems to render his civil policy out of date, binding and limiting it to the context of his times. But, despite appearances in the West in the late twentieth century, time – the course of civil history (whether the truth concerning it be that it is circular or that it is linear) – has not conclusively demonstrated that states can dispense for ever with public doctrine and cult of a religious nature, this latter attended in some measure by compulsion. Before Queen Elizabeth 'did whet the laws' against the papists – that is to say, before 'reason of state' in extreme circumstances (such circumstances being capable of occurring not only between states but also inside them) was added to and imposed itself upon 'matter of conscience and religion' – Bacon writes approvingly of her conduct. In his *In Felicem Memoriam Elizabethae*, On the Fortunate Memory of Elizabeth, Queen of England, he writes that she was amongst rulers who, besides the divine favour, were also 'in some measure by their own virtue the makers of fortune for themselves'.[77] 'Her intention undoubtedly was, on the one hand not to force consciences, but on the other not to let the state…be brought in danger. Upon this ground she concluded at the first that, the free allowance and toleration by public authority of two religions would be certain destruction.'[78] These two elements should remain in balance. It was because she concluded upon the second, that the first acquired a weight not less great.

In the first *Advancement* he writes: 'The matter informed by divinity is of two kinds; matter of belief and truth of opinion, and matter of service and adoration; which is also judged and directed by the former: the one being as the internal soul of religion, and the other as the external body thereof.'[79] Bacon allows, as we see, that reason – and clearly also experience – have their due place in the conduct of policy regarding religion of the state. Recommendation under the heads of reason and experience includes distinguishing between fundamentals and things indifferent. But also such recommendation includes distinguishing between public treatment on the one hand of the 'internal soul of religion' and on the other hand public treatment of religion's 'external body'. Only the latter, the outer, that is men's words and deeds, not the inner, that is men's thoughts and beliefs, should be subject to scrutiny and control. Total penetration from the outside into the inside of men's minds and souls is impossible and attempts by public authority at such inquisition and control should be foregone. He writes, it is true, that the outer side of religion is 'judged and directed' by the inner side of it. But as we have already seen, though in more general terms, he also recognizes an opposite process. Conformity enforced upon men and accepted by them in their deeds and words, their outer side, helps to promote rectitude of belief and truth of opinion in their inner side.

CHAPTER 9

Morality and policy IV

Considerations Touching a War with Spain consists of close study of experience and of applying reason to it. The argument concerning justice combines, on the one hand, time, which is civil history; and, on the other, scholastic morality. In *Advancement* (both versions) Bacon had proposed that little was amiss in the school divines except that they lacked, and needed to study history both of nature and of time, that is to say, adequate *data*: 'Notwithstanding certain it is that if...to their great thirst of truth and unwearied travail of wit'[1] they 'had joined variety and universality of reading and contemplation, they had proved excellent lights, to the great advancement of all learning and knowledge'.[2] The civil history – the 'time' – Bacon adduces is largely that of Thucydides – the first in Bacon's civil secular canon – but that of Guicciardini – a modern and one of Bacon's wiser sort – is not neglected – these, when added to school morality in the argument of St Thomas Aquinas – 'who had the largest heart of the school divines' – have enabled him to accomplish and present an answer to the question of justice or injustice in war.

The argument is summarized in *Of Empire*. This essay, which appeared in 1612, was republished in 1625 with numerous additions. Among the latter we find:

First for their neighbours; there can no general rule be given (the occasions are so variable), save one, which ever holdeth; which is, that princes do keep due sentinel that none of their neighbours do overgrow so...as they become more able to annoy them than they were...During that triumvirate of kings, King Henry the Eighth of England, Francis the First King of France, and Charles the Fifth, Emperor, there was such a watch kept, that none of the three could win a palm of ground but the other two would straightways balance it, either by confederation, or if need were, by a war;

and would not in any wise take up peace at interest. And the like was done by that league (which Guicciardine saith was the security of Italy) made between Ferdinando King of Naples, Lorenzius Medices, and Ludovicus Sforza, potentates, the one of Florence, the other of Milan. Neither is the opinion of some of the schoolmen to be received, *that a war cannot justly be made but upon a precedent injury or provocation.* For there is no question but a just fear of an imminent danger, though there be no blow given, is a lawful cause of a war.[3]

Thus Bacon's argument, with some of the needed data, was put into print and instructed an audience before the publication of *Considerations etc.*

The latter treatise is an exercise in 'exact and precise knowledge' arising from and resulting in caution. This caution is combined with audacity and with taking 'courage to despise vain apprehensions' both in the achievement of the knowledge and also in its application – and hence in its progression – in use and action as directed to a specified objective. The procedure is the same, whether the objective Bacon addresses be that of handling and perhaps altering 'characters of dispositions' in individuals, or that of grappling with and perhaps expelling idols of the mind in individuals, or that of dealing with and perhaps managing parliaments in England, or that of challenging and perhaps successfully disposing of the menace of the King of Spain. Early in the present century Ernst Troeltsch, speaking of Bacon and Hobbes, said that the former compared with the latter was 'cautious and hesitating'.[4] This judgment obscures due recognition that in Bacon's case caution was on a par with, and matched by audacity.

'Things', he writes in *Of Counsel* (1612 and 1625), 'will have their first or second agitation; if they be not tossed upon the arguments of counsel, they will be tossed upon the waves of fortune, and be full of inconstancy, doing and undoing, like the reeling of a drunken man.'[5] 'Above all things', he writes in *Of Dispatch* (1612 and 1625), 'order and distribution, and singling out of parts, is the life of dispatch; so as the distribution be not too subtile: for he that doth not divide' – that is to say, the man who does not perceive or make distinctions as an aspect of exercising his caution – 'will never enter well into business; and he that divideth too much will never come out of it clearly'.[6] '...and generally', he writes in *Of Delays* (1625), 'it is good to commit the beginnings of all great actions to Argus with his hundred eyes, and the ends to Briareus with his hundred hands; first to watch and then to speed.'[7] 'This is well to be weighed', he writes in *Of Boldness* (1625), 'that boldness is ever blind; for it seeth not dangers and inconveniences. Therefore it is ill in counsel, good in execution... For in counsel it is good to see dangers, and in execution not to see them except they be very great'.[8]

In the matter of the Spanish Kingdom the purpose, the specific objective, is that of victory over that power and containment of it... and of planting in Britain as a consequence a monarchy in the West, this being progress in grand strategy. Early in 1624 Bacon wrote notes for advice to be given to Buckingham: 'Nay and the King will put a hook in the nostrils of Spain, and lay a foundation of greatness here to his children in these west parts.'[9] 'I am persuaded the hinge of the K. affairs, for his safety and greatness, is now in Spain.'[10] *Considerations Touching etc.* as we have said was published after Bacon's death. But it had been written for the King and for his successors. It had been written also for a parliament and for a parliament's successors. Explaining the course which was needed, invited, certainly difficult, but not impossible to complete successfully, the treatise presented the urgent business of state which would bind monarchs and parliaments together. As a piece of civil science it had been written also for the world in general.

In his projects for amendment of laws and in constructing maxims of law – enterprises which he described as 'for his particular' – Bacon was entirely on his own. He announced on the topic of law maxims: 'I have seen little in this kind, either in our law or other laws, that satisfieth me.'[11] On the other hand and by contrast, in government, that part of policy which in statement and also in action be preferred – and in the aspect of his grand strategy which as he claimed was 'the fairest', he travelled almost entirely in the company and with the aid of another. In most aspects of the 'fairest' part of the grand strategy he proceeds in agreement with Machiavelli: sometimes quoting him by name, and, if not, revealing concurrence with Machiavelli's positions. In short not only does Bacon approve and follow this Florentine's procedure in mixed history, he in addition adopts many of his findings. His many points of agreement with Machiavelli will be recounted according to the order in which they have emerged in the course of foregoing pages dealing with morality and policy and with Bacon's engagements in seeking to improve these.

But some of the cases of Bacon's adherence to Machiavelli,

whether or not explicit, have not been made as fully plain in this present argument as they could have been. The former's rendering of the Fable of *Styx* in which he follows Machiavelli's teaching that conduct of policy should be in accord with recognized necessities has been mentioned. But – also in *De Sapientia Veterum* – Bacon when interpreting *Scylla and Charibdis* stated : 'Moderation, or the Middle Way, is...in Politics only, questionable and to be used with caution and judgment.'[12] This too is Machiavelli's teaching – see *Discourses*.[13] For example again, Bacon wrote '...rigour of proceeding...tendeth not to strengthen authority, which is best supported by love and fear intermixt...'[14] This is a possible rendering of the argument in *Discourse*[15] It will be recalled that Bacon had written that 'these predominant affections of fear and hope suppress and bridle all the rest'[16] and that this is 'of special use in moral and civil matters'. For it is upon such a base that civil governments dispensing rewards and punishments are erected and conduct themselves.On the other hand, on a related but different point Bacon writes in *Of Empire* (1612 and 1625) : 'Certain it is, that nothing destroyeth authority so much as the unequal and untimely interchange of power pressed too far, and relaxed too much.' This again is Machiavelli – see *Discourses* (41.2).[17]

Next, on Bacon's point that good policy can help in making good men, Machiavelli in *Discourses*[18] observed that conduct in Rome seemed in general to improve under the rule of 'good' emperors; and he noted that subjects or citizens often followed examples set by their rulers. Machiavelli, like Bacon, insisted that every state should vigilantly watch the doings of its neighbours and that all states should always be ready for war.[19] Machiavelli like Bacon warned that societies in years of long peace could degenerate. He wrote (see *Discourses* I. Ch. 6.9): '...should heaven,...be so kind that' a state 'has no need to go to war, it will then come about that idleness will either render it effeminate or give rise to factions; and these two things, either in conjunction or separately, will bring about its downfall.'[20] In the interests of a state's internal peace in religious matters and therefore in all kinds of matters Bacon advocated the discovery and establishment of a difference between fundamentals of faith and doctrines inessential or indifferent. Machiavelli like Bacon allotted prime place in policy to the maintaining of religion:[21] Machiavelli recommended that in religion rulers should be careful to display attachment to *il fondamenti*.[22] Therefore, as regards religion at least, he adumbrated Bacon's distinction between policy – the outward man – and morality – the inner man. Bacon's advocacy of the distinction between religious fundamentals and inessentials was first made in *An Advertisement Touching the Controversies of the Church of England* (1589). In *An Advertisement etc.* Bacon in addition made this following point:

> Now concerning the occasion of controversies, it cannot be denied but that the imperfections in the conversation and government of those which have chief place in the church have ever been principal causes and motives of schisms and divisions... And therefore it is truly noted by one that writeth as a natural man, that the hypocrisy of friars did for a great time maintain and bear out the irreligion of bishops and prelates.[23]

'The one that writeth as a natural man' is Machiavelli. The latter wrote in *Discorsi III* (I.vii): 'As to religious institutions one sees here again how necessary these renovations are from the example of our own religion, which, if it had not been restored to the starting-point by St Francis and St Dominic would have become quite extinct.'[24]

Like Bacon's, Machiavelli's axioms applied indifferently in both kingdoms and estates, though Machiavelli referred to these as kingdoms or principalities and republics. Bacon quoted Machiavelli to King James on the good laws made by early kings of Rome in antiquity, laws which had contributed to the 'wonderful growth of that state in after times'.[25] Bacon quoted to King James Machiavelli's remarks on the enlightened naturalization policy of the ancient Romans.[26] In February 1607 he quoted Machiavelli in the House of Commons, explaining that iron was stronger than gold and that men not monies were the sinews of war.[27] We have already seen that early as 1605 in the text of the first *Advancement* he had cited this contention out of Machiavelli.[28]

Restore institutions to their origins – to their original principles. Machiavelli warned that in monarchies, in republics and in religions constant attention should be devoted to this need for restoration to origins. Bacon no less than Machiavelli preached this. Bacon did so in regard even to a subsidiary institution like the Court of Wards. This latter should be handled 'not by way of novelty, but by way of reformation, and reduction of things to their ancient and true institution'.[29] But he tried to apply this same precept in regard as we have seen to another and less subsidiary institution, namely to Parliament itself – at this point it being recalled that in their constitution parliaments included the monarch.

Machiavelli wrote:

I am concerned with composite bodies, such as are states and religious institutions, and in their regard I affirm that those changes make for their conservation which lead them back to their start... For at the start religious institutions, republics and kingdoms, have in all cases some good in them, to which their early reputation and progress is due. But since in process of time this goodness is corrupted, such a body must of necessity die unless something happens which brings it up to the mark... It is... essential that men who live together under any constitution should frequently have their attention called to it either by some external or some internal occurrence. When internal, such occurrences are usually due to some law which from time to time causes the members of this body to review their position; or again to some good man who arises in their midst and by his example and his virtuous deeds produces the same effect as does the constitution.[30]

Bacon's grand strategy can justly be recognized as the attempt to bring the political state in England back to its origins, restoring it to its original principles. A series of statements which he makes about parliaments indicates the decisive part which they together with the monarch must according to him be expected to play: parliaments are the means for the supply of the King's estate and for the better knitting of the hearts of his subjects to him:[31] 'the matter of Parliament is a great problem of estate'.[32] Assembling a parliament is 'the greatest cause, or as I may term it the cause of causes, as things now stand'.[33] 'I have some interest in the gentlemen of England, and shall be able to do some effect in rectifying that body of parliament men which is *cardo rerum*:[34] 'I was ever for a parliament which seemeth to me to be *cardo rerum* or *summa summarum* for the present occasions':[35] matters 'should be weighed by the beam of the kingdom'.[36] Machiavelli had pointed to two ways by which renovations could be brought about – internally by some good man and his example, or externally by the intervention of events compelling renovation to be undertaken. Bacon's strategy combined the two. In accord with his counsel parliaments would be bound to government by the sharing by them in some great matter of estate put to them by the monarch. Thereafter the course of events and the pressures induced would compel the combination to proceed as it had begun.

Next, we can note, in a surviving fragment of the treatise *Of the True Greatness of Britain* Bacon mentioned (this point as yet has not been cited in this present text) the successful invasion of Italy in 1494 by the King of France, Charles VIII. In referring to this event he went so far as to point out that here, for Machiavelli, was yet another example which the man might have used – but neglected – for illustrating his contention that iron was stronger than gold and that men not monies were the sinews of war. 'Neither is the authority of Machiavel to be despised, specially in a matter whereof he saw the evident experience before his eyes in his own times and country.' For had he not seen 'a needy and ill-provided army of the French ... make a passage only by the reputation of their swords by their sides undrawn, through the whole length of Italy (at that time abounding in wealth after a long peace), and that without resistance, and to seize and leave what countries and places it pleased them?'[37] Another instance, more striking but from antiquity, namely the defeat by Rome of the trading empire of Carthage, was missed by Machiavelli. This time Bacon missed it too. Another point urged by the former, Bacon being in expressed agreement, was that in the matter of the extent of their territories states needed to possess roots and trunks massive enough to bear the weight of branches.[38] The kingdom of Spain, Bacon argued, was a state whose branches were too heavy for the trunk. Fear between states is the most fundamental of all causes of war. This in *Discorsi* would appear to have been Machiavelli's final position. It was also Bacon's. But whereas for Bacon justified fear is a just cause for war, in Machiavelli's case justice has no part to play save in so far as justice is implied in *salus populi suprema lex*.[39]

If *Discorsi*, Book II (19, 2, 3) is consulted it will be amply evident that, except in recommending that governments should 'keep individuals poor', the 'fairest' part of the grand strategy is already sufficiently suggested in Machiavelli's instructions:

And since what history teaches about infantry is thus seen to be true, in the same way one should give credit to, and profit by, all other ancient practices. Were this done, republics and princes would make fewer mistakes, would be stronger in repelling an attack which should catch them unawares, and would not set their hopes on flight. Those who have to handle a body politic would know better how to direct its policy, whether with a view to its expanding or to holding its own: would realise that the right way to make a republic great and for it to acquire an empire is to increase the number of its inhabitants, to make other states its allies, not its subjects, to send out colonies for the security of conquered territory, to fund the spoils of war, to subdue the enemy by raids and battles, not by sieges, to enrich the public but to keep individuals poor, to attend with the utmost care to military training. And, should this method of providing for expansion not meet with their approval, they should reflect that acquisitions made in any other way spell ruin to a republic and so should bridle all ambition, provide well for the internal administration of their city-state by means of laws and customs, forbid it to make acquisitions, and look only to its defence, for which good preparation should be made...Nonetheless, as I have said elsewhere, when discussing the difference between constituting a state with a view to expansion and with a view to its maintaining the *status quo*, it is impossible for a state to remain for ever in the peaceful enjoyment of its liberties and its narrow confines; for, though it may not molest other states, it will be molested by them and, when thus molested, there will arise in it the desire, and the need, for conquest.

But the singular closeness between the grand strategy of Bacon and the conclusions of Machiavelli is further manifested because Bacon at a place which happens to be critical absorbs Machiavelli's positions without acknowledgment, putting them out as his own achievements. The conclusion of the second *Advancement*, like that of the first, consists as we have seen of indispensable statements and proposals concerning divinity and the sacred canon of scripture. But we have seen also that not only does the second *Advancement* duly omit a statement made in the first, to the effect that, as for the world of nature, studies in *Know Thyself* require the building of a speculative/theoretic part before men can proceed to an operative/ practical part. In addition we have seen that as the second version approaches its terminus, this time the second version again differing from the first, two operative/practical pieces in *Know Thyself* are presented – *Example of a Summary Treatise on the Extension of Empire* and *Example of a Summary Treatise on Universal Justice or the Fountains of Equity, by Aphorisms*. The first of these, like the second, is introduced as science. But unlike the first, the second does not present middle axioms. It is therefore the first, consisting of middle axioms, which is the more relevant here. Nothing like this first of the two trial treatises, Bacon announces, has been done before. It is executed according to a mode of procedure which he, Bacon, puts forward as new, correct and his own. No mention of Machiavelli's name is made in this trial treatise – also published as said two years later in the last essay collection under another title. There is not even a mention in the form of an allusion to 'one that writeth as a natural man' – indicating presumably that Machiavelli, though discussing church matters, was not a divine – or an allusion to 'a discourser of Italy'. But, given that some of the *data* is different for the reason that Bacon wrote in later times and did so in England, there is no axiom

presented in the contents which is not already explicitly available –
or sufficiently implied – in Machiavelli's *Discourses*.

'There is not any thing amongst civil affairs more subject to error',
Bacon writes, 'than the right valuation and true judgment
concerning the power and forces of an estate.'[40] Right valuation and
true judgment reject territorial size, material wealth and even
multitudinous armies as providing keys to a state's effective power
and to reliability in its forces. Machiavelli, too, dismisses these
features of a state's power as constituting decisive assets – see
Discourse II (10 and 19). Nevertheless the trunk must be great enough
to bear the branches, else territorial acquisitions and possessions will
constitute not strength but liability and weakness.[41] This point is
made twice in *Discourse* II (3, 30). States 'liberal of naturalisation
towards strangers are fit for empire'. On this both Bacon and
Machiavelli cite the policies of Rome in antiquity. Not only is liber-
ality in naturalization recommended but also acceptance of inflowing
populations. But the resulting amalgamated populace must be 'free'
– that is to say, it must not be oppressed by excess of taxes or other
grievous burdens. Compare *Discourse* II (2, 10). This people must
constitute 'a race of military men';[42] and be trained for war in
peacetime. Compare *Discourse* III (31). Neither mercenaries (*Discourse*
I (21, 32)), *Discourse* II (20); nor fortresses (*Discourse* II (24)); nor
artillery (*Discourse* II (17)) can be depended upon. Infantry must be
the dominant arm in battle; also, infantrymen must be native to the
state where they live (*Discourse* II (17, 18)).[43] 'No body can be
healthful without exercise, neither natural body nor politic; and
certainly to a kingdom or estate a just and honourable war is the true
exercise.' '…in a slothful peace both courages will effeminate and
manners corrupt'.[44] Compare *Discourse* I (6) and *Discourse* II (25).
'…there is that justice imprinted in the nature of men, that they
enter not upon wars (whereof so many calamities do ensue) but upon
some, at least specious, grounds and quarrels'.[45] Compare *Discourse* II
(9).

As said there is a difference in the *data*. Bacon uses Machiavelli's.
He also uses more.

Let states that aim at greatness take heed how their nobility and gentlemen
do multiply too fast. For that maketh the common subject grow to be a
peasant and base swain, driven out of heart, … and you will bring it to that,
that not the hundred poll will be fit for an helmet: especially as to the
infantry, which is the nerve of an army … This which I speak of hath been

nowhere better seen than by comparing of England and France; whereof England, though far less in territory and population, hath been (nevertheless) an over match...And herein the device of king Henry the Seventh...was profound and admirable, in making farms and houses of husbandry of a standard, that is, maintained with such a proportion of land unto them, as may breed a subject to live in convenient plenty, and no servile condition...[46]

But England is not neglected by Machiavelli. According to *Discourse* I (21): 'It is indeed the truest of truths that if, where there are men, there are not soldiers, it is their ruler's fault, not the fault of the situation or of nature. Of this there is quite a recent instance...a short time ago the king of England attacked the kingdom of France and took with him none but his own people as troops...this was due to the king's being a prudent man and to his kingdom being in good order, for in times in peace it had not dropped the institutions associated with war.'[47] The King of England is Henry VIII and the date is 1513.

It could be objected that there is an exception to the complete convergence between the trial treatise and *Discorsi* in the items they cover and the axioms they display, the exception being Bacon's discussion of the import of sea power and navies. But though Machiavelli wrote *Discourses* on the first decade of Livy's history of Rome, not on the eight books of Thucydides' history of the Peloponnesian War, Machiavelli uses and cites Thucydides as Bacon does. The story of the defeat of Athens by Sparta (Lacedaemon) is adduced amongst Machiavelli's examples in support of the axiom that men not money are the sinews of war:

gold is not the sinews of war, but good soldiers are. Gold is necessary, but is of secondary importance, and good soldiers can get it for themselves; for it is as impossible for good soldiers to fail to find gold as it is for gold to find good soldiers. That in this we are speaking the truth history shows again and again, in spite of the fact that Pericles advised the Athenians to wage war with the whole of the Peloponnese on the ground that their industry and their pecuniary resources should enable them to win it.[48]

Thucydides reports that Pericles urged that Athenian sea power provided an additional advantage. Machiavelli does not allude to this; but the point is of secondary import compared with the one which he is making. He continued: 'And though during the war the Athenians sometimes prospered, in the end they lost, so that Sparta's wisdom and good soldiery was worth more than Athens' industry and money.'[49]

Recognizing the undeniable, namely that Bacon plentifully relied upon and repeated Machiavelli's positions, it is no less evident that Bacon parted company with him in two notable respects. There were two areas in which he differed decidedly from him. Most of Machiavelli's axioms are middle axioms, for the reason that he offered specific and practical answers to specific and practical questions. But when he ascends to high generalities Bacon is less ready to follow. In *Discourse* I (2) Machiavelli recommends the mixed state as the best form of government: 'I maintain then, that all the forms of government mentioned above are far from satisfactory.' Machiavelli had mentioned principality (monarchy), aristocracy and democracy, together with their corrupt forms, tyranny, oligarchy, and anarchy. 'Hence prudent legislators, aware of their defects, refrained from adopting as such any one of these forms, and chose instead one that shared in them all...' 'In Rome the blending of monarchy, aristocracy, democracy made a perfect commonwealth...' But though he reminded himself in his 1608 jottings that he should consult books on 'monarchy mixed or aristocracy', Bacon in the House of Commons in 1610 rejected the mixed state for England as a monster inviting 'confusion and dissolution'. Again, in *Discourse* I (3) Machiavelli asserts that

in constituting and legislating for a commonwealth it must needs be taken for granted that all men are wicked and that they will always give vent to the malignity that is in their minds when opportunity offers. That their evil dispositions often do not show themselves for a time is due to a hidden cause which those fail to perceive who have had no experience of such contrariness; but in time – which is said to be the father of all truth – it reveals itself.

Bacon nowhere expressed himself in such terms. He wrote in the essay of *Goodness and Goodness of Nature* (1612, 1625): 'The inclination to goodness is imprinted deeply in the nature of man...'[50] 'Neither is there only a habit of goodness directed by right reason; but there is in some men, even in nature, a disposition towards it; as, on the other side there is a natural malignity...'[51] Resorting to civil history and to experience, Bacon reported that as far as the inner man could be judged by observing the outer, characters of dispositions were various. Some were indeed bad. But others in differing ways and degrees were good.

A second area in which Bacon parts company with Machiavelli is when the latter recommends that policy, whether in negotiation or in government, should ignore morality. Recommending – and doing so in terms of high generality – differs from admitting as Bacon did that in particular extreme cases policy will regretfully differ from and abandon morality. According to both *Advancements*:

But it must be remembered all this while, that the precepts which we have set down are of that kind which may be counted and called *bonae artes*. As for evil arts, if a man would set down for himself that principle of Machiavel, *that a man seek not to attain virtue itself, but the appearance only thereof; because the credit of virtue is a help, but the use of it is cumber*: or that other of his principles, *That he presuppose, that men are not fitly to be wrought otherwise but by fear; and therefore that he seek to have every man obnoxious, low, and in strait*, which the Italians call *seminar spine*, to sow thorns:... and the like evil and corrupt positions, whereof (as in all things) there are more in number than of good; certainly with these dispensations from the laws of charity and integrity, the pressing of a man's fortune may be more hasty and compendious. But it is in life as it is in ways, the shortest way is commonly the foulest, and surely the fairer way is not much about.[52]

At another place in *Advancement* – both versions – Bacon cited a further and similar 'evil and corrupt position' proposed by Machiavelli: 'So in the fable that Achilles was brought up under Chiron the Centaur, who was part a man and part a beast, expounded ingeniously but corruptly by Machiavel, that it belongeth to the education and discipline of princes to know as well how to play the part of the lion in violence and the fox in guile, as of the man in virtue and justice.'[53] To these instances, though he does not mention Machiavelli in the passage, should be added what Bacon writes of in *Of Truth* (1625):

To pass from theological and philosophical truth to the truth of civil business; it will be acknowledged, even by those that practice it not, that clear and round dealing is the honour of man's nature, and that mixture of falsehood is like alloy in coin of gold and silver, which may make the metal work the better, but it embaseth it. For these winding and crooked courses are the goings of the serpent; which goeth basely upon the belly, and not upon the feet.[54]

...we are much beholden, [Bacon writes in both *Advancements*] to Machiavel and others of that class, who openly and unfeignedly declare or describe what men do, and not what they ought to do.

But Bacon was not beholden to Machiavelli in that sometimes the latter had advocated conduct in policy which was morally evil.

Bacon certainly did not follow him in such advocacy of the evil arts. His indebtedness to 'Machiavel and others of that class, who openly and unfeignedly etc.' consisted of nothing more than that Machiavelli in the course of allowing and approving them had described in detail certain of the corrupt procedures which rulers indeed resorted to, and which Bacon cites as we see above as evil arts.

The sentences in the first *Advancement* which are substantially unchanged in the second, and amongst which we find the statement, 'we are much beholden to Machiavel etc. etc.', run as follows:

there belongeth further to the handling of this part touching the duties of professions and vocations, a Relative or opposite, touching the frauds, cautels, impostures, and vices of every profession, which hath been likewise handled: but how? rather in a satire and cynically, than seriously and wisely: for men have rather sought by wit to deride and traduce much of that which is good in professions, than with judgment to discover and sever that which is corrupt. For, as Solomon saith, he that cometh to seek after knowledge with a mind to scorn and censure, shall be sure to find matter for his humour, but no matter for his instruction ... But the managing of this argument with integrity and truth, which I note as deficient, seemeth to me to be one of the best fortifications for honesty and virtue that can be planted. For, as the fable goeth of the basilisk, that if he see you first, you die for it; but if you see him first, he dieth: so it is with deceits and evil arts; if they be first espied they leese their life; but if they prevent, they endanger. So that we are much beholden to Machiavel and others, that write what men do, and not what they ought to do, for it is not possible to join serpentine wisdom with the columbine innocency, except men know exactly all the conditions of the serpent; his baseness, and going upon his belly, his volubility and lubricity, his envy and sting, and the rest; that is, all forms and natures of evil. For without this, virtue lieth open and unfenced. Nay, an honest man can do no good upon those that are wicked to reclaim them, without the help of the knowledge of evil. For men of corrupted minds presuppose that honesty groweth out of simplicity of manners, and believing of preachers, schoolmasters and men's exterior language: so as, except you can make them perceive that you know the utmost reaches of their own corrupt opinions, they despise all morality.[55]

Bacon had introduced and expounded this same teaching as early as his *Meditationes Sacrae*. This was published together with the first essay collection in 1597. Here he had written:

Try all things, and hold that which is good: which induceth a discerning election out of an examination whence nothing at all is excluded. Out of the same fountain ariseth that direction: *Be you wise as Serpents, and innocent as Doves*. There are neither teeth nor stings, nor venom, nor wreaths and folds of serpents, which ought not to be all known, and as far as examination doth lead, tried: neither let any man fear infection or pollution; for the sun entereth into sinks and is not defiled. Neither let any man think that herein he tempteth God; for his diligence and generality of examination is commanded; and *God is sufficient to preserve you immaculate and pure.*[56]

In *Advancement* – both versions – though not in *Meditationes Sacrae*, Bacon thus admitted to being beholden to Machiavelli even while expressly distancing himself from him. For distance himself he most positively did when he, Machiavelli, permitted and commended evil arts in the conduct of policy. Bacon once stated in the House of Commons that 'in matters of policy ill is not to be thought ill which bringeth forth good'.[57] The context of this remark revealed that what he had in mind was different from what Machiavelli was capable of contemplating. The 'ill' Bacon referred to was an evil nothing worse than inconvenience suffered by landlords when laws against enclosures were strictly enforced. The three instances Bacon quotes for rejection in Machiavelli are taken not from *Discorsi* but from *Il Principe*.[58] But it is not the case that Bacon rejected the Machiavelli of *Il Principe* while accepting him as the writer of *Discorsi*. For one thing, most of the contents of *Il Principe* closely resemble those of *Discorsi* and therefore were as likely to be acceptable to Bacon as was so much else in *Discorsi*. Secondly, Machiavelli unlike Bacon showed himself capable of contradicting himself. On the one hand, Machiavelli makes himself clear in *Discorsi* that if rulers seek to acquire successful armies they should not oppress their subjects, an axiom with which Bacon agreed. On the other hand, in the passage quoted above from *Discorsi*, where an advance outline of Bacon's grand strategy is provided, he recommends as in *Il Principe* that rulers should keep their peoples poor. In addition to contradicting himself he showed himself capable of giving more than one answer to a question. In one place in *Discorsi* he accuses the religion of the moderns of responsibility for the inferiority of their armies when compared with those of Rome in antiquity.[59] On this observation Bacon is not silent and what he wrote in *Of Goodness, and Goodness of Nature* (1612 and 1625) does not indicate that he agrees: 'Nicholas Machiavel, had the confidence to put in writing, almost in plain terms, *that the Christian faith had given up good men in prey to those that are tyrannical and unjust...*'[60] But elsewhere in *Discorsi* Machiavelli's explanation is different – different and acceptable to Bacon: not that ancient Roman pagan religion was superior to modern Roman

Christian religion and hence encouraged more warlike men and
therefore better armies: but instead that modern armies were
inferior because often they were recruited from oppressed peoples.[61]

Despite differences which are deep it is plain that Bacon leaned
heavily upon Machiavelli – so heavily that the state of the case
cannot be better described than in Baconian terms. His knowledge
and Machiavelli's knowledge, though distinct, are not separable.
The art of Bacon and the art of Machiavelli constitute another twin
of flanking and interlocking arts. The question poses itself – why,
given that Bacon uses Machiavelli's science as his own, and given
that at the critical place in the second *Advancement*, he makes no
acknowledgment of his debt, is it not Machiavelli rather than
Bacon who, according to his claim in the second *Advancement*, has
invented civil science? An answer though not provably a correct one
lies ready at hand.

It is possible that Bacon disqualified Machiavelli on account of his
evil arts. But nowhere else does he argue that or proceed as if
Machiavelli's evil arts cancel out his good ones. An alternative
explanation, though scarcely fair to Machiavelli, is the more likely
one. Throughout his surviving writings Bacon nowhere recognizes
Miachiavelli as having been the active man duly becoming the
writer.Active men should become writers. But, also, writing men
should have been active. Machiavelli's justified pretensions both in
Discorsi and in *Il Principe* where he writes of his qualifications in
political action and experience are ignored. For Bacon Machiavelli
is a writing man only. By contrast Bacon sees himself both as active
man and writing man. He told King James that though he had been
studying laws and histories he had also been serving him – doing so
actively – in business of state, holding high offices in the realm. He
could have allowed that in this way he had activated Machiavelli
and that in doing so had tested him. But no such limited recognition
was extended.

Assuming that Bacon disqualified Machiavelli as inventor or co-
inventor of the science of policy on the grounds that he, Bacon,
discarded Machiavelli's claims to having had experience through
action in state affairs, it is arguable that nevertheless he should still
have accepted him. Writing of the branch of policy which he named
negotiation or business, Bacon stated: 'For if books were written of
this... I doubt not but learned men with mean experience, would far
excel men of long experience without learning, and outshoot them in

their own bow.'[62] In *Advancement* Book 1 (both versions) Bacon rebutted 'disgraces which learning receiveth from politiques'. Political critics protest that 'learning doth soften men's minds, and makes them more unapt for the honour and exercise of arms; that it doth mar and pervert men's dispositions for matters of government and policy, in making them too curious' (over-careful)

and irresolute by variety of reading, or too peremptory or positive by strictness of rules and maxims, or too immoderate and overweening by reason of the greatness of examples, or too incompatible and differing from the times by reason of the dissimilitude of examples; or at least that it doth divert men's travails from action and business, and bringeth them to a love of leisure and privateness; and that it doth bring into states a relaxation of discipline, whilst every man is more ready to argue than to obey and execute.[63]

Bacon rejects all such charges. Tables are turned on the accusers. A learned man in the person of Bacon must launch the charges on behalf of the critics. Being unlearned, the latter cannot mount them if left to themselves. The learned act for both prosecution and defence. The defence is that only the truly learned can be rid of the faults described: and self-styled practical men of state, men of experience, are precisely those most likely to display them.

Bacon continues a little later:

And for matter of policy and government, that learning should rather hurt, than enable thereunto, is a thing very improbable: we see it is accounted an error to commit a natural body to empiric physicians, which commonly have a few pleasing receits whereupon they are confident and adventurous, but know neither the causes of diseases, nor the complexions of patients, nor peril of accidents, nor the true method of cures: we see it is a like error to rely upon advocates or lawyers, which are only men of practice and not grounded in their books, who are many times easily surprised when the matter falleth out besides their experience, to the prejudice of the causes they handle. So by like reason it cannot be but a matter of doubtful consequence, if states be managed by empiric statesmen, not well mingled with men grounded in learning. But contrariwise, it is almost without instance contradictory, that ever any government was disastrous that was in the hands of learned governors…it hath been ordinary with politique men to extenuate and disable learned men by the names of *pedantes*.[64]

But 'let a man look into the government of the bishops of Rome, as by name into the government of Pius Quintus and Sextus Quintus in our times, who were both at their entrance esteemed but as pedantical friars, and he shall find that such popes do greater things, and proceed upon truer principles of estate, than those which have ascended to the papacy from an education and breeding in affairs of estate and courts of princes'.[65]

Duly taking into account these judgments, Machiavelli arguably should have qualified for Bacon as at least his co-inventor in policy. But such pronouncements are less than the whole of Bacon's position. They are no more than the half of it. What he requires is learning – certainly – but he also requires experience added to learning. According to both *Advancements* it is men only of experience and lacking learning who resort to shifts when dangers arise, failing to see them afar off.[66] The point is obscured in the essay *Of Empire* (1612). There he does not write that men only of experience resort to shifts etc. But by the second *Advancement* history civil and experience have become the same thing. Civil history is for Bacon the source of learning: and experience must be added to it.

Of Studies stands first in the essay collection of 1597. It loses this dignity in the subsequent collections. But it continues to illuminate many of Bacon's other essays and much else. In 1612 the first part of the 1597 text is repeated unaltered: it runs:

Studies serve for delight, for ornament, and for ability; their chief use for delight, is, in privateness, and retiring; for ornament, is in discourse; and for ability, is in judgment. For expert men can execute, but learned men are fittest to judge or censure. To spend too much time in them, is sloth; to use them too much for ornament, is affectation; to make judgment wholly by their rules, is the humour of a scholar. They perfect Nature, and are perfected by Experience... they teach not their own use, but that [? there] is a wisdom without them, and above them, won by observation. Read not to contradict nor to believe, but to weigh and consider...[67]

Of Studies' first part as said is unchanged in 1612 and repeats what was published in 1597. The essay is added to in 1625. In 1597 and in 1612 the way in which studies serve for ability 'is in judgment'. In 1625 the way in which studies serve for ability 'is in the judgment and disposition of business'. In 1612 we find 'For expert men can execute but learned men are fittest to judge and censure.' In 1625 we find 'For expert men can execute, and perhaps judge of particulars, one by one; but the general counsels and the plots and marshalling of affairs, come best from those that are learned.' In other words, men only of practice can act upon what is counselled. But counsel which leads to marshalling of affairs for the purpose of entering into them, comes best from learned men. In 1612 we find 'To make judgment wholly by their (that is, studies') rules is the humour of a scholar. They perfect nature and are perfected by experience.' In 1625 we find

to make judgment wholly by their rules is the humour of a scholar. They perfect nature, and are perfected by experience: for natural abilities are like natural plants, that need pruning by study; and studies themselves do give forth directions too much at large, except they be bounded in by experience.[68]

Throughout its versions this essay matures. In the process the element of experience becomes stressed. It is in this element on the face of things that Machiavelli according to Bacon is defective. On the other hand he duly recognizes Machiavelli in that he was learned and uses him. He qualifies for Bacon and is richly acceptable to him as a contributor in a history of arts, letters and learning.

Bacon had written that a branch of history recording the story of human learning and arts had been neglected. The importance of this learning was, he observed, such as to entitle it to a separate history of its own. And this 'I mean to be included in civil history'. The incontestable import of Machiavelli for Bacon is witness to the extent Bacon's desiderated history of letters weighed with him in his two programmes. '...every one in some one point hath seen clearer than his fellows'. Machiavelli had seen clearer than all his fellows in many points.

Among the 1612 essays, among the new ones devoted to negotiation or business and to wisdom of state or government, Bacon presented *Of Fortune.* This essay was reprinted in 1625 with little change. In it he wrote: 'It cannot be denied, but outward accidents conduceth much to fortune...But chiefly the mould of a man's fortune is in his own hands...if a man look sharply and attentively, he shall see Fortune; for though she be blind, yet she is not invisible.'[69] Bacon affirmed in *Novum Organum*, Book 1, that in the natural order both the term and the concept, fortune, lacked correspondence with reality: in the world of nature's self-conduct under providence fortune was strictly a nothing.[70] In the area of *Know Thyself* he affirmed that there was in one respect, if not in another, as little reality attaching to fortune as was the case in the universe of nature.

Machiavelli wrote extensively about fortune in *Discorsi* and in *Il Principe*. The Romans, he said, by making good institutions and by administering them well created good fortune.[71] However there was one kind of fortune which was self-conducting and irresistible by men.

Bacon concurred on both points: '...chiefly the mould of a man's fortune is in his own hands'. That was because by seeing fortune, by knowing what was taking place around him, and by exercising appropriate foresight in his actions, a man could create good fortune. Bacon on the other hand agreed that there was another kind of fortune which was fully real, all-seeing – not blind – and impossible for men to resist with hopes of success. He termed this type not fortune but divine providence. For him the other kind, the blind kind, assumed the guise of reality and in doing so became all powerful only in circumstances where no man attempted to see her, thus making himself aware of what was taking place in events and adopting appropriate measures to control them. When men abdicate from their responsibilities as truly real rational beings, a vacuum is created. This is filled by fortune and by the spurious reality she thus acquires.

In *Discorsi* Machiavelli wrote of men creating their good fortune. Bacon wrote of men doing so because they saw her. He distinguished himself from Machiavelli in effect because of his remarks in *Of Fortune* and because of his practice in civil policy in accord with these remarks. Witness for example his penetrating and comprehensive analyses of men and events in the paper on the Council of Wales, in the speech in the Commons on naturalization, and in his *Considerations Touching a War with Spain*. As he sees himself, Bacon is the man who perceives fortune and is correspondingly active. For his civil experience, buttressed by civil histories, consists of seeing fortune and of acting on what he sees.

Seeing – thinking – doing and not least *writing* – being committed in all these, in order to direct events in the ways they want – with such a commitment men can create a body of civil science by pressing onwards and by perhaps succeeding in the case of particular instances. In the department of *Know Thyself* we already possess the form of man, including and implying common notions of what he aims to have and of what he attempts to do in state and society. In *Know Thyself* the nature of the creature man is known, and with respect to projected results this knowledge stands behind and alongside close attention to what is taking place and to what has taken place already, with the purpose of steering events in a way desired. In *Know Thyself* '...the best divinations and predictions are the politic and probable foresight and conjectures of wise men'.[72] In the universe of nature, by contrast, all is unknown. But in *The History of Winds* Bacon writes of prediction in the world of nature based on observation, that is on experience:

The purer part of Divination should be the more received and practised, in proportion as it is wont in general to be corrupted by vanity and superstition. Natural Divination is sometimes more certain, sometimes more treacherous, according to the nature of the subject with which it deals. For if the subject be of a constant and regular nature, the prediction is certain; if it be of a variable nature, and compounded as it were of nature and chance, the prediction is uncertain. But yet even in a variable subject, if rules are diligently framed, a prediction will generally hold good, and will not err much from the truth, though it does not hit the exact point of time.[73]

But this is prediction arising out of observation of nature in its normal cause and in its irregularities. It is not prediction in the third department of natural history, that is to say in arts, in nature wrought upon by man. But in the conduct of this arts department, which is experimenting, nature's normal cause and also its irregularities must, as in *know thyself*, be kept always under observation. In experimenting observation is the first step in resorting to action. Though it is true that in principle men do not and should not have a particular result in mind since nature – the nature of things in nature – is unknown; nevertheless in this realm too there will in practice be thinking and acting to some purpose – a projected possible result to emerge from experiment. That attempts at prediction are not excluded in experiments conducted in investigating the natural world is sufficiently indicated when Bacon writes in the second *Advancement* of the lessons philosophers can learn from workers in the mechanical arts; 'I give this advice as to experiments of this nature; that no one should be disheartened or confounded if the experiments which he tries do not answer his expectation. For though a successful experiment be more agreeable, yet an unsuccessful one is oftentimes no less instructive.'

But was Bacon any more successful than Machiavelli – successful, that is to say, in his actions in policy? Though Bacon ignored this, Machiavelli had been an active man in the government of Florence. Action in policy presupposes success. If failure rather than success ensues, reasons for this need to be discovered. Bacon in advance had provided one reason for his failure. Measures in civil policy he had said depend upon 'the help and consent of others'. He did not get this cooperation. Instead he met concerted action against him, producing his disgrace and downfall – though it needs to be remarked that there was not a connection between the contents of his policy and his banishment from power.

Though his confidence to all appearances remained unshaken, Bacon's civil policy failed in his lifetime. But time fully vindicated him. Within a century the subjects of the two kingdoms of England and Scotland were mutually fully naturalized. Within a century Britain, the two kingdoms at last fully united in government and in parliament (though still embracing not only distinct but also separate churches and laws) had become the power-base of the kind he had argued for, competing with others and doing so successfully largely through the exercise of sea-power. Moreover and further, just as Bacon had urged that the strategy should be adopted for its own sake, whether or not the Scots began troubles in the north; similarly in these later years the strategy started to be applied and also to be successful both in building the power-base and in the consequent unifying coordination between the 'King's Sovereignty and the Liberty of Parliament', which are 'as the two elements and principles of this estate' – in advance of and before the achieving of a unifying consolidation of the whole of Britain in and after 1707.

In England and in Scotland bitter troubles afflicted churches no less than states in the seventeenth century after Bacon's death. But Protestant state religions survived and prospered in the following century both north and south of the Border. The church of Scotland resented the tutelage of the state, it is true, holding it at arm's length. But the church of England displayed full willingness to accept it. Inside themselves these churches, especially the church of England, achieved an adequate elasticity. Outside their bounds dissenting bodies were accommodated to a limited degree – bodies that is to say, which shared, so it would be argued, the same fundamentals. A prominent quasi-fundamental which they shared was determined rejection of 'the Pope's law'. A similar claim – sharing fundamentals and notably the quasi-fundamental – could be invoked to minimize the bearing of the apparent external differences between the religious settlements of England and of Scotland. 'Religion being the chief band of human society, it is a happy thing when itself is well contained within the true band of unity.' Bacon's happy thing may fairly be said to have sufficiently prevailed until the nineteenth century, when the state consented to emancipate the adherents of 'the Pope's law', and when the state later acquiesced in the setting up of a hierarchy of popish prelates.

In the matter of amendment and recompilement of the English laws, Bacon's project 'both in state and for my particular', Common Law remained administering a securely judge-made business, and therefore a civil history, as Bacon had expressly anticipated. He had proposed to improve the course of the law by providing for better reporting of court cases. Such reforms in the law as were made did not take place until the nineteenth century. They were achieved by statute and chiefly affected criminal law. The lawyers secured the satisfactory reporting of their court cases in the same century. Law reforms played no part in the earlier triumph of constitutional consolidation. But though attention to the law was 'for his particular', Bacon as we have seen made no claim that it was his 'fairest'.

Although in power rivalry the chief struggle for Britain turned out, as it did, to be with the French Crown, also popish, but according to Bacon, less eccentrically so than the Crown of Spain, his reasoning was scarcely less valid and effective. There occurred a second hundred years' war with France, this time, not inconclusive as the first had been. '...the footing we had in France was rather a greatness of trouble unto us than of strength'. What we had was 'a broken dominion'. The style and the arms of the Kingdom of France were not formally relinquished by the British state until the start of the nineteenth century. But on both sides of the Channel this claim had long been recognized as a fiction. The second war aimed – and with success – not at acquiring parts of, or all of the lands of France, but instead at disputing French power for profit and preponderance in other regions of the world.

Doubtless it is debatable whether in the conduct and experience of eighteenth-century British rulers iron was proved to be stronger than gold. It is debatable, that is, whether expanding wealth generated power or whether increasing power led to greater wealth. But it remains unlikely that the axiom of Machiavelli and of Bacon can easily be faulted. Amongst new divisions of civil history which he introduced in the second *Advancement*, he did not as will be apparent in the next chapter, import a division comprising what came to be called economic history. It should be recalled however that just as for him states included commonwealths, so the art of empire, which is policy, included economics. Enough of the treatise *Of the True Greatness of Britain* has survived to indicate that Bacon was well capable of protecting the validity of the axiom concerning iron, and that he was aware of needed limits and qualifications. Especially it should be recognized that iron in Machiavelli's and in Bacon's usage stood not so much for armed might and material force, though it included these, as for force intellectual and force moral, these being displayed in keen wits and resolute wills.

In natural philosophy/science, if we stand with Bacon in his times and look into the future, the man's confidence was proved right, but in general terms only. First, natural philosophy/science would burgeon and flourish. Second, it would do so by combining actions with thoughts. Here his example helped men in later years. In civil science, by contrast, his confidence and vision proved correct even in particulars. In some of these particulars, since he so closely followed Machiavelli, he was proved wrong, it is true. For example, Bacon unduly played down mercenaries, artillery and fortresses. But in *Of Vicissitude of Things* (1625) he argued that unpredictable aspects of the future included not only cataclysms in nature and turmoils in religion but changes in military procedures.[74] Though proving so largely right in civil science, it cannot be said that as in the case of natural philosophy/science men followed an example he had set in the policy he had tried to enact and in the counsels he wrote down both for his own day and for posterity. The essays, Ranke wrote: 'show wide observation and calm wisdom, and like his philosophical works are a treasure for the English nation... what better legacy can one generation leave to another than the sum of its experiences which have an importance extending beyond the fleeting moment...?'.[75] Beginning as the essay *Of the Greatness of Kingdoms* in 1612 this counsel became part of the 'philosophical works' in 1623 when it was expanded, translated into Latin, and added to *Advancement*. In 1625 this counsel, rendered back into English, became the essay *Of the True Greatness of Kingdoms and Estates*. We have no evidence that rulers of England, Bacon's successors, resorted to and consulted this particular treasure when they embraced the courses he had planned and argued for. But Bacon did not claim that only he could truly perceive realities outside himself and in consequence achieve what could turn out to be successful. Civil historians could see realities outside themselves. Therefore civil statesmen should be capable of doing the same.

Even with respect to his own lifetime it is easy – too easy – to pronounce that Bacon failed in everything he undertook. One late twentieth-century scholar has produced this comment: '...the attacks in the parliament of 1621 on the delays and expense of justice in Chancery suggest how little Bacon had done in his own court, to which he was appointed in 1617. The good intentions he trumpeted seem to have produced little more than self-righteous and unsolicited advice from the sidelines – the parallel with his vaunted scientific activity is striking.[76] Bacon could have admitted that failures in persuading were in themselves failures in science. Logic and rhetoric were sciences. Nevertheless another late twentieth-century scholar has commented more perceptively and less unsympathetically. There is still no conceding on his part that there could have been things in what Bacon had to say which transcend time and place. But this writer rightly contends that in matters of government and of law he was 'the clearest-sighted discerner of the critical problems of the monarchy in the early seventeenth century...No man perhaps so completely.'[77] How is it possible to decide that diagnosis of problems, not applied and confirmed by the achievement of solutions, is complete and correct? It can properly be concluded to be complete and correct through attentive reviews and ruminations on the part of civil historians coming afterwards – perhaps long afterwards – upon events men experienced prior to and subsequent to Bacon's diagnoses. In his lifetime Bacon's successes were restricted to correct diagnoses. These latter are not cures. But they are in themselves successes. This, while we think only of his lifetime, is a consideration which applies no less in Bacon's natural than in his civil science.

CHAPTER 10

Civil history of letters – civil history mixed

Amid differences between the reviewed and the original *Advancement of Learning* change is to be observed in the treatment of civil history. By the time the final *Advancement* was published Bacon had been deprived of power in the state. But he had held high places in it since 1604. In the final *Advancement* civil history is handled for its own sake and also because it provides *data* for advance in moral, civil and ecclesiastical sciences. In the final version the teaching is fuller and more affirmative than it is in the original book. Bacon makes changes in arrangement. He also makes additions. There are foretastes of these in the first *Advancement* or elsewhere. Some of them are substantial. If there are substantial anticipations as there are in 1605, and as there are at another and earlier date when he wrote at a time when the Queen was still reigning, why does the work in this field in the second version amount to a difference or constitute an advance? The answer as said is that the later work is fuller and more affirmative – a circumstance which can scarcely be considered apart from the career he had been pursuing in government and in the law. His treatment of civil history in 1623 is fuller and more affirmative both in arrangement and in content. Even in themselves and leaving aside his career in civil experience these differences scarcely suggest that preoccupation with *Know Thyself* – man's knowledges of man – has slackened. *Novum Organum* has been published with procedure in its second book for establishing the metaphysics of nature. But the handling of civil history in this, the second version of *The Advancement of Learning* indicates what we know to have been the case in his public career, namely the unflagging pursuit of the parallel programme.

As in the first version Bacon divides civil history into three: memorials, perfect histories and antiquities. Memorials in 1605 are civil history 'unfinished'; that is, commentaries or registers, the latter in the shape of 'public acts, as decrees of council, judicial proceedings, declarations and letters of estate, orations and the like, without a perfect continuance or contexture of the thread of the narration'.[1] In 1623 he states that 'Registers have a twofold character; for they either contain titles of things and persons in order of time, such as are called Annals and Chronologies; or collections of public acts, such as edicts of princes etc. etc. etc.'[2] He continues as before. Apart from this minor change we find no alterations under this head. In 1605 'Antiquities' are 'remnants of history' rescued from 'the shipwreck of time'. 'Industrious persons, by an exact and scrupulous diligence and observation', collect *data* 'out of monuments, names, words, etc. etc. etc.'.[3]

An addition in 1623 has already been quoted – namely, that the results of these labours are 'well worthy to supersede the fabulous accounts of the origins of nations, and to be substituted for fictions of that kind'. He also adds, as we have seen, that these industrious persons 'are entitled to the less authority, because in things which few people concern themselves about, the few have it their own way'.[4] It is enough to note that in this perhaps uncharacteristic remark, he does not state that men are in the right if they neglect to concern themselves with matters like the origins of nations. Looked at from his angle, the results of such labours are not relevant. In 1623 as in 1605 he outlined the historical enterprise he himself had undertaken and by the former date had published to the extent that he had found possible. This is a history, not of the origins of a nation, but of the origins of the union of two nations under one crown.

Perfect histories are the finished article – not perfect in the sense that they are faultless – but perfect in that they are neither unfinished like memorials, nor defaced like antiquities. In 1623 many changes and additions are introduced under the head of perfect histories. As before they are divided into histories of times, histories of lives, and 'narrations or relations of actions'. Contents under these heads are as before. But Bacon now adds two sub-sections for histories of times: 'History of Times is either Universal or Particular; whereof the latter contains the deeds of some kingdom, commonwealth, or people; the former those of the whole world.' Secondly as stated in the first *Advancement* 'narrations or relations of actions' 'cannot but be more purely and exactly true than histories of times...' But he now recommends that more than one account covering the same action is desirable. As already noted, this is because of the likelihood of bias. Here a sub-division not in classification but in practice is proposed.

In the first *Advancement* perfect civil history is divided as said into three species – times, lives and actions. In the second version, also as said, this threefold arrangement is retained. But to this division Bacon adds another. This also is tripartite. Civil history remains the name of the genus as a whole, but it 'may rightly be divided into three species. First, Sacred or Ecclesiastical; next, that which we call Civil History (using the generic term specially); lastly, the History of Learning and the Arts.'[5]

In the 1605 version ecclesiastical history had received treatment by itself and on its own. In the version of 1623 civil history has swallowed it up. This operation had been foreshadowed in practice. In the writer's practice when in power matters ecclesiastical are included under policy. They are part, that is to say, of matters civil. But it should be noted that history 'sacred or ecclesiastical' does not include histories incorporated into the sacred canon of Holy Writ. These latter histories are excluded as learning not human but divine. But it should also be remarked that Bacon, always seeking material, resorts as copiously to these sacred histories, properly so called, as he does to civil histories whether inside or outside his secular civil canon of Greeks and Romans.

In the first *Advancement* Bacon had written about a history of Learning and the Arts: 'History is natural, civil, ecclesiastical, and literary, whereof the three first I allow as extant, the fourth I note as deficient.'[6] History natural, as will be recalled, though absent according to the second version, is granted to be extant according to the original. Regarding history of letters Bacon wrote in 1605: 'For no man hath propounded to himself the general state of learning to be described and represented from age to age, as many have done the works of nature and the state civil and ecclesiastical; without which the history of the world seemeth to me to be as the statue of Polyphemus with his eye out; that part being wanting which doth most show the spirit and life of the person.'[7]

Elsewhere in the original version, not when he was handling the topic of civil history, but on another occasion, we find a further statement in which he advertises the same project: '... to those that seek truth and not magistrality, it cannot but seem a matter of great profit to see before them the several opinions touching the foundations of nature; not for any exact truth that can be expected in those theories...' (but) 'in the meantime it is good to see the several glosses and opinions upon nature, whereof it may be every one in some one point hath seen clearer than his fellows. Therefore I wish some collection to be made painfully and understandingly *De antiquis philosophis*, out of all the possible light which remaineth to us of them. Which kind of work I find deficient...Neither do I exclude opinions of later times...'[8] In *Parasceve*, published with *Novum Organum* in 1620, the project is played down. But it is not abandoned: 'that may perhaps be of some assistance to an inquirer which is the ruin and destruction of a believer; *viz.*, a brief review, as in passage, of the opinions now received, with their varieties and sects; that they may touch and rouse the intellect, and no more'.[9]

Civil history of letters and arts is not envisaged as restricted to writings in some way pertaining to civil affairs as strictly defined. On the contrary, history of letters will include all ascertainable attempts in the study of nature. Indeed when writing about his natural and experimental histories just previously to the publication of the second *Advancement*, Bacon expresses himself as if suggesting that there might profitably be overlap between such civil history of letters and the 'arts' sections of previous and existing natural histories. This would be an overlap in that civil history of letters would partly consist, as he wrote here, of 'natural history and the experiments of arts'.[10] A compilation of this kind would be *civil* history. It would be civil history because, first, it would be the 'arts' sections which would chiefly matter, and only men in civil societies could conduct these 'arts'. Second, as pointed out earlier – albeit needlessly – nature could not collect histories of herself. Only men in civil societies could do so.

What Bacon has to say in 1623 in the second *Advancement* about literary history, the history of learning and the arts, now a subsection or species of civil history as a *genus*, and about the absence and need of such a thing, is an expansion and an addition. *Historia Literaria*, now pleaded for with more urgency and force, would enable men to take comparisons and to investigate relative merits – 'it may be every one in some one point hath seen clearer than his fellows'. 'The argument is no other than to inquire and collect out of the records of all time what particular kinds of learning and arts have flourished in what ages and regions of the world;...' 'The occasion and origin of the invention of each art should likewise be observed;...' 'To these should be added a history of the sects, and the principal controversies...' 'Above all things (for this is the ornament and life of Civil History), I wish events to be coupled with their causes.' 'For the manner of compiling such a history I particularly advise that the matter and provision of it be not drawn from histories and commentaries alone; but that the principal books written in each century,...be themselves taken into consultation;...' 'With regard to the use of the work,...I consider that such a history as I have described, would very greatly assist the wisdom and skill of learned men in the use and administration of learning; that it would exhibit the movements and perturbations, the virtues and vices, which take place no less in intellectual than in civil matters; and that from the observation of these the best system of government might be derived and established'. 'For everything is subject to chance and error which is not supported by examples and experience.'

Learning and philosophy may be and must be assisted by studying their past. Everything is subject to chance and error which is not supported by examples and experience. What this comes to is that Bacon's announcement – 'knowledges are as pyramides whereof history is the basis' – should be enriched in content. According to teaching consistently expounded in and after 1605, philosophy/ science must be founded on historical *data* whether of the human or the natural kind. And this, as he elaborates and stresses in 1623, should include examination of ways in which this *data* has been handled in the past.'[11] He himself helps in providing this *Historia Literarum*, which, as he argues, is needed. He made no claims for his contributions in this department. We nevertheless recognize what he has bequeathed in his works no less than in his counsels. *De Sapientia Veterum* is such a contribution. Also he assists in promoting the same project 'as in passage', that is to say, while in transit. The 'general and faithful perambulation of learning'[12] whether in the two *Advancements* or in the first book of *Novum Organum*, where he 'purged and swept and levelled the floor of the mind',[13] contains a wealth of descriptions and judgments of the procedures and achievements of ancient and modern schools, sects or systems of philosophers.

The second *Advancement* retains the calls made in the first for a 'Primitive or Summary Philosophy', *Philosophia Prima*, a First Philosophy, as an instrument for advancing learning: 'it is good, before we enter into the distribution and partitions of knowledge to erect and construct one universal science as the main and common way'.[14] But pleas for a history of letters replace, or rather outstrip, requests for *Philosophia Prima* in the distribution of Bacon's attention as he expressed it. This notion of *Philosophia Prima* was not pursued in *Novum Organum*. It remained true that 'it is the duty and virtue of all knowledge to abridge the infinity of individual experience, as much as the conception of truth will permit, and to remedy the complaint of *vita brevis, ars longa*;[15] which is performed by uniting the notions and conceptions of sciences'. But this was done better by observing the rule, as Bacon did throughout, 'that all partitions of knowledges be accepted rather for lines and veins than for sections and separations; and that the continuance and entireness of knowledge be preserved'.[16] It was done better, also, by observing and recording, as he recommended, 'the distributions and partitions of knowledge'[17] throughout time and space in a history of letters. It looks as if *Philosophia Prima*, a First Philosophy, if it arrived at all, would come not first but last.

To the request for *Historia Literaria* and to the examples he provided of the way to fulfil it, Bacon makes another addition. Civil history is now exalted to the status of a *genus*. But it remains a sub-section or species of itself. Under a separate head in a new chapter he writes: 'I come next to Civil History properly so called – *Historia Civilis Specialis* – whereof the dignity and authority are pre-eminent among human writings. For to its fidelity are entrusted the examples of our ancestors, the vicissitudes of things, the foundations of civil policy and the name and reputation of men. But the difficulty is no less than the dignity.'[18] Again as we have seen there had manifestly been an anticipation of this: 'history, of all writings, deserveth least taxation, as that which holdeth least of the author, and most of the things themselves ... history possesseth the mind of the conceits which are nearest allied unto action ...' These words from an earlier time point safely to the pre-eminence and dignity of the subject. The statement about its difficulty is something new.

Having proclaimed in a new chapter civil history's dignity, authority and difficulty, he states at the close of this chapter: 'I will now pursue the divisions of civil history, and those of the different kinds; for the species will be exhibited more clearly under several heads, than under one head 'curiously' (over-carefully) 'traced through all its members'.[19] Rearrangements and additions have been imported into the 1623 version in the shape of further distinctions

together with talk of *genera* and *species*. '...history possesseth the
mind of the conceits which are nearest allied unto action...' He
wrote now to promote the dignity and authority of civil history by
proposing more writing of it and a consequent further use of it for
action and practice. Distinctions have proliferated, but they should
not dominate and thus perplex men. Instead he holds back. For
example, each of the two first heads of the new triplet – ecclesiastical
history and literary history – could, like the third – civil history
proper – have been sub-divided into times, lives, and 'narrations or
relations of actions'. Distinctions have been increased, but they have
also been controlled.

There are two further differences of consequence in the treatment
of this topic between the first and second versions of the *Advancement
of Learning*, though neither of these occurs at this place. Both have
been earlier referred to in this text. In the second version but not in
the first he writes: 'For I consider history and experience to be the
same thing...' In this statement a distinction is not added, instead
for the sake of more writing and subsequent action and practice it is
taken away. 'History' here, it is true, is both natural and civil. The
statement is a novelty though it is doubtless prefigured in Bacon's
practice, at all events in matters civil. Secondly, when writing in the
first version about 'characters of dispositions' under the head of
morality or doctrine concerning man segregate, he proposes 'history,
poesy, and daily experience' as supplying sources for study.
'And in truth I cannot sometimes but wonder that this part of
knowledge should for the most part be omitted both in morality and
policy, considering it might shed such a ray of light on both sciences.'
In the second version he adds that the 'best provision and material'
for achieving this improvement 'is to be gained from the wiser sort
of historians'. Livy, Tacitus, Herodian, Philip de Commines and
Guicciardini are introduced. Civil history supplies 'foundations of
civil policy'. It does the same for what Bacon holds to be a missing
but suppliable branch of morality.

But even at the place where he elaborates and ramifies doctrine
about civil history in the second version of *Advancement*, yet another
distinction is introduced, this being of consequence so weighty that
he does not leave it to be no more than implied. In 1623 he writes of a
'Division of Civil History into Pure and Mixed', this being a sub-
section of history civil as a species, that is to say histories of the

conduct of civil governments. The first version of *Advancement* contains observations about two kinds of 'history manifoldly mixed'.

I cannot likewise be ignorant of a form of writing which some grave and wise men have used, containing a scattered history of those actions which they have thought worthy of memory, with politic discourse and observation thereupon: not incorporate into the history, but separately, and as the more principal in their intention...So also is there another kind of history manifoldly mixed, and that is history of cosmography...[20]

In 1623 these statements are strengthened and clarified:

Of the mixed there are two principal kinds; the one taken from Civil science, the other principally from Natural. For some men have introduced a form of writing consisting of certain narratives not woven into a continuous history, but separate and selected according to the pleasure of the author; which he afterwards reviews, and as it were ruminates over, and takes occasion from them to make politic discourse and observation...Another kind of Mixed History is the History of Cosmography; which is indeed mixed of many things; of Natural History, in respect of the regions themselves, their sites and products; of History Civil, in respect of the habitations, governments, and manners of the people; and of Mathematics, in respect of the climates and configurations of the heavens, beneath which the regions of the world lie.

Mixed history, as Bacon shows, is an achievement of the moderns. The first type of this mixture – taken from civil science – separate and selected pieces of narrative – these reviewed, ruminated and resulting in politic discourse and observation – this, as a later statement makes evident, describes Niccolò Machiavelli's *Discourses on the First Decade of Livy* (1531). Speaking of this type in 1623 he writes: 'Now this kind of Ruminated History I greatly approve, provided that the writer keep to it and profess it.' In the first *Advancement* he extends approval but with less acclaim: 'some grave and wise men have used it'. 'But mixtures are things irregular, whereof no man can define.'[21]

No one more than Bacon disapproved of snap judgments and jumping to conclusions. Is it plainly true that this civil mixed history, in Bacon's judgment, is primarily Machiavelli's? Why not the civil mixed history of, for example, Justus Lipsius (1547–1606)? Lipsius was a devotee of Tacitus. So was Bacon. The answer is that 'some men have introduced a form of writing etc. etc....' Machiavelli is not alone. Lipsius and others are not excluded. But while Bacon at another place further on in *Advancement* refers by name to Machiavelli in connection with mixed history civil and also on other occasions outside *Advancement*; he never on any occasion mentions Justus Lipsius or anyone else of this class. Bacon was addicted to Tacitus. He was also a devotee of Livy.

As for the other type of mixed 'history or science', Bacon writes that we may congratulate our own age upon it. 'For this great building of the world has in our age been wonderfully opened and thorough-lighted ... the learning of these our times, not much giving place to the two former periods or returns of learning (the one of the Grecians, the other of the Romans)', in some respects far exceeds them.[22] His outline of a second principal kind of mixed history, a type doubly mixed, combining both natural and civil *data*, is possibly a reference to Jean Bodin (1529 or 1530–96). The description answers to the contents of Bodin's two books, *Methodus ad Facilem Historiarum Cognitionem* (1566) and *Les Six Livres de la République* (1576). But this is speculation. At all events Bacon fails to pursue the second type of civil mixed history with much marked interest. Elsewhere he writes that the impact of 'regions' upon men's characters and dispositions, and also upon learning and the arts, ought to be looked into. *Of Vicissitude of Things* (1625) touches on these matters.

But it is the first kind of mixture, Machiavelli's, not the second sort, which engages his closer attention. The wonderful opening and thorough-lighting of this great building of the world, which marks out the present age and exalts current learning in some respects above that of the two former periods or returns of learning – those of the Greeks and Romans – this consists of discoveries of new lands and results in maps of new places and new maps of old. It results in cosmography. But as regards other branches of natural history – and natural *data* is the ingredient distinguishing this second from the first mixed history – the recent opening and thorough-lighting of the world's framework amounts to little more than an opportunity offered. It is not yet an opportunity seized and exploited.

It is not, then, the second but the first type of civil mixed history upon which Bacon concentrates his interest. Further, as he presents things in his final version of *The Advancement of Learning*, this first kind is an achievement of the moderns which though it does not tilt judgment in their favour against the ancients and their achievements in the writing of civil history pure, nevertheless places them ahead of the ancients in the matter of the use to which civil history can be put and of the action to which it can point. The situation is now like this: civil history pure, the record of events in and for the times of antiquity, is excellent, and though this can be and ought to be supplied and continued, it stands in no need of being improved and is in any case beyond the reach of attempts to do so. Civil history pure, the comparable recording in and for the period of modernity is extant and indubitably improvable. More is needed because most modern writing is weak. Bacon in supplying and continuing the achievements of the ancients remedies the mediocrity of the moderns. Civil history mixed is extant. More is needed, not because it is weak and improvable, but because it is strong, and needs little improvement. Bacon greatly approves it. He provides more of it.

In the final *Advancement* Bacon not only elaborates this mixed history civil concept. He also omits – conceivably in the cause and course of this elaboration – but this is speculation – a section in which he had dwelt in the original version on the pre-eminence of the ancients in the writing of civil history pure. In 1623 the statements which follow have vanished: 'For the history of times (I mean of civil history), the providence of God hath made the distribution: for it hath pleased God to ordain and illustrate two exemplar states of the world for arms, learning, moral virtue, policy and laws; the state of Grecia and the state of Rome...' Greece and Rome in these matters are examples of excellence; but not only in these ways; they are exemplary also in history writing. They provide Thucydides, Xenophon, Livy, Polybius, Sallust, Caesar, Appianus, Tacitus and Herodian. The enduring status and stature of these is such that as we have seen he wants their texts 'to be kept entire without any diminution at all, and only to be supplied and continued'. All this disappears.[23]

This disappears. But the disappearance can scarcely indicate change of mind. In the second *Advancement* we find his explicit general approval of mixed history civil. This had previously been approved only in somebody else's – Machiavelli's – practice of it. But also in the second *Advancement* we find the explicit elevation of civil history, proper and pure, to supremacy among human writings of all kinds. Previously it had been raised to this status only in Bacon's acclaim for it in the normal practice of civil historians – that is to say, when he pronounced that their achievements in comparison with those of poets and philosophers contain 'least of the author and most of the things themselves, etc.' Unmistakably Bacon still holds in 1623 that Greece and Rome in antiquity excelled in the writing of this civil history proper and pure.

Machiavelli's mixed history, his amalgam of civil history infused with politic discourse and observation, assumes without question the high quality of Livy upon whose history of Rome he chiefly hinged his work. Indeed, Machiavelli had preceded Bacon in selecting much the same secular canon; citing six of the nine by name, evidently and extensively studying a seventh, Polybius, and mentioning an eighth, Caesar, though as man of action in civil or military affairs, not as civil historian. Such resort would have been impossible if Livy's achievement and that of the rest had not been both extant and the embodiment of the highest standards. Machiavelli postulates Livy's excellence and that of the others. So does Bacon. According to the first *Advancement* Titus Livius is the best historiographer known to the memory of man.[24] The judgment is not withdrawn in the second. There is no necessity: there is not even the possibility of withdrawing it.

Civil history pure is not a form which is now disposable and dispensable because it is antiquated. The extreme statement in the first *Advancement* that mixtures are things 'irregular whereof no man can define' does not reappear. He omits it. But there was a reason for uttering it, namely the protection of civil history pure. The requirement to guard history in its pure state is asserted in the first *Advancement* more plainly than in the remark that 'mixtures are things irregular whereof no man can define'. The passage in the first *Advancement* runs in full like this: 'for it is the true office of history to represent the events themselves together with the counsels, and to leave the observations and conclusions thereupon to the liberty and faculty of every man's judgment. But mixtures are things irregular whereof no man can define.'[25] He warns that civil history mixed should advertise itself as such and be kept distinct from civil history pure. In the second *Advancement* he greatly approves civil mixed history, but provided the writers of it, he says, 'keep to it and profess it'. He continues: 'for a man who is professedly writing a Perfect History to be everywhere introducing political reflections, and therefore interrupting the narrative, is unseasonable and wearisome. For though every wise history is pregnant (as it were) with political precepts and warnings, yet the writer himself should not play the midwife.' In other words, however inseparable in some men's practice, civil history pure and civil history mixed must be kept apart.

In any case without civil history pure there can be no civil history mixed. Not only does the extant pure history which the ancients have bequeathed remain irreplaceable, without more histories pure there cannot be further histories mixed. Bacon offers his contribution in civil history pure, *The History of the Reign of King Henry the 7th*, extending his secular exemplar canon. This, his own creation, would be available in its turn for use by practitioners in civil history mixed. In his *History of the Reign of King Henry the 7th* he follows his own injunctions regarding civil histories pure. The book is almost – if not entirely – devoid of 'observations', 'conclusions' and 'political precepts and warnings'. These, with singular exceptions later to be noted, Bacon leaves to the liberty and faculty of every man's judgment.

According to the first *Advancement* the succession of times had run from a state of affairs in remotest antiquity of which histories are not available: 'As to the heathen antiquities of the world, it is in vain to note them for deficient. Deficient they are no doubt, consisting most of fables and fragments; but the deficience cannot be holpen; for antiquity is like fame, *caput inter nubila condit*, her head is muffled from our sight.'[26] The succession of times had proceeded next through an epoch when the providence of God had ordained exemplar states and exemplar histories. It had emerged thirdly into a period in which civil history writing survived in most current practice though specimens of it were usually of poor quality. But even in the first *Advancement* Bacon had provided an alternative version of a similarly threefold succession of times, consisting first of fables, next of recorded history and last of mixed history. This alternative rendering of the past has been noticed and consulted already in connection with *De Sapientia Veterum*, but as yet not cited in full: 'it is generally to be found in the wisdom of the more ancient times, that as men found out any observation that they thought good for life, they would gather it and express it in parable or aphorism or fable. But for fables, they were vicegerents and supplies where examples failed: now that the times abound with history, the aim is better when the mark is alive.' 'And therefore', he continued, 'the form of writing which of all others is fittest... is that which Machiavel chose wisely and aptly for government; namely, discourse upon histories or examples.'[27] This alternative vision of a progression of times, present in 1605, reappears in 1623. The other one is laid aside.

Bacon makes no citations from Machiavelli's *History of Florence*, thus not showing whether he knew that Machiavelli had written 'simple rehearsals', that is to say, narrative civil history. Of moderns 'whereof there are some few very worthy', he cites as we have seen Philip de Comines and Guicciardini, not Machiavelli's *History of Florence*. Nor does he betray awareness that Machiavelli has also produced 'fanciful imitations', that is, poetic creations. He did so, for instance, in *Mandragola*. Also it is not apparent from his surviving writings that Bacon recognized that the author of the *Discourses* and of *The Prince* held office as Principal Secretary of the Florentine Republic for more than twelve years. In Machiavelli's *Dedication* of *Discorsi* he asserts that he had had long experience of political affairs. Bacon makes no reference to this. In what survives of his pronouncements upon Machiavelli we have seen that he does not reckon him active among active men who have become writers.

But in *Advancement* (both versions) he contributes not one but two descriptions of the *Discourses*. On the second occasion the author is mentioned by name. Bacon welcomes the form of writing

which Machiavel chose wisely and aptly for government; namely discourse upon histories and examples. For knowledge drawn freshly and in our view out of particulars knoweth the way best to particulars again. And it hath much greater life for practice when the discourse attendeth upon the example, than when the example attendeth upon the discourse. For this is no point of order, as it seemeth at first, but of substance. For when the example is the ground, being set down in an history at large, it is set down with all circumstances, which may sometimes control the discourse thereupon made, and sometimes supply it, as a very pattern for action; whereas the examples alleged for the discourse's sake are cited succinctly and without particularity, and carry a servile aspect towards the discourse which they are brought in to make good.[28]

As we have seen already Bacon writes elsewhere that 'we are much beholden to Machiavel and other writers of that class, who openly and unfeignedly declare or describe what men do, and not what they ought to do'. The actions thus declared or described may, according to the standards of morality, be good or bad. In this statement Bacon is grateful for description of deeds which are bad. But this is at another place and in another discussion, where he argues that it is impossible for men to combine the innocence of doves with the wisdom of serpents, as commanded to do in the canon of sacred scripture, if they are ignorant of, or fail to take account of, the nature of evil. But by now we are aware that, both when he admits it and when he does not, Bacon was more abundantly beholden to Machiavelli than in the one respect recited above. Bacon was beholden to him for a procedure. He was beholden to him further in that he adopts in his own works and counsels in policy, the results Machiavelli has obtained as a result of the way he has proceeded. Adopting Machiavelli's conclusions is for Bacon another way of approving the procedure. In the first *Advancement* we see the approving description of Machiavelli's procedure. In the second *Advancement* we see an even stronger expression of approval. Both before and after the approving description in the first *Advancement* Bacon has been employing the procedure in his own civil policy. The stressed and more positive approval in the second version of *Advancement* is announced after he has been using and testing Machiavelli's way. Explicitly approving this latter, Bacon is also recommending his own works and counsels.

Civil history mixed is his instrument for promoting the grand strategy. For pursuit of his purpose civil history mixed is his *organum*; and it is as he shows a *novum organum*, moderns having invented it. He offers prominent examples. *View of the Differences in Question betwixt the King's Bench and the Council in the Marches* (1606) is civil history mixed. This paper respects internal perils, those which menace the political constitution of the state in England, and not only in England. This document presents as we have seen portions of English civil history and also portions of that of other states, together with review and rumination; that is to say, thinking in the shape of discourse, observation and recommendations. In civil history mixed he offers also his speech in the House of Commons of February 1607 concerning naturalizing the Scots. This respects internal dangers and also peril from outside. As we have seen it presents sections of internal and of foreign history, these reviewed and ruminated into discourse and observation.

Also in civil mixed history he presents *Considerations Touching a War with Spain*. To peril threatening from outside the realm Bacon in this piece applies as we have seen 'that which leadeth all men, experience and reason': he provides 'experience' in the shape of sections collected out of civil history, native and foreign, ancient and modern. He adds his further thinking – 'reason' – in the form of discourse

and observation. The term 'observation' covers the seeing and also
the statement of what is seen. In both ways 'observing' is the first
step towards acting.

All three of the above ventures in civil history mixed, and
especially the latter two, relate to the main and 'fairest' part of the
grand strategy. Mixed civil history is again employed in the sub-
science or sub-strategy. In proposals to King James for handling his
parliaments, Bacon's counsels respect internal constitutional threats.
The counsels recommend parrying these by fixing attentions, that of
the King and those of parliaments, upon peril from abroad. As we
have seen, the proposals consist of sections from the history of
parliaments, mixed and mingled with discourse and observation.

In matters ecclesiastical, a distinct but indispensable and all-
pervading branch of policy, Bacon offers two exercises in civil mixed
history – *An Advertisement Touching the Controversies of the Church of
England* (1589) and *Considerations Touching the Better Pacification and
Edification of the Church of England* (1604). These supply sections or
episodes out of the sacred canon of scripture, and also items selected
out of church history. These items, from whichever of the two sources
they are taken, lead to discourse and observation aimed at achieving
peace in the religion of the state.

In the fields of policy, not as government but as law, Bacon's
Maxims of the Law and his *Example of a Summary Treatise on Universal
Justice or the Fountains of Equity, by Aphorisms* are both of them mixed
history civil. How these two pieces differ the one from the other
requires to be pointed out if not elsewhere then here. The first
restricts itself to maxims and relates exclusively to the Common Law
of England. The second while early in its text promising maxims fails
to provide any. Further, the field covered in the second work is
wider. Bacon handles in it both English and Roman law. In the first
Advancement he had promised both maxims and also other guidance
regarding laws. There he had complained as we have seen 'that all
those which have written of laws, have written either as philosophers
or as lawyers, and none as statesmen'. Those writing as philosophers
produce axioms of too high a generality. Those writing as lawyers
'write according to the states where they live what is received law,
and not what ought to be law...' What is needed, what a statesman
could provide, and what he himself announced that he could
produce, is a set of middle axioms or maxims.

But at the same time in *Advancement* he continued like this:

the wisdom of a lawgiver consisteth not only in a platform of justice but in the application thereof; taking into consideration by what means laws may be made certain, and what are the causes and remedies of the doubtfulness and incertainty of law; by what means laws may be made apt and easy to be executed, and what are the impediments and remedies in the execution of laws; what influence laws touching private right of *meum* and *tuum* have into the public state; and how they may be made apt and agreeable; how laws are to be penned and delivered, whether in Texts or in Acts; brief or large, with preambles, or without; how they are to be pruned and reformed from time to time, and what is the best means to keep them from being too vast in volumes, or too full of multiplicity and crossness; how they are to be expounded, when upon causes emergent and judicially discussed, and when upon responses and conferences touching general points or questions; how they are to be pressed, rigorously or tenderly; how they are to be mitigated by equity and good conscience, and whether discretion and strict law are to be mingled in the same courts or to be kept apart in several courts; again, how the practice, profession, and erudition of law is to be censured and governed; and many other points touching the administration, and (as I may term it) animation of laws. Upon which I insist the less, because I propose (if God give me leave), having begun a work of this nature in aphorisms to propound it hereafter...[29]

This work, proposed in the first *Advancement*, was propounded in the second. *Example of a Summary Treatise on Universal Justice etc. etc.* presents ninety-seven aphorisms. In these Bacon offers guidance as promised on many of the points he had listed in the first version. But his neglect to fulfil the undertaking to make more law maxims – this project was even repeated in Aphorism VI of this example of a summary treatise – contrasts sharply with his plentiful success in providing axioms, aided by Machiavelli, in the other region of policy. Witness for example the contents of the twin example of a summary treatise, that touching *The Extension of Empire*.

In *Maxims of the Law*, in its *Preface*, he had written:

I do not find that... I can in any kind confer so profitable an addition unto that science [viz. the law], as by collecting the rules and grounds dispersed throughout the body of the same laws: for hereby no small light will be given, in new cases and such wherein there is no direct authority, to sound into the true conceit of law by depth of reason...[30]

Later, in *A Proposition... Touching the Compiling and Amendment of the Laws of England*, he had announced

For the treatise *De Regulis Juris*, I hold it of all other things the most important to the health, as I may term it, and good institutions of any laws:

it is indeed like the ballast of a ship, to keep all upright and stable;... In this I have travelled myself, at the first more cursorily, since with more diligence, and will go on with it...[31]

But despite Bacon's insistence on the capital import of these rules or law maxims, the *Example of a Summary Treatise on Universal Justice etc. etc.* fails to complete the work begun in *Maxims of the Law* and referred to with decided flourish in *A Proposition etc. etc.* It can scarcely be irrelevant to recall at this point that though law as he admitted and indeed claimed was Bacon's 'for my particular', it was not what he called the 'fairest' element in his grand strategy when he had outlined the latter in the summer of 1608.

Notwithstanding the marked differences between *Maxims of the Law* and *Example of a Summary Treatise on Universal Justice etc. etc.* – to which indeed yet another can be added – viz. that though the middle axioms in the former qualify as aphorisms, many aphorisms in the latter cannot qualify as middle axioms – these two works share three features in common. First, they relate not to government, but to that distinct yet inseparable part of policy which consists of law. Second, they are exercises in civil mixed history. Third, in both of them the *data*, the history, is omitted. In this singular last feature they set themselves apart from all Bacon's other ventures in mixed history.

In *Preface* to *Maxims of the Law* Bacon recognizes the omission and comments upon the anomaly. He writes:

whereas it might have been more flourish and ostentation of reading to have vouched the authorities, and sometimes to have enforced or noted upon them; yet I have abstained from that...I have resolved not to derogate from the authority of the rules by vouching of the authority of the cases, though in mine own copy I had them quoted...[32]

The reason he gives for this procedure is that he follows the examples of 'Mr Littleton and Mr FitzHerbert, whose writings are the institutions of the laws of England'.[33] But – whether Bacon tells us so or not – it is plain in the case of *Maxims of the Law* and also in that of *Example of a Summary Treatise on Universal Justice etc.* that the *data* had indubitably been collected and that it had also been set out in the first place. Without *data* before his eyes Bacon could not have achieved either his 'rules' or 'grounds' in the one or his ninety-seven aphorisms in the other. In each case Bacon decided to exclude the *data*, the history, from what he published.

As for the essays, pieces which are civil and/or moral, these increasingly converge upon the civil mixed history pattern. We have urged in a previous chapter that Bacon continued with his experiments in *traditio* – in delivery, that is to say, in the form of writing. The alternatives as we saw lay between treatises and essays. But experimenting went further. It included experimenting with the form which he gives to his essays. The 1597 essays consist of strings of disconnected aphorisms. The essays of 1612 and of 1625 retain Bacon's unmistakable and characteristic aphoristic stamp. But he newly imports 'discourse of connection and order'. He introduces into them structure and a degree of internal coherence.

Nor, if we compare the last with the first collection, is this the sum of the change which he presents in the essays. Bacon increasingly incorporates civil historical examples. Of the ten original essays (1597) five started life without material of this kind and failed to acquire any in subsequent reissues. But the other five beginning without any examples from civil history are found to contain these in their final version (1625). One of the essays – *Of Faction* – began to acquire such examples in the second collection (1612). Of the twenty-three essays which first appeared in 1612 eleven provided no civil history at that date, but included civil history when they reappeared in 1625. Eight of the rest contained some civil history at the former date and included more civil history in 1625. Only three displayed such material in 1612 and showed no increase of it when they were published for the second time. Thirteen new essays appeared in the 1625 collection. Of these only three lack civil historical examples. These are, first, *Of Truth*. This, however, quotes the sacred canon of scripture. The second is *Of Adversity*. But this essay quotes the sacred canon together with poets. The third of these essays is *Of Gardens*. Bacon employed more and more civil historical examples. He also, though to a lesser extent, increasingly cited incidents out of his own experience. Material of this latter type occurs in the new essays of 1625 and also in additions to earlier essays republished at that date.

On the face of things, therefore, the essays present an exercise on Bacon's part which is sharply different from, and even the opposite to what he provided in *Maxims of the Law* and in *Example of a Summary Treatise on Universal Justice etc*. In the two latter the *data*/history – for law is a civil history – being once present was later taken away. In the former the *data*/history being once absent was subsequently added. But such a judgment would be facile. The 'observation' presented in the essays, for which civil historical material was later supplied, had in the first instance and in the nature of the case arisen out of ruminating civil histories. The essays as stated started life as disconnected aphorisms. But of the aphoristic way of writing Bacon wrote: 'For first it trieth the writer, whether he be superficial or solid: for aphorisms, except they should be ridiculous cannot be made but of the pith and heart of sciences ... there remaineth nothing to fill the aphorisms but some good quantity of observation ... no man can suffice, nor in reason will attempt, to write aphorisms, but he that is sound and grounded.'[34] To be sound and grounded is to be sound and grounded in civil histories. This soundness and groundedness we know Bacon had acquired.

We recognize therefore that Bacon in 1597 did not spin out essays *ex nihilo*. However when describing Machiavelli's procedure in 1605, he stated that part of its merit was that knowledge was drawn from particulars 'freshly and in our view', with the consequent advantage that such knowledge 'knoweth the way best to particulars again' – that is, to advancement of such knowledge. The change imported into the essays, which was progressive, and which consisted of discourse more connected and of civil history examples more numerous – the change consists of the circumstance that, since discourse becomes linked with particulars 'freshly and in our view', the advancement of learning according to Bacon's judgment is more sharply projected and more effectively provided for.

If we seek to summarize Bacon's definitions of civil mixed history together with its virtues, and if we take into account his employment of it for the sake of its attendant advantages – resorting for the purpose of the summary not only to his statements but to his practice – we shall find that the summary will comprise more than half a dozen points. First there are the definitions in *Advancement*. We recall the definition offered in 1605: 'I cannot likewise be ignorant of a form of writing ... containing a scattered history of those actions ... thought worthy of memory, with politic discourse and observation thereupon', these latter 'not incorporate into the history, but separately, and as the more principal in ... intention ...' We recall likewise the definition made in 1623: 'some men have introduced a form of writing consisting of certain narratives not woven into a continuous history, but separate and selected'; these the author 'reviews, and as it were ruminates over, and takes occasion from them to make politic discourse and observation'. Now this kind of

Ruminated History – *nos sane magnopere probamus* – 'we greatly approve provided that the writer keep to it and profess it'.

Next there are two happy and fecund qualities which Bacon attributes to civil mixed history when in both *Advancements* he describes Machiavelli's way: 'Knowledge drawn freshly and in our view out of particulars knoweth the way best to particulars again.' To this Bacon adds: 'And it hath much greater life for practice when the discourse attendeth upon the example, than when the example attendeth upon the discourse.' Nor, he writes, is this a point only of order. It is a point of substance. 'For when the example is the ground, being set down in an history at large, it is set down with all circumstances, which may sometimes control the discourse thereupon made, and sometimes supply it, as a very pattern for action; whereas the examples alleged for the discourse's sake are cited succinctly and without particularity, and carry a servile aspect towards the discourse which they are brought in to make good.'[35]

A fifth and a sixth point follow. These are not explicit either in Bacon's descriptions of civil mixed history or in his employments of it. However they are implicit in the latter. They are also implied in his comments in *Novum Organum*, Book I, upon the situation of Greek philosophers in antiquity and upon the consequent paucity of their achievements: 'a narrow and meagre knowledge either of time or place which is the worst thing that can be, especially for those who rest all on experience'.[36] By contrast, civil mixed history as practised by Machiavelli and by Bacon displays a double universality. Particulars, *data*, are sought for and collected as widely as possible in time and in place. Likewise discourse and observation are presented by both of them as being applicable always and everywhere without limit. Needless to say, in some instances when Bacon employs mixed history civil, there are bounds to universality which are imposed by the nature of the case. In these instances he is concerned with all times, but not with all places. The *data* provided in English Common Law is limited. Observations and maxims derived from the civil history, which is the English Common Law, are likewise limited in their application to the English Common Law. *Data* derived from the history and experience of English parliaments can be drawn from no other source. Similarly, discourse and observation are restricted in their applicability to these parliaments.

But in the rest of the instances cited – the paper on the Council of Wales, the speech on naturalizing the Scots, *Considerations Touching a*

War with Spain, the pieces in 1589 and in 1604 aiming at peace in the church, *Example of a Summary Treatise on Universal Justice etc.* (this latter being based upon available known laws and systems of equity but restricted inevitably to English law and to Roman law) and also the essays civil and moral – in all these exercises Bacon's *data* is so little 'circumscribed by place and time', that in the range of its collection it is universal. Similarly his 'discourse' and his 'observation' in the range of their applicability are proffered as being unreservedly valid in all places and in all times – valid, it being understood so long as experience continues to confirm what is offered in the 'discourse' and in the 'observation', not intruding itself in a contrary sense, thus modifying what has gone before.

But while Bacon follows Machiavelli in renouncing insularity in space and in time when he resorts to civil mixed history, he adds yet one more point to the list of features which define it and constitute its creative qualities. He gives it a further dimension of universality, this time a universality in the range of topics it is capable of constructively handling. In nearly all the things which Bacon said required to be done – because of lack, deficiency or improvability arising from the fact that an art which was extant was not lacking in elements of soundness – he himself attempted to make a contribution. Mixed civil history is a case in point except that it needed no improvement and suffered neither deficiency nor lack. But like the Greek and Roman exemplar canon in civil history pure it could be supplied and continued. What was needed and what he provided were yet more examples of a procedure which was promising. In his hands it was a way of improving other things.

In what has been described so far Bacon's mixed history has been devoted to contributions in the branch of policy which concerns government and laws. But in both *Advancements* he also uses mixed history when handling another branch of policy, negotiation or business, explaining as seen above that Machiavelli's form of writing was fittest, too, for this other topic in Civil Science. He added that the histories – providing material – most proper here were histories of lives, not histories of times, the former being 'more conversant in private actions.'[37]

But there are three areas, if not in policy, yet in *Know Thyself* in which according to indications on his part this proceeding could be resorted to. Morality, he maintained, required a new dimension to be added to it. He argued that in the matter of characters of dispositions and in that of passions 'better rules' could be discovered 'for the treatment of the mind'. He proposed that materials for making rules of this kind were available in civil historians and poets.

Similarly, given that history of letters was seriously undertaken – as he said it ought to be – he wrote that 'with regard to the use of the work...I consider that such a history...would very greatly assist the wisdom and skill of learned men...' Learned men perhaps would discover that 'every one in some one point hath seen clearer than his fellows'. But also the wisdom and skill of learned men would be assisted in 'the use and administration of learning'. For 'everything is subject to chance and error which is not supported by example and experience'. This suggests that civil history of letters pure should engender civil history of letters mixed, providing discourse, observation and rules. For he continues by pointing out that movements and perturbations, virtues and vices, 'take place no less in intellectual than in civil matters; and that from the observation of these the best system of government might be derived and established'.

This last statement – 'that from observation of these the best system of government might be derived and established' – is certainly less than clear. Some will wish to relate it to Bacon's posthumous *The New Atlantis*, his vision of an institution established by government for furthering natural philosophy/science. But alternatively and more convincingly, since in the past prior to the notion of state organization of learning as advertised by Bacon, there had scarcely been government intervention in such an area – the phrase can be interpreted as the search for and the use by learned men severally of a framework of directing axioms conducive to learning's advancement.

Judging by Bacon's remarks, operations in yet another area of art, that of medicine, could be bettered by similar procedure. 'Those very philosophies which physicians,...rely on (and medicine not founded on philosophy is a weak thing) are themselves of little worth'[38]...'the science of medicine, if it be destituted and forsaken by natural philosophy, is not much better than an empirical practice.'[39] In comparison with statecraft, therefore, where civil history is at hand with available aid, physicians cannot expect much betterment in their art till natural philosophy becomes feasible through collection of natural history.

In the meantime, on the other hand, – pending such progress –

the art of medicine can be improved, the way open to it being the procedure of mixed history. 'Medicine is a science which hath been...hitherto more professed than laboured, and yet more laboured than advanced.'[40] Hippocrates kept narratives of cases, relating the nature of the disease, treatment and success or failure in cure. This practice should be revived. Since Hippocrates is looked upon as father of his art, 'I shall not need to go abroad for an example from other arts; as from the wisdom of the lawyers, who have ever been careful to report' cases and decisions for future instruction. 'This continuance of medicinal history I find deficient; especially as carefully and judiciously digested into one body.'[41] If we join together these remarks about Hippocrates, the father of medicine, who 'kept narratives of cases, etc.'; and further statements about him in the *History of Life and Death*, it would appear that Hippocrates, living in antiquity, is the exception to Bacon's judgment that mixed history is a procedure conceived and employed solely by moderns. According to The *History of Life and Death*: 'Hippocrates of Cos...lived 104 years, and by the length of his life approved and credited his own art. He was a man of wisdom as well as learning, much given to experiments and observation, not striving after words or methods, but picking out the very nerves of science and so setting them forth.'[42]

'Let a man look more deeply into the prescripts and ministrations which physicians use, and he shall find the most of them full of vacillation and inconstancy, devices of the moment, without any settled or foreseen course of cure.' The picture offered to Bacon by the proceedings of physicians is comparable with that presented by men of politics with their 'fine deliveries, and shifting of dangers and mischiefs, when they are near', rather than 'solid and grounded courses...' Whether or not Bacon bracketed together the proceedings of those who tend men's natural bodies with those who concern themselves with policy, it is evident that Machiavelli could do so. For in the *Preface* to his *Discourses* he wrote 'For the civil law is nothing but a collection of decisions, made by jurists of old, which the jurists of today have tabulated in orderly fashion for our instruction. Nor, again, is medicine anything but a record of experiments, performed by doctors of old, upon which the doctors of our day base their prescriptions.'[43]

But it is profitless to expend time and print listing fields – three of them – into which mixed history procedure could have been, but as far as we know was not – despite indications of the possibility – imported by Bacon, when three areas remain into which he manifestly did extend it. When discussing his proposals for *Historia Literaria*, we cited *De Sapientia Veterum* as a contribution of his in this field. Also we have noted that each of his divisions of history civil, including civil history of letters, was capable as he indicates of sub-division. *De Sapientia Veterum*, as it turns out, is not a history of letters pure. It is a history of letters mixed. It is concerned predominantly with moral and civil topics. In these topics – and even in natural philosophy/science – the most ancient poets had 'in some one point seen clearer than [their] fellows'. Indeed poets in this instance had seen clearer in a multitude of points than philosophers had been capable of doing. A special characteristic of *De Sapientia Veterum* distinguishing it from other exercises in mixed history is that since it handles not history but fables, it offers not discourse and observation, but interpretation and observation. Though derived from interpretation, such observation conduces to action no less than does observation in mixed history of the more normal type.

Secondly, in terms not of their appearance in time but of their order of mention in this argument, Bacon employs mixed history in the realm of divinity. In divinity he proposed as we have seen three works profitably to be undertaken: first, a treatise on the function of reason in divine learning; second, a work exploring the differences between fundamentals and matters indifferent. Thirdly, since 'in divinity many things must be left abrupt',[44] he desiderated 'a concise, sound, and judicious collection of annotations and observations on particular texts of scripture, neither dilated into common places, nor chasing after controversies, nor reduced into method of art, but entirely unconnected and natural'.[45] Bacon furnished an example of what he desired of this kind when he published his *Meditationes Sacrae* (1597). As he said it should, it consists of aphorisms. But also, since the canon of sacred scripture is a history, *Meditationes Sacrae* is an exercise in sacred history mixed.

Literary history mixed and also sacred history mixed lie – at any rate partly – within the region of *Know Thyself*, but in a third case he emerges altogether from the region of *Know Thyself* and applies the procedure outside it. Beginning as an instrument applied in more fruitful areas, mixed history overflows in the end into regions as yet barren: into the fields, that is to say, of the universe of nature. Just as a civil history of letters and arts was intended from the start to embrace studies of nature, so civil history mixed in the end also did so. Explicitly explaining the procedure, Bacon wrote to the Revd Fr Fulgentius in 1625:

I wish to make known to your Reverence my intentions with regard to the writings which I meditate and have in hand...not hoping to perfect them, but desiring to try...I work for posterity;...these things requiring ages for their accomplishment...As for...the natural history...And those portions which I have published concerning Winds and concerning Life and Death are not history pure: because of the axioms and greater observations that are interposed: but a kind of writing mixed of natural history and a rude and imperfect intellectual machinery.[46]

According to Bacon's classification Machiavelli's *Discourses*, his mixed history, is history: it constitutes one of Bacon's·divisions of civil history as he examines the subject in his reviewed *Advancement*. There he wrote of 'a division of civil history into pure and mixed'. But Machiavelli's book is also science – or strongly adumbrates science: Bacon says so in the same reviewed version: 'in which kind of history or science we may congratulate our own age'.[47] It is true he refers here not to Machiavelli's amalgam but to the other mixture – the 'history of cosmography'. On the other hand he remarks in the first version, this time when writing of Machiavelli's mixture: 'which kind of ruminated history I think more fit to place amongst books of policy...[48]than amongst books of history.' Policy is Bacon's designation for philosophy civil. How can the *Discourses* be two things simultaneously – history, even if history mixed – and also science, or rather science suggestively and acceptably adumbrated? Machiavelli's book can be both or can suggest both because, when the purpose and the way of achieving it are described and expounded, as Bacon described and expounded them to Fulgentius, rational knowledge, philosophy, axioms, on the one hand, and the *data* or history on the other are distinguished and set apart. But when the aim and the procedure for achieving it are pursued in thought and in action, the *data* and its use are inseparable. Together they constitute science.

In *Advancement* in its second version the notion that mixed history can be science – not indeed science's apex which according to Bacon's avowed aim is metaphysics, but nevertheless science – is both commended and also recommended. Mixtures are no longer 'things irregular'.[49] Now they are things 'whereof a man can define'. In the 1623 version, after he had been practising it, the idea of mixed history is highly commended for handling civil knowledge – which relates to man congregate, to policy. In the second *Advancement*, though with little change it is true from the first Bacon writes that 'Mathematics is either pure or mixed'.[50] The latter, the mixed, is useful since it can play a part as adjunct to natural history and natural philosophy. The former, the pure, is useless, since it encourages the mind's bent to abstractions: 'For it being the nature of the mind of man (to the extreme prejudice of knowledge) to delight in the spacious liberty of generalities, as in a champion region, and not in the inclosures of particularity, the Mathematics of all other knowledge were the goodliest fields to satisfy that appetite.'[51] But in natural knowledge, when discussing *desiderata* for future work on natural *data* in the revised *Advancement*, he writes: 'I shall…make a…Division of Natural History, into Narrative and Deductive.'[52] A natural history which is inductive can only be a natural history which is mixed. When, a few years earlier, Bacon had presented *Novum Organum* to King James, he told him he hoped he could get help in the compiling of a natural and experimental history…[53] But a natural history which is experimental can be no other than a natural history which is mixed.

This is what he told Fr Fulgentius when describing his operations in *History of Winds* and *History of Life and Death*. It should be mentioned that the latter, the *History of Life and Death*, is not an enterprise in the history of medicine. It was an inquiry into the conditions of life and death, of duration and extinction, of bodies natural, throughout the whole range of animate and of certain inanimate creatures: '…the true ways of natural death, which deserve to be well and carefully considered. For how can a man, who knows not the ways of nature meet and turn her?'[54] In relation to the bodies natural of men, Bacon explained, 'the present inquiry is not instituted for deaths from suffocation, putrefaction, and divers diseases, which belong to the history of medicine'.[55] Instead it was an investigation into the ways of nature. Without successful search into these ways, medicine though it could as we have seen be improved, was nevertheless condemned to remain 'not much better than an empirical practice'. What he envisaged and what he produced in this piece and in the *History of Winds* and in the *History of Dense and Rare* was a combination of recorded observations on the history, including experiments, with 'the axioms and greater observations' to be constructed out of them.

Bacon's recognition and use of Machiavelli's mixed history – his identifying of it with science – occurs first as we have seen in his own practice in policy. But striking all the same is a testimony which Bacon embedded in his aphorisms in *Novum Organum* Book I, where as we know the priority is, if not exclusively, in sciences of nature. The implication is plain that mixed history applies and can be productive in all sciences. In *Novum Organum* Book I (Aphorism CIII) he argued that: '...from the new light of axioms, which having been educed from these particulars, by a certain order and rule, shall in their turn point out the way again to new particulars, greater things may be looked for. For our road does not lie on a level, but ascends and descends; first ascending to axioms, then descending to works.'[56] Bacon's rendering given in 1605 of Machiavelli's procedure in his *Discourses* – 'for knowledge drawn freshly and in our view out of particulars knoweth the way best to particulars again. And it hath much greater life for practice etc. etc.' – tallies fifteen years later with *Novum Organum*. In an earlier aphorism (Aphorism XXIV) the phrasing approximates to identity: 'axioms duly and orderly formed from particulars easily discover the way to new particulars, and thus render sciences active'.[57]

CHAPTER II

Civil history of the reign of
King Henry the 7th

Expounding mixed history's merits and potentialities, as he does, approving them and exploiting them, Bacon in no way relaxes his call that histories pure both civil and natural must be accumulated without delay. 'For it is the true office of history to represent the events themselves together with the counsels, and to leave the observations and conclusions thereupon to the liberty and faculty of every man's judgment.'[1] The part to be played by history mixed is valuable. But so also is the part to be played by history pure. Thus the two must be kept apart. His own *History of the Reign of King Henry the 7th*, as said, is lacking – though not completely as will be seen – in such observations and conclusions. But the point behind the drive in Bacon's insistence on history pure is the primacy of purity of information. Purity of text, that is, exclusion of 'observations and conclusions', while desirable, is secondary. The ancient civil historians of Bacon's civil secular canon had often not been sparing in offering their generalities. Whether or not historians, civil or natural, employ their liberties and faculties in making observations and in drawing conclusions as part of their text is a consideration subsidiary to the providing on their part of valid information. Nevertheless it is desirable that history pure and history mixed should be plainly distinguished.

The two histories pure, civil history pure and natural history pure – their purity consisting primarily of purity of information – are similar for Bacon in more than one way. Both must be shaped according to sequences of time. Coupling events with their causes 'is the ornament and life of civil history'.[2] The same is true of natural history. In this department, too, without time sequences there can be no coupling of causes and consequences. In the final *Advancement* he speaks as we have seen of inductive history natural. But he speaks, too, of narrative history natural. Further, history civil and history natural do not differ but are similar because both of them contain material wrought upon by man together with *data* which is unwrought. Natural history is comprised of nature in a regular course; of nature in its irregularities; and of nature intercepted by man's action and cajoled or trapped into an engagement with him resulting in greater or less success in terms of his avowed aims. Civil history is no different. Livy, for example, presents men in an ordinary course, men who are not ordinary but remarkable, and men wrought upon by government with greater or less success in terms of a purpose.

Nevertheless the two pure histories differ. They are different because history civil under Bacon's handling has a distinct priority. Its dignity and authority are pre-eminent among human writings. It has this pre-eminence because, first, when stating that 'history possesseth the mind with the conceits which are nearest allied unto action' and that it 'holdeth use to man's life', it is evident in the place where he says so that the reference is to history civil. As we have allowed, it is not implausible to argue that he could have said the same of history natural. But evidence in confirmation is lacking, at any rate at the time when he made the statement. Secondly, civil history is material which unlike the *data* for nature is extant and available. Thirdly, it is material which is not only extant but sound. He finds little cause to doubt its validity and integrity. This is not the case in the arena of the world of nature: 'For I want', he writes, explaining that there is a requirement in this area which hitherto has not been fulfilled, 'this primary history is to be compiled with a most religious care, and as if every particular were stated upon oath.'[3] In civil history by contrast, the proficiency of the ancients and the worthiness of a few moderns guarantee their reliability, the more especially since their findings received confirmation for Bacon in experience garnered in his own times.

It has to be added that in his case civil history has priority in yet one more respect. 'Natural history is in use two-fold. For it is used either for the sake of the knowledge of the things themselves that are committed to the history, or as the primary material of philosophy.'[4] Civil history is similarly two-fold in its use. It is used either for the sake of the knowledge of the men whose words and deeds are recorded in the history, or it is used as the primary material for philosophy. But the first of these two uses has a dimension in the case of civil history which leaves it superior to the first use ascribed to natural history.

Human actions and human failures in action as unfolded in narrative form, these not only provide items – *exempla* – which constitute primary material for philosophy, they are also *exempla* in another use of this term. Axioms and precepts respecting man in general, though based on numerous particular individuals, are made by observing men in their averagely normal ways of proceeding. But civil history like natural history consists not only of a regular or ordinary course; and of material (in this case men) wrought upon by art (in this case policy); it comprises in addition particulars (in this case human individuals) who are extraordinary, remarkable and protruding from the norm. As is not the case in natural history, individuals – those with memorable good acts to their credit, with remarkable bad acts to their names, or with notable omissions in conduct associated with their reputations – these human instances possess the power when encountered in life or when depicted in histories to evoke imitation or avoidance by other men. It is plain that here we have a belief which Bacon shared. Throughout his life he manifestly respected the power of examples no less than he worked for the truth of his precepts. In this intention he included the efficacy of examples set by himself, whether in civil matters or in his attempts to launch inquiry into the secrets of nature. It was therefore, he held, a function of civil historians to present examples and to do so persuasively.

In this he follows historians comprising his secular canon and indeed, until times comparatively recent, the vast majority of others, including for example Machiavelli in his *History of Florence*. Livy in the earliest pages of his history of Rome, *Ab Urbe Condita*, had written:

What chiefly makes the study of history wholesome and profitable is this, that you behold the lessons of every kind of experience set forth as on a conspicuous monument; from these you may choose for yourself and for your own state what to imitate, from these mark for avoidance what is shameful in the conception and shameful in the result...no state was ever greater...none more righteous or richer in good examples than Rome.[5]

Rhetoric and civil history in this its alternative use are thus related partners for Bacon as they had been and continued to be for others.

'…the business of rhetoric', whether in speeches, sermons, poems, addresses and writings of all other kinds,

is to make pictures of virtue and goodness, so that they may be seen. For since they cannot be showed to the sense in corporeal shape, the next degree is to show them to the imagination in as lively a representation as possible, by ornament of words. For the method of the Stoics, who thought to thrust virtue upon men by concise and sharp maxims and conclusions, which have little sympathy with the imagination and will of man, has justly been ridiculed.[6]

However, the business, one of the businesses, of civil historians, is to do the same; that is, to make pictures of virtue and goodness, or of their contraries, so that they may be seen – but with a difference. This time they are presented 'to the sense' in truly corporeal shape.

In Bacon's case this practice in no way dethroned the primacy of axioms. He did not waver in working for them. These as achievements of reason transcend time and place. They are applicable in all times and places. They are superior to other intellectual constructs and other forms of mental and literary exercises. The course of civil history was prone to repeat itself. Following good rather than bad examples might help to steer civil history's self-repetitions into more rather than less desirable outcomes. But if this on its own had proved effective as an instrument for improving civil policy, there would have been no need for civil history's newer function of providing foundations for civil policy – newer and also truer. For if men elicit axioms from civil history they induce it to perform a work of reason. In the *Preface* to *Discorsi* Machiavelli complained of the lack of a due appreciation of history. He claimed to be remedying this by proceeding in a new way. There was nothing new in offering examples out of the past for imitation or avoidance. His readers would scarcely have been unaware that in this respect history had not lacked appreciation. Elsewhere, as said, he himself pursued this common practice of civil historians, ancient and modern. But a new way was in *Discorsi*. Machiavelli argued that he did as jurists and physicians tried to do. He tried to find rules. Bacon was no different.

Yet Bacon affirmed repeatedly that the potency of dead or living examples to move men can surpass that of precepts. These examples, too, in their own fashion transcend time and place. 'History possesseth the mind of the conceits which are nearest allied unto action.' He proceeded to write that it, history, 'imprinteth them so, as it doth not alter the complexion of the mind neither to irresolution nor to pertinacity'. Civil history could and should provoke students, while fending off both irresolution and pertinacity, into the making of axioms by launching themselves into organized interplay between theory and practice. But alternatively and sometimes to no less effect history can promote activity in its students to imitate – or to avoid – notable deeds done by men in the past. To civil history's fidelity are entrusted not only the foundations of civil policy, it is also committed to presenting the examples of our ancestors. Indeed 'examples of our ancestors' stands first in Bacon's list of civil history's duties. Moreover the import and impact of the others – vicissitude of things – foundations of civil policy – the name and reputation of men – since these are conveyed in human and corporeal shape have the correspondingly more emotive effectiveness. Almost simultaneously with the final *Advancement* (1623) the author published *The History of the Reign of King Henry the 7th* (1622), Henry 'being one of the most sufficient kings of all the number'.[7] He was also King James's ancestor. Bacon offers ancestor to heir as an example in some ways to be imitated, in others not.

In his recommendations and achievements, Bacon thus presents another triad of flanking interlocking arts – distinct yet not to be divided. Civil history can be placed between moral and civil knowledge on the one hand, and rhetoric on the other, as participating of both. On the one side, civil history and moral and civil knowledge interpenetrate; civil historians depend on moral and civil knowledge and their criteria; if not, they cannot know what examples to present: moral and civil knowledge depend on civil history; if not, these knowledges will forfeit one of the ways in which they can be promoted, namely through the presentation of examples. On the other side, civil history and rhetoric interpenetrate: civil history depends on rhetoric, for without this science to assist historians their portrayal of examples will lack force and fall flat: rhetoric when employed in other addresses written or spoken depends on civil history, since for the purpose of stirring men's imaginations (and minds through imaginations) it cites corporeal examples from the past. Bacon does not mention this in the passage quoted where he criticizes 'the method of the Stoics': there he writes only of ornament of words as the agent of persuasion, contrasting it with the Stoics' 'concise and sharp maxims and conclusions'. Nevertheless he knows it since he practises it. He does so extensively for example in the first Book of *Advancement* (both versions). In making axioms, it is true, examples are forbidden to dance attendance upon discourse like slaves. Elsewhere they are expected to do so.

By contrast with history civil, history natural can play no part in this needed and sometimes fruitful prodding of men. Bacon it is true imports bees, ants and spiders, and also tortoises, basilisks and owls, into his arguments. Spiders spin webs out of their bellies. Their webs are exquisitely rational, but vacuous and flimsy like the achievements of philosophical sects, schools and systems. Ants collect particulars but do nothing with them but in due course eating them: they resemble the practical men who boast how practical they are.

But the bee takes a middle course; it gathers its material from the flowers of the garden and of the field but transforms and digests it by a power of its own. Not unlike this is the true business of philosophy; for it neither relies solely or chiefly on the powers of the mind, nor does it take the matter which it gathers... and lay it up in the memory whole, as it finds it; but lays it up in the understanding altered and digested.[8]

Bacon does not point out that the activities of bees do not succeed in altering and increasing the bounds of their accomplishments – that is to say, their wax and their honey remain the sum total of their products.

As for tortoises, since they remain safe inside their shells, they teach that two nations living within one island should be wholly united within one state.[9] As for basilisks, they help men to understand that 'it is not possible to join serpentine wisdom with the columbine innocency except men know exactly all the conditions of the serpent'.[10] For 'as the fable goeth of the basilisk, that if he see you first, you die for it, but if you see him first he dieth: so it is with deceits and evil arts, which, if they be first espied they leese their life; but if they prevent, they endanger'.[11] Referring to owls in the *History of Life and Death* Bacon points out that: 'It is strange how men, like owls, see sharply in the darkness of their own notions, but in the daylight of experience wink and are blinded.'[12] The lesson owls teach is that men must recognize, remain aware of, and strive to overcome the idols of their minds.

The conduct of bees, ants, spiders, tortoises, basilisks and owls does not impugn the validity of this difference between civil and natural history in that the one unlike the other teaches moral or civil philosophy by example. Bees and tortoises set a good example to philosophers. Ants, spiders, basilisks and owls set bad but nevertheless helpful and warning examples to philosophers. But all bees, all tortoises, all ants, all spiders, all basilisks and all owls do this, not outstanding individual specimens endowed with special qualities. This is not a distinction without a difference. For it is only exceptional men who provide examples of conduct which move others to imitate or to avoid, this being a matter of common experience. Their examples are inherently potent. If a creature other than a man teaches a man lessons – a spider is said to have encouraged King Robert the Bruce to persevere – this is an event to be looked upon as accidental.

A concluding difference distinguishing history civil from history natural remains to be remarked. While the former welcomes and requires alliance with rhetoric, the latter, according to Bacon, rejects this alliance.[13] Time is precious. It was wrong to waste it by efforts to improve style in presenting *data*. It matters more to collect it since there is so little of it. In this Bacon – in his collections and in his mixed history treatments of natural *data* – fails to follow what he enjoins. This is because he is incapable of writing clumsily, unpleasingly or ineffectually.

When in 1622 he published the *History of the Reign of King Henry the 7th*, this, as things turned out, concluded the enterprise he had so long projected, namely that he would write and that he would publish a civil history. Though Charles, Prince of Wales, expressed interest in Bacon's researches into the reign of King Henry VIII, these labours were not completed. Thus the original scheme which covered extensive sweeps of time became curtailed. The plea for such a history was retained in 1623 in the second *Advancement*. Perhaps others could be persuaded to embrace the undertaking of the rest of the story. Just as others could translate into practice the element which was 'the fairest' in his civil policy and grand strategy; so others perhaps could complete his civil history of 'times refined in policies' and 'new and rare variety of accidents and alterations', thus providing 'the best parts for observation'.[14] His own completed book was primed to promote his grand strategy. Later histories written by others recording the reigns of Henry VII's successors should be similarly primed. However what was foregone in quantity was compensated for in the quality of Bacon's achievement.

In the first *Advancement* Bacon refers to Henry VII as 'being one of the most sufficient kings of all the number'. But in the matter of 'new and rare variety of accidents and alterations' he points the sharpest of contrasts in the second *Advancement* between Henry VII and his son and successor. Of the first he writes *Qui unus inter antecessores reges consilio enituit*: he was the one amongst his predecessors as kings who shone in policy. Whereas of Henry VIII he wrote: *licet magis impetu quam consilio administratae*:[15] he allowed things to be administered rather by passion than by policy. Of Henry VIII he wrote at another place: '... the acts of that King were (commonly) rather proffers and fames than either well-grounded or well-pursued'.[16] Judging by these statements it looks as if Bacon's *History of the Reign of King Henry 8th* – if it had been written – would have provided examples rather of what ought to be avoided than examples of courses which deserved to be imitated. But this is speculation, especially since in yet another place (indeed in two) Bacon commends this king's conduct of relations with neighbouring states.[17] In any case the book was not written. One reason could have been that the writer faced a shortage of suitable material. He wrote in 1623 to Sir Toby Matthew: 'Since you say the Prince hath not forgot his commandment touching my History of Henry 8th, I may not forget my duty. But I find Sir Robert Cotton, who poured forth what he had in my other work, somewhat dainty of his materials in this.'[18] In the history which was successfully published, the account of Henry VIII's predecessor, there was a wealth to be garnered of *exempla* of both kinds – items for the making by others of axioms in civil history mixed – and examples to be imitated or avoided which were presented by the author himself in this civil history pure. Despite the tribute to Henry VII in the matter of policy, this account of his rule was by no means uncritical.

There were as he explained three kinds of perfect civil histories pure; histories of times, histories of lives, and 'narrations or relations of actions', the latter composed by men contemporary with the events they described, or by writers who took part in these or similar events. The secular canon contained civil histories of all three kinds. All three sorts were needed. The third variety, 'narrations or relations of actions', produced by writers contemporary with what they recounted was likely, he conceded, to be foremost of the three 'in verity and sincerity'. But in the company of all others, whether practising in ancient times, or writing in epochs long after his death, he recognized that historiography cannot be confined and restricted to this species of it. Furthermore, again in a universal and perennial company of civil historians, Bacon showed himself aware that 'narrations or relations' made by contemporaries were not always more reliable than the other two kinds. In general all three varieties were needed. In the particular instance of England all three sorts were defective or lacking. It is scarcely likely that Bacon would have argued that the three pure forms of civil history had always been and must always be practised in such a way that there was no overlap between them. The book he produced in 1622 combined in itself all three varieties of civil history pure.

It was a history of times. When describing what was desirable, and when proposing what he himself considered undertaking to remedy a lack, he wrote in *Advancement* (both versions) that 'from the Uniting of the Roses to the Uniting of the Kingdoms' there had run

a portion of time wherein, to my understanding, there hath been the rarest varieties that in like number of successions of any hereditary monarchy hath been known. For it beginneth with the mixed adoption of a crown by arms and title; an entry by battle, an establishment by marriage; and therefore times answerable, like waters after a tempest, full of working and swelling, though without extremity of storm; but well passed through by the wisdom of the pilot, being one of the most sufficient kings of all the number.[19]

Not only was this book a history of such times – of the memorable outset, generation and thrust of them – it was also a history of a life – the life of the King. The story ended with his death. In *Of the True Greatness of Kingdoms and Estates* (1625) Bacon referred to his book as a 'life'.[20] In addition, both by title and by content it comprised a 'narration or relation of actions'. It was a record of the reign of a ruler. The writer of this record was not contemporary with this ruler and with what he did as 'wise pilot'. But Bacon was a man of state and of state experience.

The History of the Reign of King Henry the 7th strictly obeyed what its author called 'regular history's' 'so strict laws'. As said he employed the science of rhetoric as did the members of his civil secular canon. In accord with standards set by these exemplar historians of ancient Greece and Rome, the prior and central topics dealt with are matters of state. Counsels and speeches are provided. Events are coupled with their causes. Bacon's book is no 'bare continuance and tissue of actions without the causes and pretexts, the commencements and occasions, the counsels and orations'. Too often, he had said, the history 'of times representeth the magnitude of actions and the public faces and deportments of persons, and passeth over in silence the smaller passages and motions of men and matters'. Bacon did not pass over these latter in silence. He sought to pursue 'the true and inward resorts of business' and to unravel and expound its 'real passages'.

The history of the church had been absorbed into the history of the state according to the second *Advancement*. Doubtless had there been major occurrences worthy of mention in this field in Henry's times, Bacon would not have omitted them. However he recorded that

the King was desirous to bring into the house of Lancaster celestial honour; and become suitor to Pope Julius to canonise King Henry the Sixth for a saint…Julius referred the matter (as the manner is) to certain cardinals to take the verification of his holy acts and miracles: but it died under the reference. The general opinion was, that Pope Julius was too dear, and that the King would not come to his rates. But it is more probable, that the Pope who was extremely jealous of the dignity of the see of Rome and of the acts thereof, knowing that King Henry the Sixth was reputed in the world abroad but for a simple man, was afraid it would but diminish the estimation of that kind of honour, if there not a distance kept between innocents and saints.[21]

In one signal respect Bacon departs from a prescription – a 'so strict law' – this time a new one which he had laid down himself. Throughout nearly all of his book he faithfully follows his injunction that general conclusions and the making of general observations should be omitted from civil histories pure, and that histories pure and histories mixed should be kept clearly apart. But he offends and on two occasions brings in what he himself said ought to be left out.

Of mixed history civil he laid it down in the first *Advancement* that when it is undertaken it should be evident as the writer's 'principal intention'. In the second *Advancement* he stated that a worker in mixed history civil should 'profess it'. Clearly mixed history is not the principal intention of the *History of the Reign of King Henry the 7th*. Therefore its author made no profession in it that mixed history was what he was after. He added in the final *Advancement* that writers of perfect civil histories pure should not themselves play midwives to the 'precepts and warnings' in policy with which every wise history is pregnant.[22] It is others, he implies, who should perform this task. But we find in his history a general observation to the effect that matters of law should be noted and written about in civil histories. In the cause of what should not be excluded he thus includes what ought – he had said – to be omitted.

in my judgment it is some defect even in the best writers of history, that they do not often enough summarily deliver and set down the most memorable laws passed in the times whereof they write, being indeed the principal acts of peace. For though they may be had in original books of laws themselves; yet that informeth not the judgment of kings and counsellors and persons of estate so well as to see them described and entered in the table and portrait of the times.[23]

He goes even further. He introduces a piece of discourse and a piece of observation as if he were writing civil history mixed. He commented profusely on a statute of 'singular policy; for the population apparently' (manifestly) 'and (if it be thoroughly considered) for the soldiery and militar forces of the realm'.[24] In his thorough consideration of this statute he wrote: 'Now how much this did advance the militar power of the kingdom, is apparent by the true principles of war and the examples of other kingdoms. For it hath been held by the general opinion of men of best judgment in the wars... [again a reference to Machiavelli] that the principal strength of an army consisteth in the infantry or foot. And to make good infantry, it requireth men bred not in a servile or indigent fashion but in some free and plentiful manner.' Bacon argued that as a result of this statute England contrasted favourably with, for example, France 'where in effect all is noblesse or peasantry'. As a result of this statute in the long term 'a middle people' was encouraged in England and such men should prove 'good forces of foot'.[25]

In this instance, and indeed in his admonition that legal matters needed to be included in civil histories, Bacon in 1622 offended against his rule laid down in 1623 that midwives of political wisdom should be other than the writers of civil histories pure. In these instances his history pure seems to have been caught up into, and to a degree swept along by, his high approbation of civil history mixed. It can be said in his favour that he makes the identical two observations in what were more appropriate places. Not being able to provide other persons to do the work, he resorts to repeating his statements at other places more suitable for the making of them. He states in Aphorism XXIX of *Example of a Summary Treatise on Universal Justice or the Fountains of Equity* etc. that 'it is a misfortune even of the best historians, that they do not dwell sufficiently upon laws and judicial acts; or if by chance they show some diligence therein, yet they differ greatly from the authentic reporters'.[26] This example of a summary treatise as we have seen is a civil history mixed relating to the part of policy consisting of laws. He states in *Example of a Summary Treatise on the Extension of Empire*:

And herein the device of King Henry the Seventh (whereof I have spoken largely in the history of his life) was profound and admirable: in making farms and houses of husbandry of a standard; that is, maintained with such a proportion of land attached inseparably to them, as may breed a subject to live in convenient plenty, and no servile condition; and to keep the plough in the hands of the owners, or at least the tenants, and not mere hirelings. And thus indeed you shall attain to Virgil's character which he gives to ancient Italy: *terra potens armis, atque ubere glebae* – a land mighty in arms and in fertility.[27]

This example of a summary treatise as we know was translated into English and appears as an essay in the collection of 1625. Many of the essays converged upon a mixed history pattern.

But there are two further considerations. First, as we have seen, the priority in his thinking about civil history pure is that of purity of information, not that of text. It could scarcely have been otherwise given the habits and conduct in antiquity of the members of his civil secular canon. A second consideration is the more telling. The two types of *exempla*, though differing in principle, could turn out to be indistinguishable in practice. Items are sorted and sifted for the discovery of rules, but there could be an item which was found to embody a rule, in which case it presents itself as an example for imitation or avoidance. Bacon had explained this when describing Machiavelli's mode of proceeding in *Discorsi* when seeking such rules: 'When the example is the ground, being set down in an history at large, it is set down with the circumstances, which may sometimes control the discourse thereupon made, and sometimes supply it , as *a very pattern for action*' [emphasis added].

Civil histories should provide material for study of human passions and also of 'characters of dispositions'. Bacon's book contains such material, but not – in the case of the latter topic – at the end only, when the King's death was recorded and commemorated; but instead, and as he had recommended, 'from the entire body of history as often as such a person enters upon the stage'.[28] The function of civil histories pure – whether of times, lives, or when consisting of narrations or relations of actions – should present examples of our ancestors, the vicissitude of things, foundations for civil policy, and the name and reputation of men. 'Vicissitude of things', as Bacon defined the term in *De Sapientia Veterum* under Fable XI (*Orpheus* or *Philosophy*),[29] and under Fable XXII (*Nemesis* or *The Vicissitude of Things*),[30] and also in the last essay collection's final piece entitled *Of Vicissitude of Things* (1625),[31] comprises events, as both Bacon and Machiavelli could not but agree, which are seemingly outside men's foresight and control, and lying beyond the reach of successful policy – 'points of nature' like deluges and earthquakes but also upheavals in religions. Certain classes of events are reserved for the irresistible interventions of divine providence. 'Vicissitude of things' is not much in evidence in Bacon's book for the reason presumably that there was little to put on record under such a head. But the other three duties of a civil historian – providing examples of our ancestors, affording foundations for civil policy, and handing on the name and reputation of men – these are scrupulously and profusely attended to.

Writing as statesman for the profit of statesmen, Bacon made sure that his book contained material for *exempla* of both the needed kinds: records of foundations for civil policy which had been laid successfully in the times covered; for instance, Henry's already referred to statute 'of Singular policy;...for the soldiery and militar forces of the realm...' It should be mentioned in this connection that in 1597 while the Queen was yet reigning Bacon had successfully introduced two bills in the House of Commons for the enforcement of Henry's statute:

Mr Bacon made a motion against depopulation of towns and houses of husbandry and tillage... though it may be thought ill and very prejudicial to lords that have enclosed great grounds, and pulled down even whole towns, and converted them to sheep-pastures; yet considering the increase of people and the benefit of the commonwealth, I doubt not but every man will deem the revival of former moth-eaten laws in this point a praiseworthy thing... For enclosure of grounds brings depopulation, which brings forth first idleness, secondly decay of tillage, thirdly subversion of houses, and decrease of charity and charge to the poor's maintenance, fourthly the impoverishing the state of the realm. A law for the taking away of which inconveniences is not to be thought ill or hurtful unto the general state.[32]

In 1601 he successfully defended these acts against proposals for their repeal: 'The old commendation of Italy by the poet is *Potens viris atque ubere gleba*; and it stands not with the policy of the State that the wealth of the kingdom should be engrossed into a few pasturers' hands...the husbandman a strong and hardy man – the good footman: which is a chief observation of good warriors, etc. So he concluded the statute not to be repealed, etc.'[33]

There was also other material to be gathered by others out of Bacon's book for making yet further foundations for policy in the present and future: and in addition portrayal of King Henry's actions to be followed and imitated or to be eschewed and avoided. Though Bacon judged Henry VII 'one of the most sufficient kings of all the number', but he presents him as embodying a mixture of differing, even opposite, qualities.

Certainly his times for good commonwealths laws did excel; so as he may justly be celebrated for the best lawgiver to this nation after King Edward the First. For his laws (whoso marks them well) are deep and not vulgar; not made upon the spur of a particular occasion for the present, but out of providence of the future; to make the estate of his people still more and more happy, after the manner of the legislators in ancient and heroical times.[34]

One such action has been noticed earlier. This instance did not stand alone.

The King also (having care to make his realm potent as well by sea as by land) for the better maintenance of the navy, ordained, that wines and woads from the parts of Gascoign and Languedoc, should not be brought but in English bottoms; bowing the ancient policy of this estate from consideration of plenty to consideration of power: for that almost all the ancient statutes invite (by all means) merchants strangers to bring in all sorts of commodities, having for end cheapness, and not looking to the point of state concerning the naval power.[35]

In that part of policy which comprises attention to laws the King was politic. Bacon it is true does not include him in lists of famous lawgivers which he provides elsewhere. But here in his history he could scarcely have more decidedly stressed this quality in Henry: 'in that part both of justice and policy which is the durable part, and cut as it were in brass or marble, which is the making of good laws, he did excel'.[36] Bacon wanted from King James not so much 'the making of good laws' as their amendment. But the point could be taken as including that requirement. On the other hand, in that part of policy which concerns government or matters of state King Henry was far otherwise, though with some exceptions. He grew 'to such a height of reputation for cunning and policy, that every accident and event that went well was laid and imputed to his foresight, as if he had set if before'.[37] But, early in the book Bacon remarked: 'in his nature and constitution of mind' he was 'not very apprehensive of forecasting of future events afar off, but an entertainer of fortune by the day'.[38] Summing up at the end, he wrote:

His wisdom, by often evading from perils, was turned rather into a dexterity to deliver himself from dangers when they pressed him, than into a providence to prevent and remove them afar off. And even in nature, the sight of his mind was like some sights of eyes; rather strong at hand than to carry afar off... certain it is that the perpetual troubles of his fortunes (there being no more matter out of which they grew) could not have been without some great defects and main errors in his nature, customs, and proceedings, which he had enough to do to save and help with a thousand little industries and watches. But those do best appear in the story itself.[39]

By contrast with his conduct in matters of law, the King's proceedings in matters of government illustrated the complaint made in the essay *Of Empire* (1612 and 1625): 'This is true, that the wisdom of all these latter times in princes' affairs is rather fine deliveries, and shiftings of dangers and mischiefs, when they are near, than solid and grounded courses to keep them aloof. But this is but to try masteries with fortune...' King James VI and I and also others should take due note and mark this. At the start of the fragment on the reign of Henry VIII Bacon refers to 'that wise and fortunate King, King Henry the Seventh...' He was fortunate in two ways – fortunate because, successfully seeing her, he created his fortune: fortunate also because, when trying masteries with her, he escaped scot free. A key to the discrepancy between King Henry VII's actions in the field of law and his conduct in matters of state is suggested when Bacon explained that in matters of state he had started by being often lucky and had continued being often lucky. 'No doubt, in him as in all men (and most of all in kings) his fortune wrought upon his nature, and his nature upon his fortune.'[40]

But not all Henry's proceedings in matters of government illustrated that perilous transaction of trying masteries with fortune. 'He professed always to love and seek peace... Yet he knew the way to peace was not to seem to be desirous to avoid wars.' In this he set an example in policy for King James. Further, in concluding the book Bacon observed that as King Henry 'would sometimes strain up his laws to his prerogative, so would he also let down his prerogative to his Parliament. For mint and wars and martial discipline (things of absolute power) he would nevertheless bring to Parliament.' As an example of this procedure Bacon records a speech King Henry made to the Lords and Commons:

now that I need to make a war upon France in person, I will declare it to you myself... The French King troubles the Christian world... France hath much people, and few soldiers: they have no stable bands of foot. Some good horse they have, but those are forces which are least fit for a defensive war, where the actions are in the assailant's choice... My people and I know one another; which breeds confidence... In this great business let me have your advice and aid... Go together in God's name, and lose no time, for I have called this Parliament wholly for this cause.[41]

In this – 'letting down his prerogative to his parliament' Henry VII was setting a further good example in policy for King James; a policy which he, Bacon, encouraged and pressed the latter to adopt as an essential – as *the* essential – core and 'fairest' part of a grand strategy; binding thereby parliaments to monarchs, confirming the rights of both parties, securing supplies to governments, and all in the process of safeguarding and establishing the moral and material power of Britain. But perhaps above all as a stroke of policy Bacon adduced Henry VII's achievement in arranging the marriage of his eldest daughter Margaret with the King of Scots.

During the treaty, it is reported that the King remitted the matter to his counsel, and that some of the table... did put the case – that if God should take the King's two sons without issue, that then the kingdom of England would fall to the King of Scotland, which might prejudice the monarchy of England. Whereunto the King, himself replied; That if that should be, Scotland would be but an accession to England, and not England to Scotland; for that the greater would draw the less: and that it was a safer union for England than that of France. This passed as an oracle,...

Nevertheless, as King James and others should observe, many of King Henry's successes as ruler were rooted, Bacon was insistent, in good fortune rather than grounded in foresight which can create good fortune. Even in the source freely and frequently quoted from already, the paper written while the Queen still reigned in good felicity, Bacon remarked of Henry that:

His times were rather prosperous than calm, for he was assailed with many troubles, which he overcame happily; a matter that did not less set forth his wisdom than his fortune; and yet such a wisdom as seemed rather a dexterity to deliver himself from dangers when they pressed him, than any deep foresight to prevent them afar off.[43]

On the other hand Bacon describes an occasion when in dealings with powers across the Channel the King 'promised himself money, honour, friends, and peace in the end'. Bacon comments: 'But those things were too fine to be fortunate in all parts: for that great affairs are commonly too rough and stubborn to be wrought upon by the finer edges and points of wit.' In other words Bacon detected in the King a bent towards unrealistic refinement in calculating.[44]

Another failing was the

disposition which afterwards nourished and whet on by bad counsellors and ministers proved the blot of his times: which was the course he took to crush treasure out of his subjects' purses, by forfeitures upon penal laws. At this men did startle the more...because it appeared plainly to be in the King's nature and not out of his necessity.[45]

'Kings', Bacon commented, 'do more easily find instruments for their will and humour than for their service and honour.'[46] 'And, it may be justly suspected...that as the King did excel in good commonwealth laws, so nevertheless he had in secret a design to make use of them as well for collecting treasure as for correcting of manners.'[47] But perhaps even in this there could lie a lesson in policy for King James. Bacon remarks that Henry 'having every day occasion to take notice of the necessities and shifts for money of other great Princes abroad, it did the better by comparison set off to him the felicity of full coffers'.[48] Though not avariciously or oppressively, James should seek to possess treasure of his own in his coffers, treasure other than what parliaments could be persuaded to provide.

'Never prince was more wholly given to affairs, nor in them more of himself.'[49] He was 'governed by none'.[50] But to his counsel 'he did refer much...knowing it to be the way to assist his power and inform his judgment: in which respect also he was fairly patient of liberty both of advice and of vote, till himself were declared.'[51] 'What he minded he compassed.'[52] He 'kept state and majesty to the height, being sensible that majesty maketh the people bow...'[53] 'As for the disposition of his subjects in general towards him, it stood thus with him; that of the three affections which naturally tie the hearts of the subjects to their sovereign, – love, fear, and reverence – he had the last in height; the second in good measure, and so little of the first, as he was beholding to the other two.'[54] The relevance of these statements about King Henry VII to the sundry advices and admonitions which Bacon gave to King James VI and I should be evident from past pages in this present study. The instances and occasions of his addresses to the King require no repetition.

Bacon was adversely critical of Henry's conduct towards his nobles.

He kept a strait hand on his nobility, and chose rather to advance clergymen and lawyers, which were more obsequious to him, but had less interest in the people; which made for his absoluteness, but not for his safety. Insomuch as I am persuaded it was one of the causes of his troublesome reign. For that his nobles, though they were loyal and obedient, yet did not cooperate with him, but let every man go his own way.[55]

Observations elucidating remarks like these are to be found, as they should be according to Bacon, not in the text of his history of this king, but in the essay *Of Nobility* (1612 and 1625). Bacon's teaching in this essay on the place and function of nobles in a state follows that of Machiavelli. Nobles properly belong in monarchies, not in republics. In *Discourse* 1.55 Machiavelli had written: '... (1) that, where the gentry are numerous, no-one who proposes to set up a republic can succeed unless he first gets rid of the lot; and (2) that, where considerable equality prevails, noone who proposes to set up a kingdom or principality, will ever be able to do it unless from that equality he selects many of the more ambitious and restless minds and makes of them gentry in fact as well as in name, by giving them castles and possessions and making of them a privileged class with respect both to property and subjects; so that around him will be those with whose support he may maintain himself in power, and whose ambitions, thanks to him, may be realised.'

Bacon in his essay *Of Nobility* (1612 and 1625) wrote on similar lines but added a point of his own; namely that 'A monarchy, where there is no nobility at all, is ever a pure and absolute tyranny, as that of the Turks; ...' '... nobility attempers sovereignty, and draws the eyes of the people somewhat aside from the line royal. But for democracies' (*sic*), 'they need it not; and they are commonly more quiet and less subject to sedition than when there are stirps of nobles; ...'.[56] In monarchies a great and potent nobility adds majesty to the ruler 'but diminisheth power; and putteth life and spirit into the people, but presseth their fortune.'[57] We have seen that Bacon's complaint in his history about King Henry VII in the matter of the treatment of his nobles was that since he did not advance them, preferring clergy and lawyers, they, his nobles, did not cooperate with him. This, 'made for his absoluteness, but not for his safety'. His nobles did not assist him in keeping the people peaceable. 'It is well', he writes in the essay, 'when nobles are not too great for sovereignty nor for justice; and yet maintained in that height, as the insolency of inferiors may be broken upon them before it come on too fast upon the majesty of kings.'[58] Judging by a statement Bacon made in 1618 it seems that in this matter King James did better than King Henry: 'Your nobility in a right distance between crown and people, no oppressions of the people, no over shadowers of the crown.'[59] But it is possible that this is a case of *laudando praecipere*: 'when by telling men what they are, they represent to them what they should be...'

Civil history in its dignity and in its authority stands first among branches of human learning. By making his definitions and by drawing his distinctions, Bacon extends civil history's scope. He describes civil history of arts, letters, and sciences. Similarly he delineates civil history mixed. He identifies civil history with civil experience; thus extending the past into the present. He defines 'memorials' as civil history preparatory, civil history unfinished, comprising for example 'declarations and letters of estate': 'So again letters of affairs from such as manage them, or are privy to them, are of all others the best instructions for history, and' [though this final sentence is omitted in the second *Advancement*] 'to a diligent reader the best histories in themselves'.[60] History civil swallows up history ecclesiastical. Matters of law are to be treated in civil histories. For law is as much part of policy as government. Even the course of the law in itself becomes a civil history.

In all these instances Bacon not only extends civil history's range in definition – in counsel – in theory. But also in all these instances he extends it in his contributions – in his works – in his practice. While performing other tasks he provides pieces of the history of letters. He practises civil mixed history, even momentously extending it into studies in the universe of nature. He extends civil history into his own present, as embodied in his words, his actions, his experiences, in relation to events of his own times. Recalling his correspondence with Bishop Williams, it will not be forgotten that he writes, submits and bequeaths what he calls 'memorials' – 'declarations and letters of estate'. In both ways – in his theory, that is, and in his practice – he enhances the dignity and authority of civil history.

But for Bacon, while history civil becomes a *genus*, it remains a species within its own *genus*. For Bacon it is this civil history, 'properly so called' – *Historia Civilis Specialis* – that is to say, the history of government, but now also of laws and thus of the whole of policy – which stands highest. Similarly it is this civil history pure – that is to say, civil history devoid of observations ('For it is the true office of history to represent the things themselves, together with the counsels') – which comes first. Likewise in his case it is this civil history perfect – that is to say, not civil history 'preparatory' and 'unfinished' in the form of memorials or declarations of estate, though experience presented in these latter indeed enriches and buttresses his civil history perfect – which has the highest rank: and it is this civil history, species of its own *genus*, which is his prime and his foremost version of all human learning. Bacon's other extensions of the subject are, so to say, lateral. It is this extension alone which is, so to say, vertical. He elevates it upwards into a supremacy. It is appropriate that it is a specimen of this prime kind of history civil which in terms of the span of his life is embarked upon very nearly first among his commitments. In terms of this life span it is this kind of civil history which is his *alpha* and his *omega*. For it is a project which was very early brooded. It was not indeed brooded exclusively. Natural philosophy was also indubitably his very early preoccu-pation. Nevertheless this kind of civil history was very early brooded; and also it was very late in being offered and published in the shape of *The History of the Reign of King Henry the 7th*.

CHAPTER 12

Aims and claims – but no metaphysics of nature

The final *Advancement* announced a fully positive approval for civil
mixed history in principle. In 1605 in the first *Advancement* Bacon had
already approved its use by somebody else in practice when he
described the procedure of Machiavelli in his *Discourses*. Mixed
history is a thing produced by moderns, Bacon included. It is this
instrument – itself a *Novum Organum* – which he resorted to in seeking
to launch his grand strategy. This procedure is another recent fruit
of time. But he could scarcely have advanced with a banner
inscribed

> Ruminated histories manifoldly mixed
> But ruminated and mixed with no respite
> Certainly with results
> But seldom with results indubitably certain.

Instead in two programmes he preaches and practises science/
philosophy in its correct method – except that, as we have seen, the
term 'method' is another badge which in general and for many
purposes he does not carry. He preaches and practises science/
philosophy in its correct way, and mainly, except at the end, in
human self-knowledge. In moral, governmental and legal studies, he
preaches chiefly by practising: in natural studies, except at the end,
he preaches by straight preaching: he does so above all in *Novum
Organum*. The right procedure is claimed to be new. Results will
accumulate because applying this procedure assumes cooperation.
Conduct of the procedure will be in public and no man's private task
or secret. It will thus be inspected both in the collecting of *data* and
in validity of reasoning. Honesty of conduct in using senses and
reason is presupposed, without tricks or cheating. There will be

consortium to check and correct. Interchange of findings should take place without disputing bred of ambitions aimed at mastery; and also without disputing interminably protracted by urges to dispute.

'I must request men not to suppose that after the fashion of ancient Greeks, and of certain moderns... I wish to found a new sect in philosophy. For this is not what I am about.' 'My purpose, on the contrary, is to try whether I cannot in very fact lay more firmly the foundations, and extend more widely the limits of the power and greatness of man.'[1] The human power and greatness which he aims at is no promotion of self-assertion or ill-regulated display. '...for I am not raising a capitol or pyramid to the pride of man'.[2] Power and greatness whether manifest in a series of men segregate, or achieved in kingdoms and estates of men congregate, is to be yoked with moral conduct; and moral conduct in its turn is linked with divinity. These latter, morality and divinity, will be fortified if possible, not only by practice of them but by work on their histories, seeking out axioms. 'For it is not Saint Augustine's nor Saint Ambrose's[3] works that will make so wise a divine, as ecclesiastical history, thoroughly read and observed...' What is sought is not self-importance and self-flattery for the human race, but, instead, a rich storehouse for the glory of the creator and the relief of man's estate.

Cultivation of knowledge, religious, moral, civil, natural, is a religious and moral exercise. 'All knowledge is to be limited by religion and referred to use and action.'[4] Pursuit of knowledge is to be directed by religion and in this pursuit proceedings will be grounded in use and action, not in speculation alone. Religion directs not only the purpose – the relief of man's estate – it also dictates the frame of mind in which the search will be conducted. Men should 'consider what are the true ends of knowledge', not seeking it for what are 'inferior' ends. They should 'perfect and govern it in charity'.[5] We have seen Bacon argue that morality should be handmaid to religion. Natural philosophy would also be handmaid to religion. Each would receive benefits from the mistress and each in return would bestow benefits upon her.

Men are urged 'not to be wise above measure and sobriety,...'.[6] It is thus that this cultivation is a cooperative enterprise. Therefore – again – '...my way of discovering sciences goes far to level men's wits, and leaves but little to individual excellence'.[7] This science, he claims, 'leaves but little to the acuteness and strength of wits...':[8] '...any reader of even moderate sagacity and intelligence'[9] may

embark upon it. '...all things...shall be discovered with ease.'[10]
'...For interpretation is the true and natural work of the mind when
freed from impediments. It is true however that by my precepts
everything will be in more readiness, and much more sure.'[11]

In *Novum Organum* Book I, Bacon contrasts his own new logic for
the exploring of nature with the old logic, that of Aristotle. 'Now my
way', he explained, 'though hard to practise' (hard to practise –
but only because and not for any other reason – laziness, inattention,
disputatiousness or other moral frailties require to be mastered)

is easy to explain; and it is this. I propose to establish progressive stages of
certainty. The evidence of the sense, helped and guarded by a certain
process of correction, I retain. But the mental operation which follows the
act of sense I for the most part reject; and instead of it I open and lay out
a new and certain path for the mind to proceed in, starting directly from
the simple sensuous perception.[12]

Thinking is not excluded. It cannot be and should not be
excluded. But it is protected and directed on every side by
appropriate proceedings which consist not of thoughts but of actions.

For its own good pursuit of knowledges will proceed in alliance
with religion. Also, benefits will be mutual. Religion, as *Novum
Organum* Book I, Aphorism LXXXIX explains, will be fortified.
Religious men have wrongly feared the alliance as if men 'in the
recesses and secret thoughts of their hearts doubted and distrusted
the strength of religion and the empire of faith over the sense; and
therefore feared that the investigation of truth in nature might be
dangerous to them. But if the matter be truly considered, natural
philosophy is after the Word of God at once the surest medicine
against superstition, and the most approved nourishment for faith,
and therefore she is rightly given to religion as her most faithful
handmaid, since the one displays the will of God, the other is
power.'[13]

Three revolutions and periods of learning, Bacon maintains, have
taken place in the West. He thus introduces a framework for the
history of arts and letters. The first two revolutions and periods are
respectively Greek and Roman. A third begins after barbarians
overrun Rome's territories. This period inaugurates the moderns. It
is the epoch of the Christian nations of the West and it endures still.
But after the barbarian incursions 'by far the greater number of the
best wits'[14] concentrated their efforts in divinity and religion. Of
Greeks in the first period – referring to times after the ancient poets.

– he writes that the wisdom of their philosophers was professorial.[15] It was delivered and debated in self-instituted teaching establishments. He asserts that these Greek savants were disputatious[16] and above all that their learning lacked the indispensable preconditions in terms of which their efforts could have been endowed with roots, ballast and the capability of expanding and improving themselves, namely historical *data* upon which to make observations. Bacon passes much the same judgment on divines of the third and modern epoch. Like the Greeks whose learning they borrowed they were disputatious. They taught and debated in self-established institutions. They used little history. Mixing Greek learning with their church religion, they disfigured the latter not only with controversies but also with heresies.[17]

Of the Romans, who brought in the second revolution and period of learning, he writes neither that they were professorial and disputatious, nor that they were devoid of these failings. In different places so that he is able to pronounce, as we have seen, the identical judgment on both, he nominates Titus Livius and Julius Caesar as each of them the most eminent civil historian of all time.[18] These and others, it was evident, presented examples in their histories to be imitated or avoided. But he does not assess Roman writing and use of history civil according to his conception of its other proper employment, which is to provide foundations for civil policy, and also a basis for improvements in aspects of moral knowledge. In assessing the second period his judgment is that while some of the Romans engaged themselves in moral knowledge, many of them were occupied in public affairs, devoting their services to practice and employing their faculties in governing the state, in notable cases combining this with writing civil histories.

Temptations to call Bacon's three revolutions or periods of learning an outbreak of dialectics which anticipates Hegel can be resisted; a period chiefly contributing thinking and theory, followed by times largely displaying practice, this is to be succeeded by an epoch which binds practice and theory into one. Such a pattern is flawed. Not only did civil history writing and reading constitute thinking; in addition schoolmen came after Romans and turned out to be as obsessively addicted to thinking and theory as Greek philosophers. What the argument suggests in its drift is that if more history, that is to say reliable *data* of whatever kind, can be provided in this the third epoch of times, and granted that it is employed in a right way, disputatiousness will diminish in extent and intensity. Assent will be compelled by a mounting weight of evident, tangible and unchallengeable results in all sciences.

But in Bacon there is due recognition that in divinity and in all learning wits in this the third period are no less disposed to rivalry, rancour and contending than wits flourishing in earlier times.[19] '...oftentimes...reason [is] litigious'. Disputes will continue. Indeed they are needed in procedure which is cooperative. He writes in 1623 to the dons at Cambridge university: 'Surely the grace of the divine light will attend and shine upon you; if humbling and submitting Philosophy to Religion you make a legitimate and dextrous use of... the sense; and putting away all zeal of contradiction, each dispute with his other as if he were disputing with himself';[20] his point being that men when deliberating within themselves seek neither to manifest skills in debate nor to contradict out of zeal for contending. 'There is', he wrote in the first *Advancement*, 'a disposition in conversation to soothe and please, and a disposition contrary to contradict and cross.'[21] Worse still, while in some men there is a disposition to goodness, in others 'on the other side, there is a natural malignity'.[22] Disputes must continue and are necessary. Disputatiousness, however likely to survive, is unnecessary. Read – or listen – he enjoins in *Of Studies*, 'not to contradict and confute, nor to believe and take for granted, or to find talk and discourse, but to weigh and consider'.[23] '...logic and rhetoric make men able to contend'[24] and rightly so. But contention should not be conducted as an end in itself or with wrong motives. Bacon wrote in *Of Great Place* (1625):

Neglect not also the examples of those that have carried themselves ill in the same place not to set off thyself by taxing their memory, but to direct thyself what to avoid. Reform, therefore, without bravery or scandal of former times and persons.[25]

In policy we have seen that he attempted to practise this precept. '...as in civil business, if there be a meeting and men fall at words there is commonly an end of the matter for that time, and no proceeding at all; so in learning, where there is much controversy there is many times little inquiry.'[26]

Reviewing the course of learning and arts Bacon complains that men have seldom followed studies:

sincerely to give a true account of their gift of reason, to the benefit and use of men: as if there were sought in knowledge a couch, whereupon to rest a searching and restless spirit; or a terrace, for a wandering and variable mind to walk up and down with a fair prospect; or a tower of state, for a proud mind to raise itself upon; or a fort or commanding ground, for strife and contention; or a shop for profit or sale; and not a rich storehouse, for the glory of the creator and the relief of man's estate.[27]

Sloth, vain-glory, envy, pride, greed – it is failings like these which Bacon describes here. This condition requires to be pondered by wits engrossed with divinity and religion in this the third epoch of learning, recognizing the part these things play in misdirection of effort and consequent stalemate and stagnation. Their moral findings, together with those of the Romans for whom moral knowledge was as theology is to us, require application. This is because moral and religious qualities, though spoken of as different, are inseparable from mental capacity and intellectual achievement. The former as much as the latter are needed if men are sincerely and effectively to give a true account of their gift of reason.

Of this right way, manifoldly mixed with morality and divinity, Bacon writes like this in *Novum Organum*, Book I, Aphorism cxxvii:

It may also be asked (in the way of doubt rather than of objection) whether I speak of natural philosophy only, or whether I mean that the other sciences, logic, ethics and politics, should be carried on by this way...Now I certainly mean what I have said to be understood of them all; and as the common logic which governs by the syllogism extends not only to natural but to all sciences; so does mine also, which proceeds by induction, embrace everything. For I form a history and tables of discovery for anger, fear, shame, and the like; for matters political; and again for the mental operations of memory, composition and division, judgment and the rest; not less than for heat and cold, or light, or vegetation, or the like.[28]

The way which is offered embraces all. Doubt remains and is wholesome. He disbelieves there can be objection. The procedure is relevant in moral knowledge, in civil knowledge and in natural knowledge. The appearance of logic in company with these perhaps reflects compressed thinking. Bacon can scarcely be intending to assert that the procedure is applicable to the procedure. The message is that he has a new logic. The work, he tells King James when presenting *Novum Organum*: 'is no more but a new logic, teaching to invent and judge by induction...and thereby to make philosophy and the sciences both more true and more active'.[29] All philosophy and all sciences can be made more true because more active (that is more experimental); and also more active (that is, producing new and better axioms) because more true.

But to this declaration that the way, which is offered and which is new, embraces all, he adds two further pronouncements. These sharply modify the position. First, after stating in Aphorism CXXVII that 'I form a history and tables of discovery for anger, fear, shame, and the like...not less than for heat and cold, or light, or vegetation or the like'; he proceeds:

But nevertheless since my way of interpretation, after the history has been prepared and duly arranged, regards not the working and discourse of the mind only (as the common logic does) but the nature of things also, I supply the mind with such rules and guidance that it may in every case apply itself to the nature of things. And therefore I deliver many and divers precepts in the doctrine of Interpretation, which in some measure modify the mode of invention according to the quality and condition of the subject of Inquiry.[30]

The second pronouncement is delivered in the next aphorism. This, when taken together with what Bacon laid down about the legitimate and needed uses of the common logic, illuminates what is obscure in Aphorism CXXVII. In Aphorism CXXVIII he writes

On one point not even a doubt ought to be entertained; namely, whether I desire to pull down and destroy the philosophy and arts and sciences which are at present in use. So far from that, I am most glad to see them used, cultivated, and honoured. There is no reason why the arts which are now in fashion should not continue to supply matter for disputation and ornaments for discourse, to be employed for the convenience of professors and men of business; to be in short like current coin, which passes among men by consent...I frankly declare that what I am introducing will be but little fitted for such purposes as these, since it cannot be brought down to common apprehension, save by effects and works only. But how sincere I am in my profession of affection and good will toward the received sciences, my published writings, especially the books on the Advancement of Learning [the *Advancement* of 1605 comprised two, that of 1623 would provide nine] sufficiently show: and therefore I will not attempt to prove it further by words. Meanwhile I give constant and distinct warning that by the ways now in use neither can any great progress be made in the doctrines and contemplative part of sciences, nor can they be carried out to any magnitude of works.[31]

The 'many and divers precepts' in some measure modifying the mode of invention according to the subject matter – that is to say, topics like 'anger, fear, shame, and the like' in a man's nature, 'and again for the mental operations of memory...and the rest', subjects which perhaps include involuntary, quasi-mechanical interactions between his mind and his body – these precepts derived from applying his new logic, Bacon, it appears, either did not succeed in delivering or else he succeeded, the precepts having subsequently been lost. Studies of this kind, proposed also among items in *Catalogue of Particular Histories by Titles*, which was published together with *Parasceve* and *Novum Organum* are attempts to explore causation which later inquirers would describe as mechanistic or materialistic, though it will be recognized that such notions were not new ones in Bacon's day. When in *Novum Organum* he reports '...histories and tables of discovery for anger, fear, shame, and the like; for matters political; and again for the mental operations of memory, composition and division...not less than for heat and cold, or light, etc. ...', what Bacon projects is inquiry whether or not verifiable connections can be shown to exist between natural knowledges and moral or civil knowledges, that is to say, he invites investigation on the one hand, of possible – at least partial – ways of explaining moral or civil attitudes and conduct in terms of involuntary bodily or psychological influences or causes; and on the other, of possible – at least partial – ways of explaining bodily conditions in terms of side effects of the impact of a man's passions or 'character of disposition'. To what extent is a man's 'character of disposition' – or even the idols of his mind of the innate variety – rooted in and governed by peculiarities in his body? To what extent is the condition of his body subject to the movements of his mind?

In *Advancement* (both versions) he discussed similar or congruent questions: 'that part of inquiry is most necessary, which considereth of the seats and domiciles which the several faculties of the mind do take and occupate in the organs of the body; which knowledge hath been attempted, and is controverted, and deserveth to be much better enquired'.[32] In the second version he adds: 'Neither again is that arrangement of the intellectual faculties (imagination, reason, and memory) according to the respective ventricles of the brain, destitute of error.'[33] 'The origins of these faculties ought to be handled, and that physically...In which part nothing of much value...has as yet been discovered...'[34]

Bacon did not succeed in delivering what he wanted applying his new logic in these studies; or else the results of his efforts have not survived. It should indeed be remarked that in his *History of Life and Death* he writes: 'I now come to the affections and passions of the mind, to see which of them are prejudicial to longevity, which profitable. Great joys attenuate and diffuse the spirits, and shorten life; ordinary cheerfulness strengthens the spirits, by calling them out, and yet not wasting them.' 'Spirits', it will be understood, are the forces of life.

Sensual impressions of joys are bad; ruminations of joys in the memory, or apprehensions of them in hope or imagination, are good. Joy suppressed and sparingly communicated comforts the spirits more than joy indulged and published. Grief and sadness, if devoid of fear, and not too keen, rather prolong life; for these contract the spirits, and are a kind of condensation. Great fears shorten life. For though both grief and fear distress the spirits, yet grief causes only a simple contraction; whereas fear, through cares respecting the remedy and hopes intermixed, causes a turmoil and vexation of the spirits. Suppressed anger is likewise a kind of vexation, and makes the spirits to prey upon the juices of the body. But anger indulged and let loose is beneficial, like those medicines which induce a robust heat. Envy is the worst passion, and preys on the spirits, which again prey on the body. And it is so much the worse, because it is always at work, and (as they say) keeps no holidays. Compassion for another man's misfortune, which does not appear likely to befall ourselves, is good. But that which may by some similitude be reflected on the person pitying is bad, because it excites fear. A light shame hurts not, because it slightly contracts the spirits and then diffuses them; and therefore bashful persons are generally long-lived. But shame for a great disgrace, and of long continuance, contracts the spirits even to suffocation, and is pernicious. Love, if not unfortunate, and too deeply wounding, is a kind of joy, and is subject to the same laws as were laid down for joy. Hope is of all affections the most useful, and contributes most to prolong life, if it be not too often disappointed, but feed the imagination with the prospect of good. They therefore who set up and propose some definite end as their mark in life, and continually and gradually advance thereto, are mostly long-lived; insomuch that when they arrive at the summit of their hopes, and have nothing more to look forward to, they commonly droop and do not long survive; so that hope appears to be a kind of *leaf-joy*, which may be spread out over a vast surface like gold. Admiration and light contemplation are of very great effect in prolonging life. For they detain the spirits on pleasing subjects, and do not permit them to become tumultuous, unquiet and morose ... So much then for the motion of the spirits by the affections of the mind.[35]

But in *The History of Life and Death* and in his other two natural and experimental histories it is not the case that Bacon is using his new logic. He was employing or relying on the old logic. Further, in *The History of Life and Death* he seeks to show the effect of states of mind upon the living body; not the effects of conditions of the living body upon the mind. Furthermore, as is evident, his discourse and observation relate in this history specifically to the topic of the prolongation of life; of man certainly, but also of all creatures, 'mineral, vegetable and animal'. He considers the interactions of three entities – mind (when there is a mind), body and life (that is, livingness or spirits), not those of two entities, mind and body. Finally there can be no ignoring his confession: 'I candidly admit that some of the propositions here laid down' [he does not say which] 'have not been proved by experiment (for my course of life permits not of that), but are only derived, with what appears to me the best reason, from my principles and hypotheses (whereof I insert some and reserve others in my mind), and as it were cut and dug out of the rock and mine of nature itself.'[36]

Bacon as said either did not succeed in delivering what he proposed applying his new logic, or else the results of his efforts have been lost. Alternatively he shelved these tasks in preference for other projects in 'received sciences';[37] these others being no less an aspect of his announced plans as a whole, equally urgent, and indeed not truly separable from *The Great Instauration*. It is these latter projects, at any rate, which the world has inherited. The other projects in effect constitute a dead end. It is in connection with such abortive or aborted studies that we should understand aphorisms in *Novum Organum* declaring that natural philosophy ought to be esteemed the great mother of the sciences. '... all arts and all sciences, if torn from this root, though they may be polished and shaped and made fit for use, yet they will hardly grow.'[38] 'Meanwhile let no man look for much progress in the sciences – especially in the practical part of them – unless natural philosophy be carried on and applied to particular sciences, and particular sciences be carried back again to natural philosophy.'[39] He had continued like this: 'For want of this, astronomy, optics, music, a number of mechanical arts, medicine itself – nay, what one might more wonder at, moral and political philosophy, and the logical sciences – altogether lack profoundness, and merely glide along the surface and variety of things; because after these particular sciences have been once distributed and established, they are no more nourished by natural philosophy; which might have drawn out of the true contemplation of motions, rays, sounds, texture and configuration of bodies, affections, and intellectual perceptions, the means of imparting to them fresh strength and growth. And therefore it is nothing strange if the sciences grow not, seeing they are parted from their roots.'[40]

Active men, Bacon insists, should become writers 'as that which would make learning indeed solid and fruitful'.[41] But for whatever reason, no writings of his survive in which natural philosophy is carried on and applied to particular sciences, and particular sciences turned back again to natural philosophy.

By contrast, professions of affection and good will towards 'received' – rightly received – sciences are more than justified in his contributions to improvements in them, not only in formal publications but elsewhere. Publications made prior to *Novum Organum* are the first *Advancement*, the *Wisdom of the Ancients* and two sets of essays, 1597 and 1612; the former slight, the latter substantial. Contributions appearing after *Novum Organum* comprise, *inter alia*, a second much enlarged *Advancement*, the *History of the Reign of King Henry the 7th* and another even more substantial collection of essays. In due course Bacon elevates *Advancement* in its final form to constitute a not less solid portion of the *Great Instauration* than *Novum Organum* itself.

With respect to the 'constant and distinct warning' that by present procedures no great progress can be made in 'the doctrines and contemplative parts of sciences nor can they be carried out to any magnitude of works'; this indeed stands. But it relates to man's knowledge of nature including his body; not to his knowledge of the rest of himself – his mind, his will and their joint products. In this latter field advance can proceed. Bacon proceeds in it, 'doctrines and contemplative parts' – that is to say, 'speculative/theoretic' parts – being dispensed with.

'Humanity Particular consisteth of the same parts whereof man consisteth; that is, of knowledges which respect the Body, and of knowledges that respect the Mind.'[42] 'my way... after the history has been prepared and duly arranged... regards not the working and discourse of the mind only (as the common logic does) but the nature of things also.'[43] 'I that regard the mind not only in its own faculties, but in its connection with things...'[44] While bodies are things, the mind according to Bacon is not a thing. The mind is no more a thing than God is a thing. Leaving aside, at least for a time (a time which in his case failed, so it appears, to arrive), bodies and interactions between bodies and minds and *vice versa*, Bacon's way indeed regards the working and discourse of the mind. He studies the mind 'in its own faculties'. In *Advancement* (both versions), in *Wisdom of the Ancients*, in three collections of essays and in many other places in addition, he attends to minds, to the idols besetting them, to their constitution consisting as this does of memory, imagination and reason, to their 'characters of dispositions' and to their passions. He attends not only to these, but also to the processes of reasoning and willing which come out of minds and which result in creations in all the extant, 'received' and improvable arts.

He also attends to minds in *Novum Organum*, Book I. *Novum Organum*, Book I consists of descriptions and analyses of the ways in which men use their minds in general, including examinations of the idols of their minds which entrap them. It also consists of observations on ways men have employed their minds in the past in producing doctrines of schools, sects and systems, constituting attempts to achieve truth in sciences. It is Book II not Book I which lays out the 'teaching to invent and judge by induction'. But Bacon does not apply this in studies of the natural world, and since that is so, he uses it nowhere, for nowhere else does he propose it to be applicable.

He successfully makes his contributions in natural philosophy/ science. He does so in natural history, the basement of the pyramid. He does so also in the achievement of axioms – in his *History of Winds*, *History of Life and Death* and *History of Dense and Rare*. He offered such studies as being truly scientific. But he does not achieve the ascent of his third tier, the pyramid's apex, which would reveal the form and true reality of nature including that of human bodies and their interactions with minds.

Doubtless a metaphysics of that part of nature which consisted of the human body and its interactions with the mind presented its peculiar difficulties. These would arise not only in the field of experiments but also because of the 'tacit agreement of men concerning the imposition of words and names'. The form of man according to Bacon is his rational soul or mind together with his will. But what is the form – or what are the forms – of a man's body, considered as distinct from his rational soul or mind together with his will; and in that his body consists of material substances? In *Advancement* (both versions) Bacon writes: 'to enquire the form of a lion, of an oak, of gold; nay of water, of air, is a vain pursuit: but to enquire the forms of sense, of voluntary motion, of vegetation, of colours, of gravity and levity, of density, of tenuity, of heat, of cold, and all other natures and qualities, which...are not many, and of which the essences (upheld by matter) of all creatures do consist...'[45] – such inquiry, though not as yet undertaken, is possible. Apart from this statement made in 1605 and repeated in 1623, he provides no clue how he approached, or would have approached, this matter. Success, he appears to hold, is promised in the title deeds providing the metaphysics of man. It is promised by Bacon himself. If fulfilled – and it was not – the promise would balance and complete the metaphysics of man by re-endowing him with his forfeited dominion over nature and his body.

A treatise on 'the several characters and tempers of men's nature and disposition' (the first *Advancement*) – a treatise on men's 'different characters of dispositions' (the second *Advancement*) – a treatise devoted to this topic, providing a 'scientific and accurate dissection of minds and characters', would be a boon for moral knowledge and therefore for policy. But supposing that connections between the body and the mind could be discovered and defined, the situation would be better still for morality and policy: 'ethics and politics, should be carried on according to our way…For I form a history and tables of discovery for anger, fear, shame, and the like; for matters political…' (Book I, *Novum Organum*). It was conceivable that knowledges could turn out to be 'drenched in flesh and blood' in a more than figurative fashion. The situation would be better even than that. The uniting of the sciences would presumably be within mankind's grasp.

This vision, this project, helps explain why the *Great Instauration* was conceived predominantly in terms of natural philosophy, Bacon's guess or perhaps some basic experience – 'experience; which if taken as it comes, is called accident' – [46]being that there exists a 'league' between mind and body. Proofs of the nature of this relationship would indicate the bounds of the nature of things, pointing to what could or could not be done; this moreover would be in the shape of 'real truth' and in 'progressive stages of certainty'. Indubitably if these relationships could be convincingly established, sciences would be unified under natural philosophy/science; it being not forgotten that Bacon's religious, moral, and political reasons for promoting natural philosophy/science in the first place, and for conceiving that other sciences could ultimately be united in or under this branch of studies, remain paramount.

Admittedly fulfilment would take time. But his plans included showing the way, this implying products not only in the abstract and in principle, but in procedures showing results tested in practice. The vision of this goal is never abandoned. But also it is never achieved. Not arriving there helps to explain Bacon's imprecision about what is part of and what is not part of the *Great Instauration*. 'Nothing is finished till all be finished.' This grand business was not finished. Completion was not reached. Therefore all that was done in *Know Thyself* was provisional – and not only in the matter of certainty. It was provisional also because it was work done in an interim. Indeed the interval in which interim products could be worked on and presented in *Know Thyself* threatened to extend itself to almost interminable distances. Knowledge of interactions between minds and bodies must wait upon knowledge of bodies. This in turn must attend upon wider knowledge of nature as a whole – until which time 'medical knowledge' – along with much else – could expect to be little 'better than an empirical practice'.

On the other hand Bacon's approach to his destination was from opposite directions, so to say. His religious, moral, and political concerns being paramount, he operated in extant arts which were possible of improvement, these being sound enough to merit it. Furthermore in such undertakings he was attending throughout to correct procedure for discovery in arts as yet absent. His physio-psychical and psycho-physical researches not visibly maturing, and morality not succeeding in helping policy in this way, it was a reverse operation which took place. Policy aiming to assist morality by improving it by external pressures was the alternative position which, in agreement with Machiavelli, he was able to maintain. *Of Custom and Education* makes this explicit as early as 1612 and as late as 1625. It has been cited already. 'Certainly the great multiplication of virtues upon human nature, resteth upon societies well ordained, and disciplined. For commonwealths and good governments, do nourish virtue grown, but do not mend the seeds; but the misery is that the most effectual means are now applied to the ends least to be desired.' Bacon's guess – or some basic experience – respecting a 'league' between mind and body continued to seem justified – it should be added – in the times after his death. In his first treatise Thomas Hobbes united mind and body, in effect renouncing the distinction between them altogether. But Hobbes abandoned this position in later treatises.

Bacon's *Catalogue of Particular Histories by Titles*[47] was published as already noted with *Parasceve* and *Novum Organum*. A hundred and thirty titles are listed. These fall into three groups. The first group is sub-divided. The first sub-division contains topics in the field of nature – for example, *History of the Heavenly Bodies*; *History of Winds and Sudden Blasts and Undulations of the Air*; *History of Hail, Snow, Frost, Hoar-Frost, Fog, Dew, and the like*; *Natural History of Geography*; *of Mountains, Vallies, Woods … and the like; leaving apart Nations, Provinces, Cities, and suchlike matters pertaining to Civil Life.*

The second subdivision contains titles relating to man as part of nature: for example, *Anatomical History*; *History of the Parts of Uniform Structure in Man; as Flesh, Bones, Membranes, etc.; History of Life and Death.* These relate to man's body. Titles like *History of the Intellectual Faculties; Reflexion, Imagination, Discourse, Memory, etc.* relate to his mind. But these last, together with *History of the Affections; as Anger, Love, Shame, etc.*, lie in a disputed borderland, the area of interactions and interpenetrations between mind and body which drew and enticed Bacon's attention. According to his statements, as we have seen, it is because this problematic borderland exists – 'the league between the mind and the body' – that he justified 'the consideration in general and at large of human nature to be fit to be emancipate and made a knowledge by itself…'

All these histories, whether produced by himself (*History of Winds* and *History of Life and Death* and *History of Dense and Rare*) or by others, were to be fed into the machine (Bacon calls it a machine) described in *Novum Organum*, Book II in order to be processed into metaphysics. As far as we know none of this infeeding takes place. One reason no doubt is that apart from his own efforts these histories were not written. But even his three pieces remained unused for constructing a metaphysics of nature.

A second group of titles in the *Catalogue* – like the overwhelming majority of the rest, being no more than an expression of his wishes – is constituted like this: '*Histories must also be written of Pure Mathematics; though they are rather observations than experiments. History of the Natures and Powers of Numbers: History of the Natures and Powers of Figures.*' A third group introduces the topic of the mechanical arts or *experientia literata*, learned experience. Examples in this topic in the *Catalogue* are: *History of Cookery, and the arts thereto belonging, as of the Butcher, Poulterer, etc.; History of Baking, and the Making of Bread, and the arts thereto belonging, as of the Miller, etc.: History of Leather-making, Tanning, and the arts thereto belonging: History of working in Iron; History of Architecture generally; History of Gardening.* Brief passages touching mechanical arts or *experientia literata* occur in the first *Advancement*: he writes there: 'But if my judgment be of any weight, the use of History Mechanical is of all others the most radical and fundamental towards natural philosophy; such natural philosophy as shall not vanish in the fume of subtile, sublime, or delectable speculation, but such as shall be operative to the endowment and benefit of man's life.'[48] Later in the book he proceeds: 'This part of invention, concerning the invention of sciences, I propose (if God give me leave) hereafter to propound, having digested it into two parts; whereof the one I term *experientia literata*, and the other *interpretatio naturae*: the former being but a degree and rudiment of the latter. But I will not dwell too long, nor speak too great upon a promise.'[49]

Bacon makes a footnote to *Catalogue of Particular Histories by Titles* (1620): 'I care little about the mechanical arts themselves: only about those things which they contribute to the equipment of philosophy.'[50] In the second *Advancement* he has more to say about them than he had provided in the first. Craftsmen and artisans, those who toil in mechanical arts do not make axioms: 'For all transition from experiments to axioms, or from axioms to experiments, belongs to that other part, relating to the New Organon.'[51] He notes also: 'But if men were at leisure to inquire after useful things, they ought to observe attentively and minutely and systematically all natural works and operations, and be ever eagerly considering which of them may be transferred to the arts.'[52]

Of these things it may be said generally, that the best chance of bringing down as from heaven a shower of inventions at once useful and new, is to bring within the knowledge of one man, or of a few who may sharpen one another by conference, the experiments of a number of mechanical arts... For though the rational mode of inquiry by the Organon promises far greater things in the end yet this sagacity proceeding by Learned Experience will in the meantime present mankind with a number of inventions which lie near at hand, and scatter them like the donatives that used to be thrown among the people...[53] Meanwhile I give this advice as to experiments of this nature; that no one should be disheartened or confounded if the experiments which he tries do not answer his expectation. For though a successful experiment be more agreeable, yet an unsuccessful one is oftentimes no less instructive. And it must be ever kept in mind (as I am continually urging) that experiments of Light are even more to be sought after than experiments of Fruit. And so much for Learned Experience, which (as I have already said) is rather a sagacity and a kind of hunting by scent, than a science. Of the New Organon I say nothing, nor shall I give any taste of it here; as I purpose by the divine favour to compose a complete work on that subject – being the most important thing of all.[54]

Learned experience in the mechanical arts, despite his list in the *Catalogue,* and notwithstanding remarks about digesting the invention of sciences 'into two parts, whereof the one I term *experientia literata,* and the other *interpretatio naturae*', the former topic did not for Bacon become yet another and a third programme lying alongside two others – improving arts which were improvable because they already contained something of soundness in them; and supplying arts, which so far did not exist. Two programmes were enough and proved more than enough. Without doubt Learned Experience taught philosophers indispensable 'most radical and fundamental' lessons. Above all, work in this field did not 'vanish in the fume of subtile, sublime, or delectable speculation'. Workers engaged themselves in actions. They used and depended upon experience and experiments. But if in later times men suggest that it constituted a programme and a series of projects in 'history mechanical', in mixed histories mechanical, the reply must be in the negative. For one thing, as he pointed out in *Of Vicissitude of Things* (1625), mechanical arts together with merchandise flourished 'in the declining age of a state'. He did not portray, nor did he work for a state which as he judged matters was in the throes of decline. Secondly in the man's own words, he cared 'little about the mechanical arts themselves'. They were not science. Learned experience was 'rather a sagacity' and 'but a degree and rudiment' of science. Though learned experience conducted experiments of a kind, it made no axioms. It did not make histories. In these respects it deserved no imitation. Both Bacon's programmes lay in the liberal arts. Though the liberal arts could and should indeed learn from the mechanical arts, liberal arts concerned themselves with truth. In both programmes Bacon sought truth. As we see, he again stated when discussing learned experience that experiments of Light, that is, of Truth, were more to be sought after than experiments of fruit that is, of utility. If in the process of preparing and cooking lamb chops or of planning and building a warship, a man were to discuss the truth or falsehood of the way to set about it, the man according to Bacon would be resorting to metaphor. With the exception of contributions concerning sailing ships and windmills in the *History of Winds* and the essays *Of Building* (1625) and *Of Gardens* (1625) – essays which contain sizeable elements of the civil and the moral – he bequeathed nothing in the field of mechanical arts. According to Bacon it is not the case, as the present writer has let slip, that reliable material of *whatever kind* can be turned into philosophy/science. In short learned experience should be pronounced and spelt not as *learned* but as *learnt.* The truth which Bacon sought was of the kind with which philosophers had been, were, and still remain concerned. Aspiring to excel not in technology but in philosophy whether natural or political – and indeed in both – Bacon in his two programmes declined to allow utility to substitute itself for the goal.

In his last years Bacon's plans and projects for natural philosophy/science cannot be elucidated in detail. His results can be assessed, not his intentions. In these last years nothing is so apposite as his remark: 'as in other things I am certain of my way, but not certain of my position'. He told the Revd Fr Baranzan in 1622: 'Be not troubled about the Metaphysics. When true Physics have been discovered there will be no Metaphysics. Beyond the true Physics is divinity only.' He proposed that his correspondent should provide a *History of the Heavens* and a *History of Comets*.[55] Even so, in the same letter it is not evident that for his own part he had given up being troubled about the Metaphysics. He writes: 'I do not propose to give up syllogism altogether. Syllogism is incompetent for the principal things rather than useless for the generality.'[56] Despite disparagement of metaphysics which he went on to administer in this letter, 'principal things' refers to the machinery of *Novum Organum*, Book II. He writes also: 'It is the flux of matter and the inconstancy of the physical body which requires Induction; that thereby it may be fixed, as it were, and allow the formation of notions well defined.'[57] In 1605 in the first *Advancement* he had defined physics as 'that which is inherent in matter, and therefore transitory', and Metaphysic as 'that which is abstracted and fixed. And again, that Physic should handle that which supposeth in nature only a being and moving, and Metaphysic that which supposeth further in nature a reason, understanding, and platform'.[58] In 1623 the second *Advancement* repeated this definition of the difference between physics and metaphysics. It also reaffirmed not only that a metaphysics of nature was needed: it promised that it was possible to achieve it and that it would be provided.

In 1625 when describing the *Great Instauration* to Fulgentius in a letter already quoted, he states that to the *Novum Organum* 'there is still a second part to be added – but I have already encompassed and planned it out in my mind. And in this manner the second part of the Instauration will be completed.'[59] Remarks made when discussing mechanical arts in the second *Advancement* are thus rendered intelligible. *Novum Organum* had been published in 1620. He had written in 1623 in the final *Advancement* when discussing the mechanical arts as if *Novum Organum* had yet to appear. 'As for the third part', he told Fulgentius in 1625, 'namely the Natural History, that is plainly work for a King or Pope, or some college or order: and cannot be done as it should by a private man's industry.' There followed the passage already quoted at an earlier stage about his two exercises in mixed history – in mixed natural history, *History of Winds* and *History of Life and Death*. But he went on to explain to Fulgentius with respect to these pieces that in the fourth part of the *Instauration* there 'will be shown many examples of this machine, more exact and more applied to the rules of induction'.[60]

As said we cannot do more than assess surviving results. What is plain on this showing is that remarks to Baranzan – 'Be not troubled about the Metaphysics. When true Physics have been discovered, there will be no Metaphysics. Beyond the true Physics is divinity only' – proved prophetic. In the fields of knowledge of nature it was truly science at the preliminary stage which he intended, held that he was achieving, and would succeed furthermore in bequeathing. But it was not the intended metaphysics. As corollary of this he failed to achieve levels of certainty which in knowledge of the realm of nature he had stated to be possible and had professed to aim at: 'the ordinary face and view of experience is many times satisfied by several theories and philosophies; whereas to find the real truth requireth another manner of severity and attention...'[61] In his claims and aims the department of metaphysics in the knowledge of nature, if conducted under his promised manner of severity and attention, would establish the essential forms and true differences of things.

In describing *Novum Organum* to King James he called it 'a new logic teaching to invent and judge by induction, (as finding syllogism incompetent for sciences of nature) and thereby to make philosophy and sciences both more true and more active'.[62] According to statements elsewhere, making the philosophy and sciences of nature more true and more active entailed making them more certain. He announced that he would establish 'progressive stages of certainty'.[63] But as a result willy-nilly of stopping short of metaphysics there occurred in his pieces on winds and on life and death a subsidence and demotion of truth in knowledge of things in the natural order to the lesser level of certainty obtaining in knowledges achieved in man's knowledges of man where the old common logic, as Bacon granted to be the case, was rightly implied or applied.

His starting point in the programme in the latter – man's knowledges of man – was an already possessed assurance regarding man's form and true nature. According to the evidence he nowhere discussed the standing of his contributions in these fields in terms of the degree of certainty achieved or achievable in them. It was in connection only with his new induction promised for a metaphysics of nature that he introduced and expressed notions on the topic of certainty. Nevertheless it is a fair inference that because he stopped short of producing this metaphysics the aforesaid subsidence and demotion of truth in his natural science contributions to lesser levels of certainty was indeed what took place – and that he was aware of this.

Fr Marin Mersenne (1558–1648) in his *La Vérité des Sciences contre les Sceptiques ou Pyrrhoniens* (Paris 1625) argued that Bacon [*Verulamus*] could not have succeeded in achieving the certainties announced for his metaphysics of nature even if he had tried.

Or quelques Phénomènes qu'on puisse proposer dans la Philosophie, il ne faut pas penser que nous puissons penetrer la nature des individus ni ce que se passe interieurement dans iceux, car nos sens, sans lesquels l'entendement, ne peut rien conoître, ne voyent que ce qui est exterieur, qu'on anatomise, qu'on dissolve les corps tant qu'on voudra soit par le feu, par l'eau, ou par la force de l'esprit, jamais nous n'arriveront à ce point que de rendre notre intellect pareil a la nature des choses; c'est pourquoi je croy que le dessein de Verulamus est impossible, & que ces instructions ne seront causes d'autre chose que de quelques nouvelles experiences, lesquelles on pourra facilement expliquer par la Philosophie ordinaire.[64]

Bacon showed he was aware that in addition to idols in men's minds, their 'characters of dispositions' affected their inquiries into reality. Some men were too much given to doubt; others too much inclined to credulity. But granted that these difficulties were surmountable he could have replied to Fr Mersenne that since the entire realm of nature was as yet unknown, how could men tell in advance what kind or degree of certainty would be achievable when they explored it? He could have asked his French critic what evidence he had for deciding in advance to limit man's capabilities when exploring nature's secrets.

It is plainly the case that Bacon both in offices of power and also on paper – two exercises which he did not separate – attempted civil science. More than this, in the second *Advancement* he stated that he had invented it by emancipating and distinguishing it from moral science in study and inquiry though not in the operations of practice. The *data* for civil science in civil histories and in his experience could concern itself only with the outside of men. The civil science which he made out of this *data* was similarly restricted to knowledge of the outside of men. Despite asserting in the first *Advancement* (he repeats the statement in the second) that 'moral philosophy is more difficile than policy'[65] he persists in demanding in the final *Advancement*

a full and careful treatise ... that so we may have a scientific and accurate dissection of minds and characters, and the secret dispositions of particular men may be revealed; and that from the knowledge thereof, better rules may be framed for the treatment of the mind ...[66] And in truth I cannot sometimes but wonder that this part of knowledge should for the most part be omitted both in Morality and Policy, considering it might shed such a ray of light on both sciences.[67]

He thus continues to show himself aware that the exterior appearances projected by men or by things do not comprise the whole of either of them. But for the realms covered by the Delphic oracle's directive it was Bacon himself who introduced the distinction between civil and moral knowledge, and it was Bacon himself who contributed the definition of the difference – the former for the outside, the latter for the inside of men. He did these things for the sake of action in achieving improvements in men's knowledges of themselves. When pursuing this purpose experience establishes that it is only the external aspects of men – their words and their deeds – which are observable. Even for 'the true and inward resorts of business', as presented in civil histories and in civil experience, we must content ourselves with externalities, the reason being that nothing else is securely available.

Hence civil history though exercising its prerogative of supremacy in dignity has also a pre-eminence in difficulty, presenting as it does tasks of great labour and judgment. Civil knowledge in its basic form, namely civil history, rivals and even surpasses moral knowledge in difficulty, though Bacon has pronounced the latter to be the 'more difficile'. Civil history must penetrate from the outside 'the revolutions of times, the character of persons, the fluctuation of counsels, the courses and currents of actions, the bottoms of pretences and the secrets of governments'. But hence, also, and nevertheless, a priority which Bacon allots to civil over moral science, not only because impacts made on the outside of men by custom, law and government are the surest way of affecting their conduct for the better – this being itself a judgment which is based on observation; but also because in civil science compared with moral science observations are not difficult to come by. By contrast the secrets of men's minds and wills are not less impenetrable than the secrets of their bodies, the subtleties of the structure of them and the conditions governing their health and sickness.

In the study of the world of nature Bacon proposed no distinction between the inside and the outside of things. 'The real truth' is manifestly an all-inclusive term. Fr Mersenne, when criticizing such a claim for knowledge in the realm of nature revealed no recognition of Bacon's way of proceeding in civil science. Mersenne nevertheless argued that knowledge of the outside of things in nature was the most that Bacon could hope to obtain in that realm. He could not have added, given the date of his book, that this turned out to be the sum total of Bacon's achievement. With regard to his own completed three natural and experimental histories Bacon, for his part, nowhere allowed – so far as the evidence goes – that the lower level of certainty he accepted in his other and parallel programme was operatively sufficient and operatively sufficiently productive in disclosing what was true, not only in these departments but in what he was doing in the departments of nature also. '... the ordinary face and view of experience is many times satisfied by several theories and philosophies; whereas to find the real truth requireth another manner of severity and attention...' Bacon neither withdrew this statement nor altered it by explaining that the object was not to 'find the real truth', but instead by organizing further 'experiences' – that is, experiments – to ascertain to what extent which of several theories could survive testing, and that successes like this were all that a man could aspire to compass. In continuing to hold out prospects of, and to entertain visions of a more certain type of certainty in exploring the department of nature than was available elsewhere, Bacon appeared to allow that areas of investigation in which doubting would rule as integral in all advancement in knowledges would contract in extent. For he wrote that he proposed 'to establish progressive stages of certainty'. But given that the inference made above is a valid one – namely that, since Bacon's metaphysics of nature though laid out in design was not put into practice (or else has not survived), certainties in his works in natural sciences suffered corresponding and also recognized reduction; and given (which is plain) that he did not abandon the old logic and start to work successfully in his new one, it was doubting which in the nature of the case he continued to practise in his contributions.

No metaphysics of nature – civil history supplies Bacon's masculine birth of time

Bacon conceded and affirmed that the old logic survives for use in the extant arts: 'in sciences popular, as moralities, laws, and the like, yea, and divinity... that form may have use'[1]... 'the logic which is received', is 'very properly applied in civil business and to those arts which rest in discourse and opinion...'[2] It survives also for the purpose of explaining and conveying results of the new logic if and when they arrive. '...that form' (the old logic) 'may have use... in natural philosophy... by way of argument or satisfactory reason'.[3] Creative and cooperative dispute, truly persuasive interchange of notions and experiences, as opposed to 'falling at words', fractiousness and disputatiousness, is in general commended, recommended and, save in one singular instance to be later noted, consistently attempted by Bacon. But fruitful disputing, cultivating truth in charity, cannot be conducted in defiance of logic. If any logic is involved in fruitful disputing, it will be the old logic. Even aphorism – aphoristic writing – cannot dispense with it. He told Fr Baranzan that he did not abandon syllogism: 'I do not propose to give up syllogism' (the common logic) 'altogether. Syllogism is incompetent for the principal things rather than useless for the generality.' The principal things here referred to were discoveries in the natural order.

Further, in addition to what we observe and is plain to see, having told us that the old logic serves in the extant arts, he also reminds us that he contributes extensively in these improvable extant arts. '...the intellect is not qualified to judge except by means of induction, and induction in its legitimate form'.[4] But the ancient logic is legitimate as induction in morality, in policy (the latter comprising inquiries into government and into law) and in divinity.

Nor is this the sum of the matter. In his writings even in arts up to now not extant but absent, arts concerning the natural world and men's bodies, both the ancient rhetoric and also the ancient logic continue to make their appearance. Introducing certainties less than final, he uses both these ancient arts in *History of Winds*, *History of Life and Death* and *History of Dense and Rare*. Undertakings in non-existent arts become indistinguishable from contributions in arts which were extant and improvable. Nor, it is plain, were they intended to be other than indistinguishable.

In regard to the achievements which he bequeaths a cardinal point is that in both programmes, whether in sciences of nature (the world of things, including man's body), or in knowledges of the mind (including the mind's idols, its creations, its moral and rational actions, its systems, sects, philosophies, religions, state constitutions, governments, and laws), Bacon's procedure, as he projects in it, writes about it, and applies it, stays unified and overarching by virtue of movements of overlap, interflow and cross-fertilization.

Bacon has worked, he tells King James, on *Novum Organum* for 'near thirty years'[5] before publishing it. But he has made 'pause', he has warned and explained, 'upon that which is received; and thereby the old may be more easily made perfect and the new more easily approached'. It is therefore to be expected that we should find distinctive elements which were going to the making of, and aimed at the construction of, the new induction, being used from an early date to reinforce his employment of the old. In *Know Thyself* not only was more work achieved than in natural studies, but this work started to appear earlier. Never launching into practice – so it would appear – his new way contained in Book II of *Novum Organum*, he amply shows in his undertakings in morality and in policy his discard of 'ways now in use'[6] and that the new way is continually in the making.

Bacon wrote of that part of metaphysics which concerned itself with the discovery of forms in nature: 'I do not find [it] laboured and performed: whereat I marvel not; because I hold it not possible to be invented by that course of invention which hath been used, in regard that men (which is the root of all error) have made too untimely a departure and too remote a recess from particulars.'[7] But equally in the subject-matters of the other programme – that which was concerned with *Know Thyself* and which proceeded not towards discovering a metaphysics of nature, but out of an already established metaphysics of man – he abandoned the course of invention that had been used, in that men had made too untimely a departure and too remote a recess from particulars, this being the root of all error. '…generalities, though true, have the fault that they do not well lead the way to action…'[8] He made this last statement when discussing medicine. He made similar statements throughout his pursuit of the *Know Thyself* programme. In both programmes the aim is the making of middle axioms based upon keeping close to particulars. Similarly in both programmes, differences and resemblances must equally be attended to, a balance between them being observed, but stress given to the former when entering into inquiries, and stress to the latter if inquiries are successfully to reach a decision or a conclusion.

'The use of History Mechanical is of all others the most radical and fundamental towards natural philosophy; such natural philosophy as shall not vanish in the fume of subtle, sublime, or delectable speculation, but such as shall be operative to the endowment and benefit of man's life.'[9] But this lesson is no less applicable in the *Know Thyself* enterprise than it is 'towards natural philosophy'. 'But this is that which will indeed dignify and exalt knowledge, if contemplation and action may be more nearly and straitly conjoined and united together than they have been.'[10] In both programmes this pronouncement in *Advancement* (both versions) is Bacon's alternative to the fume of subtle, sublime or delectable speculation.

'For all transition from experiments to axioms, or from axioms to experiments, belongs to that other part, relating to the New Organon.'[11] Aphorism CIII in Book I explains that: 'Our road does not lie on a level, but ascends and descends; first ascending to axioms, then descending to works.'[12] But interplay between experiments and axioms, that is to say, contrived and calculated interchange between thinking and acting, theory and practice – this belongs as much in the programme for human nature as it does in projects for exploring the natural order.

Machiavelli's mixed history had shown the way to Bacon's *History of Winds* and *History of Life and Death* and *History of Dense and Rare*. But not only had the Florentine launched a procedure for Bacon he had also launched a procedure within a procedure. He wrote as we know of Machiavelli's work: 'For knowledge drawn freshly and in our view out of particulars knoweth the way best to particulars again.' Machiavelli had done more. He presented the correct relationship between thinking, discourse or axioms on the one hand, and examples, particulars or history on the other. '...it hath much greater life for practice when the discourse attendeth upon the example, than when the example attendeth upon the discourse. For this is no point of order, as it seemeth at first, but of substance.' The course which Machiavelli resisted and which should be resisted by others is when 'the examples alleged for the discourse's sake are cited succinctly, and without particularity, and carry a servile aspect toward the discourse which they are brought in to make good'.[13] Bacon identified this latter way with the conduct of Aristotle. Bacon imports Machiavelli's correct relationship between discourse and example into inquiries concerning the natural world.

But in truth, assuming a man is setting out to create sciences, it seems that all the above points – onwards, that is, from 'the root of all error being too untimely a departure and too remote a recess from particulars' – and indeed other and further points will be involved in, or derived from, or subsumed by yet another but more basic point. Machiavelli's *Discorsi*, though mixed civil history, was nevertheless civil history. As we have seen it was not natural history, but civil history, as the context indicates, which Bacon had in mind when he wrote while the Queen was still reigning:

> The books which are written do in their kinds represent the faculties of the mind of man; Poesy his imagination; Philosophy his reason; and History his memory. Of which three faculties least exception is commonly taken to memory; because imagination is oftentimes idle, and reason litigious. So likewise History of all writings deserveth least taxation, as that which holdeth least of the author, and most of the things themselves. Again, the use which it holdeth to man's life, if it be not the greatest, yet assuredly is the freest from any ill accident or quality. For those which are conversant much in poets, as they attain to great variety, so withal they become conceited; and those that are brought up in philosophy and sciences do wax (according as their nature is) some of them too stiff and opinionate, and some others too perplexed and confused. Whereas History possesseth the mind of the conceits which are nearest allied unto action and imprinteth them so, as it doth not alter the complexion of the mind neither to irresolution nor pertinacity.[14]

Bacon wrote these words when discussing his plans in civil history writing. These plans were to remedy England's notable deficiency in this field and to improve the general mediocrity prevailing in this art in and for modern times. If in this passage he was not thinking exclusively of civil history, it is plain that whatever history he was considering, civil history was not only not excluded from his thoughts, but was to the fore in them. In this passage not poetry only, but philosophy is compared to its disadvantage with history. We know from other early writings that Bacon's judgment of philosophers was to say the least a low one. Further, as we shall see, what he said about philosophers in these early writings tallies closely with his remarks about them in the above quoted passage. Relying on Bacon's own judgments, expressed in Bacon's own words, it is legitimate to infer and to propound that qualities which Bacon perceived in, and attached to histories of the civil affairs of men, were imported by him into plans for histories of the world of things in nature. Histories hold 'least of the author, and most of the things themselves'. Histories embody particulars and these reside outside men's minds.

It can be objected that civil histories are about men and that men are not things. But civil histories are also about things which men make – governments, laws, plans and policies in peace and war. This consideration introduces the second and related point. Civil histories recount actions: they record words, discourse, disputations, arguments, only as these are connected with actions. Affected by civil history's usefulness because of its inherent activating force, consisting as it does of accounts of the proceedings of people other than, and outside a man's self; and because also of its capacity to make men beware in their own actions of irresolution and pertinacity, Bacon, beginning to be immersed in policy in a public career, and proceeding in it with the aid of his civil histories, transferred and imported these creatively propelling properties of civil histories into operations to be undertaken by himself and others in natural histories.

Policy is a great part of philosophy and civil history and civil experience are a great part of policy, providing as they do its indispensable foundations. Not only is policy, thus founded, a great part of philosophy, policy in the situation to which Bacon addresses himself is the decisive part of philosophy. For natural science is to imitate and emulate policy. Both are to consist both of thinking and of doing. They will be different only in that in policy the doing consists of actions precipitated by such speaking as consists of counsel, command or judgment – of words, that is, which are 'but as inducements and passages to deeds'.[15] Uncontentious argument is not excluded. It will be constructive given that it is employed to achieve agreement producing and providing action. In natural sciences the doing part, as not in policy, will employ the hand for handling things outside the mind of the handler. Hands in policy, if used, are moved only as an aspect of rhetoric in addresses directed to and amidst other men. In natural sciences hands and other instruments will be used in action directed towards and amidst things. But in natural sciences as in policy, the first step in all doing – in all acting – will consist of observing what is outside a man; and in all sciences all subsequent steps will begin with observing what is outside a man.

The preface to *Novum Organum*, reads: 'Let there be therefore (and may it be for the benefit of both) two streams and two dispensations of knowledge; and in like manner two tribes or kindreds of students in philosophy – tribes not hostile or alien to each other, but bound together by mutual services; let there in short be one way for the cultivation [the ancient common logic], 'another' [Bacon's new logic] 'for the invention, of knowledge. And for those who prefer the former... I wish that they may succeed in their desire... but if any man, not content to rest in and use the knowledge which has already been discovered, aspire to penetrate further; to overcome, not an adversary in argument, but nature in action;... I invite all such to join themselves'... with me, that we may find the other (more certain as he ever protests) but still kindred way.[16]

As mentioned already a number of Bacon's small pieces – which he did not publish – can be reliably dated as having been written before or soon after he published the first *Advancement*. *De Interpretatione Naturae Proœmium* and *Valerius Terminus* have been cited already. Another was *Temporis Partus Masculus* – The Masculine Birth of Time. *Temporis Partus Masculus* contains a single brief reference to history. It is, however, as should be noted, a history in itself. It is a history of letters. Likewise, *Redargutio Philosophiarum – Refutation of Philosophies* – is in effect a history of letters. As for *Valerius Terminus*, this like *Redargutio Philosophiarum* contains references to the requirement that men pay attention to particulars – to history. On the other hand, another early piece, *Cogitationes de Scientia Humana*, Thoughts on Human Knowledge, is found to contain or to echo precisely the points made by Bacon in his paper written concerning civil history at a time when the Queen still reigned in good felicity.

In *Thoughts on Human Knowledge*, written soon after her death, there is no mention of civil history, as being of its nature devoid of faults so often evident in philosophy and in poetry. Instead, in this

piece, natural history takes civil history's place as being manifestly
no less free from the shortcomings Bacon describes in philosophy and
in poetry.

'If we are to have a purer Natural Philosophy', he argued in
Cogitationes de Scientia Humana, Thoughts on Human Knowledge.

its foundations must be solidly based in Natural History, and a Natural
History which is both copious and accurate. A philosophy derived from any
other source is as unstable as water and as gusty as wind, and has no
bearing on the active side of philosophy and human needs. To make the
point still more clear, a Natural History resting on insufficient research and
insufficient testing begets two faults and, as it were, two diseases or
corruptions of theory. The first results in sophistry, the second in poetry.

[In *Refutation of Philosophies* Bacon classed Plato and Aristotle as
Sophists.]

Take first a man who, on the basis of commonplace observations, constructs
a specious theoretical system and relies for the rest on his discursive and
argumentative ingenuity. His discoveries may be so fortunate as to win a
great reputation, but he himself is nothing more than a survivor of the old
sophistic school. Take again a man who conducts a thorough and carefully
controlled investigation of a portion of the field. If he is puffed up by this
and allows his imagination free play he may be led to interpret the whole
of nature after the pattern of the little bit he knows. His philosophy then
passes into the realms of fancy or dreaming and consigns him to the
category of the poet.[17]

'We should therefore', Bacon continues, 'recognise the depth and
penetration of that saying of Heraclitus, who protested against those
who sought their philosophy in their own private worlds instead of
in the great public world. Such men have only a touch of Natural
History, but yet indulge themselves in endless speculation with only
a feeble capacity to distinguish between the two'[18] – between, that is,
what is speculation inside themselves and what outside themselves,
is natural history.

Of this weakness the most astonishing example is Aristotle. He was a great
man, financed by a great king, familiar with natural and civil history, the
author of a notably accurate *History of Animals*, who moreover, as is clear
from his *Problems* and *Parva Naturalia*, had devoted much thought to all sorts
of researches, and who even allowed the senses their proper role.
Nevertheless his Natural Philosophy is divorced from things; he notoriously
deserted experience; and, however men may seek to hedge and quibble,
produced as a result of his mighty exertions something much closer to Logic

than to Physics or Metaphysics. Thus it came about that Aristotle with his impetuous and overbearing wit was a sufficient authority unto himself, despised his predecessors, compelled experience to lend a servile support to his own views and led her about like his captive slave. Now I myself have not the ability to fashion a statue of Philosophy and set it up: but I might aspire to prepare a base for such a statue and I recommend to men as the first essential the recognition of the usefulness and dignity of Natural History.

'My idea, however, is very different' – from what has been understood hitherto as natural history. 'The kind of natural history I am seeking is one from which natural causation can be understood, on which philosophy can be based, which is faithful to sense-evidence, and proved by works.'[19]

Like civil history natural history will bear 'on the active side of philosophy and human needs'. Like civil history natural history which is 'both copious and accurate' will dispel 'two diseases or corruptions of theory'. It will dispel that of the sophist or philosopher. The sophist or philosopher, succeeding in escaping from irresolution, makes up his mind too quickly or too firmly, and thus becomes 'stiff and opinionate', that is to say, he exemplifies pertinacity. Also natural history will banish the diseases and corruptions of the poet when he becomes puffed up, allowing his imagination too much play. Heraclitus protested against men who make philosophy out of their private worlds inside their minds, instead of out of 'the things themselves'. Such men can scarcely distinguish their own private worlds from the things or persons outside them. Of these men the signal example is Aristotle. His natural philosophy is divorced from things. He deserted experience, that is, the things outside himself. He was a sufficient authority unto himself and within himself. 'Now I myself have not the ability to fashion a statue of Philosophy and set it up: but I might aspire to prepare a base for such a statue and I recommend to men as the first essential the recognition of the usefulness and dignity of natural history.'

From an early date Bacon concentrated a powerful interest both in civil history and in natural philosophy/science. The latter preoccupation is manifest in *Temporis Partus Masculus*, a piece which takes the shape of a history, a history of letters. History of letters as we have seen becomes a branch or species of the *genus* civil history in the second *Advancement*, Bacon in the meantime having made contributions to it in bits and pieces while doing other things, and having described and recommended it in the first *Advancement*. He early adopts this form to express his judgments on all pre-existing exponents of natural philosophy/science. But his explicit interest in history while the Queen was still reigning was shown only in the department of history civil. The latter, he claimed, was preferable both to philosophy/science and to poetry, since faults likely to be found in examples of these two are less evident in histories civil. Accordingly, 'Histories', he wrote in *Of Studies*, 'make men wise.'[20] The histories which do so are civil histories. Wisdom and science for Bacon are interchangeable terms. *Of Studies* was the first essay in the first collection of essays. The year in which this was published was 1597. In *The Advancement of Learning* (1605) the merits of history civil have come to characterize history natural. Therefore men must proceed in collecting history natural. History is to be of first concern in all pursuits in all sciences – not only in moral, governmental, legal and divine – but in natural sciences. All advancement depends upon progress in historical knowledge – in history pure or mixed, in history pure and mixed. It means advancement in what can be done with history and in what cannot be done without it.

Temporis Partus Masculus as said is a history of letters. In it Bacon denounces all natural philosopher/scientists as having been wrong in every respect. That they have all been at fault in all respects and that nothing is to be learnt from them, this message in this piece – *Temporis Partus Masculus* – is the one and only major surviving instance in which the author expresses himself not only magisterially and disputatiously, but also and in addition in abusive and reviling language. As we have seen in *Advancement* (not only in the second but also in the first version) he has in mind a different kind of history of letters. This is not disputatious, and the message is not that they, the natural philosophers, have all been wrong in all respects. '...I proceed to those errors and vanities which have intervened amongst the studies themselves of the learned which is that which is principal and proper to the present argument; wherein my purpose is not to make a justification of [?judgment upon] the errors, but by a censure and separation of the errors to make a justification of that which is good and sound, and to deliver that from the aspersion of the other...'[21] Again: 'so let great authors have their due, as time, which is the author of authors, be not deprived of his due, which is, further and further to discover truth'.

Histories as the starting point and groundwork of all knowledges – this emerges as a central teaching of *Advancement* (both versions) and also of *Novum Organum*. It is this, the presence of, or the absence of histories, correctly made and correctly used, which as from 1605 in the first *Advancement*, is presented by Bacon as what is inarguably right or inarguably wrong – as the case might fall out – in the undertakings of other philosophers. But also as from 1605 in the first *Advancement* Bacon teaches that in other aspects of their work – and this applies even in the fields of natural philosophy/science – discussion whether these men have contributed something worthwhile can be profitably undertaken.

Producing but not publishing a reckless, intemperate small history of letters exposing and dismissing all other philosophers as in all ways wrong – this is *Temporis Partus Masculus*. Bacon changes this stance, signalling the change as from 1605. He changes it into a preoccupation with histories which, when they have been correctly and copiously collected, would be capable of making all philosophers right. These histories would include history of letters neither rancorous nor disputatious. Civil histories in general contain least of the author and most of the things themselves: accordingly history of letters and arts in particular would contain least of the author's opinions and conclusions on the nature of men and things and most of those of other people: 'so let great authors have their due[22]... it may be every one in some point hath seen clearer than his fellows[23]...' In this explicit advocacy of history of arts and letters Bacon recommends and substitutes leadership for magistrality – or as he put the matter in *Refutation of Philosophies* – 'candour for arrogance'.[24] Aristotle would be a beneficiary of this change.

Pursuit of sciences thus entails a dual cooperativeness – a cooperation with other workers present but also past, provided they could be found to have had something to contribute, which he admitted as from the first *Advancement* to be a possibility. But it also entails a cooperation with materials as presented in histories – materials, whether concerning persons or things, residing indubitably apart from and outside the minds of the men observing them. The closer this latter – and also the former – cooperation could be brought, the more fruitful the results which would accrue.

Audacity unsupported by caution was not Bacon's way. He stigmatized audacity thus unescorted as boldness in the essay entitled *Of Boldness* (1625). Nevertheless, while invoking caution in order to buttress audacity, it is legitimate, putting matters at their lowest, that we should add to the priorities of civil history over natural history which have been examined already, a temporal priority of the former in the history of Bacon's mind, thus leading to and resulting in an otherwise perhaps absent predominant commitment to natural history in the sphere of natural philosophy/science. This is the place at which to add this further priority, since we examine interflow, overlap and cross-fertilization between *Know Thyself* and the exploration of nature. For Bacon the masculine fertilizing birth of time is civil history pure, chiefly ancient and recently recovered. This is the case not only in the programme for *Know Thyself* but in the programme for the world of nature too. Civil history's pre-eminent dignity among human writings, affirmed or rather reaffirmed in the final *Advancement*, includes paternity of history natural. Since civil histories make men wise, natural histories shall do so likewise. 'Truth of story' – truth of civil history – will procreate 'truth of nature'.[25] The latter is made to acquire the dignity, authority and pre-eminence of the former.

'You may', Bacon wrote in *Refutation of Philosophies*,

be inferior to Aristotle on the whole, but not in everything. Finally, and this is the head and front of the whole matter, there is at least one thing in which you are far ahead of him – in precedents, in experience, in the lessons of time. Aristotle, it is said, wrote a book in which he gathered together the laws and institutions of two hundred and fifty five cities; yet I have no doubt that the customs and example of the single state of Rome are worth more than all of them combined, so far as military and political science are concerned. The position is the same in natural philosophy. Are you of a mind to cast aside not only your own endowments but the gifts of time? Assert yourselves before it is too late. Apply yourselves to the study of things themselves. Be not for ever the property of one man.[26]

Since history natural has been graced with the dignity and pre-eminence of history civil, and given that Bacon has delivered, as he has done in *Advancement* (1605), his considered prescriptions for natural philosophy/science, it follows that civil history's dignity and pre-eminence among human writings provides grand-paternity for natural philosophy/science itself.

He meditated a project to remedy a deficiency in civil history peculiar to his native country. He combined this with a purpose to elevate a mediocrity present in modern civil history as a whole; thereby continuing and supplying an exemplary canon bequeathed by exemplar states in antiquity. In doing these things he found his entrance into plans consisting of histories which would provide foundations for the natural philosophy/sciences which – not only in his judgment, but in judgments and experiences of many later observers – had hitherto been absent throughout time and space.

Furthermore, having established the point in the first *Advancement* that the foundations of all the pyramids of knowledge will always be histories, the order of events is not that concern with histories recedes as science – as distinct from history – gets made. In and after *Novum Organum* (1620), despite the claims and aims associated with that work, science in the shape Bacon wanted it, which was metaphysics, did not get made as we have seen. But concern with history in no way receded. On the contrary, parallel with aims or attempts to make metaphysics, he continued to stake claims for natural histories radiating the resonance of his early remarks about the intrinsic merits of civil history, placing it in its prerogative of high advantage in comparison with philosophy and poetry, and dating from the time when the Queen still reigned in good felicity.

In *Parasceve* (published with *Novum Organum*) we find:

'If all the wits of all the ages had met or shall hereafter meet...; if the whole human race had applied or shall hereafter apply themselves to philosophy, and the ...earth had been or shall be nothing but academies and colleges...; still, without a natural and experimental history...no progress...could have been or can be made. Whereas...let such a history be once provided...and let there be added such auxiliary and light-giving experiments as in the...course of interpretation will present themselves or will...be found out; and the investigation of nature...will be the work of a few years.'[27]

In Aphorism xcii of Book 1, *Novum Organum* Bacon states: 'the strongest means of inspiring hope will be to bring men to particulars; especially to particulars digested and arranged in my Tables of Discovery...since this is not merely the promise of the thing but the thing itself...'

According to Aphorism cxxx, the last aphorism in *Novum Organum*, Book 1:

I am of opinion that if men had ready at hand a just history of nature and experience, and laboured diligently thereon; and if they could bind themselves to two rules – the first, to lay aside received opinions and notions; and the second, to refrain the mind for a time from the highest generalizations, and those next to them – they would be able by the native and genuine force of the mind, without any other art, to fall into my form of interpretation. For interpretation is the true and natural work of the mind when freed from impediments.[28]

Historia Naturalis et Experimentalis ad condendam Philosophiae, containing *The History of Winds*, was published as part of the *Instauration* in 1622: 'It comes therefore to this', he wrote, 'that my Organum, even if it were completed, would not without the Natural History much advance the Instauration of the Sciences, whereas the Natural History without the Organum would advance it not a little. And therefore, I have thought it better and wiser by all means and above all things to apply myself to this work.'[29]

In *Parasceve*, published with *Novum Organum* two years previously, he had stated his intention to proceed with his original design. Others therefore were urged to work on histories.[30] Urging men to join in such undertakings, he delivered these instructions:

> they who shall hereafter take it upon them to write natural history should bear this continually in mind – that they ought not to consult the pleasure of the reader, no, not even that utility which may be derived immediately from their narrations; but to seek out and gather together such store and variety of things as may suffice for the formation of true axioms. Let them but remember this, and they will find out for themselves the way in which the history should be composed. For the end rules the procedure.[31]

He urged others to cooperate. He himself continued in his enterprises in natural history, producing pieces already referred to. 'I have thought it better and wiser by all means and above all things to apply myself to this work.'[32] This echoes the early confession in *Thoughts on Human Knowledge*: 'And I myself have not the ability to fashion a statue of philosophy and set it up: but I might aspire to prepare a base for such a statue, and I recommend to men as the first essential the recognition of the usefulness and dignity of natural history.'[33] Nevertheless it cannot be stated with confidence, as a noted scholar has stated, that the task of collecting natural histories came to assume in Bacon's mind such exclusive urgency that he abandoned plans to achieve his metaphysics. As we have seen evidence is in short supply. That being so, the conclusion is a rash one.[34]

On the other hand this evidence reveals full correspondence being maintained between judgments made in the last years about the inherent propelling capabilities and force of histories – histories completed by the 'auxiliary and light-bringing experiments which arise in the course of interpretation'[35] – and the much earlier statements about history's unique prerogatives – statements which were occasioned by Bacon's plans to write a portion of the history of England. Judgments delivered in the previous reign, it will be recalled, were in respect of civil history pure. They were made before he expressed his approving notice of civil history mixed. He produced histories in the final years which were, natural histories mixed. But they were more than merely the means, starting point and groundwork; they partook of the end and of the thing itself. These tributes illustrate, and in illustrating confirm, the original force and the enduring thrust of Bacon's earliest recorded recollections on history – civil history – when he claimed while the Queen still reigned that it makes men wise; and when he compared it – also while she yet reigned – to its advantage not only with poetry but with philosophy itself.

In Bacon's hands civil history did more than these things for natural history and with it. As we have seen, he had extended civil history to include a history of arts and sciences, a branch which can be deemed to share something of civil history proper's supremacy in authority and dignity. He expected, he wrote, a judgment by posterity to the effect that he did no great things, but that he made less account of things that were accounted great.[36] Aristotle was accounted great. Bacon succeeded in making less account of Aristotle. But he did not dismiss him altogether. The history of arts and sciences explored by Bacon in *De Sapientia Veterum*, and also as a side-product in the course of attending to other matters, serves in the case of the latter incidental contribution (though certainly not in the case of *De Sapientia Veterum*, where, by implication, Aristotle is dismissed 'among the greater gods' who deal in 'abstract philosophies'[37]) to reprieve and rehabilitate Aristotle – partially, it is true, and certainly not wholly. Reproaches and condemnation remain. But nevertheless he is reprieved to the extent that Bacon gives him a place in his plans and purposes in his programme for the world of nature. Since, however, these remained plans and projects, and failed to mature, it is not possible to know how much of Aristotle would have survived Bacon's resort to him.

For the programme in *Know Thyself*, antiquity had handed down complete intact products – poetry, civil histories, the common logic, rhetoric, aphorism – there being no need nor possibility either of improving them or of dispensing with them. In the other programme, the state of things is different. Nevertheless, given Bacon's considered, and in the second *Advancement* emphasized, decisions concerning history of letters; and given that two provisos are recognized, contributions made by antiquity in natural philosophy/science need not be dismissed as absent, or if present, derisory. Yet another description in the first *Advancement* of Bacon's notions for a history of letters runs like this:

A just story of learning, containing the antiquities and originals of knowledge and their sects; their inventions, their traditions; their diverse administrations and; their flourishings, their oppositions, decays, depressions, oblivions, removes; with the occasions and causes of them, and all other events concerning learning, throughout the ages of the world; I may truly affirm to be wanting. The use and end of which work I do not so much design for curiosity, or satisfaction of those that are lovers of learning; but chiefly for a more serious and grave purpose, which is this in few words, that it will make learned men wise in the use and administration of learning.[38]

The two provisos are, first, that it be recognized that ancient natural philosophers such as Democritus and Aristotle offer for posterity not complete intact products, but, instead, possible guidelines in the administration, that is to say, in the conduct and advancement of learning. The second proviso is that such guidelines require to be discovered and elucidated in a history to be achieved in the future by others. This history, *inter alia*, would no doubt locate and assess Bacon's own efforts, while he himself in his lifetime apart from producing *De Sapientia Veterum* did no more than contribute to such a history *en passant*. It would compare his own with the aims and achievements of others. Contrasted with such guidelines for a programme concerning the world of nature – which are only possible ones at that, and which were to be illuminated by workers chiefly in the future – the *data* afforded by the past for *Know Thyself* provides the bounty Bacon displayed and also abundantly and fruitfully used not only in that programme, but also, if less abundantly, in his programme for nature.

Interflow and overlap between his programmes is largely cross-fertilization. But the latter is fertilization from the side of *Know thyself* into the arena of studies of nature. The further point is that the energies of civil history in fertilizing natural history are paralleled and echoed in a perceptible impact of civil philosophy – civil history's offspring – upon a proper conduct of natural phil-

osophy when Bacon was arguing for it in *Novum Organum*, Book I.
'...no one', he wrote in the second *Advancement*, 'should be
disheartened or confounded if the experiments which he tries do not
answer his expectation. For though a successful experiment be more
agreeable, yet an unsuccessful one is oftentimes no less instructive.'[39]
This is among lessons taught by practitioners conducting experiments in the mechanical arts. It is a lesson to be learnt by philosophers
in whichever of Bacon's programmes they engage themselves. We
have observed already that despite Bacon's insistence that the
natural world is unknown, he assumes that in investigations and
experiments conducted regarding it, as in those in policy, a specific
end or aim will be held in view: and that such statements regarding
disappointments confirm this.

Inquiries and projects in civil knowledge present their peculiar
and frustrating difficulties. They often disappoint 'the lighter
breezes of hope'.[40] Civil *phenomena* are hard to isolate either from
mutual interactions or from interventions from outside. Bacon's
positions regarding the deity and human free will themselves
precipitate expectations of irregularities. In policy controlled
conditions can be achieved only by self-controlled men conducting
themselves cooperatively. More often than not a different state of
affairs prevails in which men display little self-control and small
cooperation, the result being that events flow from passions and
short-sightedness. But this experience gained in civil affairs is
presented by Bacon in *Novum Organum* Book I as advice for those
working in things natural: '...putting aside the lighter breezes of
hope, we must thoroughly sift and examine those which promise
greater steadiness and constancy. Nay, and we must take state-
prudence too into our counsels, whose rule is to distrust, and to take
the less favourable view of human affairs.'[41]

The above quotation is from Book I, Aphorism XCII. Aphorism
XCIV, Book I, also refers to 'state prudence'. The lesson here is offered
as a less discouraging one:

Next comes a consideration of the greatest importance as an argument of
hope; I mean that drawn from the errors of past time, and of the ways
hitherto trodden. For most excellent was the censure once passed upon a
government that had been unwisely administered. 'That which is the worst
thing in reference to the past, ought to be regarded as best for the future.
For if you had done all your duty demanded, and yet your affairs were no
better, you would not have even a hope left you that further improvement

is possible. But now, when your misfortunes are owing, not to the force of circumstances, but to your own errors, you may hope that by dismissing or correcting these errors, a great change may be made for the better.' In like manner, if during so long a course of years men had kept the true road for discovering and cultivating sciences, and had yet been unable to make further progress therein, bold doubtless and rash would be the opinion that further progress is possible. But if the road itself has been mistaken, and men's labour spent on unfit objects, it follows that the difficulty has its rise not in things themselves, which are not in our power, but in the human understanding, and the use and application thereof, which admits of remedy and medicine. It will be of great use therefore to set forth what these errors are; for as many impediments as there have been in times past from this cause, so many arguments are there of hope for the time to come.[42]

The censure referred to, 'once passed upon a government' was inflicted by Demosthenes (383–322 BC). We have seen that Bacon had made this point earlier and had mentioned Demosthenes by name when instructing the King on how to handle his parliaments. Bacon had argued that difficulties in dealing with parliaments had their rise not in the things themselves, that is, in parliaments, but in the human understanding, namely in that of King James.

Aphorism XCVII, already quoted early in this argument, again enlists 'state prudence', that is, civil philosophy, to assist natural philosophy, this time citing the part which needs to be played in the latter as much as in the former not only by caution but also by audacity:

Now if anyone of ripe age, unimpaired senses, and well-purged mind, apply himself anew to experience and particulars, better hopes may be entertained of that man. In which point I promise to myself a like fortune to that of Alexander the Great; and let no man tax me with vanity till he have heard the end; for the thing which I mean tends to the putting off of all vanity. For of Alexander and his deeds Aeschines spake thus: 'Assuredly we do not live the life of mortal men; but to this end were we born, that in after ages wonders might be told of us'; as if what Alexander had done seemed to him miraculous. But in the next age Titus Livius took a better and a deeper view of the matter, saying in effect, that Alexander 'had done no more than take courage to despise vain apprehensions'.[43]

The next aphorism, XCVIII, yet again brings in civil philosophy to play the part of preceptor and auxiliary to natural philosophy:

Now for grounds of experience – since to experience we must come – we have as yet had either none or very weak ones; no search has been made to collect a store of particular observations sufficient either in number, or in kind or in certainty, to inform the understanding, or in any way adequate. On the contrary, men of learning, but easy withal and idle, have taken for the construction or for the confirmation of their philosophy certain rumours and vague fames or airs of experience, and allowed to these the weight of lawful evidence. And just as if some kingdoms and states were to direct its counsels and affairs, not by letters and reports from ambassadors and trustworthy messengers, but by the gossip of the streets; such exactly is the system of management introduced into philosophy with relation to experience. Nothing duly investigated, nothing verified, nothing counted, weighed, or measured, is to be found in natural history: and what in observation is loose and vague, is in information deceptive and treacherous.[44]

Aphorism CI presents, though less explicitly, another case where civil prudence intervenes on behalf of progress in natural philosophy/ science:

But even after such a store of natural history and experience as is required for the work of the understanding, or of philosophy, shall be ready at hand, still the understanding is by no means competent to deal with it off hand and by memory alone; no more than if a man should hope by force of memory to retain and make himself master of the computation of an *ephemeris*. And yet hitherto more has been done in matter of invention by thinking than by writing; and experience has not yet learned her letters. Now no course of invention can be satisfactory unless it be carried on in writing. But when this is brought into use, and experience has been taught to read and write, better things may be hoped.[45]

In civil histories civil experience has been taught to read and write. Elsewhere this is made very clear.

Aphorism CIV is as telling as any of the above:

the understanding must not however be allowed to jump and fly from particulars to remote axioms and of almost the highest generality... and taking stand upon them as truths that cannot be shaken, proceed to prove and frame the middle axioms by reference to them; which has been the practice hitherto; the understanding being not only carried that way by a natural impulse, but also by the use of syllogistic demonstration trained and inured to it. But then, and then only, may we hope well of the sciences, when in a just scale of ascent, and by successive steps not interrupted or broken, we rise from particulars to lesser axioms; and then to middle axioms, one above the other; and last of all to the most general. For the lowest axioms differ but slightly from bare experience, while the highest and most general (which we now have) are notional and abstract and without solidity. *But the middle are the true and solid and living axioms, on which depend the affairs and fortunes of men* [the present author's added emphasis]; and above them again, last of all, those which are indeed the most general. Such I mean as are not abstract but of which those intermediate axioms are really limitations. The understanding must not therefore be supplied with wings, but rather hung with weights, to keep it from leaping and flying. Now this has never yet been done; when it is done, we may entertain better hopes of the sciences.[46]

In both programmes Bacon conducts 'Experiments of Light'. Experiments of light are experiments of truth not experiments of utility. It is only because they are the former and not the latter that they can promote the glory of God and the relief of man's estate. '...it must ever be kept in mind (as I am continually urging) that experiments of Light are even more to be sought after than experiments of Fruit'.[47] Preoccupation in the short term with discovering utilities frustrates possible achievement in the long term. Here again policy provides a lead. For in this latter realm, not only as historian of King Henry VII but in his proceedings as man of state, Bacon argues for measures 'not made on the spur of a particular occasion for the present, but out of providence of the future'.[48] His grand strategy if and as it succeeded would carry a plentiful flow of benefits. Immediate advantages should be sacrificed. In the long term many more advantages could accrue from restraint.

The evident priority granted in *Novum Organum* (both books) to knowledges of nature requires no justifying. Nor should Bacon's earnest cravings to promote them be played down. No such shortfall in recognition of what is plain is intended in this argument. Preoccupation with histories natural and with axioms to be made therein and therefrom became as deep as his absorption in histories civil and in proceeding from them to axioms in civil science. Extant arts like medicine and policy were extant because men throughout the ages could not do without them. They were extant because demanded by the human condition. All the same, what is most lacking and absent – in this case knowledges of nature based on plentiful histories of nature – must be regarded as the one end it is most desirable to achieve. For if a man is denied the possession of something it is impossible for him to estimate the proportions and implications of possessing it. A man in any case is endowed with a corporeal frame. This, with its unexplored interactions with his mind, forms part of the natural order.

Bacon had written in *Novum Organum* Book i, Aphorism cxxix:

Further, it will not be amiss to distinguish the three kinds and as it were grades of ambition in mankind. The first is of those who desire to extend their own power in their native country; which kind is vulgar and degenerate. The second is of those who labour to extend the power of their country and its dominion among men. This certainly has more dignity, though not less covetousness. But if a man endeavour to establish and extend the power and dominion of the human race itself over the universe, his ambition (if ambition it can be called) is without doubt both a more wholesome thing and a more noble than the other two. Now the empire of man over things depends wholly on the arts and sciences. For we cannot command nature except by obeying her.[49]

He echoes here what he had written in *De Interpretatione Naturae Proæmium*, that early piece in which he had sought to assess his abilities and to sort his ambitions, in both cases, as it turned out, inconclusively. There as in *Novum Organum* Book I Aphorism cxxix it is discovery of arts and sciences, bestowing control for man in the universe of nature, who have – or rather who deserve – first place in repute as benefactors of mankind. On the other hand, it would be remiss not to point out that in the essay *Of Honour and Reputation* such benefactors have no place in 'the true marshalling of the degrees of sovereign honour... '[50] In order as Bacon gives them these degrees are one and all those of eminence in the realm of what Bacon would expound, conduct, construct and invent as the science of policy. 'In the first place are *conditores imperiorum*, founders of states and commonwealths;... In the second place are *legislatores*, lawgivers; which are also called *second founders*, or *perpetui principes*, because they govern by their ordinances after they are gone'; In 'An offer to the King of a Digest to be made of the Laws of England' Bacon had suggested to James in 1621 that if he would accept this offer, he too could aspire to this degree of 'sovereign honour'.[51] 'In the third place', the essay continues, 'are *liberatores*, or *salvatores*, such as compound the long miseries of civil wars, or to deliver their countries from servitude of strangers or tyrants.'[52] And so the list proceeds. Next to rulers, Bacon's list defines 'degrees of honour in subjects... ' These are 'First *participes curarum*, those upon whom princes do discharge the greatest weight of their affairs; their *right hands*, as we call them. The next are *duces belli*, great leaders; such as are princes' lieutenants and do them notable services in the wars. The third are *gratiosi, favourites*; such as exceed not this scantling, to be solace to the sovereign and harmless to the people. And the fourth, *negotiis pares*, such as have great places under princes, and execute their places with sufficiency.'[53]

This essay appeared in 1597. It had no place in the 1612 collection. It appeared in 1625 heavily embellished with what it had

previously lacked, namely examples – that is to say, names of
characters gathered from civil histories, exemplifying the categories
Bacon had provided in 1597. All these are rulers – Bacon mentions no
names in this class of subjects – who acquired fame in government or
in law – for example, King Henry VII of England. Here despite the
praise given this king as lawgiver in his *History* (1622), in this essay
(1625) Bacon does not award him repute amongst the lawgivers.
Instead he prefers to recognize Henry's renown as belonging in
another category, that of 'such as compound the long miseries of
civil wars, or deliver their countries from servitude of strangers or
tyrants'.[54]

   The character and contents of the essay *of Honour and Reputation* are
explicable. Bacon argued that hitherto there had been no acceptable
natural history and no valid natural philosophy/science, and that
what he planned to contribute in both areas would be novel.
Achievements in this field in the most ancient antiquity were
unknown and unknowable save through the mysteries of the poets.
In subsequent times nothing more had been available than points
made which could possibly be helpful to later investigators. The
wording, together with the views it conveys if closely attended to,
both of *De Interpretatione Naturae Proœmium* and in *Novum Organum*
Book 1 Aphorism CXXIX indicates that, up to the present and
compared with what Bacon had it in mind to achieve, the roll of
honour in a prospective history of letters boasting names of men who
had been masters in knowledges of nature and in consequent benefits
had been a blank. In the future, if Bacon had his way, a history of
letters would be different. Wording in *De Interpretatione Naturae
Proœmium* runs as follows:

Now among all the benefits that could be conferred upon mankind, I found
none so great as the discovery of new arts, endowments, and commodities
for the bettering of man's life. For I saw that among the rude people in the
primitive times the authors of rude inventions and discoveries were
consecrated and numbered among the Gods. And it was plain that the good
effects wrought by founders of cities, law-givers, fathers of the people,
extirpators of tyrants and heroes of that class, extend but over narrow
spaces and last but for short times; whereas the work of the Inventor,
though a thing of less pomp and show, is felt everywhere and lasts for ever.
But above all, if a man could succeed, not in striking out some particular
invention, however useful, but in kindling a light in nature – a light which
should in its very rising touch and illuminate all the border-regions that
confine upon the circle of our present knowledge; and so spreading further

and further should presently disclose and bring into sight all that is most hidden and secret in the world, – that man (I thought) would be the benefactor indeed of the whole human race, – the propagator of man's empire over the universe, the champion of liberty, the conqueror and subduer of necessities[55]

– necessities imposed this time not as in civil policy by the activities of men, but by the processes of nature. As will be seen if it be consulted, *Novum Organum* Book I Aphorism CXXIX, quoted above, echoes the earlier text.

Though evidence does not suffice to establish that Bacon declined to recognize achievements of others in natural history and natural philosophy/science in order to bolster his own plans in that field, it remains scarcely debatable that in the process of attempting to promote his case in *Novum Organum* for the possibility of advances in knowledges of nature, and in arguing his procedure there for achieving them, Bacon plays down what he calls 'arts which rest in discourse and opinion'[56] – 'sciences popular...'[57] – 'arts which are now in fashion' and which 'supply matter for disputation and ornaments for discourse, to be employed for the convenience of professors and men of business...'[58] Though explicitly pronouncing that the two programmes are on the same level and that they are of equal import, he nevertheless by clear implication disparages his own contribution in the improvable extant arts.

But, also in *Novum Organum*, he himself cancels this appearance, correcting and dispelling it not only by explicit declaration in Aphorism CXXVIII but also in his numerous achievements referred to in this aphorism. If we doubt the declaration, we should consult the achievements. Deprivation of knowledges of nature in no way diminishes the value of knowledges already available in terms of histories and experience which are accessible. Nor – for this would be a distinction without a difference – can furthering sciences which are extant be other than adding new discoveries in them. '...for to invent is to discover that we know not...'[59] In sciences which are extant but improvable 'mastering an adversary in argument' – by logic and by rhetoric – sincerely giving a true account of our gift of reason, to the benefit and use of men – successfully disputing without zeal of contradiction – in such a way that future movement is not foreclosed – such operations conducted by Bacon in his career in statecraft and in the law can scarcely be other than the advancement of learning.

True, he plays down in *Novum Organum* his contribution in improving extant arts. True, he gives highest place in *Novum Organum* to men who achieve reputation and honour by inventing arts and sciences hitherto lacking. Nevertheless, in his improvements of extant arts Bacon activates and fructifies the old common logic. He extends its use, employing it in his natural experimental histories. His use of it both there and in extant arts is powered by his practice of his emerging mode or rule. The sharpness, even asperity, adopted in distinguishing the new induction from the old – 'their form of induction, I say, is utterly vicious and incompetent'[60] – this in his practice becomes muffled and blunted. The business was 'really to instruct and suborn action and active life'.[61] Whether engaged in the old arts and extant sciences or in the new – as in his natural experimental histories – he tries to 'bring down' the way he is introducing to 'common apprehension' by 'effects and works'.[62] '…everything is subject to chance and error which is not supported by examples and experience'.[63] 'The intellect is not qualified to judge etc.…';[64] but the intellect will be disciplined by the senses in experience/experiment. Whether old or new, all philosophy and every science will be made more true because more active – that is, more experimental; and also more active – that is, producing new and better axioms – because more true.

It is tempting but plainly illegitimate to conclude that Bacon invents civil science as from his point of view a secondary and minor product of attempts to invent natural philosophy/science – that in advance he awards himself, so to say, a consolation prize in view of possible failure to prove that he had founded natural philosophy/science by establishing results in this field derived from Book II of *Novum Organum*. Bacon explains, it is true, that civil science was a means to an end for him. But he also maintained that inventing civil science was an end in itself. He makes this clear both by what he does and also by what he says: '…the improvement of that which we have' is 'as much an object as the acquisition of more'.[65] Here we should recall his argument in *Novum Organum*, Book I and in *The History of Winds* that nothing can be studied to fruitful effect exclusively in itself and that observations should be kept in play over more fields than one – even over more fields than one simultaneously so far as this is possible. He wrote: '…my design is rather to advance the universal work of Instauration in many things, than to perfect it in a few'.[66] Pursuit of progress in any one area, in this case in *Know*

Thyself, is a means of projecting for advances in others. Like Christopher Columbus (1438–1506) he expressed his convictions that because men could see nothing but sea it did not follow that no land was available and waiting to be discovered. There the parallel between Bacon and the Viceroy of the Indies ends. In both programmes Bacon remained fully aware of what he wanted to invent. In *Know Thyself* – and markedly in civil policy – he effectively invented what he wanted.

Bacon, in those extant arts which he judged deserving of, and thus capable of improvement, practised all his precepts for advances in sciences, whether human or natural. He achieved more in these extant arts than in those not yet extant, but which he promised to make available. Here there is a paradox. Given that men have secured the needed natural histories, the putting into operation of *Novum Organum* Book II, establishing nature's metaphysics – producing knowledge of nature's 'true reality' – including that of men's bodies – doing so in certainties – resulting in progressive stages of certainty – this, Bacon assures men, would be easy. Making civil philosophy, on the other hand, is difficult. He is equally explicit about this. 'Civil knowledge is the hardliest reduced to axiom.' That is because 'of all others (it) is most immersed in matter' – that is to say, in civil histories and in a man's own civil experience, material, as not elsewhere, so richly abounds.[67] Not only is civil philosophy difficult; civil history out of which the former must be made is itself difficult. 'I come...to Civil History...whereof the dignity and authority are pre-eminent about human writings...But the difficulty is no less than the dignity.'[68] It will be recalled in this connection that Bacon was able to complete only the first portion of his planned project in civil history writing. In this project, as in his grand strategy as a whole, the aim of elucidating Henry VIII's 'confusion' – other than by his remarks in a source where we have suggested there lies a clue – was not fulfilled.

With one breath Bacon had asserted that 'moral philosophy is more difficile than policy'.[69] But with another breath he had declared that in difficulty civil history together with civil policy, surpassed everything else. In truth the respective predicaments were identical. Both moral philosophy and also civil history and civil philosophy must penetrate the inside of man from the outside. Bacon would appear to have set little store by introspection as procedure for detecting what goes on inside other minds. There was little to choose between the respective difficulties. Bacon's second breath prevailed over his first breath because it was in the second area that he most practised. He continued to demand help for policy from progress in moral knowledge. But by practising in the fields of civil history and civil policy he could serve the two purposes simultaneously. Striving for betterment in the field of policy could carry with it improvement in the adjacent and inseparable field of morality.

The numerous and grave faults of most civil historians in modern times offer proof of the difficulty of their task. 'In no sort of writings is there 'a greater distance between the good and the bad.'[70] ... 'Civil History', he wrote – not in the first – but in the final *Advancement*,

is beset on all sides with faults; some (and these are the greater part) write only barren and commonplace narratives, a very reproach to history; others hastily and disorderly string together a few particular relations and trifling memoirs; others merely run over the heads of events; others, on the contrary, go into all the minutest particularities, and such as have no relation to the main action; some indulge their imaginations in bold inventions; while others impress on their works the image not so much of their minds as of their passions, ever thinking of their party, but no good witnesses as to facts; some are always inculcating their favourite political doctrines, and idly interrupting the narrative by going out of the way to display them; others are injudiciously prolix in reporting orations and harangues, and even in relating the actions themselves; so that, among all the writings of men, there is nothing rarer than a true and perfect Civil History.[71]

This passage is comparable with similarly severe judgments delivered by Michel de Montaigne (1533–92) in his essay on books in the section he devoted to civil histories. Yet neither Bacon nor Montaigne were exponents of historical pyrrhonism. In each case the dignity of civil history was salvaged, redeemed and established by the excellence achieved and handed on by the ancients. Bacon had his secular canon. He also had his civil experience. This latter operated to confirm the contents of the canon, while the canon in its turn operated to inspire and direct the experience. As for Montaigne, he concluded that: 'The only good histories are those written by men who were themselves at the head of affairs, or took a share in the conduct of them, or at least had the good fortune to direct others of a similar nature. Of this kind are almost all the Greek and Roman histories.'[72]

Small wonder nevertheless, that given the observer's difficulties – whether he be man of state or civil historian – or as in Bacon's case

– the two combined, and given also the difficulty of the civil philosophy which he tries to make, we obtain conclusions in the latter of a lower order of certainty than what Bacon promised could be achieved if men would operate the machinery of *Novum Organum*, Book II in investigating the world of nature. Quarts cannot be extracted from pint pots, nor silk purses fashioned out of sows' ears. And yet it was amongst these difficulties and amidst these lesser certainties that Bacon chiefly dwelt. 'For indeed', he had told Isaac Casaubon in 1609, 'to write at leisure that which is to be read at leisure matters little; but to bring about the better ordering of man's life and business with all its troubles and difficulties... this is the thing that I aim at.'[73] It was amidst these troubles, difficulties and what was provisional, that he was mostly productive. *Novum Organum*, Book II was a dead letter. As for his natural histories, the natural mixed histories, which he bequeathed, these share the lesser certainties and the greater dignities but also the graver difficulties of his attainments in human self-knowledge.

Confessions of difficulty, uncertainty and of the provisional, the three usually, as is to be expected, going hand in hand, are presented in all three of Bacon's Natural and Experimental Histories. According to the *History of Winds*: 'Winds are generated in a thousand ways, as will be made evident in the ensuing inquiry; whence it is no easy matter to fix observations on so variable a subject. Those however which are here laid down may generally be held for certain.'[74] Again: 'Rules are either particular or general; but here both kinds are provisional. For as yet I do not pronounce certainly upon anything.'[75] According to the *History of Life and Death* 'From the neglect of observations, and the complication of causes, it is difficult to discover any rule for the length and shortness of life in animals. Some few things however I will note.'[76] Again: 'This matter requires a deeper investigation and a longer explanation than pertains to the present inquiry.'[77] In the *History of Dense and Rare* we find: 'Meanwhile I fully admit that to calculate the proportions and quantities of matter existing in different bodies, and to find by what industry and sagacity true information thereof may be procured, is a very difficult thing...'[78] Again: 'With regard to the comparative expansion of pneumatical and tangible bodies, though it be a thing difficult to be discovered, yet I have... etc.'[79] Appropriately in the final notes in this the last of his natural and experimental histories he talks of 'approximations' and employs marks of interrogation: 'Increase of

weight in metals. *Approximations.* Conversion of iron into copper. Increase of lead in cellars (?) Conversion of quicksilver into gold (?).'[80]

His masculine birth of time had been civil history. For him it was
the most masculine and the most fertilizing of all births. He affirmed
with equal assurance that among births it was also the most difficult.
The natural histories which civil history fertilized shared in their
birth civil history's honours together with its uncertainties and its
difficulties.

The critic could point out that in policy – civil history's offspring
– a major question about procedure would appear to have been
answered for Bacon and that his difficulties in the field of policy
ought to have been eased in consequence. 'Seek out and gather
together such store and variety of things as may suffice for the
formation of true axioms...'[81] He writes here primarily of procedure
for inquiries into nature. But how much constitutes sufficiency? How
far in collecting particulars is it necessary to go before safely making
an axiom? Bacon stressed the error and danger of jumping to
conclusions. He urged men to resist temptations to do so:

In the history which I require and design, special care is to be taken that
it be of wide range and made to the measure of the universe. For the world
is not to be narrowed till it will go into the understanding (which has
been done hitherto), but the understanding to be expanded and opened till
it can take in the image of the world, as it is in fact. For that fashion of
taking few things into account, and pronouncing with reference to a few
things, has been the ruin of everything.[82]

No doubt this is true. But the question remains: how far, granted
that a man is not pronouncing with reference to too few things, is it
necessary to go? Redemptus Baranzan read *Novum Organum* and
seems to have confronted the author precisely with this question.
Bacon's reply was chiefly expostulatory: 'With regard to the
multitude of the Instances by which men may be deterred from the
attempt; this is my answer, – First, what need to dissemble? Either
a store of Instances must be procured or the business must be given up.
All other ways, however enticing, are impassable. Secondly, (as you
yourself also observe), the Prerogatives of Instances... will diminish
the multitude of them very much.' Prerogative instances are the first
instances to be inquired into as being the more likely to hasten the
work in induction. He adds other arguments without true success in
giving the answer.[83]

But with respect to government the question is answered for Bacon in that he avails himself so much of the work of Machiavelli. 'Civil knowledge is the hardliest reduced to axiom.' True, but Machiavelli had sorted out much of the 'matter' in which civil knowledge is so deeply 'immersed'. He had complained that

in constituting republics, in maintaining states, in governing kingdoms, in forming an army or conducting a war, in dealing with subjects, in extending the empire, one finds neither prince nor republic who repairs to antiquity for examples. This is due in my opinion not so much to the weak state to which the religion of today has brought the world, or to the evil wrought in many provinces and cities of Christendom by ambition conjoined with idleness, as to the lack of a proper appreciation of history ... Though the enterprise is difficult, yet, with the help of those who have encouraged me to undertake the task, I think I can carry it out in such a way that there shall remain to another but a short road to traverse in order to reach the place assigned.[84]

Bacon was the man who inherited and entered upon what was but a short road to traverse. Machiavelli maintained that the Christian religion stood in constant need of restoration to its origins. So did Bacon. Machiavelli complained that politics in his times consisted too much of ambition conjoined with idleness, the idleness referred to being a neglect of the learning freely available in civil histories. So did Bacon. Machiavelli stated that the making of civil policy out of civil history was difficult. So did Bacon.

Further, in laws a reply is provided to the question what constitutes a sufficiency of particulars before it is proper for the inquirer to launch into the making of axioms. In the sphere of laws the question answers itself. Materials for laws, first English, and then English and Roman, are extensive and numerous. There are therefore enough for advance to be feasible in one way. But materials are also in the nature of the case sufficiently limited for progress to be possible in another way. Law, at least English Common Law, is a history – a civil history pure. There is not too little of this history, nor also is there too much. Bacon shows no sign that these considerations either in the field of government or in that of laws lessen the difficulties of his work in policy.

But leaving matters in this way and on this note creates an impression which is the reverse of what is required, suggesting a conclusion other than the one which is correct. Lesser certainties and greater difficulties will be incurred and these will be accepted. But they recede and pale when balanced against another consideration. The most difficult difficulties are those presented by the idols of the mind. Civil histories and also the civil experience absorbed and conducted by the man of state like himself offer a field for possibly successful exercises against idols of the mind – if only because civil histories, as contrasted with other human writings, present realities in the shape of other men and women. Admittedly common sense comes to the aid of the philosopher in such an instance. It comes to the aid of Montaigne. Bacon, too, as Macaulay diagnosed, was not ill-endowed with common sense.

In luminous additions in the final version of the essay *Of Friendship* (1625) Bacon wrote: 'a fruit of friendship is healthful and sovereign for the understanding...' Friendship can make a man wax 'wiser than himself'. 'Heraclitus said well in one of his enigmas *Dry Light is ever the best*. And certain it is that the light that a man receiveth by counsel from another, is drier and purer than that which cometh from his own understanding and judgment; which is ever infused and drenched in his affections and customs.'[85] But civil histories, including 'the orations and the epistles'[86] *et al.* of a man of state like Bacon, are pre-eminent among human writings in that they possess and perform something of the same function as friendship, affording comparable services.

This helps to explain what otherwise can seem arrantly implausible in pretensions that undertakings in civil history and civil policy assist enterprises in exploring the secrets of nature – in claims that study and practice in civil history promote the making and use of natural history – in claims that inventing civil science constitutes a constructive stage in discovering natural science. It is this which helps to explain not only why Bacon dwelt so much in the department of *Know Thyself*, but also why he was able to do so acquiescently. In this area idols of the mind arrayed themselves less formidably. They could be engaged on terms less than fatally unequal.

CHAPTER 14

Bacon and his markers I

In Book i, *Novum Organum* Bacon identified, named and judged three systems, sects or schools in natural philosophy/science. He devoted *Novum Organum* to the enterprise of advancing sciences of nature. But it will be recalled that Book i straddles both programmes, and that with respect to both Books he deplored sharp separations between sciences. He called the three systems, sects or schools, the Rational or Sophistical, the Empirical, and the Superstitious. This is a contribution to a history of letters, learning and arts made by Bacon *en passant* and in transit, as inquirer not as believer, which as he explained was lacking and needed to be undertaken. The names or labels are those affixed by himself. None of the three described itself in the terms which he allotted to it. But he offered guides for identifying the schools. The Rationals were Aristotelians. The Superstitious had connections with Plato. The Empiricals were alchemists.

It is not at once clear why he classed alchemists as constituting a system, sect or school. But he confronted the idols of the theatre as much as the other three idols. The idols of the theatre were, he argued, the least difficult of the four to eradicate. They were nevertheless idols. They consisted of false or inadequate philosophies. It was, he maintained, the idols of the market place which misled and obfuscated men's minds with words and names. But so did the idols of the theatre. Philosophical schools, sects or systems could be recognized as employing and propagating their specialized terms, modes and traditions of discourse. In this the alchemists were no exception. A late-twentieth-century scholar has described alchemists of the sixteenth and seventeenth centuries as a Tower of Babel, a company of *magi* composed of practitioners each of whom voiced a rival claim for his experiments. But this scholar also maintains that alchemists displayed a measure of order and control in their use of concepts and verbal procedures. He adduces as a helpful comparison the proceedings of late-twentieth-century civil historians in Europe and elsewhere. 'We should not', he writes, 'identify disunity with chaos. Perhaps historical studies today with a mingling of formal and informal approaches may be used as a good modern analogy of the alchemical world of the sixteenth and seventeenth centuries.'[1] It can be added that Bacon's other two schools of natural philosophy, the Rational and the Superstitious, were neither centralized nor internally integrated and harmonious in his times.

It is not immediately plain why Bacon called alchemists Empiricals. Light is shed on this point by statements he makes elsewhere. At earlier stages in this argument a remark of his has been more than once cited: medical knowledge 'if it be destituted and forsaken by natural philosophy, it is not much better than an empirical practice'.[2] Elsewhere in *Advancement* (both versions) he wrote: 'For many operations have been invented, sometimes by a casual incidence and occurrence, sometimes by a purposed experiment, and of those which have been found by an intentional experiment, some have been found out by varying or extending the same experiment, some by transferring and compounding diverse experiments the one into the other, which kind of invention an empiric may manage.'[3] In *Novum Organum* itself he wrote: 'my course and road, as I have often clearly stated, and would wish to state again, is this – not to extract works from works or experiments from experiments (as an empiric), but from works and experiments to extract causes and axioms, and again from those causes and axioms new works and experiments, as a legitimate interpreter of nature'.[4]

When Bacon employs the terms 'an empiric', 'The Empirical' sect or school, he describes a man who (or a class of men which) does not restrict himself (or itself) to thinking and disputing, but instead engages in practice and in conducting experiments. But the terms as he uses them are invariably badges of reproach and disapproval. Practice and experiments alone and on their own are as futile and fruitless as procedures consisting only of thinking and disputing.

Of the three sects, schools or systems which Bacon listed and judged at this place in Book I, *Novum Organum* it is only the sect, school or system affiliated to Plato which surpasses Empiricals in the extent to which it earns his censures. Plato is placed bottom because theology is not science. In any case Plato's theology was erroneous. But the Empirical school fared little better at his hands. This latter school, he wrote, 'has its foundations not in the light of common notions (which though it be a faint and superficial light, is yet in a manner universal, and in the formation of which many things have been taken into account) – but in the narrowness and darkness of a few experiments'.[5] Comparing these men to their disadvantage with the Rationals, he implies that it is the latter, the Rationals, who have preserved foundations in the light of common notions. Aphorism LXVI transforms an implication contained in Aphorism LXIV into a deliberate pronouncement.

The school of Empiricals bestow 'much diligent and careful labour on a few experiments...' But they have 'hence made bold to educe and construct systems; wresting all other facts in a strange fashion to conformity therewith'.[6] Carried away by these activities they produce conclusions 'more deformed and monstrous'[7] than those propounded by the Rationals. Empiricals–alchemists produce, he states, 'very little out of many things',[8] offering too little which is rational and fruitful out of too much that is practical and experimental. '...my course and road, as I have often clearly stated, and would wish to state again, is this – not to extract works from works or experiments from experiments (as an empiric), but from works and experiments to extract causes and axioms, from those causes and axioms, new works and experiments, as a legitimate interpreter of nature'.[9] Out of all their practice and experiments, alchemists fail to achieve productive axioms. They misapply or underplay the rational faculty. Even toilers in mechanical arts – who also produce no axioms – obtain tangible useful results. Despite the Empiricals' addiction to practice and experimenting – and despite the circumstance that Bacon had long since passed out of his early disputatious phase, he can propose nothing favourable to say of this school of natural philosophers in *Novum Organum*. He remained as unimpressed by them as did Edward Gibbon when writing about alchemists more than a century later in *The Decline and Fall of the Roman Empire*.[10] Like an empiric outside a school or sect, the Empirical school in Bacon's eyes deserves no place in a history of letters and arts. Whether or not this school performed many experiments or instead only a few – on this point he expresses himself less than clearly –[11] this school gives no guidance for advancing learning either in *Know Thyself* or in the unknown territories of the natural order.

The Rational school, that of Aristotle, was certainly also at fault. 'For creation', according to Book II's concluding aphorism, 'was not by the curse made altogether and for ever a rebel, but in virtue of that charter "In the sweat of thy face shalt thou eat bread", it is now by various labours (not certainly by disputations or idle magical ceremonies, but by various labours) at length in some measure subdued...' If as seems indicated 'idle magical ceremonies' refers to the proceedings of the Empirical school, 'disputations' evidently refers to those of the Rational school. This latter 'snatches from experience a variety of common instances, neither duly ascertained nor diligently examined and weighed, and leaves all the rest to meditation and agitation of wit'.[12] In some of Aristotle's works 'there is frequent dealing with experiments'.[13] But too much credit should not accrue to him on this account. For

he had come to his conclusion before; he did not consult experience, as he should have done, in order to the framing of his decisions and axioms; but having first determined the question according to his will, he then resorts to experience, and bending her into conformity with his placets leads her about like a captive in a procession; so that even on this count he is more guilty than his modern followers, the schoolmen, who have abandoned experience altogether.

Rationals, the school of Aristotle, produce, he claims, too much out of too little – too much which is rational – but scarcely fruitful – out of too little which is active and experimental.

Nevertheless, with their faults, Rationals stand highest in this league of three in Bacon's estimate – not only above the Superstitious school but also above the Empiricals. He places them highest not because of their sway in the world but because of the quality of their performance. They are lost, but unlike the other two, not lost beyond reprieve or rehabilitation. Rationals, he wrote, do not ignore the light of common notions. But it is not on this ground that they are granted superior status. 'The light of common notions, which though it be a faint and superficial light, is yet in a manner universal, and in the formation of this' (light) 'many things have been taken into account'.[14] Bacon refers to the notions in common currency for the carrying on of human living both in thought and action throughout – it would appear – all times and places. The light of common notions is not the light of reason. The phrase has reference to basic assumptions or categories which reason employs, and in the case of men acclaimed or self-acclaimed as philosophers, attempts to clarify, to improve or even to alter. His remarks about common notions are in themselves favourable. Attributing linkage with them to the party of Rationals is on the face of things to the Rationals' credit in his judgment. But this is not so. Bacon does not waver in proclaiming that for exploring nature common notions are useless. Nature is unknown. On the ground of retaining common notions in these explorations the Rationals, though not like the other schools dismissed on all counts, will fare as ill as the others do.

On the other hand, at this place in *Novum Organum* we find explicit self-revelation of what he manifested throughout in his practice – namely, that while never slackening in attending to idols of the mind, Bacon nevertheless holds that the light of common notions, though hitherto faint and superficial, is yet in a manner universal, and has reference to many things. But the area in his practice which this light legitimately illuminates, being in a manner universal and pertaining to many matters, is the area of *Know Thyself*. Bacon's self-linkage with common notions, absent and rejected for knowledge of the world of nature, is present, apparent and recognized in the programme for man's knowledges of man. In ways, many of them indispensable, common notions are properly inseparable from the form of men, from his speculative/theoretic dimension. With respect to man's knowledges of man, Bacon's position is that the light of common notions can be rendered less feeble and more penetrating not only by resort to the reasoning faculty but also by devoting attention less cavalier and more assiduous to action in collecting and correctly using civil historical *data*.

According to *Novum Organum-Preface*: '...by these means', that is to say by means of the contents of *Novum Organum* (both books) 'I suppose that I have established for ever a true and lawful marriage between the empirical faculty and the rational faculty, the unkind and ill-starred divorce and separation of which has thrown into confusion all the affairs of the human family.'[15] He did not proclaim in this statement that what he wanted was union of two schools, Empiricals and Rationals, alchemists and Aristotelians. Both of these were at fault, though not equally so. Instead, what he required was marriage of two faculties or capacities inside all minds at work.

In following this usage he was not alone. As others did in his times, when Bacon used the word 'empiric' as a substantive, it was a term of disapproval and dismissal. An empiric (the word being both Greek and Latin) was a physician whose knowledge was based in his own practice alone. But 'empirical' as employed above and as an epithet was different. He wrote of an empirical *faculty* (emphasis added) – of a man's experiencing and experimenting capability. As applied to a capability and an activity, and only as thus applied, Bacon rescued a term of reproach and blessed it with his approval. He decidedly aimed to promote in men the exercise of their experiencing and experimenting capacity. The divorce of this from the faculty of reasoning had, as he said, thrown all the affairs of the human family into disarray – all their affairs, and not only their enterprise of interpreting the world of nature for common use and benefit. Both the areas where Bacon fostered a programme had suffered.

Capabilities, distinct yet not properly divisible are equally indispensable: on the one hand, applying the senses in observations of actions or experiments, one's own or those of others; and on the other hand the applying of reason. Since the operation of either a man's senses embarked into action or of his reason inside his head is inadequate singly, each will be exerted to correct and empower the other. Nevertheless it is plain to Bacon, and he makes this equally clear to others, that if applying the rational faculty is stinted, it is not only not possible to transform use of the empirical capacity in experience into a productive force in the shape of axioms; it is also impossible to accumulate experience which is usable for that purpose. Bacon 'rested all on experience'.[16] But it is no less the case that he rested all on reason.

According to Aphorism LXXXII, *Novum Organum*, Book 1:

There remains simple experience; which, if taken as it comes, is called accident; if sought for, experiment. But this kind of experience is no better than a broom without its band, as the saying is; – a mere groping, as of men in the dark, that feel all round them for the chance of finding their way; when they had much better wait for daylight, or light a candle, and then go. But the true order in experience on the contrary first lights the candle, and then by means of the candle shows the way; commencing as it does with experience duly ordered and digested, not bungling or erratic, and from it educing axioms, and from established axioms again new experiments; even as it was not without order...that the divine word operated on the created mass. Let men therefore cease to wonder that the course of science is not yet wholly run, seeing that they have gone altogether astray; either leaving and abandoning experience entirely, or losing their way in it and wandering round and round as in a labyrinth; whereas procedure rightly ordered leads by an unbroken route through the woods of experience to the open ground of axioms.[17]

In the perspective toward the past adopted by Bacon, reason – the rational faculty – which classifies and analyses and which constitutes one of the three elements in all men's mental makeup – had been at work in all three revolutions or periods of learning in the West. It had been at work not only in these times but even earlier, though as he explained men's rational faculty had suffered a temporary eclipse during which poets had successfully substituted imagination to fulfil tasks performed in earlier and in later times by reason. Use of the rational faculty which comprised the exercise of human intelligence with the assistance and cooperation of the human will would not be jettisoned, he promised, at the precise moment of a possible flowering of this third epoch. On the contrary, his work, he tells King James when handing him *Novum Organum*, is a new instrument 'tending to enlarge the bounds of Reason and to endow man's estate with new value,...'[18] He hoped, he said, that 'the wheel, once set on going, men shall suck more truth out of Christian pens, than hitherto they had done out of heathen'. Reason preoccupied with divinity in this present age need not slacken in that department. But the bounds of its preoccupations can be widened by incursions, through still allied with divinity, into all other fields. This, his new instrument, he tells James, is the same argument as that of *The Advancement of Learning*, but 'sunk deeper'.[19] It is an instrument to extend reason, truth, and also certainty; though in this correspondence he did not write of this last commodity.

In this same exchange he also told King James that *Novum Organum* 'as by position and principle, doth disclaim to be tried by anything but by experience and the resultats of experience in a true way'. Moreover, he seeks help from James 'in setting men on work for the collecting of a natural and experimental history, which is *basis totius negotiae*' – an indispensable ground work for the whole business.[20] Nevertheless the notion of an excess of reasoning is not possible to contemplate. Reason is like charity of which he wrote in the essay *Of Goodness And Goodness of Nature* (1612 and 1625) that it 'admits no excess but error'.[21] In the case of reason the error which needed to be abandoned in the present and avoided in the future was reasoning exercising itself suspended in the air, depriving itself of contact with *data* – history/experience; and neglecting to apply such sources in action.

Pyrrhonians or sceptics are another brand of philosophers alluded to by Bacon: he does so in both *Advancements*, in *Cogitata et Visa* (Thoughts and Conclusions), in *Novum Organum*, in *Essays* and also elsewhere. Ancient scepticism embodied in the works of Sextus Empiricus had remained unknown throughout most of the Christian epoch. His works became available in Latin soon after the middle of the sixteenth century and appeared in the original Greek in 1621. Bacon as earlier noted does not refer to Sextus Empiricus by name but he frankly and forcefully admits to going part of the way with sceptics. Furthermore, these latter are omitted at the point in *Novum Organum* where adverse judgment is administered as we see to three schools, Rationals, Empiricals and Superstitious.

Elsewhere in *Novum Organum*, Book 1, Bacon describes the sceptical school: 'The doctrine of those who have denied that certainty could be attained at all, has some agreement with my way of proceeding at the first setting out; but they end in being infinitely separated and opposed. For the holders of that doctrine assert simply that nothing can be known; I also assert that not much can be known in nature by the way which is now in use. But then they go on to destroy the authority of the senses and understanding; whereas I proceed to devise and supply helps for the same.'[22] Their approach, he explained, 'is a fairer seeming way than arbitrary decisions; since they say that they by no means destroy all investigation..., but allow of some things to be followed as probable, though of none to be maintained as true; yet still when the human mind has once despaired of finding truth, its interest in all things grows fainter; and the result is that men turn aside to pleasant disputations and discourses and roam as it were from object to object, rather than keep on a course of severe inquisition. But, as I said at the beginning, and am ever urging, the human senses and understanding, weak as they are, are not to be deprived of their authority, but to be supplied with helps.'[23]

Bacon was Bacon. He was neither an Aristotelian, nor an Alchemist, nor a Platonist, nor a Pyrrhonian. Nevertheless, not only Pyrrhonians, but also Aristotle require to be placed among Bacon's fixed markers. As for the former he could write of them with acclaim and even with ardour:

We cannot...deny that if there be any fellowship between the ancients and ourselves, it is principally as connected with this species of philosophy: as we concur in many things which they have judiciously observed and stated about the varying nature of the senses, the weakness of human judgment, and the propriety of withholding or suspending assent; to which we might add innumerable remarks of similar tendency. So that the only difference between them and ourselves is, they affirm 'nothing can be known by any method whatever'; we, 'that nothing can be perfectly known by the methods which mankind have hitherto pursued'. Of this fellowship we are not at all ashamed.[24]

As for Aristotle, both he and Bacon were decidedly Rationals. Furthermore in many matters Bacon took Aristotle's side. At an early stage in this study we have seen that this is so. If this claim – that the Pyrrhonians and Aristotle are Baconian markers no less than the others – seems on the face of things unwarranted, the situation with respect to them does not differ from that obtaining in the case of the others.

The sacred canon of inspired divinity was a marker – the first of them all. But Bacon did not use it as many divines employed it before his time, in his time, and afterwards. In the first *Advancement* he complained of much of what they did with it. In this the second *Advancement* differs little, though his treatment is less complete. Amongst these complaints one related to form. Another concerned content. With respect to form: 'This is that method which hath exhibited unto us the scholastical divinity; whereby divinity hath been reduced into an art'[25] – a human art. This scholastical divinity had become as much a protestant exercise as a popish one. In scholastical divinity

men have sought three things, a summary brevity, a compacted strength, and a complete perfection; whereof the two first they fail to find, and the last they ought not to seek. For as to brevity, we see in all summary methods, while men purpose to abridge, they give cause to dilate. For the sum of abridgement by contraction becometh obscure; the obscurity requireth exposition, and the exposition is deduced into large commentaries, or into common places and titles, which grow to be more vast than the original writings whence the sum was at first extracted. So we see the volumes of the schoolmen are greater much than the first writings of the fathers…And for strength, it is true that knowledges reduced into exact methods have a show of strength, in that each part seemeth to support and sustain the other; but this is more satisfactory than substantial…it is plain that the more you recede from your grounds, the weaker do you conclude: and as in nature the more you remove yourself from particulars the greater peril of error do you incur, so much more in divinity, the more you recede from the Scriptures by inferences and consequences, the more weak and dilute are your positions.[26]

As to 'inferences and consequences' Bacon also made the point that it was these latter, 'wherewith the schools labour', which breed the 'fury of controversies, wherewith the church laboureth'.[27] Moreover it was these 'inferences and consequences' which overlooked and blurred the perception and establishment, pressed for by Bacon, of a distinction between matters essential and those which were indifferent. 'And as for perfection or completeness in divinity, it is not to be sought; which makes this course of artificial divinity the more suspect. For he that will reduce a knowledge into an art, will make it round and uniform: but in divinity many things must be left abrupt...' This is the argument we have met before – his argument regarding the better way to impart information; whether it should be in 'method' or in aphorism. The latter in the case of the message of the sacred canon, as in other things, was the preferable course.

With respect to the content of the message of this sacred canon Bacon expressed no doubts that in terms of God's purposes towards men it was in every way completely sufficient. But...'the inditer of them did know four things which no man attains to know': and which he had not deigned to impart as part of the canon's content. These are 'the mysteries of the kingdom of glory, the perfection of the laws of nature, the secrets of the heart of man, and the future succession of all ages'. But some inquirers try to discover information on these matters in the sacred canon, though such information is not present in it. In Bacon's judgment the divine 'inditer' was aware of what he did when he arranged the omissions. In all four of them it was for men's welfare that revelation concerning them was withheld. In the case of the first, 'the mysteries of the kingdom of glory', Bacon observed: 'in the mind whatsoever knowledge reason cannot at all work upon and convert is a mere intoxication, and endangereth a dissolution of the mind and understanding'.[28] The second, 'the perfection of the laws of nature', was something men were bidden to find out for themselves in their natural philosophy/science. The same applied in the cases of the third and the fourth – 'the secrets of the heart of man' and 'the future succession of all ages'. Men must wait for the secrets to appear in the open. They must also wait for the succession of times to unroll itself, in each instance adjusting if need be their knowledges in *Know Thyself*, that is to say in their civil histories, in their morality and in their policy.

The exemplar canon of secular civil histories was a marker. According to Bacon these civil histories, since they were not infrequently written by men of civil experience, acquired thereby an enhanced quality. Conversely, study of such civil histories improved the civil experience of the men who studied them. But the state Bacon served and worked for, the United Kingdom of Britain, though in no process of decline, was as yet no exemplar state, a sign of this being that it produced no exemplar histories. In his work in *The History of the Reign of King Henry the 7th* Bacon went far towards continuing his civil secular canon. The book was designed to remedy both institutions and also the condition of civil history. More than his aborted treatise, this book should count as an item of grand strategy. Until this latter was completed by later men, Britain could be no exemplar state. This she became, replacing Machiavelli's and Bacon's exemplar which was Rome in antiquity.

Another marker was Machiavelli's *Discorsi*. But Bacon was no Machiavellian. The position which came to characterize Machiavellianism in much subsequent parlance – that policy ignores, defies and even despises morality – was precisely the feature in Machiavelli's contribution which Bacon rejected. According to Lord Acton: 'The main principle of Machiavelli is asserted by his most eminent English disciple: "it is the solecism of power to think to command the end, and yet not to endure the means".'[29] Given that the argument of the present study is acceptable, a man need not quarrel with the statement that Bacon was Machiavelli's most eminent English disciple. But Acton misreads Bacon's words about 'the solecism of power' cited from the latter's essay *Of Empire* (1612 and 1625).[30] The words refer not to what Bacon called Machiavelli's evil arts but instead to Bacon's own morality and policy, these latter explicitly excluding Machiavelli's evil arts.

The case of another marker, the Common Law, is no different. Bacon was watchful of, and critical of certain proceedings of the common lawyers. In particular he resisted their claims to dictate in the realms of state policy, that is to say in what, according to him, were properly matters of government as distinguished from matters of law. Common lawyers in his times and afterwards returned his reproaches, holding that he deviated from their notions which they insisted were correct in such matters and that therefore they should prevail. As Ranke observed 'The English, contemporaries and posterity alike, have taken the side of Coke.'[31] Macaulay contended in his essay that Bacon introduced 'new corruptions'[32] in government and presumably also in law; though in truth these were doubtfully corruptions and doubtfully new.

Bacon extolled, practised and recommended the virtues of sustained doubt as Pyrrhonians did. For this he warmly commended them, rating them foremost among all the philosophers of antiquity. But they destroyed 'the authority of the senses and understanding.'[33] On this count he decisively rejected them. Bacon was a Rational, and as will be seen, his resolved positions coincided with those of Aristotle in many ways scarcely to be dismissed as trivial. He showed as we have noted near the outset of this whole argument that he was aware of this and accepted it. Nevertheless he explained that time did not invariably deliver only what was true and excellent. Time also bequeathed less worthy items. Driftwood or *débris* floats easily in the stormiest conditions. Plato and Aristotle, Bacon argued, survived in this way after the fall of Rome in the turbulent and barbarous beginnings of the third and present epoch.[34] To these specimens of flotsam Bacon could have added Empiricals/Alchemists with no inconsistency.

He continued to insist that Aristotle used insufficient *data*. But he levelled a weightier charge. Shortage of materials could scarcely be blamed entirely upon him. Here it was the moderns who were the more culpable since they had failed to seize the widened opportunities recently afforded 'this great building of the world has in our age been wonderfully opened and thorough-lighted'.[35] Aristotle's graver fault was that he misused such *data* as was available to him. 'There is none' (and not Aristotle) 'who has dwelt upon experience…as long as is necessary.'[36] 'For he had come to his conclusion before'…[37] That is to say, he did so too soon. It was for these reasons that Bacon classed his work as dross drifting on the tides of time. He in addition accused Aristotle of neglecting and opposing what he, Bacon, came to see as the constructive attitude to other thinkers – the attitude, that is, which was implied in his pleas for a history of letters, learning and arts. This was precisely the approach on Bacon's part from which he, Aristotle, would benefit, Bacon applying it in his case: '…it may be every one in some one point hath seen clearer than his fellows'.[38] But Bacon maintained that this philosopher 'as though he had been of the race of the Ottomans, thought he could not reign except the first thing he did he killed all his brethren'.[39]

Always Bacon said, both a yes and a no to markers. In addition to differing from them it can be contended that he was also unjust in the case of two. In that of Machiavelli Bacon assumes a superiority over him in civil policy on the grounds, so it has been hazarded earlier in this study, that Machiavelli lacked political experience. But the latter had been an active politician and had made this clear in *Discorsi*. Edmund Whittaker writes like this about Bacon and Aristotle: 'It must not be forgotten that the attitude of Francis Bacon towards Aristotelianism had been to a great degree anticipated in the attitude of Aristotle himself towards the doctrines of his predecessors. In direct opposition to Plato, who held that the deceptions of sense justified scepticism of sense-information, and made intuition the ground of all true knowledge, Aristotle insisted in the strongest terms on experiment and observation as the sources of our understanding. 'The principles which lie at the basis of any particular science', he wrote, 'are derived from experience ... thus it is from astronomical observation that we derive the principles of astronomical science'. Essentially a naturalist, he poured scorn on ἀπειρία – that is, the state of those who devote themselves entirely to abstract reasoning from intuitive postulates, and are indifferent to facts.'[40]

Dialogues though profitable in results to those who initiate them can also be inconclusive in that less than justice is done to those who are made partners in them. Rawley, Bacon's chaplain, wrote of him: 'For though he was a great reader of books, yet he had not his knowledge from books, but from some grounds and notions from within himself'.[41] Notions in his mind facilitated Bacon's dialogues. But notions, as he himself insisted, shelter idols. Bacon made no claim always to dispel these latter. If it is argued that Bacon has been unjust to two predecessors it can be argued equally that he has received scant justice from posterity. In the case of the *Essays*, for example, it looks as if whereas he sought to translate literature into science, much of posterity has rated his science as if it were literature.

A canon of inspired scriptures – a secular canon of ancient civil histories – the *Discorsi* of Machiavelli – the Common Law of England – the natural philosophy/science of Aristotle – Pyrrhonian radical scepticism – these six were Bacon's self-chosen markers. In no case relinquishing, still less surrendering his independence and identity to them, and remaining in his dealings with all of them first and foremost himself, it was in and with this self-imposed context and with the aid of its components that he assailed idols of the mind and strove to promote the advancement of learning, this being conducted in two distinct inseparable programmes. Each marker was distinct but no marker was sharply separable from others.

The above is the order these six markers stand in. Were it not that, in Bacon's rating, the sacred canon was learning which was not human but divine, the secular canon of civil histories would have stood first. The above order is not that provided by the sequence of times and occasions at which they were adopted. No sequence of this kind can be established. Nor is this order that of the apportionment and distribution, according to time's measure, of his attention. This too is impossible to ascertain. The order, the above order, is that of the quantity and quality of reckoning and repute which Bacon continued to attach to them, and to credit them with, in the course of directing and conducting his undertakings as a whole.

Here it should be added that the works of the ancient poets of Greece are not among Bacon's markers. Indeed, judgments both hasty and weak might conclude that in *De Sapientia Veterum* caution forsook him and that audacity prevailed to excess. But as in relations with his markers he continued to know what he was at and lost no control. 'Not but that I know very well', he wrote in *De Sapientia Veterum*'s Preface,

what pliant stuff fable is made of, how freely it will follow any way you please to draw it, and how easily with a little dexterity and discourse of wit meanings which it was never meant to bear may be plausibly put upon it. Neither have I forgotten that there has been old abuse of the thing in practice;…All this I have duly examined and weighed; as well as all the levity and looseness with which people indulge their fancy in the matter of allegories; yet for all this I cannot change my mind.[42]

He cannot change his mind. The argument is based on his conception of the course which had been taken by the history of letters, arts and sciences. In the first *Advancement* he had explained, as we have seen, that '…it is generally to be found in the wisdom of the more ancient times, that as men found out any observation that they thought was good for life, they would gather it and express it in parable or aphorism or fable. But for fables, they were vicegerents and supplies where examples failed: now that the times abound with history, the aim is better when the mark is alive. etc. etc.'[43]

In *De Sapientia Veterum*'s Preface he writes:

in the old times, when the inventions and conclusions of human reason (even those that are now trite and vulgar) were as yet new and strange, the world was full of all kinds of fables, and enigmas, and parables, and similitudes: and these were used not as a device for shadowing and concealing the meaning, but as a method of making it understood.... for as hieroglyphics came before letters, so parables came before arguments.

He admits that parables were capable of being employed for the purpose of concealing meanings. But he preferred to contemplate, and to work with the alternative, namely that they were used in order that meanings might be revealed.[44] He adds further argument. Some of the stories are 'so absurd and stupid' that if imagination alone had been at work it could scarcely have invented them. True, imagining is thinking. 'But when a story is told which could never have entered any man's head either to conceive or relate on its own account, we must presume that it had some further reach'.[45] He explained also that close study reveals that the meanings which lay behind the stories also lay behind them in time: that what was embodied in the fables as allegory was something which, not as allegory, had preceded them.[46]

As Bacon concludes his Preface he indicates how it came to be that he interpreted the fables in terms of things which he learned already from other sources: that is to say in terms of what he appropriated out of his markers. He makes confession in his own fashion of what earlier in this study we have already noted as having been the way he proceeded. His confession makes sense because reason, according to him – and indeed the whole of human nature – had always and everywhere been the same save that in primitive times in Greece reason's operations were veiled; veiled not to conceal things, but to make them evident:

Upon the whole I conclude with this: the wisdom of the primitive ages was either great or lucky; great, if they knew what they were doing and invented the figure to shadow the meaning; lucky, if without meaning or intending it they fell upon matter which gives occasion to such worthy contemplation. My own pains, if there be any help in them, I shall think well bestowed either way: I shall be throwing light either upon antiquity or upon nature itself. That the thing has been attempted by others I am of course aware, but if I may speak what I think freely without mincing it, I must say that the pains which have been hitherto taken that way, though great and laborious, have gone near to deprive the inquiry of all its beauty and worth; while men of no experience in affairs, nor any learning beyond a few commonplaces, have applied the sense of the parables to some generalities and vulgar observations, without attaining their true force, their genuine propriety, or their deeper reach. Here, on the other hand, it will be found (if I mistake not) that though the subjects be old, yet the matter is new; while leaving behind us the open and level parts we bend our way towards the nobler heights that rise beyond.[47]

He took four groups – a *corpus* of holy scriptures which was ancient; a succession of ancient civil historians; a profession of modern lawyers; a school of philosophers not only ancient but also modern. He took also two markers who were single workers – Machiavelli and Aristotle, the latter ancient, the former modern. Retaining mastership though abandoning magistrality, he sought to make these hold discourse within themselves by discussing them within himself. The discourse concerned procedures when these could be ascertained. It also concerned conclusions when these were available. He tested these procedures and these conclusions in the findings of his experience. History – civil history – and experience (his own) are the same thing. 'One age', Bishop Williams rightly told him in 1625, 'hath not bred your experience.'[48] The past had bred it. So, too, had the present. History of learning and correctly conducted experience in learning and arts (his own) are the same thing. '...the true order of experience...first lights the candle, and then by means of the candle shows the way.'[49] Markers, he taught, required to be 'supplied and continued'. In this way, that is, by correctly conducted experience (his own – 'first lights the candle, etc.') he supplied and continued them. For all this the evidence is abundant. Even the first marker which otherwise could not be supplied and continued could arguably have been extended in this fashion. But it is not presumed in these pages to examine and pronounce upon Bacon's 'religious experience'. Such exercises are *ultra vires*. The outside of Bacon, his words and deeds, expressed his inside. But not all of it, and never enough of it to justify confident pronouncements about it.

He disclaimed belonging to any ancient or surviving sect, school or system of philosophy/science. He stated that it was not his purpose to found a new one. He did not set out to establish a new school of civil historians. He aimed to supply and continue an old one. He succeeded in doing so not only writing civil history himself but by extending civil history's procedures into inspection of the realms of nature. Though ranged beneath the inspired scriptures, his civil secular canon, foremost both in itself among human letters and also foremost among his human markers in dignity and authority, stood ready to hand already displaying and fulfilling many of his stated requirements. In this matter we invoke his dispersed remarks, at the same time being instructed by him to reject sharp separations. His remarks are of general application. A charge that they are wrenched out of context holds little water in his case. Even when writing in method, not in aphorisms – the latter being the deliberately contextless way of communicating – the thinking transcends and is resistant to embowment in contexts.

For a start '... All History, walks upon the earth ... whereas poesy is as a dream of learning;'[50] So also, he held, is extant philosophy. Further, producing civil histories is in sweat and laboriousness, this being the condition laid down in the inspired canon for all advance in arts and sciences.[51] The difficulty of writing civil history was witnessed to in that 'among all the writings of men there is nothing rarer than a true and perfect Civil History'.[52] Travail – intensive and also extensive labours – together with civil history's characteristic path for proceeding which was that it walks upon the earth – secured that such work did not 'vanish in the fume of subtile, sublime, or delectable speculation'.[53]

Following the earliest poetry of the Greeks which according to Bacon had preserved an otherwise lost pre-existing learning, it had been this form and way – civil history – which alone had advanced it, carrying it out of the past through the present and in Bacon's hands into the future. Surviving human learning which exhibited something of soundness had so far been displayed only by primitive Greek poets and in later antiquity by Greek and Roman civil historians. But it was only the efforts of these historians which indicated the way by which learning could be promoted. Civil historians of his canon had not been content to grope in the dark. They tried to light candles. They travelled part of the way towards uniting 'the empirical faculty' with 'the rational faculty'. This latter was truly a faculty, a constituent part of the composition of the human understanding. But though Bacon called it such, the empirical faculty was, properly speaking, not a faculty. It was ability – that backed by decision – to undertake action. Would they but try, all men were capable of this.

The first part of action, the first stage in it, consists of observing – of observing particulars: this first step was taken by Bacon's civil historians. 'We must lead men to the particulars themselves.'[54] The historians did this: they led themselves and other men to the particulars. '...instances' must be 'duly ascertained and diligently examined and weighed'.[55] Historians complied with both these requirements. A too early recess from particulars was a mistake: so also was a too high ascent away from particulars into generalities.[56] The historians avoided these errors. 'Men on their side must force themselves for a while to lay their notions by and begin to familiarize themselves with facts.'[57] True, the historians were ignorant of idols of the mind. But they observed particulars outside themselves. True, they worked with common notions and took for granted the common logic. But such procedures were legitimate in the fields of *Know Thyself*. They combined use of common notions with observing; not obtruding as substitutes for observing, their own preconceptions concerning what they examined, weighed and recorded.

...'all that premature reasoning which anticipates inquiry is only rejected'.[58] Amongst these civil historians there had been men of inquiry and of action in their own right in the fields of policy, sharing a similar rejection. The utterances of 'speculative men' of active matters like Phormio's 'argument of the wars' to Hannibal, were 'but dreams and dotage'.[59] The historians did not purvey dreams and dotage. Active men should become writers 'as that which would make learning indeed solid and fruitful'.[60] Experience must be 'taught to read and write'.[61] These active men wrote histories. Experience 'learned her letters' in their books.[62] In these latter they recorded courses of action in policy. These recordings instructed and incited both themselves and others to take further action, in doing so discouraging irresolution and pertinacity.

In these ways Bacon's civil historians exercised, illustrated and advocated an empirical faculty. At the same time they employed their rational faculties. Discussing poetry Bacon mentioned reason and history in the same breath. He wrote that both reason and history buckle and bow down the mind to the nature of things.[63] Civil history – whether writing it or reading it – is thinking. History and experience are the same thing. The experience demanded was experience 'duly ordered and digested, not bungling or erratic'.[64] This the historians provided. They coupled events with their causes.[65] They handled particulars 'in their series and order'[66] – the series and order being that of men's conduct of action in policy, their own and that of others.

Those who have handled sciences have been either men of experiment or men of dogmas. The men of experiment are like the ant, they only collect and use: the reasoners resemble spiders, who make cobwebs out of their own substance. But the bee takes a middle course; it gathers its material from the flowers of the garden and the field, but transforms and digests it by a power of its own. Not unlike this is the true business of philosophy; for it neither relies solely or chiefly on the powers of the mind, nor does it take the matter which it gathers from natural history and mechanical experiments and lay it up in the memory whole, as it finds it; but lays it up in the understanding altered and digested. Therefore from a closer and purer league between these two faculties, the experimental and the rational (such as has never yet been made) much may be hoped.[67]

This league between faculties which eluded natural philosophers was adumbrated by civil historians. They took the middle course between the ants and the spiders. But they did not make webs out of their own substance as spiders did. They relied neither solely nor chiefly on the powers of the mind. Instead, they duly took action in observing and gathering materials. But also they were not like ants, leaving these materials as they found them. They laid them up in their understanding altered and digested. 'Exact investigation of details combined with reflective treatment'[68] – this is Ranke's description of Bacon's civil history, the *History of the Reign of King Henry the 7th*. His description applies not less aptly to the achievement of Greeks and Romans in Bacon's secular, civil canon.

Writing this time not of poets in the most distant Greek past but of natural philosophers who lived in Greece later than these poets but earlier than Plato and Aristotle, he explained:

The more ancient of the Greeks (whose writings are lost) took up…a position between…two extremes – between the presumption of pronouncing on everything, and the despair of comprehending anything; and though frequently and bitterly complaining of the difficulty of inquiry and the obscurity of things, and like impatient horses champing the bit, they did not the less follow up their object and engage with Nature; thinking (it seems) that this very question, viz. whether or not anything can be known was to be settled not by arguing, but by trying. And yet they too, trusting entirely to the force of their understanding, applied no rule, but made everything hard thinking and turn upon perpetual working and exercise of the mind.[69]

Like these ancients Bacon's civil historians took the better and middle course, not presuming to pronounce on everything and not concluding despairingly that nothing could be known. Though perhaps not airing difficulties as these ancients did and as Bacon also did, and though not claiming a formal rule for application; they nevertheless rejected arguing in favour of trying. Their trying however was less ineffectual than that of these ancients. The historians did not fall back at the last on new resorts to meditation and agitation of wit. Instead they engaged in actions, engaging this time not with nature but with observed courses of policy conducted by men like themselves.

Whether or not such procedure took a strictly narrative form, ἱστορία in Greek, *historia* in Latin, 'history' and 'story' in English meant inquiry – investigation. To civil history's 'fidelity is entrusted' the faithful and true observing and recording of truth. In his civil secular canon, history, Bacon held, had not been entrusted with this duty in vain. For him the purpose of such inquiry was instruction of the writer and of readers. In witnessing to civil history's purpose of inquiry in order to instruct he shared the company of predecessors like Thucydides, Cicero, Livy, and of a successor like Edward Gibbon. Statements made by Cicero and by Livy have been cited at an earlier stage. As for Thucydides, he explained that 'whoever shall wish to have a clear view both of the events which have happened and of those which will someday, in all human probability, happen again in the same or a similar way – for those to adjudge my history profitable will be enough for me. And, indeed, it has been composed, not as a prize essay to be heard for the moment, but as a possession for all time.'[70] Gibbon's position as he stated it was that: 'History...undertakes to record the transactions of the past, for the instruction of future ages'. Later he wrote that the Emperor Julian was 'instructed by history and reflection'. 'The experience of past faults, which may sometimes correct the mature age of an individual, is seldom profitable to the successive generations of mankind.'[71]

In common with numerous predecessors and many successors civil history's instruction, according to Bacon, is largely directed to the conduct of civil affairs. It consists of lessons in the import and necessity of action, this being the primary element in the instruction imparted. Secondly, it offers guidance on ways to act; either by suggesting that men imitate or avoid examples presented in past deeds; or else – in the cases of Machiavelli and of himself – because in addition civil history supplies material for constructing civil policy's foundations. This inquiry and instruction in the times of antiquity is first pursued in civil affairs – or so it would appear in terms of what has survived. It was extended in ancient times to inquiry and instruction into things and occurrences of the natural world. Such extension and projection of civil history, as inquiry and instruction, into the world of nature should be done over again by and for the moderns. But it should be done better. As we have seen, Bacon disqualified and dismissed extant natural histories both ancient and modern. History repeats itself, but it can be made to do so in a better shape because with improved procedure and therefore with truer results. The achievement of the historians of Bacon's civil secular canon in establishing that 'history, of all writings, deserveth least taxation', and that it 'possesseth the mind of the conceits which are nearest allied unto action' – could have been enough in itself to account for two features of the endeavours he devoted to exploring the universe of nature: namely, his already quoted assertions that for explaining nature histories suffice and that further steps and stages could perhaps be superfluous; and second, his protestations that the procedure he proposes for advancement of knowledges in the natural order does not require to be interpreted literally and rigidly – that he is not advertising tight inflexible *formulae*, departure from which is impermissible.

With respect to the third and fourth markers a substantially relevant point is that they share the characteristics of the second. They were histories. Machiavelli worked with common notions and took for granted the common logic. He was ignorant of the idols of the mind. But his discourses on Livy and other civil histories consist of observing and pondering the observations recorded in these writings. Machiavelli's labours result in a history of letters, arts and learning in the department of government in peace and war. In this he consults and compares opinions, leaving out and not including his own. But in this undertaking he also constructs his own further observations. In this way he provides axioms and proposes foundations for civil policy. The *Discorsi* 'walk upon the earth'. Few would dissent from Bacon's statement that 'we are much beholden to Machiavelli and other writers of that class, who openly and unfeignedly declare or describe what men do, and not what they ought to do'. His undertakings did not 'vanish in the fume of subtile, sublime, or delectable speculation'. Manifestly his objective is further action scorning irresolution and pertinacity – action by others, that is to say. His inquiries imply instructions.

But also the aim is to encourage, so Machiavelli admitted, further researches by others on the lines correctly laid down. Thus supplies

and continuations were invited. Like civil historians familiar to
Bacon and himself he went part of the way towards uniting the
empirical and rational faculties. But he went further in this matter
than they did. It is true that Bacon does not recognize him as a man
of action. But Machiavelli went further than writers of pure civil
histories did. In writing not pure but mixed civil history his axioms
exemplified 'the office and work of Reason'.[72] Bacon as we have seen
adopted many of Machiavelli's axioms.

Bacon rejected the philosophers' profession as the latter had been
understood hitherto. Instead, preferring the society of a company of
civil historians, not only pure but also mixed, he joined them. But he
also embraced and practised the profession of the Common Law,
reaching the highest eminence in it. In the course of his practice as
we have said he alluded more than once to the Common Law as
constituting in itself a history. This being so, this law, this profession
and its conduct, comprise a history civil. For he classed law as part
of policy. His statements that English common law with its record of
judgments running through time was a history conform with this
position – namely that law is part of policy. He found fault with civil
historians as too often neglecting matters of law. Law, though it was
the part of policy which was junior to government, was nevertheless
indispensable. If the law as a chain of events in a succession of times
is itself a history, this circumstance compensates in a degree, at any
rate in Bacon's own case, for the defect he noticed in civil historians
who, when concentrating on civil policy's senior partner, government, neglected the junior, which was law.

Common lawyers, like Roman lawyers, made axioms – maxims.
In this way, making their mixed history, they combined empirical
and rational faculties as Machiavelli combined them when dealing
in his mixed history with the branch of policy which concerned
conduct of government in peace and war. Bacon rejected the maxims
of the lawyers, deciding to construct his own. But like the civil
historians Common lawyers travelled part of the way to achieving
union of the faculties in other respects. Their profession in a process
of thinking and acting down the centuries constituted another fruit
of time – not only another civil history proper, but also another
history of letters, arts and learning – also another secular canon –
and therefore for these reasons another marker – a marker moreover
which did not so much invite as demand supply and continuation.
Lawyers' inquiries in successive cases were self-instruction and

instruction for others coming afterwards. Lawyers were ignorant of idols of the mind. They used common notions and took for granted the common logic. But of necessity they observed what went on outside their minds, forcing themselves to 'lay their notions by and begin to familiarise themselves with facts'. They digested these facts into order and in every case embraced a parallel and appropriate commitment to action. Action in this profession in the nature of things required resolution without pertinacity. In Law Reports lawyers were active men becoming writers. In these reports, though Bacon complained of poor quality, experience nevertheless learned her lessons in literacy. Lawyers were committed to walking upon the earth and to trying to ensure, what men were entitled to expect, namely that their efforts did not result in dreams and dotage or 'vanish in the fume of subtile, sublime, or delectable speculation'.

We have seen that the third marker (Machiavelli) and that the fourth marker (the Common Law) share the characteristics of the second marker (the secular civil canon). Like this latter they consisted of civil histories. But the same is true of the first marker (the sacred canon of inspired divinity). The inspired scripture is a history. The history displayed in it is that of the operations of divine providence. '... the Holy Scriptures', Bacon wrote in *Advancement* (final version), 'are the principal sources of information in theology'.[73] Since to this extent the inspired canon is for him synonymous with divinity – it follows that divinity – which is knowledge of divine matters in so far as these have been revealed – is itself a history. 'Wherefore from these three fountains, Memory, Imagination, and Reason, flow these three emanations, History, Poesy, and Philosophy...:[74] Nor do I think that any other division is wanted for theology... theology... consists of either Sacred History, or of Parables, which are a divine poesy, or of Doctrines and Precepts, which are a perennial philosophy...'[75] But the books of the sacred canon, in that they comprise as they do a single entity and form a whole, manifest a history which is also single and undivided. This history, single and undivided, is a civil history. It is in no way a natural history. Bacon like Augustine of Hippo declined to take *data* for natural philosophy from the sacred canon. The sacred canon is the civil history of the works of divine providence in its dealings with men's religious, moral and civil concerns.

The sacred *corpus* relates to sayings and doings of men whether or not these are recorded in books plainly consisting of histories. But though in a manner unaccountable to reason, in every place presented in the record these words and deeds are directed and controlled by divine providence. Thus the information contained in the record is simultaneously both a history of men and also a history of divine providence. That it should be possible that the information provided concerning words and deeds could simultaneously be products in every case of two kinds of mind and will – the mind and will of deity and the minds and wills of men – was a tenet of religion and a matter of faith. That the senior partner in this cooperation of energies, distinct yet indivisible, was divine providence – senior partner since always either sooner or later it secures its purposes – was yet another tenet of religion and another matter of faith.

According to Bacon the sacred canon displayed in its record the proceedings of divine providence. Further, the providing of this record for men giving guidance for this world and for the next, was a dispensation of divine providence. Further, the sacred *corpus* taught as a matter of faith that this superhuman force is operative, omnipotent, and despite all appearances to the contrary, invariably benevolent and beneficent, not only in events recorded in the *corpus* but also and no less in everything that has occurred in the past everywhere and always, and in everything that was to occur everywhere and always in the future. Certainly in all this Bacon is not to be regarded as standing alone. The doctrine of providence was an integral part both of the popish and of the protestant position. But further, if as Bacon proposed, teachings ought to be divided into fundamentals on the one hand and matters indifferent on the other, for Bacon this teaching could scarcely have been other than a fundamental. Governance by divine providence, its benevolence and its beneficence – in the face of every appearance to the contrary – was for Bacon a matter of faith. But also, such belief acquired confirmation in experience for Bacon as historian.

The sacred canon, the first marker, displayed and fulfilled as did others many of Bacon's stated requirements. It did not 'vanish in the fume of subtile, sublime or delectable speculation'. It did not indulge in dreams and dotage. Consisting of a civil history, it walked upon the earth. It contained and exhibited particulars. It handled these 'in their series and order'. '...and as in nature, the more you remove yourself from particulars the more peril of error you incur; so much more in divinity...' In it the rational and the empirical faculties – this time of the deity – are conjoined and married together in all proceedings not only in what is recorded in this canon, but in all events everywhere and always. In this 'closer and purer league between ... two faculties' divine providence resembles its creature, the bee, rather than the spider or the ant. Active men, but also an active deity, should become writers. In the canon divine providence had become a writer and had learned its letters. This civil history certainly inspires and incites to action to be embraced without irresolution or pertinacity. In this *corpus*, if a man inquires, he will obtain instruction for action from a source which is indubitably outside himself. The sacred document by definition contains no idols of the mind. It is free from their corrupting effects. 'Be it known ... how vast a difference there is between the Idols of the human mind and the Ideas of the divine.'[76] A man indeed will find in the canon common notions and even endorsement of the common logic: 'It is true that in sciences popular ... yea, and divinity (because it pleaseth God to apply himself to the capacity of the simplest), that form may have use.'[77] The canon exhibits and mediates the ideas of the divine: not all of them, but a sufficiency of them for the life and purposes of men. This sufficiency by divine dispensation can be received by men, penetrating through their idols despite the power of these latter: and not only so: it can assist in the dispersal of idols in men's study of everything else in both programmes.

CHAPTER 15

Bacon and his markers II

Giambattista Vico (1668–1744) as has been noted earlier was an avowed disciple of Francis Bacon. Further, like the latter, Vico worked with markers and Bacon was one of them. Vico openly professed that he had adopted four.[1] These were Plato and Tacitus in antiquity and, among moderns, Bacon and Hugo Grotius. Vico did not fail to perceive that Bacon's work was presented in two programmes. It was in that of man's knowledges of man that he affiliated himself to him. Recognizing that up to and in his times the English had chiefly noticed Bacon's programme for nature,[2] he, Vico, for his part, turned to what Bacon had achieved in *Know Thyself*. Moreover, Vico's book, *Scienza Nuova* – The New Science (in two editions) – consisted of a history, a civil history, which like Bacon's historical works, both civil and natural, was to be inquired into for the purpose of instruction. In the course of Vico's book he described what he was producing as a 'rational civil theology of divine providence'.[3] But Bacon no less than Vico presented a rational civil theology of divine providence, though without resorting to Vico's resounding terminology. True, as we have said, in terms of reasoning the mechanics of combination between the divine and the human were incomprehensible and impenetrable, and with this Vico would not have disagreed. Both nevertheless affirmed that rationality was recognizable in the results.

Acceptance of the part played by divine providence in the governance and coordination of the natural universe and in the governance and coordination of mankind's dealings in moral and civil affairs was a plainly expressed element in Bacon's position. When describing 'History of Providence' in his analysis and classification of civil histories in *Advancement* he showed himself critical in his appraisal of them in *Advancement*'s final version.[4] In his own works he improved upon such histories.

Some of Bacon's statements on divine providence have been cited in this study. The wisdom of God is the more admirable, he wrote, 'when nature intendeth one thing, and providence draweth forth another'.[5] He writes this in *Advancement* (both versions) when discussing and endorsing Aristotle's distinctions between material and efficient causes on the one hand, and formal and final causes on the other. 'Prometheus clearly and expressly signifies Providence.'[6] This statement in *De Sapientia Veterum* regards both the natural and the civil order. The lesser providence, which is man, cooperates according to Bacon with the greater providence, which is deity, in two programmes – knowing and controlling nature, and knowing and controlling himself.

one thing singled out by the ancients as the special and peculiar work of Providence was the creation and constitution of Man. For this one reason no doubt was, that the nature of man includes mind and intellect which is the seat of providence; and since to derive mind and reason from principles brutal and irrational would be harsh and incredible, it follows almost necessarily that the human spirit was endued with providence not without the precedent and intention and warrant of the greater providence. But this was not all. The chief aim of the parable appears to be, that Man, if we look to final causes, may be regarded as the centre of the world; insomuch that if man were taken away from the world, the rest would seem to be all astray, without aim or purpose...[7]

Writing on the topic of the moral and civil order as exhibited in the course of civil history Bacon states: '...all the works of Divine Providence in the world are wrought by winding and roundabout ways – where one thing seems to be doing, and another is doing really – as in the selling of Joseph into Egypt, and the like'.[8] While discussing faults to be observed in civil histories he asserted: '...such being the workmanship of God, as he doth hang the greatest weight upon the smallest wires...it comes therefore to pass, that such histories do rather set forth the pomp of business than the true and inward resorts thereof'.[9]

Besides discussing the nature of the *data* Bacon addresses himself to the providential provision of it:

For the History of Times (I mean of civil history) the providence of God hath made the distribution: for it hath pleased God to ordain and illustrate two exemplar states of the world, for arms, learning, moral virtue, policy, and laws; the state of Grecia, and the state of Rome; the histories whereof, occupying the middle part of time, have more ancient to them histories which may by one common name be termed the Antiquities of the World: and after them, histories which may be likewise called by the name of modern history.[10]

To these examples two more will now be added. They are taken from Bacon's civil history of the reign of Henry VII, the work which conformed with his prescriptions for what a civil history which was pure and also perfect ought to be. It is not likely that he regarded recognition of this feature, divine providence, as sharply dividing his work from that of members of his civil secular canon whose achievements he was supplying and continuing: 'In this fourteenth year also' (of the reign of the King) 'by God's wonderful providence, that boweth things unto his will, and hangeth great weights upon small wires, there fell out a trifling and untoward accident, that drew on great and happy effects.'[11] The reference is to a foray between Englishmen and Scots which so much displeased King James IV that he proposed a marriage treaty between Henry's daughter Mary and his son. This treaty took place. It led to union of the crowns. Next, the Lady Katherine, wife of Henry's son Arthur, became contracted in marriage to the second son, Henry, the future King Henry VIII, upon Prince Arthur's death; 'the secret providence of God ordaining that marriage to be the occasion of great events and changes',[12] those namely which Henry VIII was to make in the religion of the state by his insistence on obtaining annulment of his marriage with the Lady Katherine.

Discrepancies between what men intend to do and think that they are doing and what transpires as the result of their efforts, are a familiar aspect of civil and other experience. Man proposes and God disposes. Vico was content in his Rational Civil Theology to observe that such dispositions were beneficent. He had a vision only of the past, not of the present or future. Bacon's studies of providence were not confined to a vision of the past as Vico's were. Bacon argued that men making and employing science, the civil science of policy, could control, at least in a degree, the consequences of their actions and therefore the present and future. The Fable of the *Sphinx* taught – and according to Bacon still teaches – that 'whoever has a thorough insight into the nature of man may shape his fortune almost as he will, and is born for empire.'[13] The essay *Of Fortune* (1612 and 1625) claims that fortune, though herself blind, is not invisible.

In the plans and projects of his grand strategy Bacon aimed to descry fortune. Civil experience and its conduct imply, and consist of, perceiving and handling what is outside a man's self – that is to say, the words and deeds of others. Difficulties abound but in *Know Thyself* these, he argued, lie more in the mind of the perceiver than in what is perceived and handled. By contrast in studies of nature, as we have seen, difficulties exist not only in the mind but in the things it grapples with. But difficulties incurred in the *Know Thyself* department – and there are many – do not include that of seeing an extra dimension consisting of fortune/providence in addition to perceiving men, their words and deeds. Fortune/providence acts no otherwise than through the minds and wills of men – their wisdom and folly – their successes and failures.

Bacon's argument involved penetrating below the appearances of events and their surface to detect the 'true and inward resorts' of business.[14] It implies ability to grasp the direction which events were taking in the present and were likely to assume or were capable of assuming in the future. As he pictured and noted it in his 1608 jottings 'the bringing of the King low by poverty and empty coffers' was not being planned as a conspiracy. Instead it was a trend lurking in a long and deep current of affairs. Similarly when he noted 'the greatness' of the lower house in parliament, this greatness was as likely to be potential and future as actual and present. He explained in his paper on the Council of the Marches that changes in states could occur through no conscious purpose in the men making them and that men might find themselves regretting such changes when they had taken place. But there was nothing ineluctable and impossible to contend with in these drifts and trends. Such drifts and trends, till the times when they became irreversible, did not represent courses laid down by divine providence. These latter could be known only by looking back upon a past which could no longer be undone. Because men could perceive them, drifts and trends could also be controlled, even forestalled. '…all the works of divine providence in the world are wrought by winding and roundabout ways – where one thing seems to be doing, and another is doing really – as the selling of Joseph into Egypt and the like'.

But Bacon as he here expounds the Fable of *Pan* immediately adds another statement: 'So also in all the wiser kinds of human government, they who sit at the helm can introduce and insinuate what they desire for the good of the people more successfully by pretexts and indirect ways than directly; so that every rod or staff of empire is truly crooked at the top.' In the Fable of *Pan*, Bacon points out, this god is represented as carrying a staff which has a crook at the top.[15] It is not claimed that there can be equality of proportion between the greater providence and the lesser. The former encompasses all, foresees all, and cannot fail. The latter, encompassing what it can, predicts, and certainly is capable of failure. Nevertheless, statesmen, as the lesser providence, by imitating the greater can cooperate with it. In such courses if planned and pursued by wise pilots 'winding and roundabout ways' and 'rods or staves of empire ... truly crooked at the top' imply no divorce of policy from morality. Deviousness there will be, in such exercises, but no evil arts. In grand strategy means are also ends and ends are also means. Both the one and the other will in themselves be good and equally unexceptionable, as he explains to the King in 1615.[16] Nothing more is expected or required than a capacity, nourished in civil history, to perceive more than lies closely under a man's nose, and to calculate as most men neglect to do in terms not of one but of two or more moves ahead: 'he is for the greater and deeper politician that can make other men the instruments ...'.[17]

Both Vico and also Bacon profess to see the patterns and purposes of the proceedings of divine providence. Vico defined these patterns and purposes as the bringing about successively of an Age of Gods, an Age of Heroes, and an Age of Humanity. Similarly since Bacon came near to identifying theology with a civil history, this being the record of the doings of providence displayed in a sacred canon; conversely, given this doctrine of providence, he saw civil history – the whole of it – as a theology. He like Vico sees patterns and purposes. He saw not three ages but four.

It is true that (as already quoted) he wrote:

For the history of times (I mean of civil history), the providence of God hath made the distribution: for it hath pleased God to ordain and illustrate two exemplar states of the world, for arms, learning, moral virtue, policy, and laws; the state of Grecia, and the state of Rome; the histories whereof, occupying the middle part of time, have more ancient to them histories which may by one common name be termed the Antiquities of the World and after them, histories which may be likewise called by the name of Modern History.[18]

This providential distribution of times adds up to a sum consisting of three. It is also true that Bacon wrote of *three* (emphasis added) revolutions or periods of learning – Greek, Roman, and Christian. Nevertheless he saw in all not three ages but four.

His first was an exceedingly remote period whose achievements were lost to the memory of mankind; save that in a second antiquity the earliest Greeks had contrived to embody fragments of these achievements in their poetry. They had veiled such fragments in fables. Regarding the first and the second periods Bacon had reminded himself in his 1608 jottings to proceed 'with some better respect' (better respect, that is, than is commonly bestowed upon Greek philosophers) 'to the Aegiptians, Persians, Caldes, and the utmost antiquity and the mysteries of the poets'.[19] After the fables of the Greeks there had come another antiquity. This had embraced the Greek philosophers but it had also been described and reported upon by the Greek and Roman historians of his civil secular canon. Last, the present age of Christian modernity had arrived.

Vico professed to descry not one series of his triplet, but also the repetition of it in a second series. For his part Bacon as we have seen also presented a vision of civil history which was cyclical and repetitive. According to the Fable of *Orpheus; or Philosophy* which has been quoted already at an earlier stage:

But howsoever the works of wisdom are among human things the most excellent, yet they too have their periods and closes. For so it is that after kingdoms and commonwealths have flourished for a time, there arise perturbations and seditions and wars; amid the uproars of which, first the laws are put to silence, and then men return to the depraved conditions of their nature, and desolation is seen in the fields and cities. And if such troubles last, it is not long before letters also and philosophy are so torn in pieces that no traces of them can be found but a few fragments, scattered here and there like planks from a shipwreck; and then a season of barbarism sets in, the waters of Helicon being sunk under the ground, until, according to the appointed vicissitude of things, they break out and issue forth again, perhaps among other nations, and not in the places where they were before.[20]

Nevertheless, Vico but also Bacon, their visions grounded in faith but also in civil historical experience, contended that divine providence's proceedings invariably had been benevolent and beneficent. But here the similarity ends.

First, while both of them presented rational civil theologies of divine providence, Bacon, as Vico did not, envisaged in his counsels and in his works regarding the world of nature what amounted to a rational *natural* (emphasis added) theology of divine providence.

Secondly, in Bacon's case, portions of his rational *civil* (emphasis added) theology consisted of the sacred canon, covering in its contents events extending from the earliest and dimmest period up to the beginnings of the latest and Christian epoch. Thus the sacred canon was itself an instrument of the continuity provided by divine providence. This, the sacred canon, was an additional and parallel providential distribution of times, performing for Bacon like a bonus. Vico on the other hand, while not repudiating its authority, excluded the sacred canon from his vision.

However the grand difference between them is that Vico showed himself to be but little concerned with what men did and ought to do. His preoccupation was with providence's patterns and purposes. He recounted the words and deeds of men in order to show how they, passive under God's hand, were overruled to good effect by the divine proceedings. Bacon by contrast displayed concern not only with providence's patterns and purposes but also with the part to be played by men; that is to say, with what men ought to think and to do with respect to knowledge and control both in the world of nature and in that of *Know Thyself*. In the three ages which followed the first one he perceived features and instances of morality and policy which were common to all three. But since the poets of the second age had succeeded in handing on the wisdom of their predecessors, these features and instances must have been common to all four ages including the first one. This is where divine providence, the providential distribution of times, entered his vision. It had provided continuity. According to Bacon these common features and instances treated as *data* could be and should be transformed in the present fourth age into science, a science in middle axioms which would induce action. This science would teach that if a man were to do this, he could aim and expect to achieve that. Such axioms implied that events were not beyond men's control. Divine providence, though only, it is true, as interpreted in the fourth age by Bacon himself, had in the fables of the most ancient Greeks secured a continuity between the lost and buried arts of the first age and what came after. More important, in the third age of antiquity divine providence had ordained and made illustrious not only exemplar states in all that pertained to the arts of policy, but, of equal consequence, it had provided for exemplar historians to hand these latter on. Men according to the sacred canon were enjoined not only to know the true God but also to search for and find the truths of nature and the truths of *Know Thyself*. Divine providence in the continuity of civil history had provided the means whereby such knowledge, at least in the world of *Know Thyself*, could be achieved. The imperative, given that it was obeyed by men in the production of the required sciences, could perhaps terminate the tyranny of seemingly endless circular motion in civil history, whereby men, according to Vico however far they had progressed, were condemned to retreat anew to their starting point and begin all over again.

However the imperative and the injunctions or instructions on how to obey it were not the only messages delivered by Bacon with regard to the future. He delivered two different kinds of messages in this regard. Each was equally clearly articulated. Each was equally forcefully presented. There is nothing to choose between the clarity and the force with which in each case these were conveyed. In his science of policy he assumed some predictability and control in events. In his teaching about vicissitudes he recognized no less the unpredictable. He does not see this recognition as invalidating his science. This is for the reason that it is the same divine providence which on the one hand intervenes with the unpredictable and on the other utters in the sacred canon the imperative to know nature and to *Know Thyself*. Teaching about the unpredictable is to be found in *Of Vicissitude of Things* (1625). In this essay he writes: 'The great winding-sheets that bury all things in oblivion, are two; deluges and earthquakes.'[21] He also wrote in the essay: 'The greatest vicissitude of things amongst men, is the vicissitude of sects and religions. For those orbs rule in men's minds most.'[22] Such events, some in nature and one in particular brought about by men – namely religious upheavals, blot out all that goes before. But not only do they cause what preceded them to be lost to view, they in addition supervene in the course of events in a manner which is beyond foretelling. Bacon does not expressly state that this is the case. But that he means it to be understood that catastrophic and unpredictable interventions are part both of the civil and of the natural order is unmistakable.

Vico does not point out that Bacon provided two messages regarding the future and its predictability. Vico restricts himself to adopting one of them, namely the doctrine of vicissitudes. He does not argue that vicissitudes, catastrophes natural or human, separate his three ages, intervening in each case so that all must start afresh. None the less he showed no continuity between his three ages. He postulated three kinds of reason prevailing in turn in each of his three epochs. He called each of them 'reason'; though they present little or nothing in common. For Vico reason had a history. It changed. He did not follow Bacon's teaching that one and the same reason had been present and operative in all the ages of civil history – even though in the most ancient Greek times this one and the same reason had been concealed in fables and had become 'the mysteries of the poets'.

Bacon's second message presents a rendering of restoring institutions to their first principles which is disconcerting. It presents yet another combination of caution and audacity which also is disconcerting. It is not possible to argue – as if to save the situation – that if we look more closely his doctrine of vicissitudes implies no duality of approach. It can be proposed, for instance, that by advances in natural knowledge including progress in medicine, the causes and consequences of floods, of earthquakes, of pestilences, of droughts, and of famines, could according to Bacon be discovered, thus enabling prediction of them. Given the provision of adequate experimental natural histories of the *phenomena* in question it should be possible to devise and to apply preventive measures. The argument is invalid since Bacon makes no proposal of this kind. In regard to 'the greatest vicissitude of things amongst men' it is true that he offers recommendations aimed at anticipating and preventing uncontrollable upheavals in religions. 'Surely there is no better way to stop the rising of new sects and schisms than to reform abuses, to compound the smaller differences, to proceed mildly and not with sanguinary persecutions, and rather to take off the principal authors by winning and advancing them than to enrage them by violence and bitterness.'[23] He refers again *inter alia* to the danger signal which he had found in Machiavelli and quoted in *An Advertisement*: '...when the holiness of the professors of religion is decayed and full of scandal, etc., ... you may doubt the springing up of a new sect.'[24] But all this carries little conviction since Bacon mentions Mahomet publishing his law. The Mahometan outbreak and upsurge had been – as he put it in his interpretation of the Fable of *Nemesis: or the Vicissitude of Things* – among 'sudden and unforeseen revolutions of things'.[25] Mahomet publishing his law was scarcely the mere springing up of a new sect. Bacon's precautionary measures savour of little more than what he would have advised for smooth running in all religions of state.

Nor is it convincing to suggest that *Of Vicissitude of Things*, introducing man passive under divine providence, appears only in the last collection of essays; and to infer from this that perhaps by that time Bacon had lost faith in the other message, that namely which portrays the duty of man to conduct himself actively under divine providence. He writes at the end of the essay: 'But it is not good to look too long upon these turning wheels of vicissitude, lest we become giddy... '[26] Besides, we are aware that in 1621 he had himself suffered under a full discharge of the furies of Nemesis. The suggestion that he had grown fainthearted and that he had changed his approach holds no water. First, vicissitude – the full doctrine of it – is expounded under the fables interpreted in *De Sapientia Veterum*. This was in 1609 at the start of Bacon's career in policy. Under *Nemesis; or the Vicissitude of Things* he writes:

Nemesis, according to the tradition, was a goddess, the object of veneration to all, to the powerful and fortunate of fear also... The parents of this goddess were Ocean and Night; that is, the vicissitude of things, and the dark and secret judgment of God. For the vicissitude of things is aptly represented by the Ocean, by reason of its perpetual flowing and ebbing; and secret providence is rightly set forth under the image of Night. For this Nemesis of the Darkness (the human not agreeing with the divine judgment) was matter of observation even among the heathen... Nemesis again is described as winged; because of the sudden and unforeseen revolutions of things.[27]

Further, *Orpheus or Philosophy* as we have seen explicitly refers to the doctrine of vicissitude. But secondly, showing that despite experience thereof there had been no falling off in purpose. The final essay collection, indeed contains *Of Vicissitude of Things*, but it bulges also with the 1612 policy essays. Bacon places them there in reinforced shape, providing additional *data*.

At this point a close similarity and indeed an actual connection between *Of Vicissitude of Things* and Machiavelli's *Discourse* II ch. 5 can be observed. Machiavelli wrote in this *Discourse*:

To those philosophers who want to make out that the world is eternal, I think the answer might be that, if it really were as old as all this, it would be reasonable to expect there would be records going back further than five thousand years, did we not see how the records of times gone by are obliterated by divers causes, of which some are due to men and some to heaven. Those which are due to men are changes in religious institutions and in language. For, when a new religious institution comes into being, i.e. a new religion, its first care is, for the sake of its own reputation, to wipe out the old one; and, when the founders of a new religion happen to speak a different tongue, the old one is easily abolished. This becomes clear if we consider the measures which Christianity adopted *vis à vis* Paganism; how it abolished all pagan institutions, all pagan rites, and destroyed the records of the theology of the ancients.

The causes due to heaven are those which wipe out a whole race and reduce the inhabitants in certain parts of the world to but a few. This is brought about by pestilence or by famine or by a flood and of these the most important is the last alike because it is more widespread and because those who survive are all of them rude mountaineers who have no knowledge of antiquity and so cannot hand it down to posterity; ... That these floods, pestilences and famines happen I do not think anyone can doubt, for plenty of them are recorded everywhere in history, their effect in obliterating the past is plain to see,

Continuing, Machiavelli wrote:

and it seems reasonable that it should be so. For, ... when every province is replete with inhabitants who can neither obtain a livelihood nor move elsewhere. Finally since all other places are occupied and full up, and when the craftiness and malignity of man has gone as far as it can go, the world must needs be purged in one of these three ways, so that mankind, being reduced to comparatively few and humbled by adversity, may adopt a more appropriate way of life and grow better.

On the other hand Machiavelli points out that with respect to human causes which can bury the past the upsurge and victorious spread of Christianity had not succeeded 'in wiping out altogether the record of what outstanding men of the old religion had done; which was due to the retention of the Latin language, for this they had to retain so that they might use it in writing down their new laws.' In *Of Vicissitude of Things* Bacon took Machiavelli to task for 'traducing' in this *Discourse* 'Gregory the Great, that he did what in him lay to extinguish all heathen antiquities.'[28] But though Bacon complained, Machiavelli had made it plain that the Christians had refrained from, or purposely not succeeded in wiping out the records of the past altogether. Machiavelli, anticipating Bacon, thus recognized the occurrence of vicissitude which blots out the past. In his judgment perhaps this had obscured or obliterated more ages and revolutions or periods of learning than Bacon was able to allow for. But further, as Bacon was to do, he proposed that where catastrophic interventions had been caused by heaven, chastisements such as these had despite every appearance served a beneficent purpose. In addition, in the case of vicissitude brought about by man, the triumph of the Christian church, he again anticipated

Bacon. For Machiavelli in his work recognized and made full use of the continuity between at least the last age of antiquity and the new age of Christianity. He had been able to furnish and marshal *data* from this last age of antiquity. Helped by this *data* Bacon had been encouraged to build a science of policy, offering in this the basis for foresight.

Finally Bacon adopts and uses two markers who are not civil historians – the deity being included among these latter – but philosophers. It is because they are not historians but philosophers that the term 'finally' is deliberately chosen. They, Aristotle and the Pyrrhonians, are preceded for Bacon by all the other markers. He attached himself to the Pyrrhonians because in his caution he prescribed doubting as leading to thinking which when combined with action could lead to the advancement of knowledge. On the other hand the very existence of the Pyrrhonians, past and present, was standing proof that divorced from history/experience and action, intellectual endeavour, proceeding from and promoting doubt, was self-defeating and that, given this divorce, the aim of advancing knowledge was as good as renounced. The Pyrrhonians, past and present, proved in a prospective history of letters that philosophy as thinking alone – meditation and agitation of wit – is barren and that it renders the advancement of learning a dead end. This exhibition in a prospective history of letters had occurred both in antiquity and also in modern times. While not availing himself of this example as strengthening his case, Bacon shows himself to be aware of it. He stated that 'when the human mind has once despaired of finding truth, its interest in all things grows fainter; and the result is that men turn aside to pleasant disputations and discourses and roam as it were from object to object, rather than keep on a course of severe inquisition.'[29]

Holding that the human mind could and should 'keep on a course of severe inquisition', for this reason and also, as will be seen, for others, Aristotle for Bacon precedes the Pyrrhonians as marker. Certainly Aristotle is condemned by Bacon in that he charges him with having misused history in three ways. He commits a threefold offence against history's dignity and authority. First, according to Bacon, in the making of axioms he misused such history as he acquired. In an excess of audacity over caution history – experience – *data* – was handled like 'a captive in a procession'[30] and dragged along to support conclusions which had been come to prematurely.

Bacon explained that in this matter Machiavelli had done better. Secondly, Aristotle, according to Bacon, did not avail himself of enough history, and could have acquired more. Perhaps as already suggested the present and Christian age was more culpable in this respect than Aristotle had been. But the complaint made by Bacon who is preceded in this by Thucydides implies nevertheless an accusation. Thirdly, in a prospective history of letters, Aristotle according to Bacon neglected to look for helps in the achievements of other workers and on the contrary conducted himself like the Ottomans, rejecting all who differed from himself.[31] In these faults Bacon wrote that he perceived an 'impetuous and overbearing wit'.[32] Resulting from offences against history's dignity and authority, what Aristotle revealed in his work was most of himself and least of the things he was inquiring into.

Nevertheless, granted these charges and that Bacon did not withdraw them, Bacon stood with Aristotle in that the latter was a 'Rational'. A 'Rational' in Bacon's idiom was no term of reproach. In the exercise of the Rational faculty Aristotle 'classified and analysed'.[33] 'Philosophy' deals 'with abstract notions derived from [these] impressions [particulars]; in the composition and division whereof according to the law of nature and fact its business lies.'[34] Empiricals (Alchemists) and Superstitious (Platonists), not being Rationals, each received dismissal at Bacon's hands. Aristotle did not know about idols of the mind. But nor at that date did anybody else. Even if incorrectly, he nevertheless united the empirical and rational faculties. Even if incorrectly, he nevertheless used history. He made axioms – even middle axioms – though again incorrectly.

Bacon stood with Aristotle against Democritus. He approved Democritus only because the latter, not being concerned with final causes, had been able to devote undivided attention to material and efficient causes. 'For the handling of final causes mixed with the rest in physical inquiries, hath intercepted the severe and diligent inquiry of all real and physical causes.'[35] 'the natural philosophy of Democritus…who did not suppose a mind or reason in the frame of things, …seemeth to me…in particularities of physical causes more real and better enquired than that of Aristotle and Plato…'[36] Bacon also proclaimed his agreement with Democritus 'that the truth of nature lieth hid in certain deep mines and caves…'[37] Also he warned in Aphorism xlv of *Novum Organum*, Book i, that 'the human understanding is of its own nature prone to suppose the existence of more order and regularity in the world than it finds'.[38] Nevertheless Bacon stood with Aristotle in proceeding as if enough of the world of nature would be accountable in the end to human reason, and that 'in the frame of things' there would be found to be a conformity with 'a mind or reason'.[39]

Aristotle is blamed – this time not in the first but in the second *Advancement* – because: 'he left out the fountain of final causes, namely God, and substituted Nature for God'. This charge looks like yet another of Bacon's counts against the Greek philosopher. But the former had not objected when, similarly, Machiavelli had used the terms *Fortuna* or Heaven; and another consideration, again to be found not in the first but in the second *Advancement*, serves to exculpate Aristotle. Bacon in the version of 1623 introduces mention of his own 'rational natural theology of divine providence': 'Democritus and Epicurus', he wrote,

when they proclaimed their doctrine of atoms, were tolerated so far by some of the more subtle wits; but when they proceeded to assert that the fabric of the universe itself had come together through the fortuitous concourse of the atoms, without a mind, they were met with universal ridicule. Thus so far are physical causes from drawing men from God and Providence, that contrariwise, those philosophers who have been occupied in searching them out can find no issue but by resorting to God and Providence at the last.[40]

Bacon did not class Aristotle with Democritus and Epicurus. He, Bacon, did not invoke the orthodox difference in divinity, popish and protestant, between deity immanent in the creation and deity transcendent over it – the two modes being distinct yet not separable. Nevertheless for him, Bacon, Aristotle had come within a stone's throw of presenting a 'rational natural theology of divine providence'.

Bacon stood with Aristotle against Plato: 'Plato...in his opinion of Ideas...did descry that forms were the true object of knowledge, but lost the real fruit of his opinion by considering of forms as absolutely abstracted from matter, and not confined and determined by matter.'[41] Aristotle, unlike Plato, taught that forms were 'confined and determined by matter'. Bacon agreed with him.

Given that Plato had had to be corrected by Aristotle in his handling of this matter, and given that Bacon agreed with Aristotle in the manner in which he had done so, Bacon and Aristotle were in accord that 'forms were the true object of knowledge', and further that this knowledge was attainable. It followed that Bacon stood with Aristotle against the Pyrrhonians. When Bacon rejected in *Advancement* (both versions with few changes) 'the received and inveterate opinion that the inquisition of man is not competent to find out essential forms or true differences:'[42] the received and inveterate opinion here referred to is that of the Pyrrhonians. '...they are ill discoverers that think there is no land when they can see nothing but sea'.[43] The opinion regarding this incompetence of man was 'inveterate' because it was deeply rooted to such an extent that manifestly it was recurrent. The dates of Pyrrho of Elis are as ancient as those of Aristotle. But the position reappeared in the New Academy, for example, and in Sextus Empiricus. The opinion was 'received' in addition to being 'inveterate' because it had recently cropped up again in a pyrrhonism of modern times. 'And though', according to *Of Truth* (1625), 'the sects of philosophy of that kind be gone, yet there remain certain discoursing wits which are of the same veins, though there be not so much blood in them as was in those of the ancients.'[44] Here Bacon mentions no names. That of Michel de Montaigne perhaps comes to mind. However Bacon provides no indication that he judged Montaigne to have been a Pyrrhonian.

Bacon, then, stood with Aristotle against the Pyrrhonians in rejecting their contention that 'the inquisition of man is not competent to find out essential forms and true differences...', agreeing with him that there could be better discoverers – that is, explorers like the Greek and himself – than those who concluded that because they saw nothing but sea there could nowhere be land. What Bacon taught was that the inquisition of man is indubitably competent in this respect. The opening aphorisms of *Novum Organum*, Book II are devoted to forms: for example, Aphorism I: 'On a given body to generate and superinduce a new nature or new natures, is the work and aim of Human Power. Of a given nature to discover the form, or true specific difference, or nature-engendering nature, or source of emanation (for these are the terms which come nearest to a description of the thing) is the work and aim of Human Knowledge...'[45] For example, Aphorism II:

In what an ill condition human knowledge is at the present time, is apparent from the commonly received maxims. It is a correct position that 'true knowledge is knowledge by causes.' And causes again are not improperly distributed into four kinds: the material, the formal, the efficient, and the final. But of these the final cause rather corrupts than advances the sciences, except such as have to do with human action. The discovery of the formal is despaired of. The efficient and the material (as they are investigated and received, that is, as remote causes, without reference to the latent process leading to the form) are but slight and superficial, and contribute little, if anything, to true and active science. Nor have I forgotten that in a former passage I noted and corrected as an error of the human mind the opinion that Forms give existence. For though in nature nothing really exists beside individual bodies, performing pure individual acts according to a fixed law, yet in philosophy this very law, and the investigation, discovery, and explanation of it, is the foundation as well of knowledge as of operation. And it is this law, with its clauses, that I mean when I speak of *Forms*; a name which I rather adopt because it has grown into use and become familiar.[46]

For example, Aphorism III:

If a man be acquainted with the cause of any nature (as whiteness or heat) in certain subjects only, his knowledge is imperfect; and if he be able to superinduce an effect on certain substances only (of those susceptible of such effect), his power is in like manner imperfect. Now if a man's knowledge be confined to the efficient and material causes (which are unstable causes, and merely vehicles, or causes which convey the form in certain cases) he may arrive at new discoveries in reference to substances in some degree similar to one another, and selected beforehand; but he does not touch the deeper boundaries of things. But whosoever is acquainted with Forms, embraces the unity of nature in substances the most unlike; and is able therefore to detect and bring to light things never yet done, and such as neither the vicissitudes of nature, nor industry in experimenting, nor accident itself, would ever have brought into act, and which would never have occurred to the thought of man. From the discovery of Forms therefore results truth in speculation and freedom in operation.[47]

For example, Aphorism IX:

From the two kinds of axioms which have been spoken of, arises a just division of philosophy and the sciences; taking the received terms (which come nearest to express the thing) in a sense agreeable to my own views. Thus, let the investigation of Forms, which are (in the eye of reason at least and in their essential law) eternal and immutable, constitute *Metaphysics*; and let the investigation of the Efficient Cause, and of Matter, and of the Latent Process, and the Latent Configuration (all of which have reference to the common and ordinary course of nature, not in her eternal and fundamental laws) constitute *Physics*.[48]

Experts will no doubt correctly maintain that the Aristotelian and Baconian definitions of 'form' differ, and we note that Bacon explained that he adopted the name 'form' 'because it has grown into use and become familiar'.[49] A point more relevant and instructive is that the two philosophers were agreed that mankind was capable of achieving a true knowledge of things as things truly are.

It will be observed from aphorisms quoted above that Bacon stood with Aristotle in that he not only supported him in asserting the possibility of achieving knowledge of formal causes, but that he also accepted as sound Aristotle's description of the other three causes. On this matter he wrote not only in *Novum Organum*, Book II as above, but also in *Advancement* (both versions). As recounted early in this study he approvingly described in both *Advancements* 'the received and sound division of Causes; the one part, which is Physic Enquireth and handleth the Material and Efficient Causes; and the other, which is Metaphysic, handleth the Formal and Final causes'.[50]

Certainly similarities do not suffice to have made Aristotle into a marker for Bacon. Nevertheless, like the latter Aristotle took all knowledge for his province. Like Bacon Aristotle served and instructed a king, though this was at an earlier stage in Alexander of Macedon's career than was the case when Bacon instructed King James. Aristotle worked as Bacon did in two programmes, the one for the world of nature and the other for the realm of *Know Thyself*. Aristotle's procedure, as Bacon's did, straddled both programmes. Evidently it was chiefly in Bacon's programme for nature that Aristotle served as a marker, and the endorsing of Aristotle's quadrilateral of causes applies the more readily to the natural realm, in the which as we know he was not able to proceed to his announced and desired end. However we lack evidence – and it is not clear – that in *Know Thyself* Bacon rejected the quadrilateral. Operations in the two departments were respectively conducted by him as we know in opposite directions. In nature they were conducted in the direction – though he did not reach his goal – of discovering forms: in *Know Thyself* they were conducted and proceeded from an already known form, that of man. But in *Know Thyself* Aristotle's causes are arguably no less applicable for Bacon and therefore no less 'sound'.

The formal cause of man is his soul or mind. Though Bacon used the sacred canon as giving man's formal cause, his teaching about the soul is both biblical and Aristotelian. For he went to work with the notion that there are two kinds of soul – a rational soul implanted in man by the creator and made in his image; but also an irrational soul. Like the rest of the animate creation man likewise possesses an irrational soul. This irrational soul is the 'internal principle of movement and sensibility which holds bodies together and gives them life'.[51] For information regarding man's rational soul Bacon resorts to the sacred canon. His teaching concerning irrational souls is the same as that of Aristotle. The final cause of man in Bacon's terms is the glory of God and the relief of man's estate. Man's efficient cause is constituted by plans and projects which he devises to this end – for instance in policy when he recognizes, and acts with respect to necessities. Man's material cause for Bacon is not his body – though indeed he had designs to investigate border lands of interpenetration between minds and bodies – but instead the situations and circumstances in which and to which man's plans and projects are applied.

As we have seen, Bacon writes approvingly of Aristotle's *Rhetoric*.[52] He disallows Aristotle's logic for discovering the metaphysics of nature, arguing that only the applying of his own logic could successfully discover these latter. But Book II of *Novum Organum* discusses procedure only, though certainly providing illustrations of how the procedure should be applied. Nevertheless Book II, like Book I, consists not of works but of counsels. In the end Bacon accepted Aristotle's logic both for *Know Thyself* and also for nature, since there, as things turned out, he got no further than natural and experimental histories, stopping short of metaphysics. He asserts that the ethics of Plato and also of Aristotle are much admired, but that Tacitus provides 'livelier and truer observation of morals and institutions'.[53] He recounts that in policy Aristotle examined 255 state constitutions, but claims that, living when he did, he was precluded from examining the state constitution of Rome and that this latter would have proved more instructive than the others.[54] Bacon makes no references to Aristotle's *Politics*. On the other hand at the end of *Ethics* (*Nicomachean*) Aristotle mentions that he had collected state constitutions to provide the material for his study of politics, showing here as elsewhere that for him, as for Bacon, ethics and politics though distinct were not separable. Bacon as we have seen refers to Aristotle as having made this collection of state constitutions. It should be remarked at once that since Bacon had disallowed Machiavelli's candidature to have invented civil policy, it is inconceivable that he would have allowed Aristotle's. The latter had served a king but not, like Bacon, as his premier minister of state.

With respect to the Pyrrhonians, the last marker, it should be recalled in advance that in Bacon's case fostering doubting approaches to all accepted knowledge was an aspect of his caution – with which caution he habitually combined audacity. He revealed this audacity even in the choice of markers, though this remained continually combined with caution. In no case, as we have seen, were markers accepted or used precipitately. They were not swallowed whole, thus precluding thorough examination and subsequent discrimination in digestion and application. Doubt, then, was a component of Bacon's caution.

The Advancement of Learning contains two major pronouncements on doubt; the one in the first book, the other in the second. Changes between 1605 and 1623 are minimal. According to the first of the two:

Another error is an impatience of doubt, and haste to assertion without due and mature suspension of judgment. For the two ways of contemplation are not unlike the two ways of action commonly spoken of by the ancients; the one plain and smooth in the beginning, and in the end impassable; the other rough and troublesome in the entrance, but after a while fair and even. So it is in contemplation; if a man will begin with certainties, he shall end in doubts; but if he will be content to begin with doubts, he will end in certainties.[55]

According to the second pronouncement on doubt in *Advancement*: 'I will subjoin two appendices of Physic, which regard not so much the matter as the manner of inquiry; namely *Problems of Nature* and *Dogmas of Ancient Philosophers*.'[56] Regarding *Dogmas of Ancient Philosophers*, Bacon appends a passage, which has been quoted earlier in this study, exemplifying the valuable part he ascribes to the civil history of letters. In respect of *Problems of Nature*, while still comparing them with *Dogmas of Ancient Philosophers*, he proceeds:

The first is an appendix to nature manifold or scattered; the other, to nature united or summary. Both relate to the skilful proposing of *Doubts*, which is no despicable part of science. Problems deal with particular doubts; Dogmas with general ones, concerning first principles and the fabric of the universe. Of Problems there is a noble example in the books of Aristotle; a kind of work which certainly deserved not only to be honoured with the praises of posterity but to be continued by their labours; seeing that new doubts are daily arising. In this however there is a caution to be applied, which is of great importance. The registering and proposing of doubts has a double use; first it guards philosophy against errors, when upon a point not clearly proved no decision or assertion is made (for so error might beget error), but judgment is suspended and not made positive;

secondly, doubts once registered are so many suckers or sponges which continually draw and attract increase of knowledge; whence it comes that things which, if doubts had not preceded, would have been passed by lightly without observation, are through the suggestion of doubts attentively and carefully observed. But these two advantages are scarcely sufficient to countervail one inconvenience which will include itself, if it be not carefully debarred; which is that a doubt if once allowed as just, and authorised as it were, immediately raises up champions on either side, by whom this same liberty of doubting is transmitted to posterity; so that men bend their wits rather to keep the doubt up than to determine and solve it. Of this examples everywhere occur, both in lawyers and in scholars, who when a doubt has been once admitted will have it remain for ever a doubt, and hold to authority in doubting as much as in asserting; whereas the legitimate use of reason is to make doubtful things certain and not certain things doubtful. Wherefore I say that a *calendar of doubts* or *problems in nature* is wanting, and I would wish it to be taken in hand; if only care be taken that as knowledge daily increases (which it certainly will, if men listen to me) those doubts which are clearly sifted and settled be blotted out from the list.

To these statements in *Advancement*, Aphorism LXVII of *Novum Organum*, Book I should be added: 'A caution must also be given to the understanding against the intemperance which systems of philosophy manifest in giving or withholding assent; because intemperance of this kind seems to establish Idols and in some sort to perpetuate them, leaving no way open to reach and dislodge them. This excess is of two kinds.' Bacon connects these two kinds not only with schools but with two kinds of 'characters of dispositions', the latter helping to promote or to establish the former:

The first being manifest in those who are ready in deciding, and render sciences dogmatic and magisterial; the other in those who deny that we can know anything, and so introduce a wandering kind of inquiry that leads to nothing; of which kinds the former subdues, the latter weakens the understanding. For the philosophy of Aristotle, after having by hostile confutations destroyed all the rest (as the Ottomans serve their brothers), has laid down the law on all points; which done, he proceeds himself to raise new questions of his own suggestion, and dispose of them likewise; so that nothing may remain that is not certain and decided: a practice which holds and is in use among his successors.

Continuing, he writes:

The school of Plato, on the other hand, introduced *Acatalepsia*, at first in jest and irony, and in disdain of the older sophists, Protagoras, Hippias, and the rest, who were of nothing else so much ashamed as of seeming to doubt about anything. But the New Academy made a dogma of it, and held it as a tenet. And though theirs is a fairer seeming way than arbitrary decisions; since they say that they by no means destroy all investigation, like Pyrrho and his Refrainers, but allow of some things to be followed as probable, though of none to be maintained as true; yet still when the human mind has once despaired of finding truth, its interest in all things grows fainter; and the result is that men turn aside to pleasant disputations and discourses and roam as it were from object to object, rather than keep on a course of severe inquisition. But, as I said at the beginning, and am ever urging, the human senses and understanding, weak as they are, are not to be deprived of their authority, but to be supplied with helps.[57]

In the second pronouncement on doubt in *Advancement* Bacon expressed a yet further solidarity with Aristotle: '*Of Problems*, there is a noble example in the books of Aristotle, etc. etc.' Like all save the first of the preceding markers Aristotle deserved and needed to be 'supplied and continued' here in the field of his *Problems*. This statement regarding Aristotle and his *Problems* is echoed in Aphorism LXVII above: 'He' (Aristotle) 'proceeds himself to raise new questions of his own suggestion, and dispose of them likewise: ... a practice which holds and is in use among his successors.' But here, in this passage, it is plain from other points that he makes in it that we are back with the charges with which we have by now become familiar. Aristotle is 'intemperate' – 'ready in deciding' – his science is 'dogmatic' and 'magisterial'. While the science of the Pyrrhonians 'weakens' the understanding, that of Aristotle 'subdues it'. In one and the same matter – on one and the same point – Aristotle on the one hand is blamed (in *Novum Organum*, Book I, Aphorism XLVII) and on the other hand praised (in *Advancement*). As we have pointed out in an earlier chapter, Bacon's plans and purposes in his last years are difficult to be sure about. But he could have embraced both the above positions simultaneously. The date of *Novum Organum* is 1620: that of the second *Advancement* is 1623: in this latter we find repetition of the praise extended to Aristotle and his *Problems* in 1605. It could be granted on the one hand that both he and other workers could be depended upon to avoid the offences committed by the Greek philosopher against the dignity and authority of history. On the other hand some connection with, and some dependence upon Aristotle's *Problems* can be observed in *Sylva Sylvarum* – Wood of Woods – a collection of natural history and experiments published after Bacon's death by his chaplain, Rawley.

Of the schools of radical scepticism – that is, of Pyrrho of Elis and of his successors, Bacon wrote: 'if there be any fellowship between the ancients and ourselves it is principally as connected with this species of philosophy'. 'Of this fellowship', he declared, 'we are not at all ashamed'.[58] Their lesson for Bacon consisted of revealing 'the varying nature of the senses, the weakness of human judgment, and the propriety of withholding or suspending assent'.[59] Weakness of the senses and fallibility of the intellect set traps for men of science, and, so the Pyrrhonians argued, invalidate their findings. Here there was forceful backing and encouragement for Bacon's temperamental and procedural caution. Pyrrhonians for him were markers. But we have seen his response to them: 'as I said at the beginning and am ever urging, the human senses and understanding, weak as they are, are not to be deprived of their authority; but to be supplied with helps'.[60] Consequently, when as in the case of other markers Bacon supplied and continued the contribution of the Pyrrhonians, there was a change in his proceedings. The difference is that, whereas in the case of the others supply and continuance consisted of providing works similar in kind, what Bacon added in the Pyrrhonians' case was of a kind which was in sharp contrast with theirs. Goods which the Pyrrhonians had offered were almost as old and almost as recurrent as any item in a prospective history of letters. By contrast, Bacon's supply and continuance of them would have been a novelty in such a history. There can scarcely be question that, with respect to the programme for the universe of nature, the crowning item in this providing of supply is *Novum Organum*, Book II. 'For it has come to pass, I know not how, that Mathematic and Logic, which ought to be the handmaids of Physic, nevertheless presume on the strength of the certainty which they possess to exercise dominion over it.'[61] He rejected such aids in opposing the Pyrrhonians. His own procedure (the 'machine' consisting of *Novum Organum*, Book II) would enable him to achieve certainties, and would do so in the following manner: 'the induction which is to be available for the discovery and demonstration of sciences and arts, must analyse nature by proper rejections and exclusions; and then, after sufficient number of negatives, come to a conclusion on the affirmative instances':[62] thinking, speculation, will be disciplined by observation in experimenting – by sense perceptions. Finding out in sufficient instances what a thing is not, will enable a man to succeed, so Bacon proposes, in finding out what it is. Had he been able to establish what he thus advertised in this Book II, displaying this in a course consisting of actions and works, he would have made a contribution which would have been novel not only in a prospective civil history of letters, but novel also in terms of his own preceding counsels and works.

In a preliminary fashion – in chapter 12 above – the aims and claims of Bacon with regard to his *Novum Organum*, Book II have been described. These aims and claims concerned knowledges to be provided in his programme for nature. This, the second part of *Novum Organum*, was to be used for inquiries into the universe of nature – *and only in this area* – though this latter embraced not only everything in nature but in addition (since this was part of nature) man's body, together with a territory of possible interactions between bodies and minds. It was noted in chapter 12 that according to all surviving evidence he did not substantiate these aims and claims in his actions and works. But the description falls short of presenting the force of his claims in a duly stark outline. In chapter 12 the failure was stressed. Now in a concluding chapter, it is necessary to stress the claims. Resort has been made throughout this study to the never bettered collection and edition of Bacon's writings provided by Messrs Spedding, Ellis and Heath. Resort will now be made to commentary provided in these volumes. In some respects this commentary has not been improved upon by subsequent scholars.

'Absolute certainty', writes Robert Leslie Ellis of the claims associated with *Novum Organum*, Book II: 'and a mechanical mode of procedure such that all men should be capable of employing it, are thus two great features of the Baconian method' (*sic*).[63] This absolute certainty, explains Ellis, is guaranteed because the procedure whereby it is attained is presented as infallible. It is also a mode of proceeding which, being mechanical, is within the capacity of nearly everybody. Ellis adds a third feature, this being the procedure's novelty. 'By this method' (sic), Ellis continues, 'all the knowledge which the human mind is capable of receiving might be attained, and attained without unnecessary labour. Men were no longer to wander from the truth in helpless uncertainty. The publication of this new doctrine was the *Temporis Partus Masculus* (The Masculine Birth of Time)'.[64]

'That the wide distinction', Ellis continues,

which Bacon perceived to exist between his own method and any which had previously been known has often been but slightly noticed by those who have spoken of his philosophy, arises probably from a wish to recognise in the history of the scientific discoveries of the last two centuries the fulfilment of his hopes and prophecies. One of his early disciples, however, who wrote before the scientific movement which commenced about Bacon's time had assumed a definite form and character – I mean Dr Hooke – has explicitly adopted those portions of Bacon's doctrine which have seemingly been as a stumbling block to his later followers. In Hooke's *General Scheme or Idea of the Present State of Natural Philosophy* (published posthumously in 1705) which is in many respects the best commentary on Bacon, we find it asserted that in the pursuit of knowledge, the intellect 'is continually to be assisted by some method or engine which shall be as a guide to regulate its actions, so as that it shall not be able to act amiss. Of this engine no man except the incomparable Verulam hath had any thoughts, and he indeed hath promoted it to a very good pitch'. Something however, Hooke admits, still remains to be added to this engine or art of invention to which he gives the name of philosophical algebra. He goes on to say 'I cannot doubt but that if this art be well prosecuted and made use of, an ordinary capacity with industry will be able to do very much more than has yet been done, and to show that even physical and natural inquiries as well as mathematical and geometrical will be capable also of demonstration; so that henceforward the business of invention will not be so much the effect of acute wit, as of a serious and industrious prosecution.' Here the absolute novelty of Bacon's method, its demonstrative character, and its power of reducing all minds to nearly the same level, are distinctly recognised.[65]

Ellis at a later stage writes: 'Very few of those who have spoken of Bacon have understood his method' (*sic*), 'or have even attempted to explain its distinguishing characteristics, namely the certainty of its results, and its power of reducing all men to one common level'.[66] 'Bacon is to be regarded, not as the founder of a new philosophy, but as the discoverer of a new method. (sic) At least we must remember that this was his own view of himself and of his writings.'[67] All this is well said. However throughout the five volumes devoted to Bacon's philosophical works no mention is made of his claim to have cultivated a special relationship with the Pyrrhonians. Indeed, save in the transcripts of Bacon's own writings – and consequently in the index of contents – there is no reference to this latter school anywhere in these volumes.

Pyrrhonians were justified in pointing to the traps set for the learned by the fallibility of their senses and of their reasoning. Nor is apology owed by Bacon to posterity for having been attracted into the fellowship of these people. But the Pyrrhonian position in itself is a trap – a trap into the jaws of which the learned can fall. Encompassed by argument to the effect that the sole certainty is that there can be no such thing as certainty, the trap for the learned consists of allowing themselves to over-react. René Descartes (1596–1650) can be counted among those who have thus over-reacted. Thomas Hobbes should perhaps also be included. Confronted by the Pyrrhonian threat – the threat whereby reasoning is enlisted to undermine the empire of reason – Descartes' preoccupation was not only with the possibility of certainty but also with its necessity.[68] A prospective history of letters could show that just as dogmatists tend, in reaction, to breed Pyrrhonians, similarly Pyrrhonians tend, in reaction, to engender dogmatists.

In this latter respect Bacon is the same as Descartes: 'If a man will begin with certainties, he shall end in doubts; but if he will be content to begin with doubts, he will end with certainties'.[69] This statement, first made in 1605 in the original *Advancement*, has become by 1620 in *Novum Organum* a pronouncement much stronger: 'I propose to establish progressive stages of certainty.'[70] But though in this respect Bacon can be classed with Descartes, the Pyrrhonians constituting for him as for the Frenchman a threat and a challenge, he, Bacon, while likewise over-reacting, did not fall into the Pyrrhonian trap. He showed all willingness to do so and every intention – even determination – to fall into it. In all conscience he worked hard enough in thirty years of effort. Rawley, his chaplain, had seen those numerous drafts. Therefore it is not possible to conclude that in this matter audacity got the better of caution. According to purpose and plan he committed himself to the trap. But purpose and plan – his machine as he himself called it – lacked fulfilment in actions and works. Bacon escaped because what was set out in *Novum Organum*'s Book II as due to take place did not happen.[71]

Bacon was not saved because – as Marin Mersenne correctly pointed out – *Novum Organum*, Book II, would not work. Nor was he saved because he explicitly allowed that other less rigid forms of procedure might produce the same results. He owed salvation first and foremost to the circumstance that *Novum Organum*, Book II engendered no offspring resulting from his use of it. But also, secondly, he attained and deserved this salvation because of the contribution he made in *Know Thyself* and in the overflow and continuation of this latter which were embodied in his natural experimental histories. Referring again in this connection to commentary by the editors of Bacon's collected works, comment which proves indispensable has been noted; also an omission. Next we find myopia. Writing of Bacon's natural and experimental histories James Spedding observes: 'I suppose that if they' (the natural experimental histories) 'had all perished together and never been heard of, the progress of mankind in the interpretation of nature would have been unaffected by the accident. And when I consider what might have been the fruits of the same time and industry spent on subjects of history, morals, politics, and law, I cannot but feel that the *res humani generis* did in fact lose by his devotion a good deal more than it gained'.[72] But it was precisely in history, morals, politics and law, that Bacon produced the major part of his works. What suffered, if there is to be complaint, was not history, morals, politics, and law, but contributions in knowledges of nature.

Prior to and also after the publication of *Novum Organum* and its Book II Bacon was buoyed in many writings by his notion that history – civil history – was foremost not only in dignity but also in authority – that is to say, civil history contained and displayed more of truth than other forms of human writing whether directed to inquiries and instruction or to anything else. He nevertheless showed himself to be content in these writings, which included the natural experimental histories, with less certain and more modest certainties, these being encompassed with difficulties, but nevertheless remaining sufficiently operatively productive. Truth, he ingeminates, is the daughter of time. On occasion he uses the terms 'time' and 'civil history' synonymously. More than once he employs the phrase 'in the memory of times' to mean 'civil history shows men that, etc.' *In Felicem Memoriam Elizabethae* – On the Fortunate Memory of Elizabeth Queen of England – provides an early example of Bacon's equating of 'times' or 'time' with civil history: 'But if I should enter into her praises...in order to give them a lustre and a beauty peculiar and appropriate, I should have to run into the history of her life, – a task requiring both more leisure and a richer vein. Thus much I have said in few words, according to my ability. But the truth is that the only true commender of this lady is time', that is, a complete version of the whole of civil history: 'which so long a course as it' (civil history) 'has run, has produced nothing in this sex like her, for the administration of civil affairs'.[73] A much later example occurs in his argument that 'a just fear' is 'a sufficient ground' for going to war; in this case for provoking war against the King of

Spain. On this point 'it is good' he writes, 'to hear what time saith'.[74] In this instance 'time' is Thucydides, the civil historian. As argued in this study, what transpired was that it was not the 'machine' but instead that it was Bacon's history, his works in civil and in natural history, which turned out to be the masculine birth of time.

As noted in the preceding chapter, Bacon alludes to the Pyrrhonians in both *Advancements*, in *Novum Organum*, Book I, in *Cogitata et Visa*, in *Essays* and also elsewhere. But the most illuminating of his statements about the Pyrrhonian question and its urgency is made in his *Scala Intellectus Sive Filum Labyrinthi*, Scaling Ladder of the Intellect; or Thread of the Labyrinth. Of all his writings this is the only one dealing exclusively with the Pyrrhonians. It is short, but too long to be quoted in full. It is as aptly entitled as any of his writings. In it Bacon perhaps succeeds in emerging from the labyrinth, to the extent at least that he was ever able to do so. More precisely, he seems to get out of it, but then to announce an imminent re-entry. For the man who fails to perceive and resist the Pyrrhonian trap will be back inside the labyrinth. Bacon's declaration of closeness to the Pyrrhonians has been noted. But it is in this piece that the declaration is made with greater forthrightness than anywhere else: 'We cannot, however, deny that if there be any fellowship etc. etc. etc. Of this fellowship we are not at all ashamed.' But he proceeds at once to broaden the confines of the fellowship:

For the aggregate, if it consists not of those alone who lay down the above mentioned dogma as their peremptory and unchangeable opinion, but of such also as indirectly maintain it under the forms of objection and interrogatory, or by their indignant complaints about the obscurity of things, confess and, as it were, proclaim it aloud, or suffer it only to transpire from their secret thoughts in occasional and ambiguous whispers – the aggregate, I say, comprises you will find, by far the most illustrious and profound of the ancient thinkers, with whom no modern need blush to be associated; a few of them may, perhaps, too magisterially have assumed to decide the matter, yet this tone of authority prevailed only during the late dark ages, and now maintains its ground simply through a spirit of party, the inveteracy of habit, or mere carelessness and neglect.[75]

In the last statement, that regarding modern Pyrrhonians, Bacon repeats in a differing form what he had reported concerning them in the essay *Of Truth* (1625).[76] The statement preceding it could be a reference to Sextus Empiricus. 'The late dark ages' was not yet a further age of time to be added to those already attributed to Bacon's reckoning in this study. He refers to a declension following the age of the Greek and Roman philosophers and historians. Pointing to 'the narrow limits' of epochs 'favourable to learning' he writes: 'to each of the 'revolutions and periods of learning' [Greek, Roman, Christian] 'hardly two centuries can justly be assigned'. Intervening times had been dark.[77] Another and comparable instance of a judgment on Bacon's part is in *Maxims of the Law*: 'The Emperor Justinian, being rightly called *ultimus Imperatorum Romanorum*, ... chose it for a monument... to revisit the Roman laws... but the more ignorant and obscure time undertook to correct the more learned and flourishing time.'[78] Sextus Empiricus flourished in the late second century after Christ, Justinian in the sixth.

In Scaling Ladder of the Intellect; or Thread of the Labyrinth Bacon wrote:

It would be difficult to find fault with those who affirm that 'nothing is known', if they had tempered the rigour of their decision by a softening explanation. For should any one contend, that science rightly interpreted is a knowledge of things through their causes, and that the knowledge of causes constantly expands, and by gradual and successive concatenation rises, as it were, to the very loftiest parts of nature, so that the knowledge of particular existences cannot be properly possessed without an accurate comprehension of the whole of things; it is not easy to discover, what can reasonably be observed in reply. For it is not reasonable to allege, that the true knowledge of any thing is to be attained before the mind has a correct conception of its causes: and to claim for human nature such a correct conception universally, might justly be pronounced perhaps not a little rash, or rather the proof of an unbalanced mind.[79]

Here, Bacon has erected a scaling ladder of the intellect on behalf of the Pyrrhonians: and further, he appears also to emerge from the labyrinth clutching his thread:

independently of that rigid truth to which they refer, there still remains such a wide field for human exertion, that it would be preposterous if not symptomatic of an unsettled and disturbed intellect, in the anxious grasping at distant extremes, to overlook such utilities as are obvious and near at hand. For however they may seek, by introducing the distinction of true and probable, to subvert the certainty of science, without at the same time superseding the use or practically affecting the pursuit of it, yet in destroying the hope of effectually investigating truth, they have cut the very sinews of human industry, and by a promiscuous licence of disquisition converted what should have been the labour of discovery into a mere exercise of talent and disputation.[80]

There is little need to recall in this connection Bacon's persistent efforts in 'effectually investigating truth', not only in *Know Thyself* and especially in policy, but also in the natural and experimental histories. He makes no claims in his findings in these fields to have attained exhaustive, final, and 'rigid' truth. However at the end of the piece quoted above he makes known his intention to re-enter the labyrinth. He has, he goes on – 'for *penetrating into the secrets of nature* [author's emphasis added] – a *nova via*', a new road. By means of this new road he will successfully 'regulate and correct the aberrations both of the senses and of the intellect'. He states that this new road will set him apart from 'the great men alluded to'.[81]

Early in this study Bacon's remarks about inventing natural philosophy and unveiling the secrets of nature have been described as conflicting. It was stated also that a coherent picture was capable of being constructed. There are sufficient reasons for concluding that according to Bacon's notions and purposes – these being formed early in his career, and it being assumed that he did not change his mind at the last – the chief apparatus relating to the invention of natural philosophy was something which only he could and would produce. *Temporis Partus Masculus*, The Masculine Birth of Time, dates from before the publication of the first *Advancement*. This promise and project would be embodied in *Novum Organum*, Book II. True, though he does not renounce, he modifies this plan by admitting that as discoveries proceed the way of making them could change.[82] Also it is true that he allows that a procedure less defined than his own – though he does not renounce this latter – might serve.[83] When he had succeeded in activating his *Novum Organum*, Book II, other workers would be able to advance in inventing natural sciences for the reason that they could and would employ his invention, namely his induction. Sometimes he seems to indicate that by employing his induction everything discoverable would be discovered quickly. Sometimes he says, as he told Father Fulgentius in 1625, that the business would take ages to accomplish.[84] With respect to the past we have seen that according to his teaching about civil history of arts and letters contributions by past workers should be sought and that these might be found to be helpful.

Other workers could do, and could follow him in doing, the other things which have been described and discussed in this present study, and which he recommended as needed, whether in the field of *Know Thyself* or in that of inquiries into nature. Since in the event Bacon did not succeed in activating his chief thing, his apparatus in *Novum Organum*, Book II, it was these other things, which turn out to have comprised his message and his bequest for promoting the sciences – guidance for instance for the activities of the nascent Royal Society in England. These other things in his bequest were the preliminary to what, for the world of nature, he had had it in mind to do; namely the making of a procedure which would not only circumvent the illusions stemming from the weakness of men's senses and intellects, but at the same time – and with ease thus levelling men's abilities – achieve certainties. His attempt to build this latter being pursuit of the impossible, it was, despite himself and *pace* Hooke who evidently paid attention to Bacon's chief thing, though he also criticized it, these foreworks and preliminary stages and pausing-places which proved sounder, more fertile, helpful and constructive than that to which they were to be the introduction. The lighted candle for finding a path through the woods of experience which he advises in Aphorism LXXXII of *Novum Organum*, Book I perhaps and indeed probably points to the devices of *Novum Organum*, Book II. But certainly it is a pointer also to the needed preliminary stages; for example and *inter alia* not least, to *Natura...parendo vincitur*[85] – nature if she is to be understood and harnessed must be obeyed.

Delivering *Novum Organum* to King James VI and I, and perhaps speaking more wisely than he knew, he spoke of plans 'tending to enlarge the bounds of Reason and to endow man's estate with new value...'[86] On this occasion he made no mention of extending a dominion of certainty. This was in 1620. Two years later he perhaps also wrote more wisely than he knew when he told Redemptus Baranzan: 'Be not troubled about the Metaphysics. When true Physics have been discovered, there will be no Metaphysics. Beyond the true Physics is divinity only.'[87] In other words though God in the sacred canon had revealed to man his form, he had kept to himself knowledge of the forms of nature. Nor could men attain to knowledge of these forms of nature by their own efforts. Approving that Aristotle, his marker, should be supplied and continued with respect to his *Problems* (a collection of natural history and experiments), Bacon in this statement addressed to Baranzan appears to have abandoned his marker though he had earlier joined him in the higher quest for knowledge of nature's 'essential forms and true differences'.

The remark in the letter to Baranzan, together with the statements to the effect that natural experimental histories stood on the same level with, and were capable of perhaps constituting a substitute for the *Organum*, are the evidence – the sole evidence – as against Hooke and Ellis, for example, that Bacon reached truly decisive second thoughts about *Novum Organum*, Book II. As far as we know he never repudiated his *Novum Organum*, Book II. Doubting is not retracting. Doubts were part of the procedure. In the programme for discovering the secrets of nature doubts were the path to certainties. Bouts of doubts would have attended the whole of the course he had embarked upon. Bacon did not abandon plans which he had planted and long nourished in his mind. *Novum Organum* with its Book II and his civil history, recording a portion of time in which there had been 'no small variety in the affairs of a monarchy, but such as perhaps in four successions in any state at any time is hardly to be found',[88] are parallels. *Novum Organum* Book II and the civil history running from the Union of the Roses to the union of the Crowns were both of them achieved in that they were brilliantly and substantially launched. They were not renounced. But also they were both of them aborted.

It is true that in *The Natural and Experimental History for the Foundation of Philosophy* (1622) he declared 'that my *Organum*, even if it were completed, would not without the *Natural History* much advance the *Instauration of the Sciences*, whereas the *Natural History* without the *Organum* would advance it not a little'.[89] But a few lines previously, referring to 'the many wits scattered over Europe, capacious, open, lofty, subtle, solid, and constant', he had asked 'what if one of them were to enter into the plan of my *Organum* and try to use it?'[90] The point he makes here is that the plan of his *Organum* itself demands the natural and experimental history as its pre-liminary stage. Since we have no recorded words of Bacon renouncing the plan of his *Organum*, and since also it is inconceivable that his chaplain, Rawley, would not have reported so great a change, it is right to conclude that Bacon clung to his plan. And yet perhaps even in this he could have been wiser than he knew. The machine was defective. But was Bacon's judgment also and equally defective when he promised as he did in *Novum Organum*, Book I that as the successful exploration of nature proceeded wits would be levelled? He described Fortune as blind but not invisible. He practised watching and following her, 'But fortune layeth as heavy impositions as virtue; and it is as hard and severe a thing to be a true politique, as to be truly moral. '[91] In comparison with the difficulties experienced in all the parts of *Know Thyself* – civil history, moral philosophy, civil policy – including the auxiliary arts, common logic and rhetoric; and including *Know Thyself*'s flanking arts, divinity and medicine – the natural sciences in some of its branches and perhaps in many of them would prove easy. To that extent the natural sciences would promote the levelling of wits.

Notes

Chapter 1

[1] (B) Vol. IV. p. 73.
[2] (B) Vol. IV. p. 74.
[3] *The Growth of British Policy*. J. R. Seeley. Cambridge 1930. p. 2.
[4] (A) Vol. IV. p. 8.
[5] (B) Vol. I. p. 109.
[6] (B) Vol. VII. p. 373.
[7] (B) Vol. VII. pp. 532–3.
[8] (A) Vol. V. p. 559. In the first days of this present study I found the earlier statement to which Bacon refers in this passage. Subsequently I have not been able to trace this earlier statement.
[9] (B) Vol. IV. p. 145.
[10] (A) Vol. IV. p. 306.
[11] (A) Vol. IV. p. 318.
[12] (B) Vol. VII. p. 374.
[13] Years ago Ronald S. Crane undertook to relate Bacon's essays, notwithstanding Bacon's own words and those of commentators, with the rest of his work. Mr Crane's argument that the essays are an integral part of the Baconian enterprise is convincing. See *Essential Articles for the study of Francis Bacon*. Edited by Brian Vickers. Sidgwick and Jackson. London 1972. p. 272. This book includes *The Relation of Bacon's Essays to his Program for the Advancement of Learning*. (Reprinted from *The Schelling Anniversary Papers*. New York. The Century Co. 1923.)
[14] (B) Vol. IV. p. 141.
[15] (A) Vol. VI. p. 373.
[16] (A) Vol. IV. p. 292.
[17] (A) Vol. III. p. 396.
[18] (A) Vol. IV. p. 433.
[19] (A) Vol. IV. pp. 54–5.
[20] (A) Vol. IV. p. 423.

21 (A) Vol. III. p. 396.
22 *Critical and Historical Essays*. Thomas Babington Macaulay. Dent. London 1907. Reprint 1927. Vol. II. p. 378.
23 Translated as *A History of England principally in the Seventeenth Century*. Oxford at the Clarendon Press 1875.
24 Ibid. Vol. I. p. 459.
25 (A) Vol. IV. p. 112.
26 Macaulay. Ibid. p. 330.
27 Ibid. pp. 319–20.
28 Ibid. p. 320.
29 Ibid. p. 317.
30 Ibid. p. 325.
31 Ibid. p. 328.
32 (A) Vol. III. p. 367.
33 (A) Vol. III. p. 445.
34 Macaulay. Ibid. p. 380.
35 Rudolf Metz, p. 32. *Bacon's Part in the Intellectual Movement of his Time in Seventeenth Century Studies* presented to Sir Herbert Grierson. Oxford 1938.
36 Ranke. Ibid. Vol. I. p. 456.
37 Ibid. p. 457.
38 *The History of England from the Accession of James II*. Lord Macaulay. Longmans, Green & Co. London 1906, p. 35.
39 (A) Vol. VII. pp. 370–1.
40 Macaulay. *History*. Vol. I. pp. 198, 199.
41 *The Royal Society: Concept and Creation*. Margery Purver, with an introduction by H. R. Trevor-Roper. Routledge & Kegan Paul. London 1967. p. 101.
42 Ibid. H. R. Trevor-Roper's Introduction, p. xvi. He quotes Bacon (A) Vol. IV. p. 19. But see also and compare *The Debate over Science*. Michael Hunter in *The Restored Monarchy 1660–1688*. Edited J. R. Jones. The Macmillan Press Ltd 1979.
43 Macaulay. *Essay*. p. 364.
44 Ibid. p. 300.
45 *English Literature in the Earlier Seventeenth Century, 1600–1660*. Douglas Bush. Oxford 1945. p. 491.
46 *The Life and Letters of Lord Macaulay*. George Otto Trevelyan. Longmans, Green & Co. London 1923. Vol. I. p. 327.
47 (A) Vol. III. p. 19.
48 (A) Vol. III. p. 405.
49 (B) Vol. IV. p. 340.
50 E.g. (A) Vol. V. p. 22.
51 Macaulay. *Essay*. p. 389.
52 Ibid. p. 396.
53 Ibid. p. 388.
54 Macaulay. *History*. Vol. I. p. 200.

[55] Macaulay. *Essay.* p. 389.
[56] (A) Vol. III. p. 366.
[57] Macaulay. *Essay.* p. 388.
[58] Ibid. p. 391.
[59] Ibid. p. 388.
[60] Ibid. p. 392. Macaulay refers to *Novum Organum* Book I. Aphorism LV. (A) Vol. IV. p. 59.
[61] Ibid. pp. 379–80.
[62] Ibid. p. 370.
[63] Ibid. p. 376.
[64] Ibid. p. 371.
[65] (A) Vol. V. p. 89.
[66] Macaulay. *Essay.* p. 372.
[67] *History of England from the Accession of James I to the Outbreak of the Civil War 1603–1642.* Vol. III 1616–1621. London: Longmans, Green & Co. 1883. p. 396.
[68] *The Works of Francis Bacon, Lord Chancellor of England* – New edition. Basil Montague. London. William Pickering. MDCCCXXXIV. p. CCCCLXIV. CCCCLXIV.
[69] Ibid. p. 396.
[70] Ibid. p. 397.
[71] Ibid. Vol. IV. p. 104.
[72] Ibid. Vol. III. p. 395.
[73] *D.N.B.* Vol. II. p. 336.
[74] Ibid. Vol. II. p. 341.
[75] (B) Vol. IV. p. 74.
[76] (A) Vol. III. p. 352.
[77] (A) Vol. III. p. 363 and (A) Vol. IV. p. 53.
[78] (A) Vol. IV. p. 294.
[79] (B) Vol. VII. p. 120.
[80] (B) Vol. VII. p. 439.
[81] (A) Vol. III. p. 290.
[82] (A) Vol. IV. p. 336.
[83] (A) Vol. III. p. 332.
[84] (A) Vol. IV. p. 432.
[85] (A) Vol. IV. p. 27.
[86] (A) Vol. IV. p. 94.
[87] (A) Vol. VI. p. 497–8.

Chapter 2

[1] *Essai sur les Moeurs et l'Esprit des Nations et sur les principaux faits de l'histoire depuis Charlemagne jusqu'a Louis XIII.* Voltaire. Editions Garnier Frères. Paris 1963. Vol. II. p. 640. (Present writer's translation.)
[2] Ibid. Vol. II. p. 654.

[3] Ibid. Vol. II. p. 842.
[4] *Lettres Philosophiques*. Voltaire. Librairie Delagrave. Paris 1931. p. 143.
[5] (A) Vol. VI. p. 753.
[6] (B) Vol. VII. p. 532.
[7] (A) Vol. IV. pp. 93–4.
[8] (A) Vol. IV. p. 115.
[9] (A) Vol. VI. p. 463.
[10] (B) Vol. VII. p. 539.
[11] (A) Vol. IV. p. 293.
[12] (A) Vol. IV. pp. 78, 79.
[13] (A) Vol. III. p. 366.
[14] Ibid.
[15] (A) Vol. IV. p. 373.
[16] (A) Vol. III. p. 346.
[17] (A) Vol. III. p. 347.
[18] (A) Vol. III. p. 348.
[19] (A) Vol. III. p. 349.
[20] (A) Vol. IV. p. 339.
[21] (A) Vol. IV. p. 22.
[22] (A) Vol. III. p. 282.
[23] (A) Vol. III. p. 290.
[24] (A) Vol. III. pp. 290–1.
[25] (A) Vol. III. pp. 294–5.
[26] (A) Vol. III. pp. 353–4.
[27] (A) Vol. III. pp. 355, 356.
[28] (A) Vol. III. p. 356.
[29] (A) Vol. III. pp. 364, 365.
[30] (A) Vol. III. pp. 354–9.
[31] (A) Vol. VI. p. 711.
[32] (A) Vol. III. pp. 346, 367.
[33] (A) Vol. I. p. 191, (A) Vol. IV. p. 82.
[34] (A) Vol. III. p. 293.
[35] (A) Vol. III. pp. 366–7.
[36] Ibid.
[37] Ibid.
[38] Ibid.
[39] Ibid.
[40] (A) Vol. IV. p. 71. See also (A) Vol. IV. p. 17.
[41] (A) Vol. IV. pp. 86, 87.
[42] (A) Vol. IV. p. 95.
[43] (A) Vol. IV. p. 98.
[44] (A) Vol. IV. p. 101.
[45] (A) Vol. V. pp. 194, 195.
[46] (A) Vol. III. p. 367.
[47] Ibid.

[48] (A) Vol. III. p. 356.
[49] (A) Vol. III. p. 355.
[50] (A) Vol. III. p. 349–50.
[51] (B) Vol. IV. p. 145.
[52] (A) Vol. III. p. 367.
[53] (A) Vol. III. p. 370.
[54] (A) Vol. IV. p. 378.
[55] (A) Vol. III. p. 366.
[56] (A) Vol. III. p. 307.
[57] (A) Vol. VI. p. 747.
[58] (A) Vol. III. p. 367.
[59] (A) Vol. IV. p. 33.
[60] Ibid.
[61] (A) Vol. III. pp. 355, 356.

Chapter 3

[1] (A) Vol. III. p. 329.
[2] (A) Vol. III. p. 356.
[3] (A) Vol. IV. p. 292.
[4] (A) Vol. IV. p. 293.
[5] (A) Vol. IV. p. 325.
[6] (A) Vol. IV. p. 293.
[7] (A) Vol. V. pp. 503–4.
[8] (A) Vol. IV. p. 23.
[9] (A) Vol. III. p. 335.
[10] (A) Vol. IV. p. 299.
[11] (A) Vol. III. p. 330.
[12] Ibid.
[13] (A) Vol. IV. p. 295.
[14] (A) Vol. IV. p. 294.
[15] (A) Vol. IV. p. 299.
[16] Ibid.
[17] (A) Vol. V. p. 510.
[18] (A) Vol. V. p. 507.
[19] (A) Vol. V. pp. 507–8.
[20] (A) Vol. IV. p. 19.
[21] (A) Vol. III. p. 19.
[22] (A) Vol. VI. pp. 497–8.
[23] See *Against the Professors*. I. pp. 266–8.
[24] (A) Vol. III. p. 435.
[25] (A) Vol. IV. p. 69.
[26] Ibid.
[27] (A) Vol. III. p. 335.
[28] (A) Vol. III. p. 348.

[29] (A) Vol. III. p. 453.
[30] Ibid.
[31] (A) Vol. VI. p. 408.
[32] (B) Vol. I. p. 80.
[33] (B) Vol. III. p. 96.
[34] (B) Vol. III. p. 323.
[35] (A) Vol. VI. p. 498.
[36] (A) Vol. V. p. 21.
[37] (A) Vol. III. p. 333.
[38] (A) Vol. III. p. 336.
[39] (A) Vol. III. p. 338.
[40] (A) Vol. III. p. 330.
[41] (A) Vol. III. p. 341.
[42] (A) Vol. IV. p. 309.
[43] (A) Vol. IV. pp. 308–9.
[44] (A) Vol. III. p. 334.
[45] (A) Vol. IV. p. 303.
[46] (A) Vol. III. p. 334.
[47] Ibid.
[48] (A) Vol. IV. pp. 304–5.
[49] (A) Vol. IV. pp. 18, 19.
[50] (A) Vol. III. p. 334.
[51] (A) Vol. IV. pp. 303, 304.
[52] (A) Vol. III. p. 361.
[53] (A) Vol. III. pp. 361, 362.
[54] (A) Vol. VI. pp. 43, 44.
[55] (A) Vol. IV. p. 304.
[56] Ranke. Vol. I. p. 455.
[57] (A) Vol. III. p. 351.
[58] *Histories.* XII. 28.
[59] (A) Vol. VI. p. 305.
[60] (A) Vol. III. pp. 323–4.
[61] (A) Vol. IV. p. 302.
[62] Ibid.
[63] (B) Vol. V. p. 85.
[64] (B) Vol. VI. p. 165. Date uncertain.
[65] (B) Vol. VI. p. 67.
[66] (B) Vol. VI. p. 68.
[67] (A) Vol. V. p. 104.
[68] (A) Vol. IV. p. 309.
[69] (A) Vol. VI. p. 19.
[70] (A) Vol. III. p. 366.
[71] (A) Vol. VI. p. 19.
[72] (A) Vol. IV. pp. 300–1.
[73] (A) Vol. III. p. 339.

[74] (A) Vol. III. p. 342.
[75] (A) Vol. I. p. 515.
[76] (A) Vol. III. p. 335.
[77] Ibid.
[78] (A) Vol. VI. p. 415.
[79] (A) Vol. IV. p. 293.
[80] (A) Vol. VI. p. 722.
[81] (A) Vol. VI. pp. 516–17.
[82] (A) Vol. IV. p. 53.
[83] (A) Vol. I. p. 504.
[84] (A) Vol. IV. p. 302.
[85] (A) Vol. VI. pp. 17–18.
[86] (A) Vol. IV. p. 302.
[87] (A) Vol. IV. p. 305.
[88] (B) Vol. VI. p. 546.
[89] (B) Vol. VI. p. 547.
[90] (A) Vol. III. p. 342.
[91] Ranke, Vol. I. p. 459.
[92] Cicero *De Oratore*. Book II. pp. 224, 225. The Loeb Classical Library. London. William Heinemann Ltd. Cambridge, Massachusetts. Harvard University Press. 1959.
[93] (A) Vol. IV. p. 336.
[94] (A) Vol. IV. pp. 315–16.
[95] (A) Vol. IV. p. 316.

Chapter 4

[1] (A) Vol. III. p. 383.
[2] (A) Vol. IV. p. 373.
[3] (B) Vol. III. pp. 249–50.
[4] (A) Vol. IV. p. 407.
[5] (A) Vol. IV. p. 407.
[6] (A) Vol. IV. p. 407.
[7] (A) Vol. III. p. 392.
[8] (A) Vol. III. p. 383.
[9] (A) Vol. III. p. 411.
[10] (A) Vol. III. p. 394.
[11] (A) Vol. III. pp. 394–5.
[12] (A) Vol. IV. p. 110.
[13] (A) Vol. III. p. 396.
[14] Ibid.
[15] (A) Vol. III. p. 397.
[16] (A) Vol. IV. pp. 431–2.
[17] (A) Vol. IV. p. 27.
[18] (A) Vol. IV. p. 248.

[19] (A) Vol. IV. p. 12.
[20] (A) Vol. IV. p. 48.
[21] (A) Vol. III. p. 396.
[22] (A) Vol. III. pp. 468, 469.
[23] (A) Vol. VI. p. 420.
[24] (A) Vol. III. p. 387.
[25] (A) Vol. IV. p. 411.
[26] (A) Vol. III. p. 388.
[27] (A) Vol. IV. pp. 17–18.
[28] (A) Vol. IV. pp. 454–5.
[29] (A) Vol. IV. p. 455.
[30] (A) Vol. III. p. 284.
[31] Ibid.
[32] (A) Vol. III. pp. 409–10.
[33] (A) Vol. IV. p. 455.
[34] (A) Vol. III. p. 410.
[35] (A) Vol. III. p. 383.
[36] (A) Vol. IV. p. 456.
[37] (A) Vol. III. p. 302.
[38] (A) Vol. IV. p. 8.
[39] (A) Vol. IV. p. 42.
[40] Ben Jonson.
[41] (A) Vol. I. p. 11.
[42] Macaulay. *Essay.* p. 299.
[43] A. V. Ecclesiastes. Ch. 12 vv. 12–13.
[44] (A) Vol. III. pp. 327–8.
[45] (A) Vol. V. p. 79.

Chapter 5

[1] (A) Vol. IV. p. 53.
[2] (A) Vol. I. p. 162.
[3] (A) Vol. IV. p. 72.
[4] (A) Vol. IV. p. 72.
[5] (A) Vol. IV. p. 73.
[6] Thucydides. *History of the Peloponnesian War.* Book I. p. 3. Cambridge Massachusetts. Trans. C. F. Smith. Reprinted 1980.
[7] (A) Vol. IV. p. 325.
[8] (A) Vol. IV. p. 293.
[9] (A) Vol. IV. pp. 324–5.
[10] (A) Vol. VI. p. 707.
[11] (A) Vol. VI. p. 709.
[12] (A) Vol. VI. p. 711.
[13] (A) Vol. VI. p. 713.
[14] (A) Vol. VI. p. 696.
[15] (A) Vol. VI. p. 17.

[16] (A) Vol. IV. pp. 324–5.
[17] (A) Vol. VI. p. 697.
[18] (A) Vol. IV. p. 64.
[19] (A) Vol. V. pp. 461–2.
[20] (A) Vol. V. pp. 462–3.
[21] (A) Vol. V. p. 484.
[22] (A) Vol. VI. p. 695.
[23] (A) Vol. III. p. 453.
[24] (A) Vol. VI. pp. 745, 755.
[25] (A) Vol. VI. p. 757.
[26] (A) Vol. III. p. 367.
[27] (A) Vol. III. pp. 366–7.
[28] (A) Vol. VI. p. 689.
[29] (A) Vol. VI. pp. 689–90.
[30] (B) Vol. I. p. 223.
[31] (B) Vol. I. p. 240.
[32] (B) Vol. I. p. 109.
[33] (B) Vol. III. pp. 84–5.
[34] (B) Vol. IV. p. 147.
[35] (A) Vol. III. p. 218.
[36] (A) Vol. III. pp. 221–2.
[37] (A) Vol. VI. p. 691.
[38] Ibid.
[39] (A) Vol. III. pp. 366–7.
[40] (A) Vol. III. p. 355.
[41] (A) Vol. III. p. 294.
[42] (A) Vol. III. p. 334.
[43] (A) Vol. III. p. 335.
[44] (A) Vol. VI. p. 319.
[45] (A) Vol. III. p. 342.
[46] (A) Vol. VI. p. 691.
[47] (A) Vol. VI. p. 755.
[48] (A) Vol. VII. pp. 320–1.
[49] (A) Vol. III. p. 475.
[50] Ibid.
[51] (B) Vol. VI. p. 62. Date uncertain.
[52] (B) Vol. VI. p. 70.
[53] (A) Vol. IV. p. 59.
[54] (A) Vol. VI. pp. 576, 498.
[55] (A) Vol. III. p. 356.
[56] (A) Vol. III. p. 408.

Chapter 6

[1] (A) Vol. IV. p. 405.

[2] (A) Vol. III. p. 433.
[3] (A) Vol. IV. p. 78.
[4] Ibid.
[5] (A) Vol. III. pp. 417–18.
[6] (A) Vol. III. pp. 409–10.
[7] (A) Vol. IV. p. 455.
[8] (A) Vol. IV. p. 457.
[9] (A) Vol. III. pp. 417–18.
[10] (A) Vol. V. p. 3.
[11] (A) Vol. V. p. 4.
[12] (A) Vol. V. p. 5.
[13] (A) Vol. III. p. 419.
[14] (A) Vol. V. p. 6.
[15] (A) Vol. III. pp. 409–10.
[16] (A) Vol. V. p. 5.
[17] (A) Vol. III. p. 433.
[18] (A) Vol. V. p. 20.
[19] Ibid.
[20] Ibid.
[21] (A) Vol. IV. p. 94.
[22] (A) Vol. III. p. 329.
[23] (A) Vol. III. p. 434.
[24] (A) Vol. III. pp. 434–5.
[25] (A) Vol. VI. p. 525.
[26] (A) Vol. VI. p. 497.
[27] (A) Vol. IV. p. 69.
[28] (A) Vol. V. p. 21.
[29] (A) Vol. V. p. 22.
[30] (A) Vol. V. p. 21.
[31] Ibid.
[32] Ibid.
[33] (A) Vol. III. p. 435.
[34] (A) Vol. V. p. 22.
[35] Ibid.
[36] (A) Vol. V. p. 23.
[37] Ibid.
[38] (A) Vol. V. pp. 23–4.
[39] (A) Vol. V. p. 24.
[40] (A) Vol. V. p. 211.
[41] (A) Vol. VI. pp. 399–400.
[42] (B) Vol. VI. p. 189.
[43] (B) Vol. VI. p. 205.
[44] (B) Vol. VII. pp. 296–7.
[45] (B) Vol. VII. p. 371.
[46] (A) Vol. V. pp. 29–30.

[47] (A) Vol. IV. pp. 453–4.
[48] (A) Vol. III. p. 445.
[49] (A) Vol. IV. pp. 471–2.
[50] (A) Vol. III. p. 302.
[51] (B) Vol. I. p. 109.
[52] (B) Vol. IV. p. 177.
[53] (B) Vol. IV. p. 165.
[54] (A) Vol. IV. p. 410.
[55] (A) Vol. VI. pp. 633, 706.
[56] (A) Vol. IV. p. 47; and (A) Vol. IV. p. 114; and Farrington. p. 93. (*Cogitata et Visa*).
[57] (B) Vol. IV. p. 177.
[58] *Discourses* I.3. p. 353.
[59] Ibid.
[60] Ibid.
[61] (A) Vol. IV. p. 60.
[62] (A) Vol. IV. p. 82. See also (A) Vol. III. p. 291.
[63] *Discourses* I.3. p. 216.
[64] *Discourses* I.27. p. 275.
[65] (A) Vol. VI. pp. 546, 404.
[66] (A) Vol. VI. pp. 561, 431–2.
[67] (A) Vol. VI. pp. 433–4.
[68] (A) Vol. V. p. 90.
[69] (A) Vol. V. p. 88.
[70] (B) Vol. VII. p. 176. Vol. VI. pp. 20, 44.
[71] (A) Vol. VI. pp. 588, 450.
[72] (A) Vol. VI. p. 387.
[73] Ibid.
[74] Ibid.
[75] (A) Vol. VI. p. 388.
[76] Ibid.
[77] (A) Vol. VI. p. 389.
[78] (A) Vol. VI. pp. 450–1.
[79] (A) Vol. III. 302.
[80] (A) Vol. VII. pp. 471–2.
[81] (A) Vol. VII. p. 381. See also Vol. V. p. 543.
[82] (A) Vol. V. p. 89.
[83] Ibid.
[84] (A) Vol. VI. pp. 509–10. Also p. 585.
[85] (B) Vol. IV. p. 183.
[86] (B) Vol. IV. p. 182.
[87] (B) Vol. IV. p. 183.
[88] (B) Vol. IV. pp. 191–2.
[89] (A) Vol. VI. p. 432.
[90] (A) Vol. VI. pp. 502, 582.

91 (A) Vol. VI. pp. 426, 555.

92 (A) Vol. VI. p. 217.

93 (A) Vol. VI. p. 426.

94 (A) Vol. VI. pp. 516–17.

95 (A) Vol. VI. p. 408.

96 Macaulay. *Essay*. p. 328.

97 (A) Vol. VI. p. 472.

98 Edward Gibbon. *Decline and Fall of the Roman Empire*. Vol. IV. p. 396. Dent. London, Melbourne and Toronto. Everyman's Library. 1981.

99 (B) Vol. IV. pp. 73–6. See text. Also see footnotes. As will be seen, I have mostly accepted the editor's interpretations: also, that I have omitted some of the notes as being the less intelligible and the less central in Bacon's document.

100 (B) Vol. III. pp. 368–82.

101 (B) Vol. VII. p. 362.

102 (B) Vol. VII. p. 360.

103 (A) Vol. VI. p. 276.

104 (A) Vol. VI. p. 383.

105 (A) Vol. VI. p. 381.

Chapter 7

1 (A) Vol. I. p. 5.

2 (A) Vol. I. p. 6.

3 (A) Vol. III. p. 342.

4 (B) Vol. IV. p. 64.

5 (B) Vol. IV. p. 64.

6 (B) Vol. IV. p. 65.

7 (B) Vol. IV. p. 65.

8 (B) Vol. IV. p. 68.

9 (B) Vol. IV. p. 69.

10 (B) Vol. IV. p. 141.

11 (A) Vol. I. p. 11.

12 (B) Vol. IV. p. 145.

13 (B) Vol. IV. p. 147.

14 (B) Vol. VII. p. 89.

15 (A) Vol. V. pp. 194–5.

16 (A) Vol. III. p. 470.

17 (B) Vol. IV. p. 74.

18 (B) Vol. IV. p. 74.

19 Cf. *The Golden Age Restor'd*. Graham Parry. Manchester University Press. 1981. Parry does not cite these notes. E.g. that Bacon would 'amuse' the King. Force is thus added to the book's thesis.

20 (B) Vol. IV. p. 282.

21 (B) Vol. V. p. 243.

[22] Johnn Aubrey. *Brief Lives*. p. 288. Penguin Books. Lecber and Warburg. 1949. Revised in the Penguin English Library. 1972.

[23] (B) Vol. v. p. 243.

[24] (A) Vol. vi. p. 420.

[25] (B) Vol. vii. p. 87.

[26] (B) Vol. vii. p. 88.

[27] (A) Vol. vi. pp. 586–7.

[28] (A) Vol. vi. p. 444–5.

[29] (B) Vol. iv. p. 313.

[30] (B) Vol. iv. pp. 279–80.

[31] (A) Vol. i. p. 15.

[32] (A) Vol. vi. p. 551.

[33] (A) Vol. vi. pp. 399–400.

[34] (A) Vol. iii. p. 475.

[35] (B) Vol. iii. pp. 94, 95, 96.

[36] (B) Vol. iii. pp. 218, 219.

[37] (B) Vol. iii. p. 309.

[38] (B) Vol. iii. p. 308.

[39] (B) Vol. iii. p. 311.

[40] (B) Vol. iii. p. 313.

[41] (B) Vol. iii. p. 319.

[42] (B) Vol. iii. pp. 319–20.

[43] (B) Vol. iii. p. 321.

[44] (B) Vol. iii. p. 322.

[45] (B) Vol. iii. p. 323.

[46] (B) Vol. iii. pp. 323–4.

[47] (B) Vol. iii. p. 324.

[48] (B) Vol. iv. p. 280.

[49] (B) Vol. iv. p. 365.

[50] (B) Vol. iv. p. 369.

[51] (B) Vol. iv. pp. 371–2.

[52] (B) Vol. iv. p. 372.

[53] (B) Vol. v. p. 43.

[54] (B) Vol. v. p. 177.

[55] (A) Vol. iii. pp. 290–1. See also (A) Vol. vi. p. 434. (B) Vol. iv. p. 183. Jeremiah, Ch. 6. v. 16.

[56] (A) Vol. vi. p. 400.

[57] (B) Vol. vii. p. 171.

[58] (B) Vol. vii. p. 173.

[59] (B) Vol. vii. p. 171.

[60] (B) Vol. vii. p. 172.

[61] (B) Vol. iv. p. 177.

[62] (B) Vol. v. p. 30.

[63] (B) Vol. vii. p. 177.

[64] (B) Vol. vii. p. 124.

[65] (A) Vol. III. p. 476.
[66] (A) Vol. III. p. 474.
[67] (A) Vol. IV. pp. 78, 79.
[68] (A) Vol. VI. p. 410.
[69] (A) Vol. VII. pp. 47, 48, 49.
[70] (A) Vol. VII. p. 51.

Chapter 8

[1] (A) Vol. IV. p. 47.
[2] (A) Vol. IV. pp. 120–1.
[3] (A) Vol. III. pp. 351–2.
[4] (A) Vol. III. p. 351.
[5] (A) Vol. III. p. 355.
[6] (A) Vol. III. p. 351.
[7] (A) Vol. IV. p. 96.
[8] (A) Vol. IV. p. 71.
[9] (A) Vol. IV. pp. 28–9.
[10] (A) Vol. IV. pp. 68, 69.
[11] *Discourses* I.39.1.
[12] *Discourses* I.11.6. See Preface to I.3.
[13] (A) Vol. VI. p. 698.
[14] (A) Vol. IV. p. 325.
[15] (A) Vol. VI. pp. 697–8.
[16] (B) Vol. IV. p. 74.
[17] (A) Vol. VI. pp. 689–90.
[18] (B) Vol. IV. p. 147.
[19] (B) Vol. IV. p. 340.
[20] (A) Vol. VI. p. 373.
[21] (A) Vol. III. pp. 403, 404.
[22] (B) Vol. III. pp. 300–1.
[23] But here 'traditions' carries something more of a modern meaning.
[24] (A) Vol. III. p. 405.
[25] (A) Vol. III. p. 407.
[26] (A) Vol. III. p. 406.
[27] (A) Vol. IV. p. 85.
[28] (B) Vol. VI. p. 70.
[29] (B) Vol. VI. pp. 481–2.
[30] (B) Vol. VI. p. 469.
[31] (B) Vol. VI. p. 470.
[32] (B) Vol. VII. p. 441.
[33] (B) Vol. I. p. 163.
[34] (B) Vol. I. p. 169.
[35] (B) Vol. I. p. 170.
[36] (B) Vol. III. p. 323.

[37] (B) Vol. III. p. 325.
[38] (B) Vol. VII. pp. 22–8.
[39] (B) Vol. VII. pp. 460–5.
[40] (B) Vol. VII. p. 469.
[41] Ibid.
[42] (B) Vol. VII. p. 424.
[43] (B) Vol. VII. pp. 482–3.
[44] (B) Vol. VII. pp. 495–6.
[45] (B) Vol. VII. p. 483.
[46] (B) Vol. III. p. 316.
[47] (B) Vol. III. p. 323.
[48] (B) Vol. III. p. 313.
[49] (A) Vol. VI. p. 450.
[50] (A) Vol. III. p. 450.
[51] (A) Vol. IV. p. 405.
[52] (B) Vol. VII. p. 470.
[53] Ibid.
[54] (A) Vol. V. p. 79.
[55] (A) Vol. V. p. 87.
[56] (A) Vol. VI. p. 450.
[57] (B) Vol. VII. p. 469.
[58] (B) Vol. VII. p. 470.
[59] Ibid.
[60] Ibid.
[61] (B) Vol. VII. p. 474.
[62] Ibid.
[63] Ibid.
[64] (B) Vol. VII. p. 476.
[65] Ibid.
[66] (B) Vol. VIII. pp. 476–7.
[67] (B) Ibid.
[68] (B) Vol. VII. p. 478. The reference to Augustine is to *contra* Faustum XXII.74. The reference to Aquinas is to *Summa theologica*, Lecunda Lecundae. 9.40. art. 1.
[69] (B) Vol. VII. p. 481.
[70] (B) Vol. VII. p. 482.
[71] (A) Vol. VI. pp. 561, 416.
[72] (A) Vol. VI. p. 416.
[73] (B) Vol. I. p. 84.
[74] (A) Vol. V. p. 111.
[75] (A) Vol. III. p. 484.
[76] (A) Vol. V. p. 118.
[77] (A) Vol. VI. p. 312.
[78] (A) Vol. VI. p. 313.
[79] (A) Vol. III. p. 488. In the final version the statement is omitted.

Chapter 9

[1] (A) Vol. III. p. 285.
[2] (A) Vol. III. p. 287.
[3] (A) Vol. VI. pp. 420–1.
[4] *Christian Thought: its History and Application.* Ernst Troeltsch. Edited Baron F. van Hügel. Published by Meridian Books. New York 1957. p. 159.
[5] (B) Vol. VI. p. 423.
[6] (A) Vol. VI. p. 435.
[7] (A) Vol. VI. p. 428.
[8] (A) Vol. VI. p. 403.
[9] (B) Vol. VI. p. 445.
[10] (B) Vol. VI. p. 446.
[11] (B) Vol. VI. p. 70.
[12] (A) Vol. VI. p. 754.
[13] *Discourses* I.26.3.
[14] *Discourses* III.40.2.
[15] *Discourses* III.21–2, 3.
[16] (A) Vol. VI. pp. 420–1.
[17] *Discourses* I.41.2.
[18] *Discourses* I.10.7.
[19] *Discourses* III.16.3.
[20] *Discourses* I.6.9.
[21] *Discourses* I.11.1–6.
[22] *Discourses* I.12.3.
[23] (B) Vol. I. p. 80.
[24] *Discourses* III.1.8.
[25] (B) Vol. VII. p. 360.
[26] (B) Vol. III. p. 96.
[27] (B) Vol. III. p. 323.
[28] (A) Vol. III. p. 469.
[29] (B) Vol. IV. p. 285.
[30] *Discourses* III.1.2.4.
[31] (B) Vol. IV. p. 280.
[32] (B) Vol. IV. p. 309.
[33] (B) Vol. V. pp. 100–1.
[34] (B) Vol. V. p. 243.
[35] (B) Vol. VI. p. 233.
[36] (B) Vol. VII. p. 127.
[37] (A) Vol. VII. pp. 55–6.
[38] *Discourses* II.3.3.
[39] *Discourses* III.41.1.2. Ibid. II.25.1.
[40] (A) Vol. VI. p. 445.
[41] Ibid.

[42] (A) Vol. VI. p. 446.
[43] (A) Vol. VI. pp. 445–6.
[44] (A) Vol. VI. p. 450.
[45] Ibid.
[46] (A) Vol. VI. pp. 446, 447.
[47] *Discourses* 1.21.1–2.
[48] *Discourses* II.10.8.
[49] Ibid.
[50] (A) Vol. VI. p. 403.
[51] (A) Vol. VI. p. 404.
[52] (A) Vol. III. pp. 472, 473.
[53] (A) Vol. III. p. 345.
[54] (A) Vol. VI. p. 378.
[55] (A) Vol. III. pp. 430–1.
[56] (A) Vol. VII. p. 245.
[57] (B) Vol. II. p. 82.
[58] *Il Principe* by Niccolo Machiavelli. Edited by L. Arthur Burd. Oxford. Clarendon Press. 1891. See chapters XV, XVII, XVIII.
[59] *Discourses* II.2.6.
[60] (A) Vol. VI. pp. 403–4.
[61] *Discourses* II.2.6.
[62] (A) Vol. III. p. 447.
[63] (A) Vol. III. p. 268.
[64] (A) Vol. III. p. 270.
[65] (A) Vol. III. pp. 270–1.
[66] (A) Vol. III. pp. 302–3 and (A) Vol. I. p. 471.
[67] (A) Vol. VI. p. 575.
[68] (A) Vol. VI. p. 497.
[69] (A) Vol. VI. p. 472.
[70] (A) Vol. IV. p. 61.
[71] *Discourses* 1.11.5.
[72] (A) Vol. VI. p. 276.
[73] (A) Vol. V. p. 187.
[74] (A) Vol. VI. p. 515.
[75] Ranke ibid. Vol. I. p. 459.
[76] Derek Hirst. *Authority and Conflict: England 1503–1658*. Edward Arnold. 1986. p. 125.
[77] Hugh Trevor Roper. *Religion, Reformation and Social Change*. London 1967. p. 84, quoted by Anthony Quinton, *Francis Bacon*. Oxford University Press. Past Masters. 1980. pp. 73–4.

Chapter 10

[1] (A) Vol. III. p. 333.
[2] (A) Vol. IV. p. 303.

³ (A) Vol. III. p. 333.
⁴ (A) Vol. IV. p. 304.
⁵ (A) Vol. IV. p. 300.
⁶ (A) Vol. III. p. 329.
⁷ (A) Vol. III. p. 330.
⁸ (A) Vol. III. pp. 365–6.
⁹ (A) Vol. IV. p. 262.
¹⁰ (A) Vol. III. p. 133.
¹¹ (A) Vol. IV. pp. 300–1.
¹² (A) Vol. III. p. 328.
¹³ (A) Vol. IV. p. 103.
¹⁴ (A) Vol. III. p. 346.
¹⁵ (A) Vol. III. p. 356.
¹⁶ (A) Vol. III. pp. 366–7.
¹⁷ (A) Vol. III. p. 346.
¹⁸ (A) Vol. IV. p. 302.
¹⁹ Ibid.
²⁰ (A) Vol. III. pp. 339–40.
²¹ (A) Vol. III. p. 339.
²² (A) Vol. IV. pp. 311–12.
²³ (A) Vol. III. p. 335.
²⁴ (A) Vol. III. p. 274.
²⁵ (A) Vol. III. p. 339.
²⁶ (A) Vol. III. p. 335.
²⁷ (A) Vol. III. p. 453.
²⁸ Ibid.
²⁹ (A) Vol. III. pp. 475–6.
³⁰ (A) Vol. VII. p. 319.
³¹ (B) Vol. VI. p. 70.
³² (A) Vol. VII. p. 322.
³³ Ibid.
³⁴ (A) Vol. III. p. 405.
³⁵ (A) Vol. III. p. 453.
³⁶ (A) Vol. IV. p. 73.
³⁷ (A) Vol. III. p. 453.
³⁸ (A) Vol. IV. p. 383.
³⁹ (A) Vol. III. p. 367.
⁴⁰ (A) Vol. III. p. 373.
⁴¹ (A) Vol. IV. p. 384–5.
⁴² (A) Vol. V. p. 254.
⁴³ *Discourses* I. Preface. p. 206.
⁴⁴ (A) Vol. III. p. 404.
⁴⁵ (A) Vol. V. p. 118.
⁴⁶ (B) Vol. VII. p. 533.
⁴⁷ (A) Vol. IV. p. 311.

[48] (A) Vol. III. p. 339.
[49] Ibid.
[50] (A) Vol. IV. p. 370.
[51] (A) Vol. III. pp. 359–60.
[52] (A) Vol. IV. p. 298.
[53] (B) Vol. VII. p. 120.
[54] (A) Vol. V. p. 217.
[55] (A) Vol. V. pp. 218–19.
[56] (A) Vol. IV. p. 96.
[57] (A) Vol. IV. p. 51.

Chapter 11

[1] (A) Vol. III. p. 339.
[2] (A) Vol. IV. p. 301.
[3] (A) Vol. IV. p. 261.
[4] (A) Vol. IV. p. 298 and (A) Vol. IV. p. 254.
[5] Livy. Books I and II. Eng. translation by B. O. Foster. p. 7. Wm Heineman Cambridge Ltd. Mass. Harvard University Press. 1952.
[6] (A) Vol. IV. p. 456.
[7] (A) Vol. III. p. 336.
[8] (A) Vol. IV. p. 93.
[9] (B) Vol. III. p. 322.
[10] (A) Vol. III. pp. 430–1.
[11] (A) Vol. III. p. 430.
[12] (A) Vol. V. p. 231.
[13] (A) Vol. IV. p. 254.
[14] (A) Vol. VI. p. 19.
[15] (A) Vol. I. p. 509.
[16] (B) Vol. VII. p. 362.
[17] (A) Vol. I. p. 509; (A) Vol. IV. p. 306; (B) Vol. VII. p. 477; (A) Vol. VI. p. 420.
[18] (B) Vol. VII. p. 429.
[19] (A) Vol. III. p. 336.
[20] (A) Vol. VI. p. 447.
[21] (A) Vol. VI. pp. 233–4.
[22] (A) Vol. IV. p. 311.
[23] (A) Vol. VI. p. 97.
[24] (A) Vol. VI. pp. 93–5.
[25] (A) Vol. VI. pp. 93, 94, 95.
[26] (A) Vol. V. p. 94.
[27] (A) Vol. V. p. 82.
[28] (A) Vol. V. p. 21.
[29] (A) Vol. VI. pp. 720 ff.
[30] (A) Vol. VI. pp. 737 ff.

[31] (A) Vol. VI. pp. 512 ff.
[32] (B) Vol. II. p. 82.
[33] (B) Vol. III. pp. 35–6.
[34] (A) Vol. VI. p. 92.
[35] (A) Vol. VI. pp. 95–6.
[36] (A) Vol. VI. p. 239.
[37] (A) Vol. VI. p. 156.
[38] (A) Vol. VI. p. 31.
[39] (A) Vol. VI. p. 244.
[40] (A) Ibid.
[41] (A) Vol. VI. pp. 118, 119. Also, see editor's footnotes pp. 116, 117, 118.
[42] (A) Vol. VI. pp. 216–17.
[43] (A) Vol. VI. p. 20.
[44] (A) Vol. VI. p. 20.
[45] (A) Vol. VI. p. 155.
[46] (A) Vol. VI. p. 217.
[47] (A) Vol. VI. p. 159.
[48] (A) Vol. VI. p. 240.
[49] (A) Vol. VI. p. 244.
[50] (A) Vol. VI. p. 240.
[51] (A) Vol. VI. p. 242.
[52] (A) Vol. VI. p. 244.
[53] (A) Vol. VI. p. 241.
[54] (A) Vol. VI. p. 243.
[55] (A) Vol. VI. p. 242.
[56] (A) Vol. VI. p. 405.
[57] Ibid.
[58] (A) Vol. VI. pp. 405–6.
[59] (B) Vol. VI. p. 452.
[60] (A) Vol. III. p. 342.

Chapter 12

[1] (A) Vol. IV. p. 104.
[2] (A) Vol. IV. p. 107.
[3] (A) Vol. III. p. 330.
[4] (A) Vol. III. p. 218.
[5] (A) Vol. IV. p. 21.
[6] (A) Vol. IV. p. 20.
[7] (A) Vol. IV. p. 109.
[8] (A) Vol. IV. p. 63.
[9] (A) Vol. IV. p. 104.
[10] (A) Vol. IV. p. 104.
[11] (A) Ibid.
[12] (A) Vol. IV. p. 40.

13 (A) Vol. IV. p. 89.
14 (A) Vol. IV. p. 78.
15 (A) Vol. IV. p. 72.
16 Ibid.
17 (A) Vol. III. p. 350.
18 (A) Vol. III. p. 274. (A) Vol. III. pp. 333, 342.
19 (A) Vol. VI. p. 17.
20 (B) Vol. VI. p. 439.
21 (A) Vol. III. p. 435.
22 (A) Vol. VI. p. 404.
23 (A) Vol. VI. pp. 497–8.
24 (A) Vol. VI. p. 498.
25 (A) Vol. VI. pp. 399–400.
26 (A) Vol. III. p. 403.
27 (A) Vol. III. p. 294.
28 (A) Vol. IV. p. 112.
29 (B) Vol. VII. pp. 119–20.
30 (A) Vol. IV. p. 112.
31 (A) Vol. IV. pp. 112–13.
32 (A) Vol. III. pp. 369–70.
33 (A) Vol. IV. p. 378.
34 (A) Vol. IV. pp. 398–9.
35 (A) Vol. V. pp. 279–80.
36 (A) Vol. V. p. 267.
37 (A) Vol. IV. p. 78.
38 Ibid.
39 (A) Vol. IV. p. 79.
40 Ibid.
41 (A) Vol. III. p. 429.
42 (A) Vol. III. p. 367.
43 (A) Vol. IV. p. 112.
44 (A) Vol. IV. p. 115.
45 (A) Vol. III. pp. 355–6.
46 (A) Vol. IV. p. 81.
47 (A) Vol. IV. p. 265.
48 (A) Vol. III. pp. 332–3.
49 (A) Vol. III. p. 389.
50 (A) Vol. IV. p. 271.
51 (A) Vol. IV. p. 413.
52 (A) Vol. IV. pp. 416–17.
53 (A) Vol. IV. p. 417.
54 (A) Vol. IV. p. 421.
55 (B) Vol. VII. p. 377.
56 Ibid.
57 Ibid.

⁵⁸ (A) Vol. III. pp. 353–4.
⁵⁹ (B) Vol. VII. p. 533.
⁶⁰ Ibid.
⁶¹ (A) Vol. III. p. 365.
⁶² (B) Vol. VII. p. 120.
⁶³ (A) Vol. IV. p. 40.
⁶⁴ Quoted by H. G. Van Leeuwen in *The Problem of Certainty in English Thought 1630–1690*. Martinus Nijhoff. The Hague. 1963. p. 4.
⁶⁵ (A) Vol. III. p. 445.
⁶⁶ (A) Vol. V. p. 22.
⁶⁷ (A) Vol. V. p. 21.

Chapter 13

¹ (A) Vol. III. p. 388.
² (A) Vol. IV. p. 17.
³ (A) Vol. III. p. 388.
⁴ (A) Vol. IV. p. 27.
⁵ (B) Vol. IV. p. 120.
⁶ (A) Vol. IV. p. 113.
⁷ (A) Vol. III. p. 356.
⁸ (A) Vol. IV. p. 383.
⁹ (A) Vol. III. pp. 332–3.
¹⁰ (A) Vol. III. p. 294.
¹¹ (A) Vol. IV. p. 413.
¹² (A) Vol. IV. p. 96.
¹³ (A) Vol. III. p. 453.
¹⁴ (A) Vol. VI. pp. 17–18.
¹⁵ (A) Vol. III. p. 342.
¹⁶ (A) Vol. IV. p. 42.
¹⁷ Farrington. pp. 41, 42.
¹⁸ Farrington. p. 42.
¹⁹ Ibid.
²⁰ (A) Vol. VI. p. 525. Statement repeated in 1612 and 1625.
²¹ (A) Vol. III. p. 282.
²² (A) Vol. III. p. 290.
²³ (A) Vol. III. p. 365.
²⁴ Farrington. p. 133.
²⁵ (A) Vol. III. pp. 361, 362.
²⁶ Farrington. p. 115.
²⁷ (A) Vol. IV. p. 252.
²⁸ (A) Vol. IV. p. 115.
²⁹ (A) Vol. V. pp. 133–4.
³⁰ (A) Vol. IV. pp. 251–2.
³¹ (A) Vol. IV. p. 254.

[32] (A) Vol. v. pp. 133–4.

[33] Farrington. p. 42.

[34] *Francis Bacon. From Magic to Science* by Paolo Rossi. Translated from the Italian by Sacha Rabinovitch. London. Routledge and Kegan Paul. 1968. p. 215.

[35] (A) Vol. IV. p. 252.

[36] (A) Vol. IV. p. 94.

[37] (A) Vol. VI. p. 713.

[38] (A) Vol. III. p. 330.

[39] (A) Vol. IV. p. 421.

[40] (A) Vol. IV. p. 91.

[41] Ibid.

[42] (A) Vol. IV. p. 92.

[43] (A) Vol. IV. pp. 93–4.

[44] (A) Vol. IV. p. 94.

[45] (A) Vol. IV. p. 96.

[46] (A) Vol. IV. p. 97.

[47] (A) Vol. IV. p. 421.

[48] (A) Vol. VI. p. 92.

[49] (A) Vol. VI. p. 114.

[50] (A) Vol. VI. p. 505.

[51] (B) Vol. VII. p. 363.

[52] (A) Vol. VI. p. 506.

[53] Ibid.

[54] (A) Vol. VI. p. 506.

[55] (B) Vol. III. pp. 84–5.

[56] (A) Vol. IV. p. 17.

[57] (A) Vol. III. p. 388.

[58] (A) Vol. IV. p. 112.

[59] (A) Vol. III. p. 389.

[60] (A) Vol. III. p. 387.

[61] (A) Vol. III. p. 419.

[62] (A) Vol. IV. p. 113.

[63] (A) Vol. IV. p. 301.

[64] (A) Vol. IV. p. 27.

[65] (A) Vol. IV. p. 22.

[66] (A) Vol. v. p. 133.

[67] (A) Vol. III. p. 445.

[68] (A) Vol. IV. p. 302.

[69] (A) Vol. III. p. 445.

[70] (A) Vol. VI. p. 18.

[71] (A) Vol. IV. p. 302.

[72] Michel de Montaigne. *Essays.* Translated by J. A. Cohen. Penguin Books Ltd. Harmondsworth. Middlesex. 1958.

[73] (B) Vol. IV. p. 147.

[74] (A) Vol. v. p. 159.
[75] (A) Vol. v. p. 196.
[76] (A) Vol. v. p. 239.
[77] (A) Vol. v. p. 335.
[78] (A) Vol. v. p. 340.
[79] (A) Vol. v. p. 352.
[80] (A) Vol. v. pp. 399–400.
[81] (A) Vol. IV. p. 254.
[82] (A) Vol. IV. p. 256.
[83] (B) Vol. VII. p. 377.
[84] *Discourses* I. Preface. p. 206.
[85] (A) Vol. VI. pp. 440–1.
[86] (B) Vol. VII. pp. 546, 547.

Chapter 14

[1] *Science and Change 1500–1700*. Hugh Keaney. World University Library. McGraw-Hill Book Company. New York Toronto 1981. pp. 52, 54.
[2] (A) Vol. III. p. 367.
[3] (A) Vol. III. p. 361.
[4] (A) Vol. IV. p. 104.
[5] (A) Vol. IV. p. 65. See footnotes to same page.
[6] (A) Vol. IV. p. 64.
[7] (A) Vol. IV. p. 65.
[8] (A) Vol. IV. p. 63.
[9] (A) Vol. IV. p. 63.
[10] *The Decline and Fall of the Roman Empire*. Edward Gibbon. Vol. 5. Chap. 52. p. 415. Everymans Library. Dent. London, Melbourne and Toronto. Dutton. New York. 1978.
[11] Cp. (A) Vol. IV. pp. 64 and 65 with p. 63.
[12] (A) Vol. IV. pp. 64–5.
[13] (A) Vol. IV. p. 65.
[14] (A) Vol. IV. p. 65, and see footnotes to this page.
[15] (A) Vol. IV. p. 19.
[16] (A) Vol. IV. p. 73.
[17] (A) Vol. IV. p. 81. Again I avoid the word 'method'.
[18] (B) Vol. VII. p. 120.
[19] Ibid.
[20] (B) Vol. VII. p. 130.
[21] (B) Vol. VI. p. 403.
[22] (A) Vol. VI. p. 53.
[23] (A) Vol. VI. p. 69.
[24] Basil Montague. *The Works of Francis Bacon, Lord Chancellor of England*, 3 Vols. 1859. III. pp. 519–20.
[25] (A) Vol. III. p. 483.

[26] (A) Vol. III. p. 484.

[27] (A) Vol. III. p. 481.

[28] (A) Vol. III. p. 485.

[29] *Il Principe* by Niccolo Machiavelli. Edited L. Arthur Burd. Introduced by Lord Acton. Oxford. Clarendon Press. 1891. p. XXVII.

[30] (A) Vol. VI. p. 420.

[31] Ranke. Ibid. Vol. I. p. 456.

[32] Macaulay. *Essays.* p. 328.

[33] (A) Vol. IV. p. 53.

[34] (A) Vol. IV. p. 76.

[35] (A) Vol. IV. p. 311.

[36] (A) Vol. IV. p. 17.

[37] (A) Vol. IV. p. 65.

[38] (A) Vol. III. p. 365.

[39] Ibid.

[40] *Space and Spirit.* Sir Edmund Whittaker FRS. Thomas Nelson and Sons Ltd. London, Edinburgh, Paris, Melbourne, Toronto and New York. 1946. pp. 26–7.

[41] (A) Vol. I. p. 11.

[42] (A) Vol. VI. pp. 495–6.

[43] (A) Vol. III. p. 453.

[44] (A) Vol. VI. p. 698.

[45] (A) Vol. VI. p. 697.

[46] Ibid.

[47] (A) Vol. VI. pp. 698–9.

[48] (B) Vol. VII. p. 547.

[49] (A) Vol. IV. p. 81.

[50] (A) Vol. IV. p. 336.

[51] (A) Vol. IV. p. 248.

[52] (A) Vol. IV. p. 302.

[53] (A) Vol. III. pp. 333–4.

[54] (A) Vol. IV. p. 53.

[55] (A) Vol. IV. pp. 63–5.

[56] (A) Vol. III. p. 356.

[57] (A) Vol. IV. p. 53.

[58] (A) Vol. IV. p. 21.

[59] (A) Vol. III. p. 429.

[60] Ibid.

[61] (A) Vol. IV. p. 96.

[62] Ibid.

[63] (A) Vol. IV. p. 316.

[64] (A) Vol. IV. p. 81.

[65] (A) Vol. IV. p. 301.

[66] (A) Vol. IV. p. 53.

[67] (A) Vol. IV. pp. 92–3.

⁶⁸ Ranke. Ibid. Vol. I. p. 455.
⁶⁹ (A) Vol. IV. p. 39.
⁷⁰ Thucydides. Ibid. Book I. p. 41.
⁷¹ Gibbon. Ibid. Vol. II. p. 11. Vol. II. p. 371. Vol. IV. p. 237.
⁷² (A) Vol. IV. p. 292.
⁷³ (A) Vol. V. p. 116.
⁷⁴ (A) Vol. IV. p. 293.
⁷⁵ Ibid.
⁷⁶ (A) Vol. IV. p. 110.
⁷⁷ (A) Vol. III. p. 388.

Chapter 15

¹ Vico. *Autobiography.* pp. 138–9, 154. Translated by M. H. Fisch and T. G. Bergin. Comet Paperback. Cornell University Press. Ithaca and London. 1975.
² Vico. *The New Science.* Revised Translation of the Third Edition (1744). Thomas Goddard Bergin and Max Harold Fisch. Cornell University Press. Ithaca and London 1975. p. 168.
³ Ibid. p. 121.
⁴ (A) Vol. IV. p. 313.
⁵ (A) Vol. III. p. 359.
⁶ (A) Vol. VI. p. 746.
⁷ (A) Vol. VI. p. 747.
⁸ (A) Vol. VI. p. 711.
⁹ (A) Vol. III. p. 334.
¹⁰ (A) Vol. III. p. 335.
¹¹ (A) Vol. VI. pp. 198–9.
¹² (A) Vol. VI. pp. 215–16.
¹³ (A) Vol. VI. p. 757.
¹⁴ (A) Vol. III. p. 334.
¹⁵ (A) Vol. VI. p. 711.
¹⁶ (B) Vol. V. p. 189.
¹⁷ (A) Vol. VI. p. 364.
¹⁸ (A) Vol. III. p. 64.
¹⁹ (B) Vol. IV. p. 64.
²⁰ (A) Vol. VI. p. 722.
²¹ (A) Vol. VI. p. 512.
²² (A) Vol. VI. p. 514.
²³ (A) Vol. VI. p. 514.
²⁴ Ibid.
²⁵ (A) Vol. VI. p. 738.
²⁶ (A) Vol. VI. p. 517.
²⁷ (A) Vol. VI. pp. 737, 738.
²⁸ (A) Vol. VI. p. 513.

[29] (A) Vol. IV. p. 69.
[30] (A) Vol. IV. p. 65.
[31] (A) Vol. IV. p. 69.
[32] Farrington. p. 42.
[33] (A) Vol. IV. p. 293.
[34] (A) Vol. IV. p. 292.
[35] (A) Vol. III. pp. 357–8.
[36] (A) Vol. III. p. 358.
[37] (A) Vol. III. p. 351.
[38] (A) Vol. IV. p. 55.
[39] (A) Vol. III. p. 358.
[40] (A) Vol. IV. p. 365.
[41] (A) Vol. III. p. 355.
[42] Ibid.
[43] Ibid.
[44] (A) Vol. VI. p. 377.
[45] (A) Vol. IV. p. 119.
[46] (A) Vol. IV. pp. 119, 120.
[47] (A) Vol. IV. p. 120.
[48] (A) Vol. IV. p. 126.
[49] (A) Vol. IV. p. 120.
[50] (A) Vol. III. p. 354.
[51] *The Oxford Companion to Classical Literature*. Compiled and edited by Sir Paul Harvey. Oxford at the Clarendon Press. 1974. p. 46.
[52] (A) Vol. III. p. 409.
[53] Farrington. pp. 71–2.
[54] Farrington. p. 115.
[55] (A) Vol. III. p. 293.
[56] (A) Vol. IV. pp. 357–8.
[57] (A) Vol. IV. pp. 68, 69.
[58] Montague. III. p. 519.
[59] Ibid.
[60] (A) Vol. IV. p. 69.
[61] (A) Vol. IV. p. 370.
[62] (A) Vol. IV. p. 97.
[63] (A) Vol. I. pp. 23–4.
[64] (A) Vol. I. p. 24.
[65] (A) Vol. I. pp. 24–5.
[66] (A) Vol. I. p. 84.
[67] (A) Vol. I. p. 88.
[68] *The History of Scepticism from Erasmus to Descartes*. Richard H. Popkin. Assen-MCMLXIV. Passim.
[69] (A) Vol. III. p. 2.
[70] (A) Vol. IV. p. 40.

[71] In her remarkable study, *The Royal Society: Concept and Creation*, Routledge and Kegan Paul, London, 1967, Marjorie Purver makes no direct reference to *Novum Organum* Book II. But she attacks Macaulay for an 'extraordinary error' and suggests that Macaulay's essay affected Bacon's Victorian editors and translators, Spedding and Ellis. This 'extraordinary error' consists of the notion that the course Bacon proposed for the achievement of sciences of nature was '*such as leaves but little to the acuteness and strength of wits, but places all wits and understandings nearly on a level*'. Ms Purver proposes that Bacon's meaning here was that once Idols of the Theatre were eliminated God's universe in its reality would be plain for all to see, this elimination of an idol producing levelling of wits. The difficulty about such a view is first that Bacon states expressly that though Idols of the Theatre which are not innate 'but are plainly impressed and received into the mind from the play-books of philosophical systems and the perverted rules of demonstration', are indeed capable of elimination; the other three idols are not capable of being so summarily disposed of. No art, as for instance his machine in *Novum Organum* Book II, is available or constructible for getting rid of these other idols. All a man can do is to beware of them, oppose them and seek to reduce them. No doubt Bacon's machine would help in this respect. Secondly, the words quoted above and given emphasis by the present writer are Bacon's own. Their meaning is as plain as can be. They require no interpretation. Though Hooke is mentioned several times in Ms Purver's book, she does not note that Hooke read Bacon's words as Macaulay read them.

[72] (B) Vol. VII. p. 381.

[73] (A) Vol. VI. p. 318.

[74] (B) Vol. VII. p. 474.

[75] (A) Vol. II. p. 687. Latin: the collection provides no English version. For latter see *The Works of Francis Bacon, Lord Chancellor of England*. New Edition. Basil Montague Esq. London. William Pickering. MDCCCXXXIV. Vol. XIV. p. 425.

[76] (A) Vol. VI. p. 377.

[77] (A) Vol. IV. p. 77.

[78] (A) Vol. VII. p. 34.

[79] Montague. Ibid. Vol. XIV. p. 424.

[80] Ibid. pp. 424–5.

[81] Ibid. pp. 425–6.

[82] (A) Vol. IV. p. 115.

[83] E.g. (A) Vol. IV. p. 115.

[84] (B) Vol. VII. p. 532.

[85] (A) Vol. I. p. 157, (A) Vol. IV. p. 47.

[86] (B) Vol. VII. p. 120.

[87] (B) Vol. VII. p. 377.

[88] (A) Vol. VI. p. 19.

[89] (A) Vol. v. pp. 133–4.
[90] (A) Vol. v. p. 133.
[91] (A) Vol. III. p. 456.

Index

action, 60, 70, 101, 117, 121, 193, 204, 206, 219, 220, 252, 286, 288, 329, 344, 349, 360; and speculation, 102–5; and morality, 104; in policy, 122–3, 209, 289, 330; and knowledge, 263; in natural science, 289–90

Acton, J. E. E. D. (1834–1902), 124, 323

Advancement of Learning, The, 7, 8, 33, 36, 39, 42, 43, 49, 51, 55, 62, 69, 72, 77, 78, 81, 84, 87, 89, 90, 101, 102, 104, 105, 106, 107, 109, 111, 117, 133, 187, 190, 201, 203, 205, 214, 220, 224, 225, 232, 246, 249, 268, 271, 272, 286, 314, 319, 335, 338–9, 354, 356, 357, 358, 364
  1605 version, 7, 23, 24, 30, 31, 32, 46, 50, 53, 55–6, 65, 70, 96, 101, 103, 114, 154, 164, 168, 169, 173, 174, 176, 188, 202, 216, 221, 227, 228, 229, 248, 250, 261, 265, 271, 273, 275, 278, 281, 292, 293, 295, 298, 299, 321, 326, 362
  1623 version, 8, 23, 28, 31, 32, 33, 47, 50, 58, 61, 68, 69, 71, 73, 74, 75, 92, 95, 105, 113, 118, 120, 164, 168, 175, 176, 182, 197, 204, 209, 211, 212, 214, 217, 218, 219, 221, 222, 223, 224, 227, 238, 239, 241–2, 245, 248, 250, 261, 271, 273, 279, 281, 291, 292, 308, 339

Advertisement Touching the Controversies of the Church of England (1589), 129, 144, 158, 187, 194, 228, 346

Aeschines, 300

affections, *see* passions

alchemy, 313–15

Alexander of Macedon, 23, 27–8, 29, 146, 300, 354

allegory, 327

Anatomical History, 275

Andrewes, Bishop Lancelot, 7, 8, 116, 146

annals, 215

antiquarians, 58–9

antiquities, 214, 215

aphorisms, 39, 40, 175, 177, 229, 230, 231, 232, 240, 284, 322, 329, 352–4

apophthegms, 69

apparitions, *see* idols of the mind

Appianus, 53, 55, 223

Aquinas, Thomas, 185, 190

aristocracy, 200

Aristotle, 18, 23, 24, 33, 34, 35, 36, 40, 79, 80, 86, 110, 115, 148, 263, 287, 293, 294, 298, 313, 320, 328; deficiencies of, 92, 290, 291, 316–17, 324, 349–51, 356, 358; support for, 297, 321, 325, 339, 350–5, 357, 358, 367; use of history by, 349–51

armies, 128, 198–9, 203, 204, 212, 251, 253

Arthur, King, 58

artillery, 198, 212

arts, 40, 43, 44, 50, 78, 79, 82–3, 284–5, 303, 328, 359; history of, 23, 207, 216–17, 237, 263–6, 293, 297; improvement of, 45, 76, 86, 123, 272, 277, 305–7; *see also* mechanical arts; *see also* sciences

Athens, 199

Aubrey, John, 151

audacity, 23, 83, 112, 191, 293, 294, 300, 346, 349, 356, 362

Augustine, 56, 185, 262, 335

authority, 38, 69, 74, 193, 219, 220

axioms, 38, 45, 49, 105–7, 108, 118, 169, 176, 197, 200, 203, 238, 239, 240, 243, 244, 245, 246, 262, 266, 272, 276, 277, 286–7, 301, 310, 311, 315, 334, 344, 349; *see also* middle axioms

and British state, 149–50, 165–6
criticized by Harvey, 151
criticism of Lord Salisbury, 151–4
on handling of parliaments, 158–64
on greatness in kingdoms, 166–7
on theory and practice in civil and moral
  philosophy, 168–72
on relations with Spain, 176–86
on territorial expansion, 182–3
on politics and religion, 185–9
on origins of institutions, 194–5, 346
on goodness, 200, 203
on uses of learning, 204–7
on fortune, 207–8
on prediction, 209, 345, 346, 349
success of civil policies of, 209–13
achievements of, 212–13
on divisions of civil history, 214–20
and mixed civil history, 221–40, 250–1
and pure civil history, 223, 224–5, 248–9,
  250–3, 260
universality of, 233–4
gave priority to civil over natural
  history, 242
on examples in civil history, 243–5, 248,
  253
on Henry VII, 245, 248, 252, 254–9, 304
argued against enclosure of grounds, 203,
  251, 253–4
on nobility, 258–9
achievement of in civil history, 259
priority of civil history for, 260
on disputes, 265
new logic of, 263, 266–70, 279, 283,
  284–5, 306
on periods of learning, 263–5
on longevity, 268–9
on unification of the sciences, 273
unfinished work of, 274, 362, 363, 368
on mechanical arts, 270, 275–7, 279
on certainty, 279–83, 361–9
distinguished civil from moral science,
  281–2
on observation in natural science, 289,
  318, 329–30
on Aristotle, 290, 291, 297, 316–17, 320,
  321, 324, 325, 349–58
and improvement of natural
  philosophy/science, 298–306
on progress of civil philosophy, 298–302
on rulers, 303–4
on improvement of extant arts, 305–7
on making progress in a variety of fields,
  306–7
on difficulty of his projects, 307–11
on alchemy, 313–15

aimed to unite rational and empirical
  faculties, 317–19, 329, 330
attitude to Pyrrhonians, 320, 349, 352,
  355–65
criticized scholastics, 321–2
and priority of his markers, 325–6
on man's ability to shape history, 340–1
on history of learning, 342–3
on vicissitude, 345–8
and plans for natural philosophy/science,
  366–9
Bacon, Sir Nicholas, 99
Baranzan, Revd Fr, 278, 279, 284, 310, 367
Beginning of the History of Great Britain, The,
  144
bias, 71–3
Bodin, Jean (1529–96), 222
body, 48, 169, 170, 239, 275, 282, 285;
  relation with mind, 41–4, 45, 109,
  267–70, 271–5, 355, 360; and soul, 42
boldness, 112, 192, 293
Buckingham, Duke of, 173, 179, 192
Burke, Edmund, 30
'business', *see* 'negotiation'

Caesar, Julius, 53, 55, 58, 143, 223, 224,
  264
Cambridge University, 24, 86, 98, 103, 104,
  172, 174, 265
Casaubon, Isaac, 101, 147, 172, 309
Catalogue of Particular Histories by Titles, 268,
  274–7
Catholicism, 142, 186–7, 204, 210
causes, 36, 37, 64, 168, 268, 350–1, 352–4,
  365
caution, 23, 191, 193, 293, 300, 346, 349,
  356, 359, 362
Cecil, William, 99
certainty, 39–40, 263, 273, 274, 279–83,
  285, 309, 311, 320, 359, 361–9
'characters of dispositions', 14, 19, 64,
  112–15, 117, 170, 176, 191, 200, 220,
  234–5, 252, 268–9, 272, 273, 280, 357
Charles I, King, 1
chronicles, 56, 57, 64
Church of England, 143–4, 158, 183, 194,
  210, 228, 250
Cicero, 40, 66, 71, 72, 74, 86, 88, 332
civil history, 23, 29, 38, 46, 48, 49, 50, 87,
  121, 134, 137, 148, 151, 190, 200, 207,
  208, 212, 213, 264, 281, 310, 323, 325,
  326, 328, 335, 368; Bacon's role in
  undervalued, 7; deficient in England,
  7–8, 78, 287; deficiency of extant,
  52–66; mixed, 55, 221–40, 241–2,
  250–1, 259, 261, 286, 287, 297;

modern, 55, 56; law and, 62–5; divine
providence in, 65–6, 335–7, 339–48;
experience and, 68, 330; truth of, 69,
329–32; bias in, 71–3; used to improve
morality and policy, 77–8, 104–5;
Greek, 53, 63, 66, 92, 96, 222–4, 329;
rational improvement of, 122–4; in
Advancement, 214, 220; divisions of,
215–21; difficulty of, 61, 219, 281,
307–8, 311, 329; pure, 220, 222–5,
234, 241–2, 248–9, 250–3, 260, 294,
296; in *Essays*, 230–2; and science,
238–40; and natural history, 238–40,
241–3, 246–7, 289–99; examples in,
243–7, 252–3; rhetoric in, 243–4, 245,
247; extended by Bacon, 259–60; as
species within a *genus*, 259–60; lessons
of, 288, 294, 330–3; use against idols
of the mind, 312; includes canons of
law and scripture, 334–7; as a
theology, 342; and time, 363–4
civil knowledge, *see* policy
civil philosophy, 7, 38, 65, 77, 96, 98–9,
101, 109, 151, 168–72, 238, 245,
298–302, 307
civil science, 7, 29–30, 119, 147–8, 151,
212, 213, 221, 281, 302, 306, 312, 340;
see also civil philosophy; *see also* policy
'Clavis interpretationis', *see Novum Organum*
Clinias, 184, 185
Cogitata et Visa, 146, 320, 364
Cogitationes de Scientia Humana (Thoughts on
Human Knowledge), 289–90
Coke, Sir Edward, 15, 62, 323
colonization, 4
Columbus, Christopher, 307
commentaries, 56, 57, 215
Commines, Philip de, 55, 114, 220
common law, English, 62–3, 65, 106, 141,
143, 211, 228, 233, 311, 323, 325,
334–5
common notions, 316–17, 330, 333, 334,
335, 337
'commonwealth', 132, 211
Considerations Touching a War with Spain, 165,
176–7, 179–86, 190, 192, 208, 227,
233–4
*Considerations Touching the Better Pacification
and Edification of the Church of England*
(1604), 129, 130, 144, 158, 228
constancy, 67, 175
constitution, 5–6, 7, 135, 137, 154, 227
contemplation, 102–3, 105
context, historical, 6, 10–11, 18, 83
cookery, 275

Copernicus, 26, 35, 40
cosmography, 221, 222, 238
Cotton, Sir Robert, 248
Council of Wales and the Marches, 137–42,
208, 233, 341
counsel, 99, 132–4, 135, 151, 152, 206
Court of King's Bench, 137–42
Court of Wards, 194
Cupid, fable of, 95–6
custom, 118, 129

data, 38, 60, 65, 135, 171, 190, 197, 198,
214, 215, 218, 222, 230, 231, 233, 234,
239, 242, 247, 261, 264, 281, 320, 324,
335, 339, 344, 349
De Fluxu et Reflexu Maris, 146–7
De Interpretatione Naturae Proœmium
(Concerning the Interpretation of
Nature), 99–101, 102, 147, 289, 303,
304
De Regulis juris, 106, 176, 229; *see also
Maxims of the Law*
De Sapientia Veterum (Of the Wisdom of the
Ancients), 7, 8, 23, 27, 37, 68, 75, 89,
90, 92, 93, 95, 96, 97, 98, 101, 102–3,
104, 105, 106, 149, 172, 176, 193, 218,
225, 237, 253, 271, 297, 298, 327–8,
339, 347
death, 239
delivery, *see* tradition
Delphi, oracle of, 30–1, 32, 37
democracy, 200, 258
Democritus, 95, 169, 298, 350–1
Demosthenes, 71, 72, 86, 184, 300
Descartes, 362
Descriptio Globi Intellectualis (1612), 47–8, 51
despotism, 125
differences, 24, 45, 47, 48, 61, 352, 367
Dionysus, fable of, 93
Discorsi (Machiavelli), 54–5, 123, 193, 196,
197, 198, 199, 200, 203, 204, 207, 208,
226, 236, 238, 240, 244, 252, 258, 261,
287, 323, 325, 333, 347–8
discourse, 24, 221, 233, 234, 237, 287, 328
dispositions, *see* 'characters of dispositions'
disputes, 265, 284
dissimulation, 127–8
distinctions, 60, 105, 107, 175, 220
divinity, 37, 38, 42, 44, 67, 74, 82–3, 86,
110, 176, 180, 185–6, 188, 190, 197,
237, 262, 264, 265, 266, 279, 319,
321–2, 335–7; *see also* religion
Dogmas of Ancient Philosophers, 356
doubt, 39–40, 54, 266, 282, 320, 324, 325,
349, 356–62, 368; *see also* Pyrrhonians

Union of England and Scotland, 1, 4, 5, 8,
  64, 149, 154–8, 177, 210, 340
United Kingdom, *see* Great Britain
United Provinces, 178
unity, 40, 41
universality, 233–4
utopianism, 125

Valerius Terminus, 102, 104, 289
Valla, Lorenzo, 183
vicissitude, 68–9, 134, 212, 222, 253, 345–8
Vico, Giambattista (1668–1744), 95, 338,
  340, 342–5
*View of the Differences in Question Betwixt the
  King's Bench and the Council in the
  Marches* (1606), 13–42, 227
Virgil, 111

Voltaire, 26–7, 29, 71
Vulgate, 53

Wales, 137–42, 233
war, 126–7, 167, 178–85, 190–1, 193, 194,
  196–7, 198, 199, 251, 363
Whittaker, Edmund, 325
'wholes', 68
will, 44, 48, 109, 112, 169, 170, 171, 272,
  273, 282, 336
Williams, John, Bishop of Lincoln
  (1582–1650), 71–3, 259, 328
*Works of Francis Bacon, Lord Chancellor of
  England, The* (1825–34), 18
writing, 208

Xenophon, 53, 55, 71, 223